AF862137

RACE PREFERENCE PROGRAMS AND THE UNITED STATES SUPREME COURT'S STRICT SCRUTINY STANDARD OF REVIEW

RACE PREFERENCE PROGRAMS AND THE UNITED STATES SUPREME COURT'S STRICT SCRUTINY STANDARD OF REVIEW

Maurice Y. Mongkuo

The Edwin Mellen Press
Lewiston•Queenston•Lampeter

HAMLINE UNIVERSITY
JUN - 6 2006
LAW LIBRARY

Library of Congress Cataloging-in-Publication Data

Mongkuo, Maurice Y.
Race preference programs and the United States Supreme Court's strict scrutiny standard of review / Maurice Y. Mongkuo.
p. cm.
Includes bibliographical references and index.
ISBN 0-7734-5944-8
1. Government contractors--United States. 2. Government contractors--Florida--Saint Petersburg. 3. Public contracts--United States. 4. Public contracts--Florida--Saint Petersburg. 5. Affirmative action programs--Law and legislation--United States. 6. Affirmative action programs--Law and legislation--Florida--Saint Petersburg. 7. United States. Supreme Court. I. Title.

KF849.M65 2005
346.7302'3--dc22

2005053871

A CIP catalog record for this book is available from the British Library.

Front cover photo courtesy of Edgar Powell

Copyright © 2005 Maurice Y. Mongkuo

All rights reserved. For information contact

The Edwin Mellen Press
Box 450
Lewiston, New York
USA 14092-0450

The Edwin Mellen Press
Box 67
Queenston, Ontario
CANADA L0S 1L0

The Edwin Mellen Press, Ltd.
Lampeter, Ceredigion, Wales
UNITED KINGDOM SA48 8LT

Printed in the United States of America

KF
849
.M65
2005

To Susana Meshie Mongkuo
and
in memory of Peter Ndefre Mongkuo

Contents

Tables

List of Abbreviations

(BBE)	Black Business Enterprise
(HBE)	Hispanic Business Enterprise
(MBE)	Minority Business Enterprise
(MWBE)	Minority- and Woman-owned Business enterprise
(NIGP)	National Institute of Government Purchasing
(RMA)	Relevant market area
(WBE)	Woman-owned Business enterprise

Foreword

In this monograph Maurice Mongkuo provides an analysis of the outcomes of policies instituted in St. Petersburg, Florida to promote equity in the award of contracts to women and minority-owned (W/M) businesses. This research was originally conducted for St. Petersburg, which largely accounts for its format, style, and cautionary language. These features will undoubtedly make it difficult for some readers to discern the author's intent, particularly since one of the major conclusions advanced is that discrimination is not the major reason for the small volume of contracts received by W/M firms. As a consequence, this foreword is designed to facilitate interpretation of the study so that its value as a guide for the development of new strategies to reduce economic disparities can be better appreciated.

In recent years several contracting set-aside programs have been ruled unconstitutional under the strict scrutiny standard now employed by the courts. The strict scrutiny standard requires that there be a compelling state interest at stake to justify the use of racial classifications in making decisions about the allocation of some public good, and further that when race-based action is necessary to further a compelling governmental interest, such action must be narrow tailored so as not to violate the constitutional guarantee of equal protection. Narrow tailoring means that the use of race-focused interventions is justifiable only after all less intrusive methods have been exhausted.

One use of disparity studies is to determine if racial preferences have been successful in eliminating a previous pattern of discrimination. If there is observable evidence that discriminatory practices and outcomes have been eliminated, then continued use of racial preferences is not likely to stand up to legal scrutiny, and only so-called "race neutral" programs can be implemented in efforts to reduce persisting disparities. Mongkuo's study both demonstrates the state of the art in conducting disparity studies and also the limits of contemporary disparity investigations for ferreting out the root causes of persisting economic disparities. The methodology used by Mongkuo is designed, in fact, to overcome some of the problems that have arisen in previous research. Several disparity studies of contract awards in other cities that found discrimination to be a major factor contributing to the limited success of W/M businesses have been discredited in court.

As noted, Mongkuo's analysis fails to identify discrimination as a major factor contributing to the low numbers and value of contracts awarded to women and minority-owned businesses. This outcome raises some important questions. First, are Mongkuo's results driven by his methodology such that similar results would be obtained if the methodology was used to examine data for other cities? Alternatively do the results indicate that St. Petersburg officials are more committed and adept at implementing successful programs to reduce inequities than their counterparts in other cities? Finally, is there additional information that is needed to better understand the extent to which discrimination continues to be a factor affecting equity in the award of contracts?

Focusing first on methodological issues it is useful to understand what disparity studies can and cannot tell us about discrimination. Suppose, for example, that 5 percent of the contractors in a given jurisdiction who are qualified to bid on a particular type of contract are African American or, in the language of disparity studies, African Americans have an "availability" of 5 percent. An analyst would then compare this availability with the proportion of bids awarded to determine if there are significant differences between availability and "utilization." For the purposes of illustration, assume that African American contractors bid on 5 percent of the contracts and received 2 percent of the contracts and contract value, and also that there was no significant discrepancy in bids, i.e. there was no tendency for African American contractors to bid higher than non-Black contactors. In this situation, it might appear reasonable to conclude that African American contractors had experienced discrimination in the contract award process. However, since disparity studies use statistical tests to determine whether the observed differences are significant, i.e. do not just reflect random patterns, if the number of contracts examined and/or the availability and number of W/M businesses submitting bids are small, it will be very difficult for the differences to achieve the level of statistical significance necessary for an analyst to conclude that discrimination has occurred. In fact, this pattern is found in many of the specific test results that Mongkuo presents. In several instances he notes that the signs are indicative of the existence of systemic disparities but that the relationship is not strong enough for a professional economist to declare that discrimination accounts for the outcomes.

It is also important to note that disparity analyses do not provide information about why there may be a disparity between overall population representation and availability. For instance, suppose in our hypothetical case that African Americans constitute 20 percent of the population. For the purposes of long-term efforts to equalize economic opportunity it would be important to know why there is such a large gap between population representation and representation among contractors.

Disparity analysts are also concerned with the extent to which W/M businesses are discouraged from submitting bids although they have the resources to perform the contract work. The existence of policies deliberately designed to hamper bids from W/M businesses would constitute prima facie evidence of discrimination that would warrant the design of race/gender-conscious policies. Techniques used to ascertain whether such discriminatory policies exist include scrutiny of official records, interviews with officials, and interviews with W/M business owners who have submitted or attempted to submit bids. Critical issues that arise in the review of records and interviews with public officials include the quality and coverage of records and the degree of credibility that can be attached to interview information, particularly in jurisdictions where discrimination has been previously documented. In the St. Petersburg case, for example, records were only maintained for prime contractors – no records were maintained for subcontractors. It is clearly conceivable that public officials in such a situation could implement non-discriminatory procedures for prime contracts, since such policies were subject to external scrutiny, while collaborating in discriminatory behavior in the award of subcontracts. Unfortunately, there is no way to tell if such a scenario was operative in St. Petersburg and Mongkuo does not speculate on possible findings if sub-contracting practices and outcomes were examined.

Problems can also arise in interpreting information solicited from W/M business owners. Successful bidders are more likely to provide favorable assessments of policies and procedures than unsuccessful ones. Similarly, unsuccessful first time bidders are less likely to be attuned to discriminatory behavior than repeat unsuccessful bidders. Consequently, if the sample of interviewees is weighted toward successful and first time bidders, the collective assessment of the equity of policies and procedures is likely to be more positive than would be warranted if the entire population is considered. The implication of this discussion is that the relatively positive assessments offered by W/M business owners in this study should not be accepted without qualification.

The problem discussed above is an example of what economists characterize as a "selectivity bias," where information about some subset of the population under study is underrepresented. There is another type of selectivity bias that further complicates the interpretation of information from disparity study interviews. No information is available from individuals who elected not to bid because of presumptions that discrimination was operative and that their bids would be unsuccessful. Is it legitimate to suggest that such individuals are victims of discrimination? If so, how does this type of discrimination relate to that examined in disparity studies? With respect to the present investigation, these queries are relevant in part because minority interviewees disproportionately believed that race was somehow implicated in the contract award process, although not able to identify specific policies or procedures through which racism was manifested.

The differences between respondents' understanding of racism and the technical definitions embodied in disparity studies can be understood by referring to the figure below.

Forms of Discrimination that Produce Economic Disparities

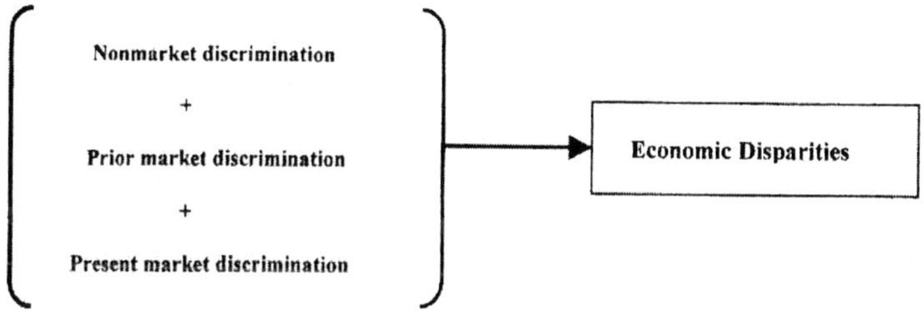

This diagram suggests that current economic disparities, in this case differences in the proportion of contracts awarded, can stem from three distinct types of discrimination. Present market discrimination would involve, for example, imposing different financial requirements and pricing schedules for W/M contractors. In the present environment in which many practices are subject to significant administrative and legal oversight, it will be very unlikely to identify "smoking guns" that unquestionably identify discriminatory behavior. Rather, current disparities are more likely to result primarily from non-market discrimination and prior market discrimination. Nonmarket discrimination would include limited institutional policies that limit access to information and experiences necessary to be successful as a business owner and governmental contractor. Prior market discrimination would include prior exclusion of W/M businesses from receiving contracts, which could contribute to an unwillingness to believe that such discrimination no longer exists, resulting in decisions not to solicit contracts. Nonmarket and prior market discrimination are examples of ways in which race can be implicated in the contract award process without any observable discriminatory behavior.

The preceding discussion raises the question, then, of what is the record of St. Petersburg vis a vis nonmarket and prior market discrimination. As background, Saint Petersburg is located on Pinellas Peninsula between Tampa Bay and the Gulf of Mexico. The city's economy is based on the manufacture of electronic and aerospace equipment, boats, and medical goods, and activities associated with telecommunications, information services, and marine research; the city's economy is bolstered by a strong tourism industry. According to the 2000 census St. Petersburg, Florida has a population of 248,000, whites are 71.4 percent of the population, blacks 22.4 percent, Asians 2.7 percent, Native Americans 0.3 percent, and Native Hawaiians and other Pacific Islanders 0.1 percent.

The first African Americans who located in what is now St. Petersburg in the late 1860s did not experience race-related problems until issues of voting arose in the 1870s. The construction of the Orange Belt railway created job opportunities for black workers as graders and as the black population expanded the first identifiable community, then known as "Pepper Town," was established. After 1900, most new Black residents established residences west of the Pepper Town area, in what became known as Methodist Town.

Throughout this period continuing into the 1960s Blacks living in St. Petersburg were the victims of institutional discrimination characteristic of the Jim

Crow segregation era. As an example, Blacks were required to sit in the balcony of the LaPlaza Theatre from the time that it opened in 1913 and faced discrimination in public accommodations. Davis Elementary School, which was built in 1910, was the only public school for Blacks until the Jordan School, also segregated, was opened in 1925. The schools attended by Blacks faced the well-known problems of inferior facilities, outdated textbooks, and discrimination in salaries and teachers and administrators suffered intimidation and retribution for voicing complaints. The segregated school system was maintained in Pinellas county for many years after the Supreme Court ruling in 1954. Class action suit filed in 1964 extended litigation and plan formation no real effort until 1971-72 to desegregate

Health services were also segregated, and Mercy Hospital was the principal health facility serving the St. Petersburg Black community until 1966. Newspaper coverage of community events was also segregated in the *St. Petersburg Times* until 1964, and the Black community was served by its own newspaper. This newspaper was an example of the type of independent Black business community that evolved that would eventually serve as the foundation for the establishment of businesses that could be potential bidders for municipal contracts. Segregation enabled a relative vibrant business community to emerge, and early Black-owned enterprises that were established included a bus company, pharmacy, a hotel retreat, a funeral home, and grocery stores. The development of a quasi-independent Black economy was necessitated by discrimination practiced by many white-owned businesses, which led to a successful selective buying campaign in 1960 that forced several retail establishments to cease engaging in overt discriminatory practices.

Voting restrictions limited the ability of the Black community to affect public policy and successful assaults on disenfranchisement did not begin until a suit was filed in 1946 to allow Blacks to vote in the Pinellas County Democratic Party primary. The major voter registration drive conducted by the St. Petersburg Non

Partisan Voters League in 1954 was another important milestone, but progress in the electoral arena was slow, as evidenced by the fact that no Black St. Petersburg citizen was elected to sit on the City council until 1970.

Overall, while the Civil Rights Movement had dramatic effects on the circumstances facing Blacks in St. Petersburg, it in no way totally eradicated the persisting effects of past discrimination. The cumulative effects of past injustices erupted in racial conflicts in the mid-1960s that were linked to similar eruptions in other cities. In St. Petersburg important events included a protest at City Hall over racist depictions of Blacks in murals and a 1968 strike by garbage collectors over wages and working conditions that paralleled the developments in Memphis that were ultimately connected to the assassination of Martin Luther King. More recently, large scale unrest occurred in 1996 following the fatal shooting of young African-American man, leading to the arrest of 20 people and 28 buildings being burned in a 25 block area.

The preceding overview suggests that the legacy of non-market and prior market discrimination is alive and well in St. Petersburg and may well be affecting contracting and other economic outcomes in ways that are difficult to identify via disparity studies. This means that community leaders must become more sophisticated in designing strategies to confront both the continuing effects of past discrimination and the new forms of racism, sometimes described as "subtle racism," that are extremely difficult to document. Developing such sophistication requires familiarity with the technical details associated with struggles around race preferences and affirmative action in the courts and administrative agencies, including disparity studies. The need for a focused community mobilization effort takes on a special urgency in Florida communities such as St. Petersburg, because affirmative action opponent, Ward Connerly, announced in 1999 that Florida was his next battleground. Conservative forces will undoubtedly be escalating their assaults on race preferences in the wake of the decisions by the U.S. Supreme Court in the University of Michigan admissions cases, (*Gratz V. Bollinger* and *Grutter v. Bollinger*, decided by the U.S. Supreme Court in June 2003). It is especially important to keep in mind that the principal author of those opinions, Justice Sandra Day O'Connor, effectively announced a 25 year sunset provision on affirmative action programs that involve race preferences. This means that there is much hard work to be done over the next quarter of a century to dramatically reduce racial economic disparities, including those in contract awards. Mongkuo's important study serves as a stark reminder of just how difficult this work will be.

James B. Stewart
Professor of Labor Studies and Industrial Relations,
African and African American Studies, and
Management and Organization
Penn State University

Acknowledgments

I wish to thank several people and organizations who contributed to the preparation of this book. I am indebted to my mentors James B. Stewart and Leon L. Haley who provided me with the inspiration, knowledge and professional guidance that enabled me to gain the broad experience to write this book. I thank the City of St. Petersburg, Florida through whose courtesy and cooperation much of the data and information processing was obtained. I am grateful to the Center for University Scholars at Jackson State University for providing funding to complete the research and bring the manuscript to camera-ready form. My thanks also go to the reviewers who provided invaluable suggestions and comments after reading the drafts of the manuscript. They are Curtina Moreland-Young of Jackson State University and Lewis A. Randolph of Ohio University. My deep appreciation to Spencer Albert and Creta Johnson of Hillsborough County, Florida for their steadfast support of, and trust in, me and my work. I am grateful to my colleagues in the College of Public Service at Jackson State University for their encouragement and support to complete this book. I thank Carolyn Divinity and Sylvia Macey for meticulously editing, typing, formatting and typesetting the manuscript for print. Of course, I thank my wife Carlene, daughter Meya and son Tafrey for their patience and understanding during the long hours required to research and write this book. Finally, I thank those persons at Edwin Mellen Press who were responsible for publishing this book: John Rupnow, Patricia Schulz and Toni Tan.

Introduction

Race preference programs are critical for increasing opportunities among minority-owned business enterprises (MBEs) to do business with government. MBEs, in turn, foster economic stability and growth in minority communities, which can lead to improving proportional equality of material well being among the various racial groups in society. Questions remain, however, about the best way to design race preference strategies. The advent of government race preference programs brought about an effort to establish set-aside or shelter market strategies to involve MBEs in government contracting. These strategies have come under judicial attack in recent years at both the state and federal levels because they do not serve a "compelling state interest" to correct discrimination in the governments' contracting process. Following the Supreme Court's decision in the landmark case of *City of Richmond v. J.A. Croson Company*[1] in 1989, the courts have rejected these programs as premised on evidence that do not offer a legally and methodologically acceptable probative explanation of the extent to which discrimination influences contract award to minority firms under the United States Supreme Court's strict scrutiny standard.[2]

---

[1]See *City of Richmond v. J.A. Croson Company*, 109 S. Ct. 706, (1989).

[2] The United States Supreme Court applies three standards (or level) of review to cases involving equal protection cases. These standards are called rational, intermediate and strict scrutiny. Each of these standards involves a two-part analysis of a government's race preference program. First, there is a determination whether the program serves a valid interest. Second is an analysis of whether the means used to fulfill the interest is consistent with the identified interest. For the rational standard, the government must show that the preference program is based on a "legitimate" governmental interest, and that there is a "minimally rational relation" between the means used to accomplish the interest and the interest itself. (*Cleburne v. Cleburne Living Center, Inc.* 473 U.S. (1985)). This is the least thorough standard of scrutiny. When the intermediate scrutiny standard is used, the government is required to demonstrate that the preference program is premised on an "important"

The intent of this study is to offer a legally and methodologically acceptable approach that governments can rely upon to generate factual predicate (objective and specific particularized findings of discrimination) for establishing compelling state interest in deciding if race preference and/or race neutral remedial policies and programs are warranted in their contracting practices under the United States Supreme Court's strict scrutiny standard of review.

Using the City of St. Petersburg as the research setting, this study combines quantitative and qualitative research methods to determine probative explanation of the extent to which discrimination influence contract awards to minority-owned firms within the framework of the Supreme Court strict scrutiny standard.

Race Preference Programs, Proportionate Representation and Equal Protection

The genesis of race preference programs in government contracting can be traced to the Civil Rights Act of 1964. Title VI of that act is essentially a protective regulatory policy that requires each federal agency to end racial discrimination in government contracting in any program or institution to which it allocates federal

---

governmental interest, and that the means chosen to accomplish this interest is "substantially" related to the interest. (*Califano v. Webster*, supra at 371, quoting *Craig v. Boren*, 438 U.S. 265, 359. (1978)). Finally, the strict scrutiny standard requires the government to show a "compelling" interest, and to demonstrate that the means used is "narrowly tailored" to achieve the interest. (*Wygant v. Jackson Board of Education*, 476 U.S. 267, 274 (1985). This is the most thorough analysis of the three standards, and it is sometimes referred to as strict in theory and fatal in fact because government preference programs rarely survive strict scrutiny. For an overview of legal and methodological issues involving race preference programs in government contracting see for example, Mitchell F. Rice and Maurice Y. Mongkuo, "Did Adarand Kill Minority Set-asides?" *Public Administration Review* Volume 58, No. 1 (January/February 1999). Gilbert J. Ginbert and Janine S. Benton, One Year Later: Affirmative Action in Federal Government Contracting After Adarand," *American Law Review* (August 1996), pp 1903-1948; G.R. Gray and B.L. Perry, "The Supreme Court's Decision: Effects on Small Business Contracting with Non-federal Public Entities," *Journal of Small Business Management* (April 1990), pp 54-59; J.D. Ward, "Response to Croson (*City of Richmond v. J.A. Croson Company*)." *Public Administration Review* (September/October 1994), pp 483-485; J.B. Hairston, "Affirmative Action Plan in Disarray after Croson." *American City and County* (June 1989), pp. 62-64; J.H. Benjamin, "The Supreme Court Decision and the Future of Race-conscious Remedies, *(City of Richmond v. J.A. Croson Company)*."

funds.[3] The Office of Federal Contract Compliance is responsible for enforcing this policy. In general, the goal of ending racial discrimination is to achieve proportionate representation for designated groups in various social roles. Proportionate representation refers to the idea that a racial group's percentage of the overall population should be equal to its share of certain social values or its occupancy of desired social roles.[4] Title VI is premised on an assumption that there are social and economic barriers that inhibit certain individuals from realizing their potential, barriers that exist even though laws or public policy itself do not assign privileges or disabilities to specific groups or individuals. For instance, the unequal distribution of market competitive attributes such as human, financial and social capital will bestow advantages and disadvantages on individuals in the competition for government contracts even when the laws and policies are neutral. Furthermore, discrimination by people and institutions external to the government may render certain firms' chance of competing and winning a contract more difficult.

Research on government contracting and business development suggests that minority-owned businesses face several challenges in competing for government contracts.[5] These challenges are related to access to, and acquisition of, social,

---

[3] Title VI of the Civil Rights Act of 1964 states "[n]o person in the United States shall, on grounds of race, color, or national origin, be excluded from participation in, be denied the benefits of, or be subjected to discrimination under any program or activity receiving Federal financial assistance", 42 USCA S2000d.

[4] Gosepath, Stefan, "Equality", *The Stanford Encyclopedia of Philosophy* (Winter 2001 Edition), Edward N. Zalta (ed.).

[5] U.S. Commission on Minority Business Development, *Interim Report, 1990 Executive Summary*, (Washington D.C.: U.S. Commission on Minority Business Development, 1990); R.E. Suggs, "Racial Discrimination in Business Transactions." *The Hastings Law Journal,* 42 (1991), pp. 1257-1323; T.G. Black, "Small Business Contracting with the Federal government." *Journal of Small Business Management* (October 1982), pp. 64-70; J.A. Cantor, "The Small Business" In The Federal Marketplace-A Study of Barriers." *Journal of Small Business Management* (January 1989), pp. 74-77; J.W. Davis, *Perceived Effects of Federal Procurement Legislation on Small Disadvantaged Businesses.* (Dissertation, School of Business Management, United States International University, 1990); see, for example Susan McManus, *Doing Business With Government* (New York: Paragon House, 1992); Nancy McCrea, *Minority Enterprise Development* (Washington D.C.: National

financial, and human capital. Social capital refers to an MBE's network linkage potential, which involves the interaction of the business owner with other vendors and sharing the market through business or trade shows, and thereby creating a competitive edge. The importance of this attribute in business formation and growth is that it provides a support network, a labor force, and access to market, government being one of the potential markets. Flora et al (1997) distinguish two type of social capital: vertical (or hierarchical) and horizontal.[6] Vertical social capital serves to maintain efficient operation of the business through the establishment of formalized hierarchical chain of command, while horizontal social capital is relevant for the development of the enterprise by perpetuating diversity and innovation in solving problems and identifying opportunities.

Lin (1999) suggests that the basic premise of social capital is to invest in social relations with expected returns.[7] The purpose of the relationship is to make productive activity possible. Much of the research that relates social capital to business success has focused on its use in human capital development, community development[8] and economic development.[9] These studies have established a strong

---

Council for Urban Economic Development, 1989).

[6] J.L. Flora, J. Sharpe, B.L. Newlon, and C. Flora, "Entrepreneurial Social Infrastructure and Locally Initiated Economic Development in the Non-metropolitan United States." *The Sociological Quarterly*, 38(4) (1997), pp. 623-645.

[7] Lin, N., "Building a Network Theory of Social Capital." *Connections*. 22(1), 28-51.

[8] L.J. Servon, "Credit and Social Capital: The Community Development Potential of US Microenterprise Programs." *Housing Policy Debate*, 9(1) (1998), pp. 115-149.

[9] V.L. Grishman, Jr., *Tupelo: The Evolution of Community* (Dayton, OH: Kettering Foundation Press, 1999); J.L. Flora, "Social Capital and Communities of Place." *Rural Sociology*, 63(4), (1998), pp. 481-506; C.M. Tolbert, C.M. Lyson, and M.D. Irwin, "Local Capitalism, Civil Engagement, and Socioeconomic Well-being." *Social Forces*, 77(2), (1998), pp. 401-427; J.L. Flora, J. Sharpe, B.L. Newlon, and C. Flora, "Entrepreneurial Social Infrastructure and Locally Initiated Economic Development in the Non-metropolitan United States." *The Sociological Quarterly*, 38(4) (1997), pp. 623-645.

positive association between social capital building and business success.[10] Support networks also play a critical role in encouraging members of ethnic groups to start and maintain a business by providing the owner with a range of assistance, including informal encouragement, dependable source of labor, and clientele. Moreover, minority businesses engaged in these activities are more likely to be exposed to new developments in the industry, and thereby increase their competitiveness. In government contracting, networking tools such as trade shows, expo marts, newspapers, pre-bid meetings, and public procurement workshops convey the desire of government to do business with minority contractors. Fratoe (1988) has found that the lack of social capital is partially responsible for the low rate of business starts and low success rate of minority businesses.[11] Thus, it would seem that in regards to government contracting, higher levels of social capital might yield higher amount of contract dollars going to minority firms.

Human capital attributes may also enhance the chance of success of a minority business owner.[12] Human capital is education, business experience, and technical capability of a business owner. Qualities such as creativity and risk-taking attributed to successful entrepreneurs are part of the human capital. Research indicates that these qualities can be attained through education and business experience. For example, Bates (1989) has asserted that educational attainment is a reflection of entrepreneurial human capital and a determinant of the potential for

---

[10] Flora et al. (1997); Servon, (1998); A.C. Cooper and C.M. Daily, "Entrepreneurial Team." In Don Sexton and Ray Smilor (eds.), *Entrepreneurship 2000*. (Chicago, IL: Upstart Publishing Company, 1997), pp. 127-150.

[11] Frank A. Fratoe, "Social Capital of Black Business Owners.' *The Review of Black Political Economy*, 16 (1988), pp. 25-32.

[12] Nancy McCrea, *Minority Enterprise Development* (Washington D.C.: National Council for Urban Economic Development, 1989); Gregory D. Wozniak, "Human Capital, Information, and Early Adoption of New Technology." *The Journal of Human Resources* (Winter 1987), pp.101-112.

business profitability.[13] Furthermore, McCrea (1989) has found that the lack of marketing skills and business plan to guide daily decisions have an adverse effect on minority entrepreneurship.[14] Technical capability is attained through training and employment that provide exposure to workplace and management issues needed to operate a successful business.

Other research indicates that minority employment is predominant in the public sector and limited in the private sector.[15] Government employment, however, does not usually translate into business potential whereas managerial experience in the private sector can be drawn upon for the decision-making and supervisory skills needed to operate a successful business. In particular, business owners who receive training on how to adequately do business with government may find a bid specification that requires them to be fully automated to expedite deliveries and services. Moreover, in response to the Paper Reduction Act,[16] most government agencies have totally converted to electronic commerce, which requires contractors to use the Electronic Data Interchange (EDI) system. Several studies have documented significant positive impact of technology use on business success, such as cost reduction, productivity gains, organizational effectiveness, and competitive

---

[13] Timothy Bates, "The Changing Nature of Minority Business: A Comparative Analysis of Asian, Non-minority, and Black-owned Businesses." *The Review of Black Political Economy* 17 (November 1989), pp. 25-42.

[14] Nancy McCrea, *Minority Enterprise Development* (Washington D.C.: National Council for Urban Economic Development, (1989).

[15] See Owen J. Smith, Mitchell F. Rice, and Woodrow Jones, Jr., *Blacks and American Government.* (Kendall Publishers, Dubuque, Iowa, 1991), Chapter 10.

[16] Small Business Administration, "Planning for EDI Implementation." *On-line Business Adviser* (June 1995), pp. 1-13; Small Business Administration, *Electronic Commerce/Electronic Exchange Data Interchange* (March 1996), pp. 1-9.

advantage.[17] Hence, it can be argued that minority firms with adequate human capital capability are better positioned to successfully compete for government contracts.

A final factor that is important to a minority business' success in obtaining government contracts is financial solvency. In principle, financial capital is debt and equity financing available to support business growth and expansion. This may include the minority business owner's credit worthiness, cash value of total asset, net worth, access to financing sources for both start-up and expansion, and cash flow. The ability to do business with governments and take on new projects requires financing. It has been commonly noted in the literature that minority businesses have had difficulty in raising financial capital sufficient enough to open, operate, and grow.[18] In addition, minority firms have had lower success rates than non-minority firms in obtaining financing and commercial loans.[19]

Furthermore, Nancy McCrea (1989) has suggested that a major limitation of minority businesses is the amount of personal and financial assets available to start and operate a successful business. Inadequate equity from these sources causes

---

[17] See for example, R.B. Cooper and R.W. Zmud, "Information Technology Implementation Research: A Technology Diffusion Approach." *Management Science*, 36(2), 1990, 31-42; G.I. Doukidis, S. Smithson, and T. Lyberes, "Trends in Information Technology in Small Businesses." *Journal of End User Computing*, 6(4), 1994, 15-25; A.E. Hartman, C.B. Tower, and T.C. Sebora, "Information Sources and their Relationship to Organizational Innovation in Small Businesses." *Journal of Small Business Management*, (January 1994); A. Holzinger, "The Virtual Future." *Nation's Business*, (May 1995), 45-47; J. Master, G.B. Hartmann, and A. Safari, "Small Business Strategic Planning and Technology Transfer: The Use of Publicly Supported Technology Assistance Agencies." *Journal of Small Business Management*, (July 1995), 26-37; P. Julien, "New Technologies and Technological Information in Small Business." *Journal of Business Venturing*, Vol. 10 (1995), 459-475; S. Schafer, "How Technology is Leveling the Playing Field." *Inc. Technology*, Vol. 4 (1995), 57-62; and A.E. Server, "Path to Wealth in the New Economy." *Fortune*, 20 February, 57-62.

[18] See Fratoe, "Social Capital of Black Business Owners;" Suggs, "Racial Discrimination in Business Transactions;" and House Government Operations Committee, U.S. Congress, *Problems Facing Minority and Women-owned Small Business Including SBA Section 8(a) Firms in Procuring U.S. Government Contracts: An Interim Report HRPT. No. 103-870* (November, 1994).

[19] Faith H. Ando, "Capital Issues and Minority-Owned Businesses." *The Review of Black Political Economy*, 16 (1988), pp. 33-49; Jawanza Kunjufu, *Black Economics*, (IL: African-American Images, 1991).

minority business owners to enter into businesses that do not require a significant amount of financial capital. This lack of equity may also mean that the businesses may be undercapitalized, and more prone to failure, particularly in contracting situations where there may be a substantial delay in payment for products delivered or services provided. Therefore, it stands to reason that the ability to receive financing will vastly improve a minority firm's opportunity in government contracting, as well as to withstand cash flow problems associated with periodic delays in payment, either by the contracting government or prime contractors.

Beyond social, human, and financial attributes that may influence minority success in government contracting is business tenure, or length of time a business has been in existence. Even though business tenure can mean many things, for the discussion here it implies a level of skills capable of sustaining fluctuations in the market as well as managing government contracts.

The discussion above suggests that race neutral contracting policies and laws may perpetuate existing inequalities of opportunity by permitting those who have superior resources to utilize those resources to maintain or augment their chances of winning contracts relative to the have-nots. Without government regulation of the marketplace, the gap between well-endowed and less-endowed firms will tend to increase. Ever since Title VI became law in 1964, race preference programs have served as the mechanism which governments have attempted to promote proportional representation through set-asides and sheltered markets to those less-endowed racial groups. The compelling argument for such programs rests on the continuing impact of previous discrimination. Recognizing that poverty is self-perpetuating both for individuals and across generations, policies that place a group in a disadvantage position can be blamed for that group's continuing disadvantage position.

Notwithstanding the compelling argument for race preference programs, opposition to these programs has been intense and based on both logical argument and the self-interest of groups not favored by the policy. Perhaps the main logical objection to race preference programs is that they seem to violate of the equal protection clause of the Fourteenth Amendment of the U.S. Constitution. According to this line of thinking, race preference programs seem to reward or penalize individuals on the basis of who they are – their racial attributes – rather than on the basis of what they can accomplish. This works against the principle of individualism, meritocracy and productivity of the American capitalist system. The self-interest argument against race preference programs is that setting aside a certain percentage of contracts by non-MBEs for designated minority groups leave fewer of the same percentage of contracts for non-MBEs. Under the strict scrutiny standard of review, governments are required to present factual predicate that the legal status of their race preference programs does not go against the logical principle and self-interest argument. In effect, the challenge for all governments considering adoption of race program programs involves not only that they must provide factual evidence of disproportionate representation in the award of contract to MBEs within particular procurement categories in the relevant market area of the particular government, but more importantly that any identified disparity is the product of racial discrimination in the award of prime and sub contracts.

Study Setting

The city of St. Petersburg is in Pinellas County Florida. The city is located on the peninsula between Tampa Bay and the Gulf of Mexico with a total area of 344.7 square kilometers (133.1 square miles). The total area is 55.2 percent water. It is connected to the main land to the north, the city of Tampa, Florida through the causeway across Tampa Bay to the east, and Bradenton, Florida in the south. The city is a seaport, and a popular destination for tourism and retirement by people from parts of the United State with colder climate. With an average of some 360 days of sunshine each year, it is nicknamed "The Sunshine City."

Historically, the city of St. Petersburg was founded by John C. Williams, formerly of Detroit, Michigan who purchased the land in 1876 and, with the help of Peter Demens, was instrumental in bringing a railroad connection to the city in 1888. The city was incorporated on February 29, 1892, when it had a population of only some 300 people. It was named after St. Petersburg in Russia, the birthplace of Peter Demens. A local legend says that John C. Williams and Peter Demens flipped a coin to see who would have the honor of naming the city. Peter Demens won and named the city after his birthplace, while John C. Williams named the first hotel after his birthplace, Detroit. The Detroit Hotel still exists downtown. Dredging of a deeper shipping channel from 1906 to 1908 opened St. Petersburg to larger shipping. Further dredging improved the port facilities through the 1910s. In 1914, the first commercial airplane service called "Airboat Line" was initiated across Tampa Bay from St. Petersburg to Tampa and back. The air service was discontinued in 1924 with the opening of the Gandy Bridge across Tampa Bay, which allowed automobile traffic between St. Petersburg and Tampa.

As of 2000 census, the city had a total population of 248,232, making it the fourth largest city in the state of Florida with 109,663 households, and 61,630 families residing in the city. The population density is 1,607 per square kilometer (4,163 per square miles). There are 124,618 housing units at an average density of 806.9 per square kilometer (2,090 per square miles). The racial make-up of the city is 71.34 percent White, 22.36 African American, 0.31 percent Native American, 2.67 percent Asian, 0.05 percent Pacific Islander, 1.07 percent from other races, 2.17 percent from two or more races, and 4.23 percent Hispanic.[20]

---

[20]U.S. Bureau of Census, *Census 2000 Summary File 1 (SF1)*.

The 1997 Economic Census reported a total of 199,133 business establishments in the City of St. Petersburg. A breakdown of the level of success of these businesses in generating sales and receipts by race indicate that White-owned firms are proportionately over-represented, while minority-owned are proportionately under-represented. For example, of the total business establishments in the City of St. Petersburg, 84.6 percent are White-owned firms generating 96.5 percent of the total business sales and receipts. Meanwhile, minority-owned firms represent 15.4 percent of the total number of business establishments in the city, but generate only 3.5 percent of the total dollars value of business sales and receipts. This under-representation exists for Black- Asian- and Pacific Islander-owned firms. For example, Black-owned firms represent 6.06 percent of the total number of businesses in the City, but they generate only 0.3 percent of the total business dollars in sales and receipts. Asian and Pacific Islanders own 3.28 percent of the business establishments in the city, but generate only 0.87 percent of the total sales and receipts. Finally, Hispanic-owned firms represent 6.12 percent of the total number of firms in the city, but they earn only 2.30 percent of the total dollar value of sales and receipts.[21] The data suggest that over 30 years after the Civil Rights movement which led to enactment of the Civil Rights Act, minority-owned firms in the city of St. Petersburg, as in many cities across the United States, continue to be disproportionately under represented in sales and receipts.

Throughout the 1990s, as in the 1960s, issues of racial economic inequity have created economic uncertainty among minority groups in St. Petersburg. This uncertainty in turn, has polarized and alienated the races in the city, and in recent years has resulted in a series of civil unrest in the city. For example, on October 24, 1996 civil unrest erupted in the city of St. Petersburg following the shooting of a

---

[21] U.S. Census Bureau, *1997 Economic Census: Minority and Woman-owned Business Enterprises.*

black motorist by a white police officer in a predominantly black neighborhood. After the unrest, the mayor asked the U.S. Commission on Civil Rights to review and assess the situation. Upon meeting with the mayor, members of city council and the director of the Southern Regional Office, the commission decided not to indict the officer. On October 31, 1996 a second civil unrest erupted stemming from the Commission's decision. The Florida Advisory Committee to the United State Commission on Civil Rights[22] promptly responded to the second disturbance by organizing a community forum in St. Petersburg that would allow members of the community, federal, state, and local officials an opportunity to discuss underlying issues that ignited the unrest. The Committee found that although there was a general perception among blacks of being persistently targeted for unfair treatment by the city's White police officers, the most urgent concern was the need to address the perceived inequity between the races in employment, housing, health care, education and business development.[23] Based on these findings, the City of St. Petersburg, as a first step, commissioned a predicate study to determine if this perception was based on factual predicate (objective and specific particularized findings of discrimination) under the strict scrutiny standard of review of the U.S. Supreme Court, which could be relied upon in establishing compelling government interest for a race preference program in the city. This book is the product of the predicate study.

---

[22] The State Advisory Committees to the U.S. Commission on Civil Rights do not have subpoena power. When a community forum is held, the Advisory Committee invites individuals representing differing points of view on an issue. Since the Advisory Committee cannot compel participation, persons invited to present information may not appear. At the conclusion of such forum, members of the audience who wish to present statements on the topic of the forum are permitted to do so.

[23] Florida Advisory Committee to the United States Commission on Civil Rights, *Executive Summary: A community Forum to Explore Race Relations in St. Petersburg, Florida*, St. Petersburg, FL, December 1996, p. 4.

Chapter One discusses the problem associated with the legal status of race preference programs, the research questions and the study objectives. Chapter Two is an outline of the research methodology. Chapter Three is an overview of the legal implications of race preference programs in government contracting. Chapter Four covers a review of past and presents contracting processes in the City of St. Petersburg. The review is aimed at providing a normative foundation for delimiting the study to the legally acceptable standard of fair contracting practices under the strict scrutiny standard of review. Chapter Five is a historical account of the development of the City of St. Petersburg's race preference program and an assessment of its effectiveness in promoting minority participation in the city's contracting process. Chapter Six is a review of anti-discrimination laws that could affect the City of St. Petersburg contracting process. The review provides an assessment of the extent to which full enforcement of applicable local, state, or federal statutory non-discrimination provisions have been achieved. Chapter Seven presents the quantitative analysis findings. Chapter Eight contains the qualitative analysis findings. Finally, Chapter Nine delineates the study conclusions and recommendations.

Chapter One

Legal Status of Race Preference Program

Determining the legal status of a race preference program is critical for governments. The legality of local and state governments' race preference programs was dramatically altered on January 23, 1989 when the United State Supreme Court, in a 6 to 3 vote declared the City of Richmond, Virginia's race preference program unconstitutional because it violated the equal protection clause of the Fourteenth Amendment of the United States Constitution. The United States Supreme Court invalidated the Richmond program because: (1) the City did not establish an adequate factual basis to justify its Minority and Woman Business Enterprise (M/WBE) ordinance, and (2) the ordinance was not narrowly tailored to its purported remedial purpose. This decision, commonly referred to as the *Croson* case, has far-reaching implications for state and local government entities. Among other things, they are required to identify the presence of discrimination in specific procurement categories in the public agency's relevant market area before establishing race-conscious programs in government contracting.

Croson required that all state and local race preference programs be prepared to withstand a strict scrutiny equal protection review. This strict scrutiny standard of review requires state and local governments to establish "compelling governmental interest" for gender- and race-based remedial policies. These policies must be based on a factual predicate, which demonstrates that past or current discrimination, either on the part of a government entity or indirectly through its prime contractors continues to affect public contracting. In a sense, the *Croson* decision requires state and local governments to conduct disparity studies to determine if a factual predicate exists for the development of remedial race-based programs.

In June 1995, the United States Supreme Court, in *Adarand Constructors, Inc. v Pena* handed down another decision which expanded the *Croson* ruling to federal gender- and race-based remedies in government contracting. What *Croson* and *Adarand* did not provide were operational definitions and methodological approaches for conducting a legally defensive disparity study.

As a result of the *Croson* decision, in 1989 the City of St. Petersburg engaged the services of a consulting firm to develop evidence of the nature and extent (if any) of discrimination against woman- and minority-owned business enterprises (M/WBEs)[24] in the relevant market area of the City, to determine if disparity existed between the availability and utilization of minority businesses, and to analyze the effect of race-neutral programs. The study findings, presented in a report entitled *City of St. Petersburg Minority Business Enterprise Disparity Study* dated June 1990 (and supplemental report dated November 9, 1990), asserted that a pattern of discrimination against black-owned business enterprises (BBEs) had resulted in

---

[24] The City of St. Petersburg Ordinance No. 2023-F (1990) defines M/WBE as a Woman Business Enterprise as WBE), Black Business Enterprise as (BBE), or Hispanic Business Enterprise (HBE) certified by the City. WBE, BBE, and HBE mean a business which is at least fifty one (51) percent owned by a woman, a black, or a Hispanic person who also controls and operates the business. In the case of corporation, at least fifty one (51) present of the stock must be owned by a woman or women, Hispanic, or black individual(s), and the corporation must also be at least fifty one (51) percent controlled and operate by a woman or women, black, or Hispanic individual(s). This definition suggests that race and gender groups eligible to participate in the City's M/WBE program are limited to woman, black and Hispanic individuals only. This definition is inconsistent with the state and federal governments' definition which also include Asian-American, Native Americans, the Eskimos, and Aleuts. Hence, since these other groups are not included in the City's program, the disparity study findings was applicable only to "defined minorities".

significant statistical disparity between the availability of such businesses and their utilization in the City's construction contracting and procurement activities.

The City Council held hearings and resolved that the disparity study findings, and anecdotal evidence of discrimination against black-owned business enterprise in construction services, provided sufficient evidence of compelling government interest in implementing race- and gender-based remedial initiatives to increase M/WBEs' participation in the City's construction contracting and procurement activities. Therefore, in 1990 the City enacted a Minority Business Enterprise Ordinance (Ordinance No. 2023-F) establishing policies and procedures intended to provide black-, Hispanic- and woman-owned business enterprises with maximum opportunity to participate in the City's construction contracting and procurement activities. Specifically, the law established participation goals of 8 percent for black-owned businesses, and voluntary goals of 7 percent for Hispanic-owned firms and 7 percent for woman-owned businesses. In 1994, the City council reviewed the performance of the M/WBE program and concluded that Hispanic- and woman-owned businesses in the City's relevant market area have been severely under-utilized in bid proposals for City contracts. As a result, the City ratified Ordinance No. 2023-F to include mandatory participation goals of 7 percent for Hispanic- and woman-owned businesses. In addition, the City council established a Sheltered Market Program in which certain construction projects were reserved for bidding amongst minority-owned businesses only.

In effect, the city required soliciting departments and prime contractors to set aside a certain proportion (based upon established goals) of City construction contracts based on availability of prime contractors and subcontractors in each category of black, Hispanic- and woman-owned business enterprise[25]. In particular, the City created a construction committee responsible for determining annual M/WBE goals and individual black-, Hispanic- and woman-owned business enterprise participation percentages for each construction project. The percentages were to be based on availability of black-, Hispanic- and woman-owned business enterprise construction contractors, and were to be included in all of the City's construction contract bid specifications and bid advertisements. All construction prime contractors submitting bids to provide construction services to the City were required to achieve and maintain participation percentages for the duration of an awarded contract.

The City's M/WBE program was to be reviewed each fiscal year, and in the event that such review indicated that parity has been achieved, the Mayor was required to sunset the program. As a result, the City solicited the services of the author of this book in July 1998, to conduct a disparity study to determine if a factual predicate exist for the continuance of the remedial race preference program. The predicate study was aimed at determining whether discrimination exists, and if so, whether it can be remedied either with a race preference program, a race neutral program, or a combination of the two.[26] In a sense, the disparity study findings was to provide the City of St. Petersburg with documented empirical evidence or data that can be used to determine whether a race preference program consistent with *Croson's* strict scrutiny standard requirement was appropriate.

---

[25] The City M/WBE ordinance does not provide an operational definition of availability. However, based on recent court decisions on the subject matter, availability is operationally defined in this study as the proportion of the number or dollar value of competitively bid contracts (or subcontracts) by racial, ethnic or gender group per procurement category.

[26] In this study, a race preference program is basically a redistributive public policy aimed at ensuring equity in the production and distribution of goods and services. A race neutral policy is distributive public policy that promotes efficiency in the production and distribution of goods and services.

In general, a predicate study involves a statistical disparity analysis which differentiates between qualified, willing, and able M/WBEs in a government entity's relevant market and the use of these M/WBEs in the government agency's procurement practices. Typically, a disparity occurs when the difference between M/WBE availability and M/WBE utilization is lower than expected[27]. The degree of difference is then assessed to determine if it is attributable to random chance or some systematic factor(s). If the latter, then the difference can be considered statistically significant, and may suggest the presence of some systematic effect[28] which may or may not be caused by discrimination.

Inference of past discrimination in the City of St. Petersburg's contracting process cannot be made until other market factors (such as the contractors' experience, human capital, financial capital and social capital) that may affect the utilization of M/WBEs are considered. This task is accomplished either by collecting and analyzing verified and corroborated anecdotal data and information from contractors in the city's relevant market area regarding unfair or disparate treatment, on the part of prime contractors doing business with the city, or manufacturers and wholesale suppliers; or by using multivariate regression procedures to sort out the relative influence of discrimination and market competitive factors on the number and dollars value of contracts awarded, or payments made, to minority contractors by the City. Such analyses should provide the City of St. Petersburg with sound

[27] In this case, a disparity exists if the difference between availability and utilization is statistically significant. Statistically significant disparity implies that the observed proportion of contract dollars (or number of contracts) awarded to a subset of available M/WBEs is different, or deviates from the proportion of utilized M/WBEs in the relevant market area with 95 percent or more certainty. In other words, we can be 95 percent or more confident that the observed under-representation or over-representation of contract dollars (or number of contracts) awarded to the particular M/WBE subgroup is produced by some systematic effect, not chance.

[28] See *City of Richmond v. Croson*, 109 S. Ct. 706, (1989), p. 730.

empirically grounded data that can be relied upon to design and implement race preference and/or race-neutral policies for each procurement category.

Consistent with the criteria in the *Croson* and *Adarand* rulings, as well as the operational definitions and methodological approaches and procedures suggested by recent Federal Court rulings on the subject matter, I addressed the following four major research questions:

1. Is there a disparity between the proportion of qualified, willing, and able minority- and woman-owned firms in the City of St. Petersburg's relevant market area and the proportion of these firms that have participated in the City's contracting process?
2. If disparities exist, are they the products of discrimination or market competitive attributes of contractors in the City of St. Petersburg's relevant market area?
3. If a disparity exists, in what procurement category should race conscious and race neutral policies be established?
4. If a disparity exists, how should the City of St. Petersburg's M/WBE policy and program be structured to remedy the effects of past discrimination, if any, and stay within the constitutional parameters of the *Croson* decision and subsequent Federal Courts interpretation of that ruling?

The above questions were translated into the following sixteen study objectives:

1. To determine whether any participant, policies, procedures, or practices discriminate or have discriminated on the basis of race, ethnicity or gender in awarding public contracts and subcontracts;
2. To assess whether the contracting system, while not actively or intentionally discriminatory, has in a "passive" manner contributed to, or participated in a system of discrimination;
3. To identify and explain the impact of any policies, procedures, or practices which, although not discriminatory, generally inhibit M/WBEs and other small businesses in competition for public contracting.

4. To assess the extent to which full enforcement of applicable local, state, or federal statutory non-discrimination provisions have been achieved.
5. To identify the distinctive five digit NIGP codes applicable to construction trades, goods, and services and professional services that the City of St. Petersburg purchases and the proportion of business that goes to those trades and services in 1991, 1992, 1993, 1994, 1995, 1996 and 1997.
6. To determine potentially and actually available firms in the City of St. Petersburg's relevant market area (RMA) per distinctive trade or service.
7. To determine why some potentially available firms (that is, firms that have the qualification and capacity to bid on prime contracts or provide subcontracting quotes to prime contractors) have not participated in the City of St. Petersburg's contracting process.
8. To measure the level of utilization of firms in each racial group for each distinctive commodity, trade or service in prime contracting and subcontracting.
9. To identify and explain how the utilization figures may be affected by any special conditions such as emergency contracts, sole source contracts, change orders, and other contract adjustments.
10. To estimate the level of disparity between availability and utilization for each race/ethnic group in each distinctive construction type, commodity, trade or service.
11. To analyze anecdotal evidence to determine whether there are forms of discrimination related to public contracting in the City of St. Petersburg's jurisdiction that should be remedied.
12. To evaluate all of the City of St. Petersburg's race-neutral policies that are ending discrimination or improving the competitive position of all small or disadvantaged businesses.
13. To assess the efficacy of race-neutral programs in relations to the necessity of race- and gender-conscious programs that might be considered
14. To determine whether the City of St. Petersburg can increase the amount of procurement subject to competitive bidding.
15. To recommend new race or gender neutral policies and/or race- and gender-preference remedies for the City of St. Petersburg, if warranted and legally defensible.

16. To provide an overview of the information, analysis and data assembled that will serve as a basis for deciding if a race preference program is warranted in the city's contracting process.

Chapter Two
Research Methodology

This chapter presents a detailed description of the research design that was used to conduct the City of St. Petersburg's predicate study. In particular, the chapter includes a description of the research phases, method of data collection, and method of data analysis.

Study Phases

The City of St. Petersburg predicate study was conducted in seven phases. The phases are: (1) a review of the legal framework for understanding race preference programs, (2) a review of City of St. Petersburg contracting procedures and law enforcement, (3) a review of the City of St. Petersburg race preference program, (4) collection of availability and utilization data, (5) disparity analysis, (6) collection and analysis of contractors survey data, and (7) collection and analysis of anecdotal evidence of discrimination.

Legal Framework

This phase involved a review and description of the key legal principles from *Croson* and subsequent related cases of the implications of race preference programs in government contracting. The purpose of this phase is to present the normative foundation of race preference program relative to the U.S. Supreme Court's strict scrutiny standard of review. In particular, the study was conducted within the framework of the landmark Supreme Court cases of the *City of Richmond v. J.A. Croson Company* (1989) and *Adarand Constructors, Inc. v. Pena* (1995), as well as following recent court decisions and rulings: *Contractors Association of East Pennsylvania v. City of Philadelphia* (July 1996), *Associated General Contractors v. City of Columbus, Engineering Contractors Association of South Florida v. Metropolitan Dade County* (September 1996), *Prior Tire Enterprise v. Atlanta Public School District* (October 1997) and *Phillips and Jordan v. Watts* (April 1998).

These cases questioned the validity of all federal, state, and local government M/WBE remedial programs and establish a "strict scrutiny" standard of review. The *Croson* decision states that this standard of review requires state and local governments to establish a "compelling governmental interest" for gender- and race-based remedial goals. These goals must be based on a factual predicate, which either demonstrates that past discrimination on the part of the government or indirectly through a prime contractor, continues to affect current public contracting. In effect, the case law requires state and local governments to conduct disparity studies to establish factual predicates for the development of remedial goals. *Croson* also requires that race preference programs be "narrowly tailored" to specific contracting procurement categories experiencing these present effects of past discrimination. The *Adarand* case expands the *Croson* ruling to federal gender- and race-based remedies in government contracting. As mentioned in Chapter One, what *Croson* and *Adarand* do not provide are detailed operational definitions and methodological approaches and procedures for establishing a "factual predicate." Therefore, subsequent disparity studies, upon which M/WBE programs are developed, are left to the interpretation of the government entity and future court rulings.

In 1996 and 1997, the five *Federal Court* rulings noted previously struck down state and local M/WBE programs because of inadequate evidence to support them. In particular, the courts identified several areas where the disparity studies presented as evidence have violated the basic principles of social science research and constitutional law. These areas include:

1. Inappropriate conceptual and operational definitions of key variables such as availability, race, and gender classifications, relevant market area specification, procurement categorization scheme, and set-aside goals setting schemes;
2. Inappropriate specification of the units of analysis; and
3. Inappropriate (or lack of) statistical tests and procedures used to establish disparity and discrimination in government contracting.

These rulings, however, have provided judicial guidelines on the acceptable data parameters, statistical procedures, and operational definitions of key concepts that should be used in conducting a legally defensible predicate study. I relied on these judicial guidelines to design the methodology for this study.

City of St. Petersburg Contracting Procedures and Law Enforcement

This phase consisted of a review and analysis of: (a) past and present public contracting processes in the City of St. Petersburg; (b) the City of St. Petersburg's legal provision prohibiting discriminatory conduct that could affect public contracting; and (c) federal and state anti-discrimination laws. The review and analysis determined whether any City officials, policies, procedures, or practices discriminate or have discriminated on the basis of race, ethnicity, or gender in awarding public contracts or subcontracts. In addition, the review evaluated whether the City's contracting system, while not actively or intentionally discriminatory, has in a "passive" manner contributed to, or participated in, a system of discrimination. The review concluded with identifying and explaining the impact of any policies, procedures, or practices, which, although not discriminatory, generally inhibit M/WBEs and other small businesses in competition for public contracting. The review and analysis were based on an examination of documents and on interviews with the City's procurement officials and policy decision makers, construction managers, inspectors, representatives of M/WBEs, and non-M/WBEs, contractor organizations, and others.

The law enforcement component of this phase of the study consisted of an assessment of the extent to which full enforcement of the City or applicable state or federal legal provisions prohibiting discriminatory conduct in public contracting has been achieved. This phase also addressed the City of St. Petersburg's M/WBE contracting procedures and legal provisions in the following two functional areas: (1) the effectiveness of the City's M/WBE policy and program operations, monitoring and reporting; and (2) the quality of the City of St. Petersburg's contracting service delivery process.

The review of the City of St. Petersburg's M/WBE policy and program included the following aspects of the City's Ordinance: (1) goal setting scheme; (2) definition of M/WBE availability and utilization of minority and women business enterprise; and (3) affirmative action and equal opportunity provisions. In addition, the review examined and summarized the City's annual progress reports on the program.

The quality of the City of St. Petersburg's M/WBE program service delivery system was assessed by soliciting the opinion of firm owners and City officials regarding the City's procurement policy and program implementation process as follows:

1. The quality of the M/WBE office assistance provided to M/WBEs.
2. The quality of the City's M/WBE certification process in general, the certification application forms, the certification appeals process, the duration of processing applications, the effectiveness of certification in creating opportunities to obtain contracts and subcontracts, and the usefulness of the practice of reciprocal certification.
3. The effectiveness of outreach efforts.

4. The effectiveness of the prompt payment provision by the City and prime contractors for products and services provided by M/WBEs.
5. The quality of M/WBE staff assistance in obtaining contracts and subcontracts.

The effectiveness of the M/WBE program operations, monitoring, and reporting was assessed by interviewing the relevant senior staff and officials of the City, community organizations, and by reviewing internal administrative reports, memoranda, forms, and other pertinent documents related to M/WBE participation in the City's contracting and subcontracting activities. In particular, the assessment focused on the following activities:

1. The effectiveness of the City's M/WBE procurement coordination and data collection management system.
2. The effectiveness of the City's M/WBE goals setting and review committees.
3. The effectiveness of the user departments' communication and compliance with M/WBE contracting and subcontracting provisions.

Contractors Survey

This phase involved a survey of contractors in the city relevant market area in order to assess the impact of race or gender on the City's contracting process and the current level of financial competitiveness of the M/WBEs and non-M/WBEs. The financial competitiveness was assessed by examining the following market competitive financial factors: cash position, net worth, total business assets, sourcing and accessing credit, and level of bonding and insurance. Meanwhile, the impact of race or gender on the City's contracting process was assessed by soliciting the M/WBEs' opinion regarding contract denial, contractor and subcontractor selection and payment for services provided. The units of analysis for this component of the study were available[29] minority and woman business owners in the City's relevant market area. In particular, the M/WBEs included were: certified M/WBEs, non-certified M/WBE's and formerly certified MBEs who have either submitted bids, quotes, proposals or have received City contracts.

Delimitation of Particular Services or Products

In this phase of the study, a delimitation was made of the particular service or products which are contracted out by the City of St. Petersburg. This delimitation is in line with the *Croson* decision which called for measurement of disparities by particular services, so as to avoid results that are over-inclusive and might mask underlying patterns. To measure particular services, the study used the National Institute of Government Purchasing (NIGP) classification which is the standard public procurement classification system across the country.[30] In order to focus on those NIGP classes where the greatest amount of purchases took place, disparity analysis was confined to those classes which represented more than 5 percent of the total number or dollars value of contracts in a particular year. If an NIGP class met the 5 percent threshold in a particular fiscal year, it was analyzed in all the nine fiscal years studied. Data from NIGP classes that did not meet the 5 percent threshold in a particular year were placed in a residual category which, because the category

---

[29] Available M/WBEs is defined in this study as minority- and woman-owned businesses in the City of St. Petersburg's relevant market area that are actively participating in the City's bidding, and quoting process. This definition is consistent with the *Dade County* case ruling which, in essence, regards these firms as meeting *Croson's* definition of qualified, able and willing.

[30] In 1983, National Institute of Government Purchasers (NIGP) conducted a survey in North America on procurement automation. Of those responding, 79 percent indicated a need for assistance in automating their procurement process, and 83 percent expressed a strong interest in a standard commodity/services code. As a result, NIGP released the first version of the NIGP Code in 1984. Since then the NIGP Code has been adopted by more than 1,400 government users and continues to grow. The Code is now available as a 3-digit class code, a 5-digit class-item code, a 7-digit class-item-group code, and a detailed 11-digit code.

represents many particular services, was considered confounding and therefore was not analyzed.

Overall, approximately 20 percent of the total number of contracts and 3 percent of the total dollar value of contracts awarded by the City of St. Petersburg were below the 5 percent threshold, while the remaining 87 percent were above the 5 percent threshold. Therefore, the sample relied upon in this study captured a large portion of the number and dollar value of competitively bid contracts awarded by the City of St. Petersburg during the period studied.

However, as discussed in Chapter Four of this book, the City also procures some contracts through non-competitive methods. The types of procurement included in this category are designated as either exceptions or exemptions by the City. The procurements designated as exception by the City include: sole source and emergency procurement; renewal procurement; procurement made as part of State blanket purchases; purchases of groceries, foodstuff and alcoholic beverage, and expendable items used in connection with restaurants or lounge business operated by the City; the purchase of merchandise for resale in City-operated retail stops; expert witness and other legal services procured through the City's Attorney's Office in furtherance of anticipated or pending litigation; professional services; artistic services or work of art; asbestos abatement and removal bids under $20,000; demolition procurement under $20,000; and purchases of goods and services used in connection with the acquisition, demolition, new construction, rehabilitation, marketing and maintenance of property identified in the neighborhood housing strategy. Meanwhile, procurement designated as exemptions by the City are: purchases of supplies and services related to construction for adapting to major sports tenant and/or operation of the multipurpose stadium being constructed in the portion of the "In Town Redevelopment Area" known as Gas Plant Area; supplies and services related to the operation of the Bayfront Medical Center; and supplies and services related to the construction for tenant improvements and/or operation of the pier. Since these exception and exemption purchases were not competitively bid by the City, and represented procurement areas where availability as defined in the Dade County decision could not be determined objectively, they were not included in the data used for this predicate study.

Since 95 percent of all City of St. Petersburg's procurement dollars are awarded through some form of competitive bid process, this analysis focused on the outcomes of that process. Outcomes were measured in terms of the number of contracts awarded and dollars awarded. When the outcome was contracts awarded, availability was measured by the proportion of total number and dollar value of bids submitted by firms owned by each racial group. For example, if a group submitted 10 percent of the bids, we expected it to obtain roughly 10 percent of the contracts awarded. When the outcome was dollars awarded, availability was measured by the proportion of the total dollar value of bids by firms owned by the particular racial group. Therefore, it would be expected that firms bidding on large contracts would win more dollars.

Disparity Analysis

In this phase of the study, a disparity analysis comparing the "availability" and "utilization" of M/WBEs in the City's contracting was conducted to identify those specific procurement categories where there exists statistically significant under-utilization, if any, of M/WBEs.

The study used two concepts of availability – potential and actual. Potentially available firms were defined as firms that have the qualification and capacity to bid on the city's prime contracts or provide subcontracting quotes to prime contractors have registered to do business with the City of St. Petersburg.[31] Meanwhile, actual available firms for prime contracts were defined as firms that had bid, or submitted quotes to the City during the study's relevant time period (that is, fiscal years (FY) 1989 – 1997)[32]. Actual available subcontractors were defined as firms that have submitted bids or quotes to prime contractors doing business with the City of St. Petersburg to provide services or goods in particular procurement categories. Actual availability was operationally defined as the proportion of the number (or dollar value) of bids or quotes submitted by contractors (or subcontractors) within a particular racial or gender group for each distinctive trade or service category according to the National Institute of Government Purchasing, Inc. (NIGP) classification system that constitutes 5 percent or more in total number or dollar value of the City's purchases.

Survey and interview of potentially available firms were conducted to determine the reasons why they have not bid or submitted quotes on City contracts. The potentially available firms were contacted through mailed survey and telephone interviews. A total of 103 firms from the City's vendor list were contacted.

Utilization was measured for distinctive commodity, trade, or service by: (a) the number of contracts awarded; and (b) the amount of dollars awarded. The measurement of utilization was made separately for prime and subcontracts. In an interview with the City of St. Petersburg procurement officials, it was revealed that the City does not have utilization data for non-M/WBE subcontractors or for M/WBE subcontractors on contracts with no goals. An attempt was made to collect this data by surveying prime contractors who have contracted with the City. However, this

---

[31] This definition includes: (a) firms in the City of St. Petersburg relevant market area that are registered to do business with the city and are competing for the city's contracts or subcontracts; and (b) firms in the City of St. Petersburg relevant market area that are registered to do business with the city, but have never competed for the city's contracts or subcontracts.

[32] These are firms that are actively competing for the city's contracts and subcontracts.

approach did not produce a statistically acceptable response rate. Therefore, no subcontracting disparity analysis was performed. Instead, a contribution to subcontracting issues was made by collecting anecdotal data, and reviewing and describing how prime contractors choose subcontractors and what data they maintain on the process.

Analysis of the utilization data also focused on identifying and explaining how the data may have been affected by any special conditions such as emergency contracts, sole source contracts, contract renewals, blanket purchases, change orders, and other non-competitive contract adjustments. In order to investigate the patterns of utilization on non-competitively bid contracts (other than state blanket purchases and sole source contracts where competition is not possible), a sample was drawn of those contracts. Although an exact comparison with utilization on competitively bid contracts was not possible because the latter contracts may be for different items and in different sizes, it was instructive to see whether different utilization patterns existed between M/WBE utilization on competitively and non-competitively bid contracts. The utilization data were displayed using interval level of measurements,[33] which allows for a statistically acceptable comparison between availability and utilization as discussed below.

Disparity ratios were calculated for each distinctive trade or service NIGP category that exhibit 5 percent or more in total number or dollar value of the City's purchases. The calculation was performed using a statistical technique called the "student t-test" for each race/gender group (that is, non-M/WBEs, blacks, Hispanics, Asians, and women) in each distinctive construction type, commodity, trade or service by the percentage of firms that bid or provided quotes (actual available firms).

---

[33] An interval level of measurement classifies a characteristic, attribute or outcome on a continuous scale. The scale has an arbitrary "zero" starting reference point. See Lawrence L. Giventer, *Statistical Analysis for Public Administration*, (Belmont, CA: Wadsworth Publishing Company, 1996).

Statistical significance test of these ratios was performed to determine whether observed disparities were due to chance or some systematic effect.

Anecdotal Evidence and Allegations of Discrimination

In this phase of the study, anecdotal evidence and allegations of discrimination were collected and assessed. The method used to gather anecdotes consisted of a combination of mail and telephone surveys and personal interviews of M/WBEs and non-M/WBEs. Firms contacted were randomly selected from the City's bidders file. In addition, an invitation was sent to appropriate groups to provide anecdotal comments regarding their experience in contracting with the City. Where possible, an attempt was made to verify the accuracy of anecdotes received through following-up by obtaining a signed affidavit and/or examining the specific contract records and interview of key City staff, City decision makers, organizations, and so forth that were involved (or participated) in the decision making process of the contract. If an anecdote could not be corroborated, it was reported as a hypothesis or lead to other information. Unverified anecdotes were not reported either as fact or used as a basis of proposed race preference remedies.

The quantity and quality of anecdotal evidence was analyzed to determine whether there exist forms of discrimination related to public contracting in the City's jurisdiction that should be remedied. Description of any pattern of discrimination or race- (or gender) specific barriers were delimited to the study's time frame (that is, from fiscal years 1989 through 1997) and the City's relevant market area. All anecdotes were specific regarding the time and place of the event, the nature of the business, and the part of the contracting process involved. In addition, description of any patterns of discrimination or the race- (or gender) specific barriers were relatively recent and as specific as possible regarding the group affected, the industry specialization areas in which the participant worked, and part of the contracting process involved.

Race-Neutral Policies

This phase consisted of a review and assessment of the City's potential race-neutral policies aimed at improving the competitive position of all small or disadvantaged businesses. This phase also examined whether the City can increase the amount of procurement subject to competitive bidding.

Policy Recommendation

This phase consisted of making policy recommendations based on the study findings. The policy recommendations involved separate evaluation of the impact of proposed or newly implemented changes to the City of St. Petersburg's procurement and MBE process for: (a) increased small dollar purchase thresholds; (b) purchase order, change order and contract amendment policies; and (c) the M/WBE Goal-Setting Process (particularly with regards to the comparison of availability and utilization, and commodity coding at the project versus the work element level). In making the recommendations, a conscious effort was made to ensure that the remedies were narrowly tailored to rectify the specific discrimination against firms owned by those groups for those distinctive commodities trade or services where discrimination was identified.

Data Collection Method

This study relied upon both obtrusive and unobtrusive methods of data collection[34]. A description of the method of data collection for each of the study phases is presented below.

---

[34] An unobtrusive method of data collection is an approach that directly removes the researcher from the set of events being studied. In this study, for example, obtaining data from the City's purchase order and bidding files or documents to measure availability and utilization represents an unobtrusive method of data collection because the conditions leading to the production of these data were not influenced the WE research team. (See David Nachmias and Chava Nachmias, *Research Methods in Social Sciences*, New York: St. Martins Press (1987).

Contracting Procedure/Law Enforcement Data

The review of contracting procedures and law enforcement relied on three techniques of data collection: (1) surveys; (2) interviews; and (3) extraction of data from procurement files (hardcopy and automated), documents, and records.

Two surveys were administered. The first survey was mailed out to a random sample of contractors (M/WBEs and non-M/WBEs) selected from the City of St. Petersburg's automated Vendors file stored in the Purchasing Department. This survey was aimed soliciting information about why potentially available contractors do not bid, anecdotal comments of discrimination and/or unfair treatment, evaluation of the City's M/WBE program, and financial capital status. The second survey instrument was used to conduct a semi-structured interview of senior staff of the City, members of the City Council, community organization officials, contractor organization officials, and representatives of M/WBEs, and non-M/WBEs regarding the City of St. Petersburg's procurement and contracting activities. The following City departments were interviewed: Finance, Purchasing, Engineering & Stormwater, Community Affairs, Legal, Administration, Utilities, and the Economic Development/MBE Office. In addition, City Council members and the City Mayor were also interviewed regarding their vision of participation of M/WBEs in the City's contracting process. The survey and interviews solicited City officials' opinion regarding the awareness and implementation of the City's M/WBE policy and program, and the City's contracting practice and law. A list of community organizations that participated in the survey/interview was provided by the Economic Development Department/Business Development Center.

Potential Availability Data

As defined earlier, a potentially available firm is a firm that has the qualifications and capacity to bid on prime contracts or provide subcontracting quotes to prime contractors. The data and information on potentially available firms were obtained from the City's vendors file. The file contains all vendors that have been either certified or registered to do business with the City or other governmental agencies in the St. Petersburg area, such as Pinellas County and the School District of Pinellas. A list of the City's vendors was obtained in automated form from the Purchasing Department Advanced Purchasing System (APS) database and Engineering Department Automated Procurement Data files.

Actual Availability Data

The contracting availability data were obtained from City of St. Petersburg's hard copy and automated bid tabulation files housed in the Purchasing Department, Engineering Department, and the Business Development Center. The actual availability data set included only purchases that are competitively bid[35]. These include sealed bids, written quotes, and verbal quotes. Excluded from this actual availability data were contracts for utilities, education, training fees, tuition, dues, publication, interest payment to financial institutions, other government agency services, payments, medical institutions and organizations, disbursements, professional trade association fees and subscriptions, other not-for-profit organization services, and City employee services. Where contracts were not competitively bid, availability was based on the particular procurement process used.

The resulting data set consisted of the following variables: (a) bid or requisition number, (b) purchase order number, (c) contractor's name, (d) contractors address, (e) bid fiscal year, (f) project description, (g) contract award status, (h) contract NIGP category, (i) contractor's racial, ethnic or gender class, and (j) contract

---

[35] In the event that the bid or quote data were on hard copy, and too large to collect in the time frame to complete the study, an optimal sample size for each relevant NIGP class with above 5 percent of total purchases was determined, and a stratified random sampling method was used to collect the data for analysis.

size (in dollars and numbers). The resulting data set was sorted by prime contractors and subcontractors separately for subsequent analysis of actual availability.

Utilization Data

Utilization was measured by the proportion of the percentage of the number of competitively bid contracts awarded to each group, and the percentage of dollars of competitively bid contracts awarded to each group. The utilization data were collected from the same sources, and using the same techniques, as collection of actual availability described above. However, the resulting data sets included only firms that have been awarded City competitively bid prime contracts or subcontracts during the study time frame. The data sets consisted of all the variables contained in the actual availability data set discussed above plus dollar amount of each contract. In order to estimate utilization based on the number of firms which have received contract awards, another data set was generated by extracting all the firms that have received contract and subcontract awards from the utilization data set. The variables in this data set were: (a) contractor's or subcontractor's name, (b) contractor's or subcontractor's address, (c) contractor's or subcontractor's primary NIGP category, and (d) contractor' or subcontractor's race/gender. These utilization data sets were stored in the computer for subsequent analysis.

Anecdotal Evidence Data

The collection of the anecdotes was conducted by relying on methodological guidelines specified by recent court decisions regarding anecdotal evidence, as well as basic principles of designing and conducting qualitative research. For example, while anecdotes have been a part of every race preference predicate study, the courts have not received them very well when the studies have been subject to litigation. The courts have taken the position that anecdotes may be useful supplement to statistical analysis, but that "only in rare cases will anecdotal evidence suffice standing alone" for a race conscious program[36]. Moreover, the courts are aware that, while some anecdotes are true (that is the incident actually occurred as reported) and are caused by discrimination, other anecdotes may be exaggerations or misunderstandings or may not be caused by discrimination.

Hence, to establish internal and external validity of a claim of discrimination, the courts suggest that the study must, at the very least, attempt to corroborate the accuracy of anecdotes where possible. For example, in *AGC v. Columbus* the court, upon review of a record of 29 interviews of local M/WBEs in the construction business and six City Council hearings with 77 witnesses, observed that:[37]

1. None of the interviewees were identified in the Predicate Study, so it was impossible for Council members who read the Predicate Study to know which evidence was redundant or to evaluate the credibility of the anecdotes reported.
2. There were no "temporal or geographical standards in gathering and recording anecdotal evidence. Many of the anecdotes selected for quotation in the Predicate Study were irrelevant because they happened in another jurisdiction or were too remote in time.
3. Interviewees were not questioned "about possible non-discriminatory reasons for adverse actions they complained about…"
4. The City did not review interview reports to assess the quality or sufficiency of the anecdotal evidence for a finding that there was pervasive discrimination in the Columbus construction industry.
5. The City's public hearings were not "impartial investigative hearings." Instead, the "purpose of the 1990 and 1992 hearings was not to investigate discrimination but to create a record to support race- and gender- based preferences.

---

[36] *Engineering Contractors Association of South Florida, Inc. v. Metropolitan Dade County, 122 F. 3rd 895 (11th Cir. 1997).*

[37] See *AGC v. Columbus, 936 F. Supp. at 1414, 1426 (S.D. Ohio 1996).*

Based on these observations, the court suggested some general standards for collecting anecdotal evidence of discrimination in government contracting. The standards as articulated by the Court are as follows:

> Such an investigation should meet minimum standards for a reasonably competent forensic investigation. The investigators should be impartial and unbiased and they should be reasonably thorough and diligent. Extra care should be taken in gathering and evaluating anecdotal evidence from advocates of race- and gender-based preferences. Such informants may be prone to exaggerate or fabricate circumstances and events or omit important details. Attempts should be made to verify claims of discrimination where it is reasonable to do so. Where knowledge of industry practices is necessary to evaluate claims of disparate treatment, such information should be obtained. The collection of evidence should not be limited to those who would benefit from race- or gender-based preferences or to members of one racial or gender group. It should include a fair sampling of all segments of the community who have relevant knowledge and who would be impacted by such legislation.
>
> The investigators should limit themselves to facts and should not solicit or report rumors or innuendos. They should obtain appropriate details. They should at least ask the fundamental questions any first-year journalism student knows to ask: "who, what, when, where, why and how?" The investigation should include the study of readily available public information on M/FBE participation in the relevant market such as local newspapers and trade publications. The investigation should be limited to the relevant time and the relevant place. It should focus on matters which are germane to the issue of discrimination and should be informed by judicially recognized methods of proving discrimination. It should not be assumed that every adverse experience of a minority or female subject was for indicia of a race- or gender-based animus or evidence of disparate treatment.[38]

---

[38] *Id at 1426.*

In *Engineering Contractors Association of South Florida, Inc. v Metropolitan Dade County*, the Court expressed skepticism, about methods and procedures used by the County's Disparity Study consultant to collect and interpret anecdotes[39]. The anecdotal evidence presented by the County in defense of its M/WBE program consisted of claims made by M/WBEs from hundreds of surveys and interviews conducted by the County's consultant, and individual trial testimonies. The court ruled that the method used to collect the anecdotes violated three general principles of the logic of scientific inquiry involved in establishing the internal validity and reliability of anecdotal evidence.

First, the objectivity of the method used to collect the anecdotes was questionable because the County did not obtain knowledge of the perspectives of both parties involved in an incident as well as knowledge about how comparably placed persons of other races, ethnicities, and genders have been treated. Second, the County did not show how, if at all, it guarded against "interviewers bias" or "response bias" during the interviewing or survey process. Third, the county made no attempt to investigate or verify the anecdotal evidence to establish the accuracy of the claims of discrimination.

Hence, the court concluded that without corroboration, it could not distinguish between allegations that in fact represent an objective assessment of the incident of discrimination, and those that are fraught with heartfelt, but erroneous, interpretations of events and circumstances. In summation, the court ruled that "the cost associated with the imposition of race, ethnicity, and gender preferences are

---

[39] *Engineering Contractors Association of South Florida, Inc. v. Metropolitan Dade County*, 943 F. Supp. 1546 (S.D. Fla. 1996)

simply too high to sustain a patently discriminatory program on such weak evidence."[40]

Finally, in *Phillips and Jordan v. Watts*, the court dismissed the anecdotes in the state of Florida disparity study as mere perceptions. In particular, the court stated:

Individuals responding to FDOT's telephone survey have described their perceptions about barriers to FDOT's bidding procedures. But FDOT has presented no evidence to establish who, if anyone, in fact engaged in discriminatory acts against Black and Hispanic businesses. The record at best establishes nothing more than some ill-defined wrong caused by some unidentified wrongdoers; and under City of Richmond that is not enough.[41]

These judicial decisions and guidelines were relied upon in designing the method used to collect and analyze the anecdotal evidence for the City of St. Petersburg predicate study. In particular, the method used was broad-based in that it attempted to acquire anecdotes from a wide variety of people (minority and non-minority) who wish to report incidents of discrimination in the public and private sectors that affect the City's contracting. In addition, every attempt was made to maintain objectivity in gathering the anecdotes.

The anecdotes of unlawful discriminatory practice in the City of St. Petersburg contracting process were derived from four major sources. The sources are:

1. Persons responding to surveys about whether discrimination has affected their decision to bid on the City of St. Petersburg's contracts;

---

[40] *Id at 1426.*

[41] *Phillips and Jordan v. Watts, 13 F. Supp. 2d 1308, 1314 (N.D. Fla. 1998).*

2. Persons responding to telephone interviews about whether discrimination has affected their decision to bid on the City's contracts;
3. Persons responding to newspaper advertisements requesting information about discrimination affecting City contracting; and
4. Persons identified by community organizations and other contractors in the City's relevant market area.

The units of analysis and the sample size of the anecdotes were determined by relying upon guidelines for maximum variety sampling suggested in the qualitative research literature[42]. The intent of the maximum variety sampling is to deliberately ensure sampling heterogeneity while observing commonalities in their experience. It is the most useful method when exploring abstract concepts such as discrimination[43]. In using the maximum variety sampling technique, the interviewees were not selected because they reflected the general population. Rather, they were selected based on common experience or knowledge in contracting with the City of St. Petersburg. The courts have not been clear as to the appropriate sample size of interviewees (or anecdotes) that is needed to establish factual predicate. However, the methodological literature on qualitative research suggests that six interviewees are adequate provided that the sample is information rich[44].

Using these methodological approaches as a guide, we selected a total of 79 firm owners and sixteen community organization representatives to be interviewed for a total sample of 95 potential interviewees. Of the total number of potential

---

[42] See Michael Quinn Patton, *Qualitative Evaluation and Research Methods*, (Newbury Park: Sage Publications, 1990); Norman K. Denzin and Yvonne S. Lincoln, Editors, *Handbook of Qualitative Research* (Newbury Park: Sage Publications, 1998); Amedeo Giorgi, *Phenomenology and Psychological Research* (Pittsburgh: Duquesne University Press, 1985); and Max Van Manen, *Researching Lived Experience: Human Science for an Action Sensitive Pedagogy* (NewYork: New York University Press, 1990).

[43] See Denzin and Lincoln, 1998.

[44] See Patton (1990); Giorgi (1985); and Van Manen (1990).

interviewees, detail interviews were conducted with eleven of the firm owners and seven representatives of community organizations. The remaining contractors and representatives of community organizations could not be interviewed for a variety of reasons such as: (a) the contractor or representative would not agree to be interviewed; (b) contact could not be made with the contractor despite repeated telephone calls; (c) the contractor or representative could not accept an interview due to a busy schedule; (d) the contractor or representative did not want to provide any information for fear of reprimand or discouragement with the City's contracting process; (e) the contractor or representative had a pending legal action against the City and would prefer not to make any comment that may adversely affect the pending case; and (f) the contractor or representative expressed having no problem with the City. The contractors that were interviewed provided a total of 13 incidents of unfair or disparate treatment in contracting with the City of St. Petersburg. Meanwhile, the community organization representatives provided 5 anecdotal comments regarding the City's contracting process.

Since the subject of these interviews was discrimination, some persons did not wish to speak on the record or be otherwise identified. In such situations, they were assured that their names will not be mentioned in the report and nothing they said would be quoted without their consent. Each interview session was conducted following a semi-structured approach involving a combination of high-quality personal case description aimed at documenting uniqueness or significantly shared patterns of commonalities existing across interviewees. In particular, notes were taken on each interview including: (a) the date, time, and location of the interview; (b) the name, address and phone number of the interviewee; (c) name and type of business; (d) number of employees; (e) gross revenue for last three years; (f) the race/ethnicity and gender of the interviewee; (d) the interviewee's business position; (e) the M/WBE certification status of the business; (f) description or discrimination of disparate treatment incident; (g) description and bid or project number of project involved; (h) names of other persons familiar with the incident (if any); and (i) name of interviewer.

For each allegation of discrimination, a recording was made of the date when the alleged incident occurred and the location. If the alleged incident occurred more than nine years ago (the study time frame) or outside of the City's relevant market area (Tampa/St. Petersburg Standard Metropolitan Statistical Area), it was considered not relevant to the study.

The record of each anecdote consisted of a detailed description of the allegation including who or what agency or firm allegedly committed the discrimination. Each interviewee was asked, unless it was obvious, why they believe the incident was caused by discrimination rather than by something else. Finally, each interviewee was asked if there were any records that would corroborate the incident.

Once the collection of the anecdotal evidence was completed, the frequency of each type of allegation was classified and estimated by race, ethnicity and gender of the persons who made the allegation; and the type of business they were in. In a situation where an allegation could not be corroborated, it was reported with the caveat that it could not be verified.

Data Analysis Method

The study relied on both qualitative and quantitative method of data analysis. The qualitative method involved verifying and corroborating anecdotes and comments obtained from surveys and personal interviews regarding the respondents' experience with the City of St. Petersburg's contracting process. Anecdotes and comments provided by the respondents were compiled, sorted, verified, validated by signed affidavits, and evaluated for consistencies and inconsistencies. The quantitative method of data analysis basically relied on descriptive and inferential statistical procedures. Descriptive statistical procedures were used to estimate the frequency distribution by race/gender category and NIGP category of: (a) the respondents' ratings on the surveys, (b) the number of potential available firms, (c) the number and amount in dollars of actual available prime contracting firms, (d) the number and amount in dollars of actual subcontracting firms, (e) the number and amount in dollars of prime contracting firms which have received contract awards, and (f) the number and amount in dollars of subcontracting firms which have received contract awards.

Six sets of data were developed and statistically analyzed. The data sets were: (a) program review survey, (b) potential available firms by race and procurement category (c) actual available prime contracting firms by race and procurement category, (d) actual available subcontracting firms by race and procurement category(if available), (e) competitively awarded prime contracts by race and procurement category, and (f) competitively awarded subcontracts by race and procurement category.

For the program review data, the frequency distribution of the responses for each item on the survey instrument was performed. The analyses performed on the last five sets of data were: (1) particular services analysis; (2) actual availability analysis; (3) utilization analysis; (4) disparity analysis; and (5) bidding analysis. Particular service analysis involved identifying the distinctive five digit NIGP codes applicable to the various products and services that the City of St. Petersburg purchases and the proportion of business that goes to those trades and services during fiscal years 1989, 1990, 1991, 1992, 1993, 1994, 1995, 1996, and 1997. Proportions were estimated by the number of contracts awarded and by the dollar amount of those contracts. Actual availability analysis was delimited to prime contractors who had participated or were actively participating in the City's competitive bidding or quoting process, and subcontractors (if the data was available) who submitted quotes to the City's prime contractors[45]. Utilization analysis involved determining the proportion of the number and the dollar value of prime or sub contracts awarded in each distinctive commodity, trade or service area with more than 5 percent of purchases during each fiscal year under study. Disparity analysis compared the proportion of the number and dollar value of contracts bid by each race, gender and ethnic group to the number and dollars amount of contracts awarded to each group per distinctive commodity, trade or services category during each fiscal year under investigation.[46] The level of significance of the difference between availability and utilization was determined by performing a student t-test.

The analysis was performed for each major procurement category with more than five (5) percent transactions during fiscal years (FY) 1989,1990, 1991, 1992, 1993, 1994, 1995, 1996, and 1997.

Disparity Analysis Procedure

A disparity analysis is a statistical comparison of the proportion of available firms to their utilization within a particular NIGP class. The intent of the analysis is to determine if the observed proportion of the number (or dollar value) of contracts awarded to particular racial, ethnic or gender group is different, or deviates, from the percentage of the number (or dollar value) of the particular group's bids for a specific NIGP class with a 95 percent or more certainty. The disparity analysis is facilitated through a statistical significance test called a t-test. In effect, the t-test allows a comparison to be made between availability and utilization to establish if an observed under-utilization of a particular racial, ethnic, or gender group is due to either chance,

---

[45] The availability analysis was limited to the distinctive trade or service categories that were awarded more than 5 percent of the City's competitively bid prime or subcontracts during each fiscal year under investigation. NIGP classes with State of Florida contract were not analyzed. In addition, NIGP classes with long term contracts were analyzed only for those years when the contracts were competitively bid.

[46] The disparity analysis was performed on prime contractors and subcontracts separately.

or some systematic effect, which according to the U.S. Supreme Court, could imply past discrimination. The underlying assumption of the test is that the absence of past discrimination in the procurement process occurs when the percentage of the number (or dollars) of contracts awarded to a specific racial, ethnic, or gender group of firms approximates, or equal, that group's proportion of the number (or dollars) of bids in the particular NIGP class.

Statistically, the t-test is based on the following hypotheses:

$H_0 : P_A - P_U = 0$ (null hypothesis)
$H_1 : P_A - P_U > 0$ (alternate hypothesis)

Where:

P_A = the proportion of the number (or dollar amount) of bids for firms in the particular racial, ethnic, or gender group within a specific NIGP class

P_U = the proportion of the number (or dollar amount) of awards for firms in the particular racial, ethnic, or gender group within a specific NIGP class.

Given these hypotheses, the t-test yields a series of test statistics with corresponding probabilities attached to each statistic. If a test yields a probability less than 0.05 percent ($p<0.05$) then we can be 95.00 percent or more confidence that the alternative hypothesis is true. In this case, the alternative hypothesis implies that the difference between availability and utilization is large enough to infer that a disparity exists within the specific NIGP class[47]. The appropriate test statistic to generate the probability is a numerical value, t, which is estimated based on the following equation:

---

[47] The Courts recommends at least 80 percent confidence level for an inference of discrimination to be made.

where:

$$t = \frac{(P_U - P_A) - 0}{\sqrt{\frac{(P_A)(1 - P_A)}{n}}}$$

P_U = proportion of the number (or dollar value) of prime (or sub) contract awards for firms in a particular racial, ethnic, and gender group within a specific NIGP class

P_A = proportion of the number (or dollar value) of prime (or sub) contract bids or quote for a particular racial, ethnic, or gender group within a specific NIGP class

n= total number (or dollar value) of contract awards

Note that P_U is calculated by dividing the total number (or dollar value) of contracts awards for a particular racial, ethnic, or gender group by the total number (or dollar) of contract awards to all utilized firms in a specific NIGP class. For example let:

$H_{\#}$ = total number contract awards to Hispanic-owned firms in a particular NIGP class

$n_{\#}$ = total number of contract awards to all firms in a particular NIGP class

$$P_U = \frac{H\#}{n_{\#}}$$

P_A is calculated by dividing the total number (or dollars value) of bids for a particular racial, ethnic, or gender group by the total number (or dollar amount) of bids for all the groups in a specific NIGP class. For example let:
H_A = total number (or dollar value) of Hispanic-owned firm bids or quotes in a particular NIGP class

n_A = total number (or dollar amount) of all the groups bids or quotes in a particular NIGP class

$$P_A = \frac{HA}{n_A}$$

The t-test is a ratio of two elements. In the numerator of the t-test equation is the difference between the observed proportion of the number (or dollar value) of contract awards for a particular racial, ethnic, or gender group relative to the total number (or dollar value) of contract awards for all the groups within an NIGP class, and the proportion of the number (or dollar value) of the observed proportion of the number (or dollar value) of contract bids for the particular racial, ethnic, or gender group relative to the total number (or dollar value) of contract bids for all the groups within the specific NIGP class. This numerator is denoted as $(P_U - P_A) - 0$. The 0 represents the hypothesized relationship between availability and utilization. The denominator, on the other hand, represents the standard error of the mean number (or dollar value) of contract bids (or quotes) of the particular racial, ethnic, or gender group in the specific NIGP class.

Since the null hypothesis assumes no difference between the proportion of the number (or dollar amount) of contracts awarded to a particular racial, ethnic, or gender group in a specific NIGP class and the proportion of the number (or dollar value) of contract bids (or quotes) of the particular group in the NIGP class, it is presumed that the proportion of the number (or dollar value) of contract awards is equal to the proportion of the number (or dollar value) of contract bids or quotes. From a statistical standpoint, we are concerned with estimating the number (or dollar value) of bids or (quotes) of a particular racial, ethnic, or gender group because, if we took numerous samples of the number (or dollar value) of bids (or quotes) of the particular group, we would generate a range of estimates. Hence, we need to account for the degree of error in establishing the availability given the number (or dollar value) of contracts awarded to a particular racial, ethnic, or gender group. As denoted in the equation above, the standard error is simply the square root of the product of P_A and $1 - P_A$ over the total number (or dollar value) of contracts awarded in the NIGP class.

In terms of drawing conclusions from calculating the t-test statistic, typically the larger the test statistic, the less likely the null hypothesis of no difference is true. Consequently, it is more probable that a difference exists between availability and utilization suggesting a greater chance or inference of some systematic effect. The decision to accept or reject the null hypothesis of no difference is contingent upon a statistical decision rule commonly referred to as the alpha level. The alpha level is the probability that an outcome or event could occur by chance. The smaller the alpha level, the more difficult it will be to reject the probability that an outcome is occurring by chance, and hence the more difficult it will be to reject the null hypothesis of no difference between availability and utilization. Since we want to be certain that the results obtained from this statistical model are valid, we set the alpha level at 0.05 percent. An alpha level of 0.05 or more implies that we are certain that we will not reject the null hypothesis of no difference between availability and utilization when in fact there is no difference.

The t-test has the capacity of generating a test statistic and corresponding probability for any sample size, and because of this capability the t-test is referred to an exact test. Since the t-test is an exact test, the test statistic for alpha level of 0.05 varies by the sample size of the number (or dollar value) of contracts awarded, or what is commonly referred to as the degree of freedom. To illustrate by example, let us use the City of St. Petersburg's Hispanic-owned firms general construction services number of prime contracts data for FY 1992:

$$t = \frac{(5.26 - 5.38) - 0}{\sqrt{\frac{(5.38)(94.62)}{19}}} = -0.0232$$

In this case, the test statistic for an alpha level of 0.05 with a sample size of 3 is 2.353,[48] which means that if an estimated test statistic, t, is greater than 2.353, we reject the null hypothesis of no difference and conclude with a 95 percent or more confidence that a statistical difference exists between availability and utilization. If, on the other hand, the estimated test statistic, t, was less than 2.353 as in our example above we would accept the null hypothesis and conclude that no statistical difference exist between availability and utilization. If an estimated t-test statistic exceeds the alpha cut-off, it is denoted by an asterisk (*), suggesting that the difference between availability and utilization is statistically significant. A statistically significant test statistic with a negative sign implies a disparity. On the other hand, a statistically significant test statistic with a positive sign suggests an over-utilization. This approach was used throughout the entire City of St. Petersburg's contracting disparity analysis.

Bid Analysis

While the disparity analysis focused on the level of contracts that are awarded to minority-owned firms, the bid analysis was aimed at determining the level of participation of minority firms in the City of St. Petersburg competitive bidding process, as well as identifying barriers that inhibit certain potentially available minority firms from actively competing in the city's contracting process.

To make this determination, a random sample of 100 contractors was selected from the city's potentially available data set and a semi-structured telephone

---

[48] This value is determined by referring to a standard t-test Table which lists the cut-off value by alpha level for different sample sizes.

interview and/or mailed survey was conducted[49]. The interview focused on soliciting the contractors' opinion regarding reasons why they have not bid on City of St. Petersburg contracts. The information gathered from these interviews was compiled and analyzed using descriptive statistical procedures. In addition, inferential statistical procedures (t-tests) were used to compare the proportion of the number of potentially available firms to the proportion of the number of actually available firms by racial, ethnic, or gender group. This analysis was aimed at determining whether a statistically significant pattern of under-bidding exists in the various genders, ethnic, or racial group of contractors in the City's relevant market area. Meanwhile, the data and information obtained from the survey and interviews was compiled and analyzed to determine whether there were barriers to bidding that might be mitigated by race neutral, or race preference means.

[49] It is important to note that M/WBEs were over-sampled in order to ensure an adequate representation of M/WBEs in the sample to be surveyed.

Chapter Three

Legal Implications of Race Preference Programs in Government Contracting

This chapter presents the normative foundation of government race preference programs relative to the U.S. Supreme Court's strict scrutiny standard of review. An understanding of this foundation was critical in defining the research variables, delimiting the units of analysis and identifying and selecting the most appropriate methods of data collection and analysis relied upon in this study.

City of Richmond v. J.A. Croson Company

Any discussion of the legal implications of race preference programs in government contracting must necessarily begin with the Supreme Court's landmark decision in *City of Richmond v. J.A. Croson Company*,[50] and its progeny. At issue in *Croson* was whether the City of Richmond's Minority Business Utilization Plan (hereinafter "Plan") which required that, on an annual basis, 30 percent of the City's construction dollars be paid to minority business enterprises[51] was violative of the Fourteenth Amendment's Equal Protection Clause.[52] The Court held that government-sponsored race preference programs must pass a strict scrutiny standard

---

[50] 488 U.S. 469, 102 L. Ed. 2d 854 (1989).

[51] *Id.* at 477. Minority businesses enterprises were defined as those which were at least 51percent owned and controlled by "minority group" members, which were defined as "[c]itizens of the United States who are Blacks, Spanish-speaking, Orientals, Indians, Eskimos or Aleuts."

[52] The Fourteenth Amendment's Equal Protection Clause provides that "[n]o state shall . . . deny to any person within its jurisdiction the equal protection of the laws." The fundamental purpose of the Clause "is to prevent the States from purposefully discriminating between individuals on the basis of race." *Shaw v. Reno*, 509 U.S. 630, 642, 125 L. Ed. 2d 511 (1993).

of review in order to comport with the Fourteenth Amendment's Equal Protection Clause. In so holding, the Court reasoned that generalized assertions of societal discrimination were insufficient to demonstrate "a compelling state interest in apportioning public contracting opportunities on the basis of race."[53] The Court further noted that Richmond's Plan failed the strict scrutiny test in that it was not "narrowly tailored" to remedy the effects of past discrimination.[54]

Croson is perhaps most significant for its exacting standards with respect to the evidence local and state governments must demonstrate before legislation containing race- and gender- conscious measures may be implemented. As the Court admonished: Absent searching judicial inquiry into the justification for such race-based measures, there is simply no way of determining what classifications are "benign" or "remedial" and what classifications are in fact motivated by illegitimate notions of racial inferiority or simple racial politics.[55]

Thus, re-affirming the view expressed in its earlier plurality decision in *Wygant v. Jackson Board of Education,*[56] the Court noted that the standard of review under the Equal Protection Clause was not dependent "on the race of those burdened or benefited by a particular classification."[57] Because notions of stigmatic harm and racial stereotyping are inherent in any type of racial classification, the Court held that a legislative body must essentially demonstrate that it has become an active or a "passive participant" in the systemic discrimination against racial and ethnic groups before race-conscious relief may be utilized.[58]

---

[53] *Croson*, 488 U.S. at 503.
[54] *Id.* at 507-09.
[55] *Id.* at 492.
[56] 476 U.S. 267, 279-280 (1986), 90 L. Ed. 2d 260 (1986).
[57] *Croson*, 488 U.S. at 494 (citing *Wygant*, 476 U.S. at 279-80).
[58] *Id.* at 492.

Compelling State Interest

In *Croson* the court stated that "It is beyond dispute that any public entity, state or federal, has a compelling interest in assuring that public dollars, drawn from the tax contributions of all citizens, do not serve to finance the evils of private prejudice."[59] In order to eradicate the effects of past discrimination based on race-conscious measures, however, the municipality must demonstrate that it is motivated by specific, particularized findings of discrimination rather than mere speculation of discrimination.[60] It was the dearth of specific evidence of discrimination which ultimately led the Supreme Court to declare that the City of Richmond failed to demonstrate a compelling state interest in apportioning public contracts on the basis of race or ethnicity.[61]

Evidence of Past Discrimination

In *Croson*, there was no direct evidence that the City of Richmond or the City's prime contractors had ever discriminated against minority-owned subcontractors.[62] Rather, the City's sole justification for its Plan was that it was remedial in nature and "enacted for the purpose of promoting wider participation by minority business enterprises in the construction of public projects."[63] Rejecting what it considered mere administrative rhetoric, the Court stated that many of the discriminatory barriers facing minority contractors cited by the City were equally formidable to "member[s] of any racial group attempting to establish a new business enterprise, such as deficiencies in working capital, inability to meet bonding requirements, unfamiliarity with bidding procedures, and disability caused by an

---

[59] *Id.*
[60] *Id.* at 498.
[61] *Id.*
[62] *Id.* at 480.
[63] *Id.* at 478.

inadequate track record."[64] Stripped of their embellishment, the Supreme Court noted that none of these so-called barriers provided a strong basis for the City's conclusion that remedial action was necessary.

Measurement of Availability

Also fatal to the City's Plan was the fact that the parameters by which the City measured the availability of MBE ("minority business enterprise") firms were arbitrarily crafted and grossly overbroad. With virtually no evidentiary support, the City's Plan required prime contractors to whom the City awarded construction contracts to subcontract at least 30 percent of the dollar value of those contracts to one or more MBEs.[65] In its original opinion in *Croson*, the Fourth Circuit Court of Appeals initially upheld the 30percent set aside figure, not by comparing it to the number of MBEs in Richmond, but rather to the percentage of minority persons in Richmond's population.[66]

The Supreme Court held that reliance on the disparity between the number of prime contracts awarded to minority-owned firms and the minority population in Richmond was further evidence of the lack of particularized findings on the issue of past discrimination.[67] Although noting that gross statistical disparities may in some instances "constitute prima facie proof of a pattern or practice of racial discrimination,"[68] the Supreme Court noted it is equally clear that "[w]hen special qualifications are required to fill particular jobs, comparisons to the general population (rather than to the smaller group of individuals who possess the necessary qualifications) may have little probative value."[69] Notably, the City of Richmond did

---

[64] *Id.* at 498-99.
[65] *Id.* at 477-78.
[66] *Croson v. City of Richmond*, 779 F.2d 181, 191 (4th Cir. 1985).
[67] *Croson*, 488 U.S. at 501.
[68] *Id.* (citing *Hazelwood School District v. United States*, 433 U.S. 299, 307-08, 53 L. Ed.2d 768 [1977]).
[69] *Id.* (citing *Hazelwood*, 433 U.S. at 308 n.13).

not even know how many MBEs in the relevant market were qualified to perform prime or subcontracting work on public construction projects.[70] Likewise, there was no evidence in the record that the City was aware of the percentage of total city construction dollars which had flowed to minority firms as subcontractors on construction jobs awarded by the City.[71] "Without any information on minority participation in subcontracting," the Court noted, "it [was] quite simply impossible to evaluate overall minority representation in the city's construction expenditures."[72]

Anecdotal Evidence

The City of Richmond also relied on certain anecdotal evidence to buttress its conclusion that there had been past discrimination in the construction industry. For example, statements in the legislative record leading to the adoption of the Plan indicated that there was racial discrimination in the construction industry "in th[e] [Richmond] area, and the State, and around the nation."[73] Likewise, Richmond's City Manager expressed his view that race discrimination still plagued the construction industry in his hometown of Pittsburgh.[74] Although recognizing that findings made by legislative bodies are generally entitled to a presumption of

---

[70] *Id.*

[71] *Id.* at 502.

[72] *Id.* at 503. The Court was equally critical of the Richmond Plan in that there were no geographic limitations to the Plan's application. The Court was particularly troubled by the notion that "[a]n otherwise qualified MBE from anywhere in the United States could avail itself of the 30percent set-aside." *Id.* at 478. Although cited as a failure in the City's evidence of past discrimination, the lack of a specific geographical limitation also spilled over into the Court's analysis of the "narrowly tailored" requirement. Once again questioning the lack of geographic limitations on the Richmond Plan, the Court noted that "[u]nder Richmond's scheme, a successful black, Hispanic, or Oriental entrepreneur from anywhere in the country enjoys an absolute preference over another citizen based solely on race. We think it obvious that such a program is not narrowly tailored to remedy the effects of prior discrimination." *Id.* at 508.

[73] *Id.* at 500.

[74] *Id.*

correctness, the Court stated that any presumptions are lost when the legislative body chooses suspect classifications to achieve its goal.[75]

Similarly, the Court found that evidence of low MBE membership in local contractors associations was also of negligible probative value.[76] Noting that there were several nondiscriminatory reasons for the dearth of minority participation in local contractors associations, the Court held that "[t]he mere fact that black membership in these trade organizations is low, standing alone, cannot establish a prima facie case of discrimination."[77] Echoing its earlier rationale concerning the proper yardstick by which to measure availability, the Court concluded that in order for such evidence to be probative, the city would have to link it to the number of local MBEs eligible for membership. If the statistical disparity between eligible MBEs and MBE membership were great enough, an inference of discriminatory exclusion could arise. In such a case, the City would have a compelling interest in preventing its tax dollars from assisting these organizations in maintaining a racially segregated construction market.[78]

Congressional Findings of Discrimination

The final predicate for the City's assumption of past discrimination had been its reliance upon earlier congressional findings of societal discrimination in conjunction with Congress' passage of the Public Works Act of 1977 ("Act").[79] Section 103(f) of the Act provided for $4 billion in appropriations in federal grant monies to state and local governments for use in public works projects.[80] The Act also contained the following provision:

---

[75] *Id.*
[76] *Id.* at 503.
[77] *Id.*
[78] *Id.* at 503-04.
[79] *Id.* at 504.
[80] *Id.* at 486.

> "Except to the extent the Secretary determines otherwise, no grant shall be made under this Act . . . unless the applicant gives satisfactory assurance to the Secretary that at least 10 per cent of the amount of each grant shall be expended for minority business enterprises."[81]

In *Fullilove*, the Court upheld the aforementioned minority set-aside provision as a valid exercise of Congress' authority under section 5 of the Fourteenth Amendment.[82] In affirming Congress' power to utilize racial classifications to ferret out societal discrimination, the Court noted that Congress, unlike the States, was a co-equal branch of the government given broad remedial powers under the U.S. Constitution to enforce equal protection guarantees.[83] The Court also emphasized that *Fullilove's* 10percent set-aside goal was not a rigid quota and that "a waiver could be sought where minority businesses were not available to fill the 10 percent requirement or, more importantly, where an MBE attempted to exploit the remedial aspects of the program by charging an unreasonable price, thsat is, a price not attributable to the present effects of prior discrimination."[84]

In rejecting the City of Richmond's premise that congressional findings of nationwide discrimination approved in *Fullilove* obviated the necessity of specific findings in the Richmond market, the Court emphasized that Congress' findings were of little probative value in Richmond.[85] First, the Court noted, "by Congress' inclusion of a waiver provision in the national program addressed in *Fullilove*, Congress explicitly recognized that the scope of the problem would vary from market

---

[81] *Id.* at 486-87 (citing *Fullilove v. Klutznick,* 448 U.S. 448, 454, 65 L. Ed. 2d (1980) (quoting 91 Stat. 116, 42, U.S.C. § 6705(f)(2)).
[82] *Croson*, 448 U.S. at 476.
[83] *Id.* at 488-491.
[84] *Id.* at 488-89.
[85] *Id.* at 504.

area to market area."[86] More importantly, the Court continued, state and local governments' mandate to implement race-conscious measures must be distinguished from Congress' powers under § 5 of the Fourteenth Amendment.[87] As the Court admonished:

> While the States and their subdivisions may take remedial action when they possess evidence that their own spending practices are exacerbating a pattern of discrimination, *they must identify that discrimination with some specificity before they may use race-conscious relief.* Congress has made national findings that there has been societal discrimination in a host of fields. If all a state or local government need do is find a congressional report on the subject to enact a set-aside program, the constraints of the Equal Protection Clause will, in effect, have been rendered a nullity.[88]

Narrowly Tailored

The second prong enunciated under *Croson's* strict scrutiny analysis is that any government-sponsored preference program must be "narrowly tailored" to serve the public body's compelling state interest.[89] The purpose of the "narrowly tailored" requirement is to "ensure that the means chosen 'fit' th[e] compelling goal so closely that there is little or no possibility that the motive for the classification was illegitimate racial prejudice or stereotype."[90] With these principles in mind, the Court held that the Richmond Plan was not narrowly tailored to serve its intended purpose.[91]

---

[86] *Id.*
[87] *Id.* at 489-91.
[88] *Id.* (emphasis added).
[89] *Id.* at 507-08.
[90] *Id.* at 493.
[91] *Id.* at 508.

Race-Neutral Alternatives

One of the benchmarks determining whether a race preference remedy is narrowly tailored is whether race-neutral alternatives to increase minority participation have been utilized. The Court found that there was no indication that the City of Richmond had ever considered race-neutral alternatives to increase minority participation in its local contracting community.[92] The Court observed that many of the so-called barriers to minority participation in the local construction market relied upon by the City were equally formidable barriers for non-minority firms as well. As an example, the Court noted that "[i]f MBE's disproportionately lack[ed] capital or [could] not meet bonding requirements, a race-neutral financing program of city financing for small firms would, *a fortiori*, lead to greater minority participation."[93] Moreover, in contrast to the lack of consideration of race-neutral alternatives underlying the Richmond Plan, that Court noted that prior to adopting the Public Works Act of 1977, Congress had expressly considered (and rejected as insufficient) race-neutral alternatives.[94]

Furthermore, the Court held that Richmond's Plan failed the "narrowly tailored" test in that the Plan randomly encompassed racial groups within its application for which "there was absolutely no evidence of past discrimination . . . ."[95] For instance, as to Spanish-speaking, Oriental, Indian, Eskimo, and Aleut persons, all of whom were included in the Richmond Plan as eligible "minorities," the Court found the Richmond Plan more consistent with an attempt to "avoid the bureaucratic effort necessary to tailor remedial relief to those who truly had suffered

---

92 *Id.* at 507.
93 *Id.* at 506.
94 *Id.* at 507 (citing *Fullilove*, 448 U.S. at 463-467).
95 *Id.* at 506.

the effects of prior discrimination" rather than a carefully drawn scheme which drew upon racial classifications only to the extent necessary. [96]

In summation, the following legal principles can be gleaned from *Croson's* application of the strict scrutiny standard:

1. a municipality has the authority to eradicate the effects of private discrimination within its own legislative jurisdiction so long as its authority is exercised within the constraints of Section 1 of the Fourteenth Amendment;[97]
2. in order to justify a program of construction set-asides or goals, the municipality or other local governmental authority must, in essence, demonstrate that it has become a "passive participant" in a system of racial exclusion practiced by the applicable local industry;[98]
3. when a municipality uses race-based measures to prohibit certain citizens the right to compete for public contracts based solely on their race or ethnicity, the court will engage in a searching judicial inquiry into the justification for the race-based measures to determine which classifications are "benign" and, therefore, "remedial," and which classifications are in fact motivated by illegitimate notions of racial inferiority or racial stereotyping;[99]
4. local governments have a compelling interest in remedying past discrimination only after specific legislative or administrative findings of constitutional or statutory violations. A generalized, bureaucratic assertion that remedial action is needed will not withstand constitutional scrutiny;[100]

---

[96] *Id.* at 508-509.
[97] *Id.* at 491-92.
[98] *Id.* at 492-93.
[99] *Id.* at 493.
[100] *Id.* at 496-97.

5. when reliance is made upon statistical disparity and special qualifications are necessary to undertake a particular task, the relevant statistical pool must be sufficiently culled to include only those firms qualified to perform the task. Those firms must be qualified, willing and able to provide the requested services;
6. if the statistical analysis includes the proper pool of eligible minorities, any resulting disparity, in a proper case, may constitute prima facie proof of a pattern or practice of discrimination.[101] "In an extreme case, some form of narrowly tailored preference might be necessary to break down patterns of deliberate exclusion;"[102]
7. if a municipality can establish a strong basis in evidence that a pattern of discrimination has occurred, the court must determine whether the measures used to remedy the discrimination are narrowly tailored to meet that goal. The use of an inflexible percentage quota is not narrowly tailored to any goal; and[103]
8. factors to be considered in determining whether a program is narrowly tailored include: (a) the basis offered for the numerical goal(s) selected; (b) whether the program provides for waivers of goals and other means of considering differing situations on a case-by-case basis; (c) whether the program only applies to minorities in the limited geographic region where the municipality is located; and (d) whether the municipality made a bonafide effort to consider race-neutral alternatives to increase minority participation, but found such alternatives ineffective.[104]

---

[101] *Id.* at 501-503.
[102] *Id.* at 509.
[103] *Id.* at 507.
[104] *Id.* at 505-08.

In the aftermath of *Croson*,[105] several municipalities have grappled with *Croson's* strict scrutiny standard in defense of their minority business preference/affirmative action programs. What has emerged from the reported decisions has been further insight into *Croson's* strict scrutiny test, particularly as it relates to the methodology for determining "availability" of women and minority

---

[105] In *Adarand Constructors, Inc. v. Pena*, 115 S. Ct. 2097, 132 L. Ed. 2d 158 (1995), the Supreme Court was faced with a suit brought by a disappointed bidder on a federal highway construction project challenging the constitutionality of a federal program which provided financial incentives to general contractors to hire subcontractors controlled by "socially and economically disadvantaged individuals." *Id.* at 2101. In finding that the program in question violated the equal protection component of the Fifth Amendment's Due Process Clause, the Court held that "federal racial classifications, like those of a State, must serve a compelling governmental interest, and must be narrowly tailored to further that interest." *Id.* at 2117.

Because *Adarand* does not alter *Croson's* requirements as to the heightened level of scrutiny which a municipality must meet in order to justify affirmative action programs, the balance of this framework will focus on *Croson* and its application.

business enterprises when determining whether a pattern of discrimination exists.[106]

Court Decisions in the Aftermath of *Croson*

Following the *Croson* decision, several lower court decisions were handed down which, in a sense, expanded on *Croson* to provide insight into the methodological requirements for conducting a legally defensible predicate study. This section will address five of the most recent and significant court decisions, beginning with the Southern District of Florida's decision in *Engineering Contractors Association of South Florida, Inc. v. Metropolitan Dade County.*[107]

---

[106] In *Monterey Mechanical Co. v. Wilson*, F.3d, 1997 WL 538757 (9th Cir. 1997), decided by the Ninth Circuit Court of Appeals on September 3, 1997, a low bidder which was not awarded a state contract because it failed to achieve the requisite percentages of work subcontracted to minority-, woman-, and disabled veteran-owned firms (and failed to demonstrate that it made good faith efforts to achieve those percentages), filed suit on the basis that the California statute creating the affirmative action program was unconstitutional. *Id.* at 2. The applicable statutory scheme permitted a bidder to excuse its noncompliance with the subcontractor participation goals if it was able to establish "good faith efforts," *e.g.* that it followed and documented the relevant statutory procedures for bid advertising and solicitation from minority, women and disabled veteran business enterprises. *Id.* at 8.

The Ninth Circuit held, among other things, that the statute at issue established classifications based on ethnicity and sex because its "good faith efforts" provision treated contractors differently by: (1) not requiring all contracting firms to advertise and solicit bids from companies identified by ethnicity or sex; and (2) implicitly imposing higher compliance expenses on contracting companies according to ethnicity and sex. *Id.* at 9-10.

Having concluded that the statute created classifications which were subject to the Equal Protection Clause, the Court proceeded to review the classifications under the strict scrutiny standard. The Court held that the statute was unconstitutional because the plaintiff/state university presented no evidence of past discrimination nor did it demonstrate that the statute was narrowly-tailored to serve its remedial purpose. *Id.* at 11-14.

Although worth mentioning, *Monterey* has marginal relevance to this framework because the state university had not performed a disparity study prior to implementing the challenged preference program. ("[T]he University . . . offered no evidence whatsoever that the University or the state had previously discriminated, actively or passively, against the groups benefitted by the statute."). *Id.* at 12.

[107] 943 F. Supp. 1546 (S.D. Fla. 1996).

Engineering Contractors Assoc. of South Florida, Inc. v. Metro Dade County.

One of the most recent decisions to address the constitutionality of a minority business preference program was the Southern District of Florida's decision in *Engineering Contractors Association of South Florida, Inc. v. Metropolitan Dade County (hereinafter "Dade County")*[108]. *Dade County* is significant not only because of its in-depth analysis of *Croson's* compelling state interest requirement. But also provided detailed explanation of factual predicate needed to fortify a race preference program.

Dade County arose out of a suit filed by a non-minority contractors association in September 1994, challenging the County's MWBE program as it related to the construction industry.[109] Asserting that the County could not demonstrate a compelling state interest in using gender, ethnic, or racial classifications as a basis upon which to award County construction contracts and that the County's program was also not narrowly tailored, the plaintiff sought a declaratory judgment that the program was unconstitutional and a permanent injunction against the enforcement of the program.[110] Following a four day non-jury trial, the Court found that the program ran afoul of *Croson* and permanently enjoined the County from using racial, ethnic, or gender criteria in: "(i) deciding whether a bid submitted for construction work is responsive; (ii) whether such a bid will be considered; [and] (iii) whether a contract will be awarded to a contractor submitting such a bid."[111]

---

[108] *Id.*

[109] *Id.* at 1552.

[110] *Id.* at 1553. Although Dade County's program encompassed several different aspects, the plaintiffs only sought relief as to, and the Court's order only addressed, the construction aspects of the program.

[111] *Id.* at 1584.

Compelling State Interest[112]

In determining that Dade County failed to demonstrate a compelling state interest in the use of race- and gender-based preferences, the Court highlighted the following infirmities in the County's Program:

1. the statistical evidence relied upon to support the County's claim of past discrimination was contradictory and inconclusive;[113]
2. reminiscent of Croson, the County relied upon unreliable data in measuring subcontracting trends;[114]

---

[112] The Court noted that there was some uncertainty as to the level of scrutiny to be applied to gender-conscious programs challenged under the Equal Protection Clause. Id. at 1556. After reviewing the existing precedent in the Eleventh Circuit and the U.S. Supreme Court, the Court concluded that gender-conscious programs appeared to be subject to an intermediate level of scrutiny, but ultimately determined that the issue was not dispositive since even under an intermediate scrutiny standard, the gender-based aspects of the County's construction program failed to pass constitutional muster. *Id.* at 1556-57.

[113] In the Court's view, focusing on the disparity between the proportion of MWBE bidders and the proportion of contract dollars those firms received did not produce any statistically significant disparities such that an inference could be drawn that the County had become a "passive participant" in the discriminatory letting of construction contracts. *Id.* at 1563.

To the extent that disparities did exist in the contract dollars being awarded to MWBE and non-MWBE firms, the Court was more persuaded by the plaintiff's position that "the disparities . . . simply reflect the fact that MWBEs tend to be newer, smaller, and less experienced firms – the majority having entered the construction industry in the last ten years – and thus are more often successful bidders on lower dollar contracts rather than higher dollar contracts." *Id.* at 1563.

The Court was similarly unimpressed with the County's use of regression analyses to explain the disparities between the total contract dollars being awarded to MWBE and non-MWBE firms. Although generally endorsing the use of regression analysis to estimate the relationship between a dependent variable and one or more independent variables, the Court found that the County's regression analyses did not produce any statistically reliable disparities. *See, e.g., id* at 1546. For example, in the area of BBE prime contracting, the regression analysis indicated a statistically significant disparity only for Standard Industry Classification 15 – general building construction – and even then, the analysis showed that the disparity had dissipated by 1993. *Id.*

[114] The firms which the Court identified as subcontractors were those firms which had filed a subcontractor's release of lien on at least one Dade County project during the years 1991-1994. *Id.* at 1566. Finding this pool of firms an unreliable source from which to measure subcontractor utilization, the Court noted that:

> The first problem is that the pool of identified subcontractors being evaluated may not in fact derive their primary source of income from subcontracting. The fact that a firm has filed a subcontractor's release of lien does not preclude that firm from

3. the MWBE marketplace analysis utilized by the County did not produce any disparities larger than might be expected in light of the fact that non-MWBE firms tended to be larger, better established and more likely to have the financial wherewithal to meet bonding, financing, and insurance requirements;[115]
4. studies relied upon by the County which allegedly measured business formation rates and revenues in the construction industry for women, Blacks, and Hispanics, as opposed to white males in Dade County, were skewed in that they were not premised on a proper regression analysis and, therefore, failed to control for neutral variables such as firm size and number of employees;[116] and
5. as opposed to supporting the County's claims of past discrimination, the County's anecdotal evidence confirmed the fact that the County's contracting process favored firms with a proven "track record" and that the contracting process was "fraught with opportunities for individuals to exercise discretion in decision making."[117]

Narrowly Tailored

Following precedent established by the Eleventh Circuit Court of Appeals, the Court examined four criteria which a municipality's affirmative action plan must satisfy before it may be considered "narrowly tailored":

> deriving most of its other income from other sources, such as prime contracting. More importantly, the sales and receipts data used in the statistical analyses come from all sources, and is not limited to sources within Dade County . . . . The Supreme Court has made it clear that an appropriate statistical evaluation must confine itself to the geographic boundaries of the jurisdiction to which the affirmative action program applies.

[115] *Id.* at 1564, 1566, 1569-70, 1571.

[116] Other variables which the Court noted should have been controlled for included: i) whether the firm or individual had ever done work specifically for Dade County; ii) the degree of reported sales which came from private sources versus public sources; and iii) whether the earnings reported were from work performed for Dade County or outside the County. *Id.* at 1573. Finally, the Court noted that the County's study did not attempt to categorize business owners into a SIC category in which they did business. *Id.* at 1574.

[117] *Id.* at 1577.

> "(1) the necessity for the relief and the efficacy of alternative remedies; (2) the flexibility of the relief, including the availability of waiver provisions; (3) the relationship of numerical goals to the relevant labor pool; and (4) the impact of the relief on the rights of innocent third parties."[118]

Examination of each of these criteria, *in seriatim*, led the Court to conclude that the County's program was not "narrowly tailored."[119]

Alternative Remedies

Aside from conclusory statements in the legislative findings that race-neutral measures were not practical given the County's limited funds, the County failed to give good faith consideration to the use of race and gender-neutral alternatives[120]. Where discriminatory conduct had been identified, the County had taken no steps to reprimand, punish or otherwise denounce the conduct.[121]

---

[118] *Id.* at 1580 (quoting *Ensley Branch, N.A.A.C.P., et al. v. Seibels*, 31 F.3d 1548, 1569 (11th Cir. 1994).

[119] *Id.* at 1583.

[120] *Id.* at 1580. At trial, the County's own employees identified several obstacles to the County's contracting process, including:

> the level of discretionary decision-making by County employees, the complexity of contract specifications, the difficulty in attaining bonding and financing, unnecessary bid restrictions, bias towards firms with a proven track record, inefficient payment procedures, and lack of information exchange and significant impediments to minority, small, and new firm participation in County contracting.

Id. These were all areas, the Court noted, in which the County could have implemented race-neutral programs to increase public contracting opportunities to those who had suffered from past societal discrimination or neglect. *Id.* at 1581.

[121] *Id.* For example, notwithstanding testimony from its own employees that the County was aware of discriminatory conduct by either isolated County employees or private equipment suppliers, there was no evidence that the County had taken steps to penalize or otherwise reprimand the offending parties. *Id.* Similarly, the County had passed no ordinances prohibiting contractors from discriminating in their selection of subcontractors or suppliers on account of race, ethnicity, or gender. *Id.*

Relationship of Relief to Prior Discrimination[122]

This inquiry, the Court noted, undertakes to "analyze the flexibility and duration of the remedy as well as the relationship of the numerical goals to the relevant labor market."[123] Although the County's program did have the requisite flexibility required by *Croson* in that waiver and appeal provisions were available after a contract had been designated for MWBE goals, the Supreme Court found that the Program was not of limited duration.[124] The Court also found that the program failed to establish an appropriate relationship between its numerical goals and the relevant market.[125]

Effect on Innocent Third Parties

The last prong of the Eleventh Circuit's test for determining whether a race preference remedy is narrowly tailored or whether the impact of the remedial efforts is unduly burdensome upon third parties.[126] Finding that the commitment of resources to prepare a bid was particularly onerous, the Court held that, on balance, it was not an "appropriate burden for a non-minority firm to expend the required level of effort in preparing what turns out to be a low bid only to be ultimately denied

---

[122] For purposes of the court's analysis, factors two and three of the *Ensley* test were considered in tandem.
[123] *Id.* at 1582 (quoting *Peightal v. Metropolitan Dade County*, 26 F.3d 1545, 1558 (11th Cir. 1994)).
[124] *Id.* Notably, the Court was unimpressed with the fact that the program's application to a particular market segment would expire when statistical evidence of a disparity ceased to exist. In this regard, the Court observed that:

> [S]imple disparity indices do not account for the myriad factors that can legitimately result in disparities, such as the availability of MWBEs that are actually qualified to perform the contract requirements [and] the size of a firm . . . . Only when these and other factors which affect the qualifications, ability, and willingness of a firm to compete for County construction work are taken into account through using appropriate data and regression analysis can the County accurately determine whether there are actual disparities in the number of willing able and qualified MWBEs and the amount of work they are performing in the local construction industry.

Id.
[125] *Id.*
[126] *Id.* at 1583.

the bid because the contractor was not able to hire a sufficient number of MWBE subcontractors to fulfill a participation goal requirement."[127] Thus, the Court held that based on the totality of the circumstances, the County's program was not sufficiently narrowly tailored to overcome the plaintiffs' Equal Protection Clause challenge.[128]

Based upon the Court's analysis, one could reasonably conclude that the following steps would be necessary before Dade County's MWBE Program could withstand a constitutional challenge:

1. formulation of a reliable statistical pool for both prime and subcontractors which includes only MWBEs which are qualified, willing, and able to provide the relevant services; the resulting statistical analysis must filter out any non-social factors which could distort the final result through the use of regression analysis;
2. statistical analysis must show identifiable discrimination in the local industry affected and must be confined to the geographic boundaries of the jurisdiction to which the program applies;
3. reliable data to support statistical analysis must be used, particularly evidence of the proportion of contract dollars awarded to minorities as subcontractors;
4. marketplace studies must also categorize business owners by the field within an industry in which they do business;
5. anecdotal evidence should not merely confirm general business trends that County contracting processes favor larger, more well-established firms; rather, anecdotal evidence should identify specific instances in which County personnel or persons in the private construction industry have engaged in discriminatory behavior leading to the deprivation of a

[127] *Id.*
[128] *Id.*

contract award to a M/WBE which is qualified, willing and able to perform;[129]

6. consideration should be given to the use of race and gender-neutral programs to sanction individuals or companies who discriminate against women, minorities, and other ethnic groups in the awarding of contracts;
7. implementation of a training program to sensitize County employees and others who do business with the County of the inappropriateness and illegality of racial and gender stereotyping;
8. standardization and centralization of the county contracting program to minimize the amount of individual discretion currently afforded by the system;
9. evaluation of technical and financial aid programs for their effectiveness; and
10. incorporation of limited duration provisions which periodically address whether numeral disparities reflect actual disparities through techniques such as regression analysis.

In *Engineering Contractors Association of South Florida v. Metropolitan Dade County,*[130] the Eleventh Circuit affirmed the district court's judgment enjoining Dade County from using racial, ethnic or gender criteria in the awarding of public construction contracts.[131] The Eleventh Circuit's opinion is perhaps most significant in that it clarifies existing law with respect to the legal standards by which race-, ethnicity-, or gender-conscious programs are reviewed. Thus, municipalities and other entities seeking to implement women and minority business preference programs, as well as the lower courts which will be reviewing the constitutionality

---

[129] It is generally recognized that "'[a]necdotal evidence is most useful as a supplement to strong statistical evidence' and 'it rarely, if ever, can . . . show a systemic pattern of discrimination necessary for adoption of an affirmative action program.'" *Id.* at 1579-80 (quoting *Coral Construction Co. v. King County*, 941 F.2d 910, 941 (9th Cir. 1991)); *O' Donnell Construction Co. v. District of Columbia*, 963 F.2d 420, 427 (D.C. Cir. 1992) (same).

[130] *Monterey Mechanical Co. v. Wilson*, F.3d, 1997 WL 535626 (11th Cir. 1997).

[131] *Id.* at 37.

of those programs, now have concrete guidelines on how such programs should be structured in order to withstand constitutional scrutiny.

The following principles can be gleaned from the Eleventh Circuit's opinion regarding the appropriate standards of review:

1. Although gender-conscious affirmative action programs may rest on a weaker evidentiary foundation than race- or ethnicity- conscious programs, a district court's factual findings as to whether an adequate evidentiary basis exists to justify both gender-conscious and race- or ethnicity-conscious programs will be reviewed under a "clearly erroneous" standard.[132] In layman's terms, this means simply that the district court's findings will not be disturbed so long as they are plausible in light of the entire factual record.[133]
2. "[A] gender preference may be upheld so long as it is substantially related to an important governmental interest." This is the so-called intermediate scrutiny standard.[134]
3. "A district court applies law to the facts when it determines whether a race- or ethnicity- An appellate court conscious remedy is narrowly tailored to serve a compelling government interest, and whether a gender-conscious program bears a substantial relation to an important governmental interest."[135] The appellate court may review the district court's application of the law to the facts *de novo* or as though the issue was before the appellate court as a matter of first impression. The *de novo* standard should be distinguished from the clearly erroneous standard.
4. With respect to delineating the constitutional boundaries of intermediate scrutiny for purposes of reviewing gender-conscious programs, the court reaffirmed two principles: First, "[u]nder the intermediate scrutiny test, a local government must demonstrate some past discrimination against women, but not necessarily discrimination by the

---

[132] *Id.* at 10.
[133] *Id.*
[134] *Id.* at 14.
[135] *Id.* at 11.

> government itself." *Ensley Branch*, 31 F.3d at 1580. Indeed, "[o]ne of the distinguishing features of intermediate scrutiny is that, unlike strict scrutiny, the government interest prong of the inquiry can be satisfied by a showing of societal discrimination in the relevant economic sector.
> Second, the intermediate scrutiny evidentiary review is not to be directed toward mandating that gender-conscious affirmative action is used only as a "last resort," but instead to ensuring that the affirmative action program is "a product of analysis rather than a stereotyped reaction based on habit."[136]

In addition, the 11th Circuit declared,

> "...we flatly reject the County's assertion that given a strong basis in evidence of a race-based problem, a race-based remedy is necessary." That is simply not the law. If a race-neutral remedy is sufficient to cure a race-based problem, then a race conscious remedy can never be narrowly tailored to the problem. (See, Croson, 488 U.S. at 509), (holding that affirmative action program was not narrowly tailored where " there does not appear to have been any consideration of the use of race-neutral means to increase minority business participation in city contracting.; id. at 509 (plurality opinion) (reserving race-conscious remedies for the "extreme case when to break down patters of deliberate exclusion"); see also, e.g., United States v. Paradise, 480 U.S. 149, 171, (1987) ("In determining whether race-conscious remedies are appropriate we look to several factors, including the efficacy of alternative remedies...."). Supreme Court decisions teach that a race- conscious remedy is not merely one of the many equally acceptable medications the government may use to treat a race-based problem. Instead it is the strongest of medicine, with many potentially harmful side effects, and must be reserved for those Contractors Association of South Florida v. Metropolitan Dade County, 122 F.3d 895 (11th Cir.,1997)

---

136 *Id.* (citation omitted) (emphasis added).

The Circuit Court then spelled out a jurisdiction's race neutral responsibilities:

> Although the County does offer some limited technical and financial aid that might benefit BBEs [black business enterprises] and HBEs [Hispanic business enterprises], even those half-hearted programs have not been evaluated for their effectiveness.
>
> Most notably, the record indicates that the County has not taken any action whatsoever to ferret out, and respond to instances of discrimination if and when they have occurred in the County's own contracting process. If such conduct has occurred – and the County's own anecdotal evidence suggests it has on at least some occasions – the County has taken no steps to inform, educate, discipline, or penalize its own officials and employees responsible for the misconduct. The first measure every government ought to undertake to eradicate discrimination is to clean its own house and to ensure that its own operations are run on a strictly race-and ethnicity neutral ordinances to outlaw discrimination by local contractors, subcontractors, suppliers, bankers or insurers. Instead of turning to race- and ethnicity conscious remedies as a last resort, then County has turned to them as a first resort. Because the County's BBE and HBE programs are not a narrowly tailored, those programs would violate the Equal Protection Clause even if they were supported by a sufficient evidentiary foundation.[137]

Finally the Eleventh circuit cautioned in evaluating statistical evidence that:

> Because they are bigger, bigger firms have a bigger chance to win bigger contracts. It follows that, all other factors being equal, and in a perfectly non-discriminatory market, one would expect the bigger (on average) non-MWBE firms to get a disproportionately higher

---

[137] *Engineering Contractors Association of South Florida v. Metropolitan Dade County*, 122 F.3d 928, (11th Circuit 1997).

percentage of total construction dollars awarded than smaller M/WBE firms.[138]

Associated General Contractors of America v. City of Columbus

Another recent case to address the constitutionality of a minority business preference program is Associated General Contractors of America v. City of Columbus.[139] The Columbus case arose out of a challenge to the City's MBE program by the Associated General Contractors' Association.[140] In 1989, the Ohio contractors' association brought suit challenging the program's recently revised participation goals and in January 1991, the City agreed to permanently enjoin its recently revised program.[141] In an attempt to establish a program which would withstand constitutional scrutiny, however, the City hired consultants and held public hearings which led to the creation of the 1993 Equal Business Opportunity Code ("EBOC").[142]

Unlike the admitted shortcomings of the City's previous program, the revised set-aside program was thought to be based on adequate evidentiary findings of past discrimination.[143] The EBOC provided for various preferences in City contracting for M/FBEs, such as subcontracting goals of 10 percent for MBEs and 7 percent for

---

[138] *Engineering Contractors of South Florida v. Metropolitan Dade County* 122 F.3d 917 (11th Circuit 1997).

[139] 936 F. Supp. 1363 (S.D. Ohio 1996).

[140] *Id.* at 1371-75.

[141] *Id.* at 1371. Columbus had had an affirmative action program in place since 1975. *Id.* at 1375. The 1975 program was designed to enforce racial composition requirements for a contractor's work force and in July 1981, provisions were added requiring prime contractors to award 10 percent of their contracts to MBEs and 2 percent to FBEs ("female business enterprises"). *Id.* In 1989, these participation percentages were raised to 21 percent and 10 percent respectively. *Id.*

[142] *Id.*

[143] *Id.* The City's consultants conducted studies on the availability and utilization of M/FBE ("minority and female-owned business enterprise") firms within the Columbus Metropolitan Statistical Area ("MSA"). The consultants measured availability based on the number of M/FBE firms in the Columbus MSA and measured utilization based on the amount of contract dollars awarded to M/FBEs. *Id.* at 1371-72.

FBEs.[144] It also provided for special programs designed to help MBEs such as publicly funded bonding, financial assistance, and technical programs.[145] Subsequent to the EBOC's enactment, the City requested that the 1991 injunction be dissolved so that the new legislation could take effect. Thereafter, a trial was held to determine the EBOC's constitutional validity.[146] Applying *Croson's* standard of strict scrutiny, the Court held that the EBOC was unconstitutional because it did not serve a compelling state interest nor was it narrowly tailored to achieve the City's goal.[147]

Compelling State Interest

In its determination that the EBOC did not serve a compelling state interest,[148] the Court highlighted the following defects in the City's statistical and anecdotal evidence:

1. the statistics utilized failed to limit the study to those contractors who were qualified, willing and able to perform the City construction work;[149]
2. the disparity studies failed to separate and distinguish prime contractor from subcontractor data, thereby leading to skewed results;[150]
3. the City's studies overstated the M/FBE availability percentage by including M/FBE companies which did not work in the construction industry, i.e. landscaping or horticultural firms, in the number of available M/FBE

---

[144] *Id.*
[145] *Id.*
[146] *Id.*
[147] *Id.* at 1441.
[148] The court opined that while gross statistical disparities may constitute prima facie evidence of a pattern or practice of discrimination, they are not necessarily conclusive because the disparity may be explained by race-neutral factors and the inference of discrimination may be rebutted by other evidence. *Id.* at 1379 (citation omitted). Anecdotal evidence, on the other hand, "is most useful as a supplement to strong statistical evidence." *Id.* (citation omitted).
[149] *Id.* at 1385, 1389.
[150] *Id.* at 1385, 1391. The court found that the combination of prime and subcontractor data was illogical because one of the principal purposes of the City's program was to implement participation goals for M/FBE subcontracting. *Id.* at 1391.

construction firms while excluding those same firms in the total number of construction firms for the industry;[151]

4. the databases used by the City's analysts contained discrepancies, overlapped geographic areas, or were inappropriately relied upon to measure the data;[152]
5. some of the City's analysts did not verify any of the research or calculations upon which they subsequently relied;[153]
6. the use of "indirect statistical analysis" was inappropriate;[154]
7. the statistical analysis based on the amount of dollars awarded was inappropriate to determine past discrimination because it did not account for the fact that there were "relatively few contracts and relatively few firms seeking those contracts, and the amounts of the contracts var[ied] greatly";[155]

---

[151] *Id.* at 1385.

[152] *Id.* at 1386-90, 1394-96, 1407-08. One such discrepancy and overlap involved one study's use of two different databases to determine the M/FBE availability percentage. *Id.* at 1386. Because one database covered a larger geographical area than the other, the court found that "this methodology mixe[d] apples and oranges" *Id.* Another discrepancy observed by the Court was that one of the sources relied upon by the City indicated a lower M/FBE utilization rate than another database which contained the same information. *Id.* at 1387-89. These discrepancies led to "questions of reliability" regarding the analyst's method of extracting data. *Id.* at 1389.

In addition, the Court found that many of the City's sources were inappropriately relied upon because they failed to measure the number of M/FBEs who were qualified, willing, and able to perform the work. *Id.* Those sources included the Bidder Registration File which was a list of all M/FBE firms that registered with the City's Purchasing Division for any project; U.S. Census Total Industry data which failed to include Subchapter C corporation data; U.S. Census Subsector Industry data which contained discrepancies in the use of Standard Industrial Classification Codes; and telephone survey information which the Court determined had "questionable value." *Id.* at 1389-90, 1394-96, 1407-08.

[153] *Id.* at 1387.

[154] *Id.* at 1400. Improper "indirect statistical analysis" was based on the City's use of improper measurements to determine the existence of discrimination. *Id.* The Court stated that the City's consultants incorrectly assumed that every contractor had an equal chance to be awarded a City contract, when in reality, the awards were based on which contractors submitted the lowest bid. *Id.*

The court suggested that instead of pulling M/FBE availability and utilization data from the various sources which it did, i.e. vendor lists and census data, etc., the City should have determined the existence of discrimination based on an analysis of bidding information for actual contracts awarded: invitations to bid, submitted bids, determinations of non-responsive bids, and the winning bidder. *Id.* Although perhaps not as explicitly stated, the court in *Dade County* also endorsed the use of bidding data in comparing the availability and utilization of MWBE firms. *See, e.g. Dade County*, 943 F. Supp. at 1562-63.

[155] *Columbus*, 936 F. Supp. at 1400.

8. it could not be inferred that the cited decline in the M/FBE utilization rates resulted from discrimination.[156] In fact, the Court concluded that it was more likely that the decline was the result of substantial M/FBE over-utilization prior to the discontinuation of the previous set-aside program;[157]
9. one study which purported to measure discrimination in the private sector was flawed because it failed to consider numerous variables which may impact M/FBE operations such as net worth, bonding capacity, and a comparison of revenues between comparable M/FBE and majority-owned companies based on size, age, and experience;[158]
10. the lack of M/FBE participation could be explained by race-neutral reasons such as career and entrepreneurial choices and a disproportionate attraction of M/FBEs to other industries;[159] and
11. the anecdotal testimony which included witness testimony from City Council hearings, interviews from the City's studies, and a record of complaints to City Council members, failed to specifically allege the existence of discrimination which could be independently verified.[160]

---

156 *Id.* at 1399.
157 *Id.*
158 *Id.* at 1409.
159 *Id.* at 1410.
160 *Id.* at 1402-07, 1411-1419.

Narrowly Tailored

In its determination that the program failed the second prong of the *Croson* test; namely, that the EBOC be narrowly-tailored to meet a compelling interest,[161] the Court determined that:

1. the city failed to enact any race or gender-neutral alternatives prior to its adoption of the EBOC program;[162]
2. the program was not of limited duration;[163]
3. the program allowed for preferential treatment of any M/FBE firm contained within City limits without regard to the

[161] The Court found that there were four factors to consider when determining if a program is narrowly-tailored:

> 1) whether the city has first considered race-neutral means to increase minority participation . . . but found those programs to be ineffective; 2) the basis offered for the set-aside percentage selected; 3) whether the program provides for waivers of preference or other means of affording individualized treatment to contractors; and 4) whether the program applies only to minority businesses who operate in the geographic jurisdiction covered by the program. Other considerations include the flexibility and duration of the relief . . . , the relationship of numerical goals to the relevant labor market, and the impact of the relief on the rights of third parties.

Id. at 1379 (quoting *Adarand Constructors, Inc. v. Pena*, 115 S.Ct. 2097, 2118 (1995); *U.S. v. Paradise*, 480 U.S. 149, 171 (1987)).

[162] *Id.* at 1436. The City's evidence concerning its race- and gender-neutral programs included: (1) a Neighborhood Commercial Revitalization Program and Neighborhood Design Assistance Center which provided financial and design assistance for the building revitalization projects; (2) the Columbus Minority Development Center which was designed to provide financial and marketing assistance to M/FBEs; (3) donations to Columbus' Chamber of Commerce to assist various minority programs; (4) testimony from the Mayor of the City of Columbus regarding various activities instituted by his administration, such as apportioning large contracts into smaller segments and updating the M/FBE directory; and (5) testimony from the City's Purchasing Department regarding various programs it pursued, such as informational advertisements in minority publications and educational programs. *Id.* at 1434-46. Despite this evidence, the Court determined that these programs failed to provide evidence of race- and gender-neutral alternatives for various reasons: (1) they provided "little or no benefit" to small construction firms; (2) there was no evidence indicating that the programs had in fact been implemented; or (3) there was "very little substance" to the programs because they were primarily informational in nature. *Id.*

[163] *Id.* at 1437.

consideration of whether that firm suffered past discrimination;[164]

4. there was no relationship between the EBOC's stated percentage goals and the availability of M/FBE firms;[165] and
5. the program would have a significant impact on non-minority firms seeking to bid on City contracts.[166]

Although the EBOC was ultimately held unconstitutional, it was found to be appropriately limited in geographical scope and appropriately flexible because it established specific M/FBE goals on a contract-by-contract basis with the inclusion of waiver provisions.[167]

In summation, based upon the Court's analysis, one could reasonably conclude that in order to successfully structure the EBOC program such that it would pass constitutional muster, the City should:

1. obtain substantial statistical evidence inferring discrimination through the proper analysis of qualified, willing, and able M/FBE participation at both the prime and subcontractor levels;
2. use appropriate databases to gather the needed statistical information, including bidding data;
3. ensure that its consultants independently verified the statistical information;
4. substantiate claims of past discrimination with verifiable anecdotal evidence specifically alleging discrimination against those groups contained in the EBOC program;

---

[164] *Id.* Under the EBOC, any M/FBE firm could participate in the plan so long as the M/FBE firm could establish that it had been in the Columbus Metropolitan Statistical Area for at least three months and that it "ever had two consecutive years in which its average earnings were less than the average for other firms in the industry." *Id.* The Court noted that the EBOC's use of a weighted average calculation for earnings, which included income from all industries in which the M/FBE participated, was improper.

[165] *Id.* at 1438-39.

[166] *Id.* at 1439.

[167] *Id.* at 1438, 1436.

5. implement race-neutral alternatives such as bonding and financial assistance programs;
6. incorporate limited duration sunset provisions; and
7. establish a relationship between the availability of M/FBE firms and the stated participation goals.

Contractors Association of Eastern Philadelphia v. City of Philadelphia

Further guidance on the application of *Croson's* strict scrutiny analysis can be gleaned from a series of opinions rendered in connection with the City of Philadelphia's MBE program. In 1989, nine contractors' associations brought an action against the City challenging an ordinance which created set-asides for black subcontractors on City public works contracts.[168] The challenged ordinance had a 15 percent goal for MBE participation (which, by definition, included all "disadvantaged" business enterprises) in city construction contracting and a 10 percent goal for WBE participation.[169]

Applying *Croson's* strict scrutiny standard, the Court issued a permanent injunction against the use of the ordinance holding that there was no firm basis for

---

[168] *Contractors Assoc. of Eastern Pennsylvania v. Philadelphia*, 893 F. Supp. 419, 423 (E.D. Pa. 1995). The district court granted the plaintiff's motion for summary judgment twice due to insufficient evidence of past discrimination. *See Contractors Assoc. of Eastern Pennsylvania v. Philadelphia*, 735 F. Supp. 1274 (E.D. Pa. 1990); *Contractors Assoc. of Eastern Pennsylvania v. Philadelphia*, Civ. No. 89-2737, 1992 WL 245851 (Sept. 22, 1992). On appeal, the Third Circuit agreed that the evidence considered by the district court was insufficient to establish a strong basis of discrimination against women and non-black minority-owned businesses; yet, it reversed and remanded as to the program's provisions regarding black-owned construction firms because the City's disparity study, which was based on post-enactment statistical evidence, "created an inference" of race discrimination. *Contractors Assoc. of Eastern Pennsylvania v. Philadelphia*, 6 F.3d 990 (3d Cir. 1993). On remand, the district court had to determine whether the ordinance's "fifteen percent 'goal' for black participation in City construction contracting [was] justified by a 'compelling government interest,' and, if so, whether it [was] 'narrowly tailored' to remedy specifically identified instances of past discrimination." 893 F. Supp. at 424-25.

[169] *Id.* The ordinance was later amended to include a 2 percent goal for handicapped-owned business enterprises ("HBEs"). *Id.*

justifying the race-based program and that the program was not narrowly tailored even if discrimination could be shown.[170]

The Court found the following problems with the City's disparity study[171] and anecdotal evidence used to justify its affirmative action program:

1. the City's statistical disparity study was not linked to any additional evidence of discrimination because the anecdotal evidence presented by the City did not provide a sufficient basis to withstand strict scrutiny;[172]
2. "unadorned speculation" that past discrimination affected current availability and qualifications of black construction firms could not justify the use of "highly suspect racial classifications";[173]
3. the City failed to account for the actual number of MBE firms which sought to participate in City contracting and incorrectly assumed that all contractors, no matter what their race, were

---

[170] *Id.* at 447. On appeal, the Third Circuit affirmed the district court's opinion, concluding that there was no strong basis for the City's assertion that discrimination occurred in City construction subcontracting opportunities, that there was no basis for establishing a 15 percent set-aside requirement applicable to all prime contracts for City construction projects, and that the City failed "to include race-neutral or less burdensome remedial steps to encourage and facilitate greater participation of black contractors, measures that the records show[ed] to be available." *Contractors Assoc. of Eastern Pennsylvania v. Philadelphia*, 91 F.3d 586, 609-10 (3d Cir. 1996).

[171] The disparity index was calculated by "dividing the percentage participation in dollars of minority groups in the public works contracts awarded by the City of Philadelphia by their percentage of availability or composition in the 'population' of Philadelphia area construction firms and multiplying the result by 100." 893 F. Supp. at 427. Minority "participation" was measured by dividing the total dollar value of prime contracts awarded to minority firms by the total dollar value of all public contracts awarded by the City of Philadelphia. *Id.* "Availability" was measured by dividing the number of MBE firms in the Philadelphia Standard Metropolitan Statistical Area ("SMSA") by the federal census figure for total number of construction firms in the Philadelphia SMSA during the same period of time. *Id.*

[172] *Id.* at 429. The anecdotal evidence consisted of testimony before the City Council which included testimony from several minority contractors, one representative from a business minority action program, another representative from a research company, and a local congressman. 735 F. Supp. at 1295-98; 6 F.3d at 1002-03.

[173] 893 F. Supp. at 429-30.

equally qualified, willing, and able to perform City construction jobs;[174]

4. race-neutral explanations existed for the utilization disparity figure cited by the City because there was a low number of certified and available MBEs during that period, and of the available MBEs, several were already participating in federal projects;[175]
5. the consultant improperly "mixed data" from sources which did not have the same geographic scope;[176]
6. the disparity study did not consider the degree of MBE participation at the subcontractor level;[177] and
7. the City's consultant failed to independently validate the City's information concerning M/WBE availability or test the

---

[174] *Id.* at 430-32. Specifically with regard to a firm's qualifications, willingness and ability to perform City contracts, the Court adopted the conclusions of the plaintiff's expert that: (1) the City relied too heavily on census data which gave no indication of a firm's qualifications, willingness, or availability; and (2) the City never considered the unique specializations of MBEs to determine if they could meet the City's needs. *Id.* at 431-32.

The Third Circuit, however, found the district court's criticism of the consultant's lack of data collection for qualified, willing, and able MBEs to be "problematic." 91 F.3d at 603. It stated that "one can normally assume that participants in a market with the ability to undertake gainful work will be 'willing' to undertake it. Moreover, past discrimination . . . may provide a reason to believe the minorities who would otherwise be 'willing' are discouraged from trying to secure the work."

[175] 893 F. Supp. at 430-31. Although the Third Circuit acknowledged that the district court was correct "in suggesting that the availability of substantial amounts of federally-funded work and the federal set-aside had an impact on the number of black contractors available to bid on other City contracts," it also recognized that the extent of the impact was more difficult to gauge. 91 F.3d at 605. Even if the disparity index was adjusted to reflect the lack of availability of black firms due to the federal projects, the Third Circuit stated that the disparity index would still suggest "substantial under-participation of black contractors among the successful bidders on City prime contracts." However, the fact that there was difficulty in even getting black contractors to bid on sheltered contracts during the relevant time period gave credence to the possibility the under-participation of these firms was attributable to a "dearth" of MBE contracting capacity.

[176] 893 F. Supp. at 431. The Third Circuit found that the district court overemphasized the fact that the City's consultant may have used "mixed data." 91 F.3d at 604. The consultant only used two sources of data in the disparity index calculation (data which came from the City itself and Census data from the Philadelphia SMSA) and, although there was a "minor mismatch in the geographic scope of the data" from these sources, the Third Circuit concluded that given the size of the disparity index calculated, it was not persuaded that the mismatch was significant. In fact, the Court found that the use of this "mixed data" may have actually led to a conservative estimate of the actual disparity.

[177] 893 F. Supp. at 434.

underlying document upon which the information was drawn.[178]

In its determination that the program failed *Croson's* narrowly-tailored prong, the Court found that:

1. there was no consideration of race-neutral alternatives;[179]
2. the 15 percent participation goal established by the City was not set for a remedial purpose because there was no evidence that any of the minorities, including blacks, had been discriminated against;[180]
3. the waiver and exemption provisions were insufficient to justify the 15 percent goal because they solely focused on MBE availability and did not at all consider whether the individual MBE in question had suffered the effects of past discrimination;[181]
4. the program was not geographically limited in scope;[182] and
5. the City's decision to extend the duration of the program without any determination that an extension was necessary was improper.[183]

---

[178] *Id.* at 437.

[179] *Id.* at 441-44. The City's position that its two discontinued race-neutral programs proved to be unsuccessful was contradicted by the City's own witnesses and exhibits; the Court found that the effectiveness of these two race-neutral programs was not even considered when adopting the challenged ordinance.

[180] *Id.* at 444-45.

[181] *Id.* at 445-46. The Court was led to the conclusion that these provisions were meant to foster "administrative convenience."

[182] *Id.* at 446.

[183] *Id.* at 447. The original ordinance was scheduled to expire in 1989 and the preamble to the original Bill proposing the ordinance provided that the ordinance could be extended for an additional period of 10 years if: (1) the extension was recommended by the Minority Business Enterprise Council; and (2) it was enacted through another ordinance. *Id.* at 446. In 1987, two years before the scheduled expiration date, the City amended the ordinance to include handicapped-owned business enterprises and, at the same time, decided to extend the expiration date until January 1, 1998. *Id.* at 446-47. The Court found that this lack of "de novo review of the appropriateness and efficacy of the program's goals" when extending the ordinance for an additional eleven and one-half years, provided additional evidence that the ordinance was not narrowly-tailored. *Id.* at 447.

Based upon the Court's analysis, one could reasonably conclude that in order to successfully structure and defend the Philadelphia ordinance, the City should:

1. obtain substantial statistical evidence inferring discrimination through the proper analysis of qualified, willing, and able MBE participation at both the prime and subcontractor levels;
2. substantiate its claims of past discrimination with verifiable anecdotal evidence;
3. account for the number of actual MBE firms which sought to participate in City construction projects;
4. use appropriate databases to gather the needed statistical information and ensure that there is no "mismatch" of geographical scope;
5. ensure that the City's consultants independently verify any and all statistical information received;
6. implement various race-neutral alternatives, such as the relaxation of prequalification and bonding requirements for disadvantaged contractors of all races; implement training and financial assistance programs to assist disadvantaged contractors of all races; and vigorously enforce anti-discrimination ordinances and the procurement department's standard contracting requirements;[184]
7. establish waiver and exemption provisions which analyze contracts on a case-by-case basis to determine whether a specific MBE firm has suffered past discrimination;
8. limit the scope of the MBE participation program to ensure that only contractors within the affected area are receiving the program's benefits; and
9. incorporate limited duration sunset provisions.

Prior Tire Enterprises v. Atlanta Public School District

The City of Atlanta recently experienced a challenge to the race preference action program utilized by the purchasing department of the Atlanta Public School

---

[184] *Id.* at 444.

(APS) District.[185] The creation of the challenged program was based on the School Board District's concern over low participation by minorities in Atlanta School District contracting opportunities.[186] Although the School Board District attempted to remedy the problem with a race- and gender-neutral program in 1985, the School Board District later determined that those alternatives were ineffective in increasing the participation of minority and female-owned companies.[187]

In 1991, the School Board District investigated the possibility of enacting race and gender-conscious remedies and retained a consultant to perform a disparity study.[188] Based on the consultant's study, the School Board District developed a program containing affirmative action participation goals of 32 percent for African-Americans, 3 percent for women, and 1 percent for both Asians and Hispanics[189]. In early 1994, an unsuccessful bidder brought a challenge to the School Board District's affirmative action program based on the Equal Protection Clause.[190] Both parties subsequently filed cross motions for summary judgment.

In determining the constitutionality of the School Board District's race preference program, the Supreme Court analyzed the constitutionality of each participation goal separately.[191] With respect to the program's provisions for Asian

---

[185] *See* Order on Motions for Summary Judgment in *Prior Tire Enterprises v. Atlanta Public School District*, Case No. Civ. 1:95-CV-825-JEC (N.D. Ga. 1997). This was an unreported decision rendered on March 27, 1997. *Id.* at 32.

[186] *Id.* at 1.

[187] *Id.* at 1-2. The race and gender-neutral program was developed in 1985; it provided education and outreach efforts for small business enterprises. *Id.*

[188] *Id.* at 2.

[189] *Id.* at 4. The program contained other methods to encourage minority participation, some of which were race- and gender-neutral, others of which were not. *Id.* The neutral measures included elimination of unnecessary restrictive contract specifications and increasing minority awareness of contracting opportunities. *Id.* The race- and gender-conscious measures "included a limited sheltered program, mandatory subcontracting requirements, a requirement that at least one minority vendor be contacted for all purchases by the School Board under $2,000 and a system of bid preferences which were to be applied to certain contracts." *Id.*

[190] *Id.* at 5.

[191] *Id.* at 4.

and Hispanic participation goals, the Court granted summary judgment in favor of the plaintiff because: (1) as acknowledged by the defendant's expert, "there was very little evidence of any disparity regarding Asians and Hispanics;" (2) there was a small number of Asian and Hispanic businesses located within Atlanta making it difficult to conduct a disparity analysis on this information; and (3) there was very little anecdotal evidence to support the School Board's claims of discrimination against these minorities.[192] Accordingly, the Court granted plaintiff's motion for summary judgment "as to the inclusion of Asian and Hispanic firms in [the School Board's] affirmative action program."[193]

In its analysis of the program's gender-conscious remedies, the Court used an intermediate level of scrutiny; namely, whether there was "an important governmental interest" served and whether the program's goals were "substantially related" to that interest.[194] Based upon the School Board's own evidence, the Court struck down the gender-conscious measures of the program, finding that those measures were not compelled by an "important governmental interest."[195] The evidence presented by the School Board which led to the Court's conclusion included the fact that: (1) "only about 5 percent of any disparity between female availability and utilization could be attributed to discrimination"; (2) white women enjoyed a higher bid success than white men; and (3) "women overwhelmingly disagreed when surveyed as to whether they ha[d] encountered discrimination in pursuing or performing public sector contracts on Atlanta."[196] Thus, the plaintiff's motion for

[192] *Id.* at 27-30.
[193] *Id.* at 30.
[194] *Id.*
[195] *Id.* at 31-32.
[196] *Id.* at 31.

summary judgment was also granted as to the program's inclusion of gender participation goals.[197]

In its analysis of the 32 percent participation goal for African-Americans, the Court denied both parties' motions for summary judgment, noting that it could better decide the validity of the evidentiary basis for past discrimination at a bench trial.[198] In its review of whether the School Board had a compelling interest in the adoption of an affirmative action program for African-Americans, however, the Supreme Court noted that the plaintiff's expert "raised serious questions" about the validity of the School Board consultant's disparity index.[199] Among other things, the Court noted that:

1. there was an underestimation of minority utilization because the amount of minority firms outside of the Atlanta area who were receiving contracting dollars may not have been included in the School Board consultant's utilization figure;[200]
2. the records used by the School Board consultant were in a "state of disarray";[201]
3. the School Board's availability figure was unreliable because it was measured by an examination of vendor application forms which did not distinguish between the levels of availability for the vendor firms or account for the minority firms' qualifications to supply products to the School Board;[202] and

---

[197] *Id.* at 32.
[198] *Id.* at 25, 29.
[199] *Id.* at 18-25.
[200] *Id.* at 18. The Court noted that measuring utilization "merely requires examining records and determining the ethnicity of the ownership of firms receiving School Board contracting dollars." The School Board's consultant, however, "verified the minority status of firms by checking the records of other City of Atlanta contracting authorities" which limited the measurement to Atlanta based firms.
[201] *Id.*
[202] *Id.* at 20-21.

4. the study failed to distinguish minority firms based on their ability to provide different types of products.[203]

The Court also reviewed the School Board's anecdotal evidence consisting of unsubstantiated testimony from School Board hearings and held that "[p]laintiff is entitled to have defendants' anecdotal evidence subjected to the test of trial before the Court determines whether it actually supports a sound basis in the evidence of discrimination."[204]

With regard to the second prong of the *Croson* standard; that is, whether the race preference program as it applied to African-Americans was narrowly tailored,[205] the Supreme Court held that it could not decide the issue unless it knew "for certain the level of discrimination which exists . . . ."[206] Thus, it denied summary judgment on this issue as well.[207] Following the court's decision on the parties' summary judgment motions, the School Board filed a Suggestion of Mootness on the basis that the challenged M/FBE program expired on May 19, 1997, pursuant to the program's sunset provision.[208] The Court denied the suggestion on May 21, 1997, the same day it was filed.[209] The parties also executed a Consent Order on May 21, 1997, wherein they agreed to a stay of the case pending the School Board's adoption of a new

---

[203] *Id.* at 21. The Court found that "[t]his criticism no doubt has some validity." If the consultant had distinguished firms on this basis, it might have found that minority firms were unable to provide the high ticket items to the School Board which may have led to the conclusion that "minorities would likely receive a disproportionately low share of contracting dollars even in the absence of discrimination."

[204] *Id.* at 24.

[205] The Court cited the same four factors relied upon by the court in *Dade County* to determine whether the School Board's plan was narrowly tailored; namely: "(1) consideration of race neutral alternatives; (2) flexibility of the plan; (3) relationship of [the] plan's numerical goals to relevant labor market; and (4) effect of [the] plan on third parties." *Id.* at 26 (citing *Peightal v. Metropolitan Dade County*, 940 F.2d 1394, 1406 (11th Cir. 1991)).

[206] *Id.*

[207] *Id.*

[208] *See* Defendants' Suggestion of Mootness dated May 21, 1997.

[209] *See* Order on Suggestion of Mootness dated May 21, 1997.

M/FBE program following which the Court would determine whether the case was moot or whether the plaintiff's Motion for Preliminary Injunction should be granted.[210] The Court also ordered the parties to file a status report within 90 days of the date of the Consent Order.[211]

On July 21, 1997, the School Board filed its status report which provided that based on a new disparity study conducted for the years 1992-97, the 1992 M/FBE program "mitigated most of the barriers to M/FBE participation" which were identified in the first disparity study.[212] The new study also reported that even though disparities still existed in some commodity codes (product supply lines), the 1992 M/FBE program helped to establish parity in the codes where there were more minority contractors available.[213] Thus, based on this new report, the School Board adopted a new race preference program on July 14, 1997.[214]

The plaintiffs argued that the new program was not actually race-neutral, and in an order the judge agreed. On January 15, 1998, she denied the APS motion and ruled for equal protection purposes, the crucial factor being that both plans drew distinctions solely on the basis of race and gender, preventing the plaintiff from competing on an equal footing when it submitted a bid for an APS contract. The APS had commissioned two new disparity studies, a revision by Davis of his earlier study on commodities and services and a second by Rodney Strong on construction. In his new study, Davis made one adjustment to the court's initial ruling and disaggregated commodities into 420 separate categories, instead of treating all purchases as a single item. When he did that, he found that there was no availability of MWBEs in some categories, over-utilization in some and under-utilization in

---

[210] *See* Consent Order dated May 21, 1997.
[211] *Id.*
[212] *See* Defendants' Status Report at ¶6.
[213] *Id.*
[214] *Id.* at ¶7.

others. In the second study on construction, availability was based on firms that actually bid. The study stated, "The determination of the availability of business for public contracting is crucial to a good disparity study. If availability is miscalculated then all inferential statistics, including disparity indexes, will be in error."[215]

The study also acknowledged that "One of the most common themes of the recent decision is that "available" firms must have the "qualifications" to perform work for a local jurisdiction."[216] Consequently, the study examined bidding files to determine the number of discrete bidders affiliated with each M/FBE group. This measure, the study noted, "incorporates all the required criteria of availability," that is, that the bidder does business within an industry group from which APS makes purchases; that the firm believes it is qualified and able to perform the work; and the firm is interested in doing the work..[217] Based on bidding, Strong found that while MWBE firms were 16.7 percent of the firms that bid, they received 24.1 percent of the prime contracts and 92 percent (476 of 518) subcontracts. Out of a total of $148,470,064 awarded, MWBEs received 35.6 percent.

The mixed results in the Davis study and the extraordinary over-utilization of MWBEs in construction created a problem for the APS. As Strong wrote in his study:

> The current posture of the APS program is legally new ground. Our research has not resulted in the discovery of any cases in which a program has been so successful that at the conclusion of the period there was no disparity within that period. It is completely unclear how courts will react to a situation in which utilization has been unclear as a result of the program. The primary question is whether APS could continue to achieve utilization of M/FBE firms absent a program. No court that we are aware of has provided substantial

---

[215] Rodney Strong, Disparity study – Construction, Atlanta Public School District, Atlanta, GA, 1998, p. 38.
[216] *Id.*, p.35
[217] *Id.*, p.39

> guidance in that area. There are no clear legal guidelines for the instant situation of the APS.[218]

In April, the day trial was to begin, the case was settled when the APS agreed not to use race, ethnic or gender criteria in making the prime contract awards or setting subcontracting goals for a period of two years and to pay the plaintiff's attorney's fees and expenses.

Phillips & Jordan v. Watts [Florida Dept. of Transportation]

On April 24, 1998, a federal district court in Tallahassee struck down the MWBE set-asides in the Florida state highway maintenance program and added to the judicial guidelines about disparity studies.

The Florida study was completed by MGT of America and it based availability on census data. Judge Stafford responded:

> The court is also unconvinced that it was appropriate to assume – as MGT did – that every firm in the selected SIC (census) codes was qualified and/or willing and able to bid on an FDOT road maintenance contract. See Eng's Contractors Ass'n, 488 U.S. at 501 – 502 (explaining that the "relevant statistical pool for the purposes of demonstrating discriminatory exclusion must be the number of minorities qualified to undertake the particular task") (emphasis in original). Common sense alone suggests reasons to question such assumptions. Do all firms in selected two-digit codes representing such large categories as transportation services (SIC 47), electric, gas, and sanitary services (SIC 49), heavy construction (SIC 16) perform road service work? The probable answer is: "No" … Is it not likely that MGT's statistical pool of qualified business was too large? The likely answer is: "Yes".[219]

The problems noted by the judge in this case was avoided by this predicate study by not basing availability on census data and disaggregating our analysis to

---

[218] Id. p.32

[219] *Id* at 20

avoid being over inclusive. Actual availability was calculated by identifying firms that have participated in the city's bidding process or subcontractors who have submitted bids or quotes to prime contractors doing business with the city. That is consistent with the Jordan & Phillips decision. The Court stated:

> Because MGT did not review actual bids on FDOT maintenance contracts, its study did not reveal (1) how many black and Hispanic-owned firms in fact submitted bids for FDOT maintenance contracts; (2) how many, if any black or Hispanic-owned firms unsuccessfully submitted bids for FDOT maintenance contracts; (3) how many, if any, black or Hispanic-owned firms submitted low bids that were rejected in favor of higher bids.[220]

With regard to anecdotes which played a substantial role in the MGT study, the court appeared to dismiss them as "perceptions." This justifies the reason why, in the St Petersburg study, verification and corroboration were an integral component of the procedures used to validate anecdotes.

There are two other issues in the Phillips & Jordan decision that warrant discussion. The case was decided on plaintiff's motion for summary judgment. Therefore disputed facts about the validity of census data, over inclusiveness, etc. could not have decided the case. What did decide the case was the judge's interpretation of a rule of law in *Croson*.

Florida had conceded that FDOT had not itself discriminated in the awarding of highway maintenance contracts, but relied on a generalized assertion that black and Hispanic-owned businesses may have been harmed by the discriminatory practices of bonding companies, or financial institutions, or prime contractors, or suppliers. FDOT's generalized allegations, however, did little to help define the

---

[220] *Id* at pp. 8-9

precise scope of the alleged harm or help to identify, with specificity, the purported wrong-doers. *Croson* had held that even where a governmental unit was not itself guilty of discrimination the governmental unit may act to dismantle a closed business system "by taking appropriate measures against those who discriminate." The court then insisted:

> It goes without saying that the identity of "those who discriminate" must be known before a governmental unit takes appropriate measures against "those who discriminate". An affirmative action program that is not focused on "those who discriminate" may well serve the illegitimate purpose of providing certain racial or ethnic groups with compensation for some ill-defined social disadvantages, but it probably will not serve the legitimate purpose of dismantling a closed business system. (emphasis in original)[221]

This language suggests that careful identification of the kind of discrimination being remedied and the identity of those who discriminate is necessary before race conscious measures can be taken. According to the Florida court "The Supreme Court's particularity requirement is not relaxed just because a claim of discrimination is supported by evidence statistical disparities."[222]

The final issue the Florida court raised goes to the subject of aggregating and disaggregating data for the purposes of calculating disparities. In the Jordan case, the court expressed concern about the effects of over-aggregating data and repeated warnings for Engineering Contractors Association about Simpson's paradox where the disparities are illusory because "Data so aggregated may disappear when the data is disaggregated.[223]

---

[221] *Id* at 15
[222] *Id* at 14
[223] *Id* at 18

In short, the new decision in *Phillips & Jordan v. Watts*, while not a binding precedent on the City of St. Petersburg study, adds to the increasing number of cases critical of the use of race preference remedies, reinforces some of the methodological decisions considered in designing this study, and adds a cautionary note about how conclusions should be drawn in the final recommendations.

Chapter Four

City of St. Petersburg Contracting Law and Procedure

This chapter covers a review of past and present contracting processes in the City of St. Petersburg's jurisdiction.[224] The review provides a normative foundation for delimiting the predicate study and a gauge for assessing the city's effectiveness in ensuring fair and constitutionally correct treatment of firms in its relevant market area. As discussed in Chapter Two, the purpose of this review is to: (a) determine whether any participant, policies, procedures, or practices discriminate or have discriminated on the basis of race, ethnicity or gender in awarding public contracts and subcontracts; (b) assess whether the contracting system, while not actively or intentionally discriminatory, has in a "passive" manner contributed to, or participated in a system of discrimination; and (c) identify and explain the impact of any policies, procedures, or practices which, although not discriminatory, generally inhibit M/WBEs and other small businesses in competition for public contracting.

The City of St. Petersburg's contracting law and procedure is contained in the City's procurement code adopted by the City Council on July 1, 1993,[225] and the City of St. Petersburg Purchasing and Material Management Policy and Procedures issued on February 1, 1989. The City's procurement code outlines general contracting and legal provision that must be followed by City officials and contractors and vendors

---

[224] An analysis of the City of St. Petersburg's contracting procedures will be performed completion of interviews with procurement officials, construction managers, inspectors, representatives of minority and woman- and non-minority-owned firms, contractor organization, vendors who are either contracting, or have contracted with the City.

[225] See City of St. Petersburg Ordinance 102-G, 1, July 1, 1993

for the procurement of supplies and services. The purchasing and materials management policy and procedures basically provide the policy and program implementation structure of the City's contracting of goods and services, and to a less extent, contracting services. The City's Engineering and Stormwater Department, utilizing their standard operating procedures, focuses entirely on consulting and construction related services. The objectives of the City's contracting procedures and law are as follows:[226]

1. to procure supplies and services of the right quality in the proper quantity at the right time from the proper source;
2. to conserve public funds by reducing costs and improving the quality of material purchased;
3. to reduce the overhead costs of buying by improving operations and procedures;
4. to reduce the volume and streamline the flow of paperwork;
5. to improve the speed of delivery to using departments by predetermining, through contracts or other appropriate means, the source of supply before the actual need for a particular material become known;
6. to have high inventory turnover, thereby diminishing excess storage and carrying expenses and inventory losses as a result of deterioration, obsolescence, and pilferage;
7. to achieve a high degree of cooperation and coordination with the using departments;
8. to maintain good records and control
9. to develop good supplier relationships in order to create positive attitudes and the desire to furnish the City with new ideas and commodities, as well as better prices and services.
10. To develop, motivate, and train personnel to fulfil the above objectives.

---

[226] See City of St. Petersburg Purchasing and Material Management Policy and Procedure Manual, February 1, 1989, p. xix.

General Contracting and Legal Provisions

The provisions of Ordinance 102-G-1 applies to contracts for the procurement of supplies and services which are entered into by the City of St. Petersburg, and the expenditure of funds by the City irrespective of the source of the funds. When the procurement involves the expenditure of federal assistance or funds, the procurement is conducted in accordance with any mandatory applicable federal or state law and regulation.

According to the City's procurement code, the City Mayor is authorized to purchase all supplies and service necessary for and incident to the proper conduct and management of the City. However, the Mayor has delegated this responsibility to the Director of Purchasing and Materials Management under the general supervision of the Mayor. The City's Director of the department of Purchasing and Material Management[227] is the principal public purchasing official for the City. The Director is appointed by the Mayor, and is responsible for the procurement of supplies and services in accordance with the provisions of Ordinance 102-G, as well as the management and disposal of supplies. In particular, the duties of the Purchasing Director include: (a) purchasing or supervising the procurement of supplies and services; (b) supervising all inventory stored in the City's Consolidated Inventory Warehouse; (c) selling, trading, or disposing of surplus property belonging to the City; and (d) establishing and maintaining programs for specification development, contract administration, and inspection and acceptance in cooperation with using departments. In effect, the City Director of Purchasing, under the directives of the Mayor, promulgates purchasing regulations governing the procurement, management, control, and disposal of any and all supplies and services procured by the City. The purchasing regulations include, but are not limited to: the responsibilities of the

---

[227] Here forth will be referred to as Director.

purchasing department, engineering department, and user agencies; application and removal from vendors lists; source selection and contracting; evaluation and award; mistakes; follow-up and contract administration; specifications; modification and termination of contracts; contract cost principle; cooperative purchasing with other jurisdictions; and surplus and obsolete material.

With regard to purchases involving other governmental entities, the City of St. Petersburg's Public Procurement Unit (that is, the City's Purchasing Department) either participate in, or sponsor, conduct, or administer a cooperative purchasing agreement for the procurement of any supplies or services with one or more Public Procurement Unit or External Procurement Activities in accordance with an agreement entered into between the participants. Such cooperative purchasing may include, but not limited to, joint or multi-party contract with other public entities and open-ended State contracts made available by the State of Florida. In addition, a City's using department, in consultation with the Director of Purchasing, may sell to, or acquire from, or use any supplies belonging to another Public Procurement Units or External Procurement Activity independent of the requirements source selection and contract formation and supply, provided that the unit comply with the legal provisions of the City's procurement code.

The City of St Petersburg's contracting and legal provisions also authorize the Purchasing Director to take affirmative measures to encourage the utilization of minority businesses when possible as sources of supplies and services items. However, the City M/WBE program is construction related and is implemented and bid through the City's Engineering and Stormwater Department. This construction related projects are referred to by the City as Capital Improvement Projects (CIP). A detail description of the administrative procedures and law for capital improvement program is presented below.

Contract Formation and Source Selection

A primary criterion for determining availability is that contractors interested in doing business with the City of St. Petersburg must participate in the City's competitive bidding process. According to the City's procurement Code, all of the City contracts exceeding $10,000 are awarded by competitive sealed bidding except for those contracts that are designated as either exempt or exception by the City[228]. The City of St. Petersburg utilizes seven major methods to award contracts. These methods include: (1) competitive sealed bidding; (2) multi-step sealed bidding; (3) competitive sealed proposals; (4) small purchases; (5) sole source procurement; (6) emergency procurement; and (7) purchases of police vehicles.

To ensure fair competition and efficiency in the source selection process, the City assigns specific duties to each individual or entity involved in the process. In particular, the Purchasing Manager maintains a uniform set of forms to serve in the bid process for: vendor notification, bid analysis and summary, bid bonds, bidder mailing list applications, invitations for bids, instructions to bidders, notices of award, and sealed bid envelopes. The using department, under the supervision of the Purchasing Manager, obtains bids on all supplies and services, and provides potential suppliers with answers to technical questions raised during the bidding process. All potential suppliers are provided the same information.

Option for Contracts or Direct Labor

Any of the City's public work or improvement may be executed by contract or direct labor, as may be determined by the Mayor. Before authorizing the direct

---

[228] On February 26, 1998, the City of St. Petersburg City Council amended the Procurement Code to increase the bid/proposal threshold to $25,000. The purpose of the amendment was to speed up the procurement cycle, reduced administrative lead time, streamline the layers of review and approval, allow department directors more discretion on small purchases, and improve productivity throughout the organization. This amendment occurred during only one of the nine fiscal years analyzed in this study. Hence, the amendment was not considered in delimiting the unit of analysis for this study.

execution of any work or improvement, detailed plans and estimates thereof are submitted to the City Council by the Mayor, and separate accountings as to each work or improvement so executed. In addition, the Mayor will require persons may perform the work or improvement to file with the City a bond with good and sufficient sureties to guarantee faithful performance of such work or contract and to completely and fully guarantee the City of any loss thereon. The City Council may, by resolution, waive the requirement for such a bond.

Fraud and Collusion by City Officers and Employees

To ensure fair competition, the Procurement Code prohibits City officers and employees from engaging in fraud and collusion in bidding and award of contracts. In particular, any officer or head or employee of any department thereof who aids or assist any bidder in securing a contract to furnish labor, material or supplies at a price than that proposed by any other bidder, or who favors one bidder over another by giving or withholding any information, or willfully misleads any bidder in regard to the character of the materials or supplies called for, or who knowingly accepts materials or supplies of any inferior grade to those called for by any contract or specifications, or who knowingly certifies a greater amount of labor performed, or the receipt of a greater amount of different kind of materials or supplies than has been actually received, or defraud the City in any other manner in relations to contracts, is guilty of misfeasance in office and removed from such office.[229]

Collusion by Contractors

The City Procurement Code also has provisions that prohibit contractors from collusion. Specifically, if at any time it is found that the person to whom a contract has been awarded has colluded with any other party for the purpose of circumventing any other competing bidder, or has entered into any arrangement by which he has

---

[229] See *Laws of Florida* (1931), Chapter 15505, 17(a); *Laws of Florida*, Chapter 69-1557, 1; *City of St. Petersburg Ordinance No. 744-F*, 1, 5-17-84.

made a higher or lower bid than some other person for the purpose of dividing the contract or profits therefrom between two or more bidders, then the contract so awarded shall be null and void.[230]

Awarding of Bids and Proposals

After the bids have been received and examined for completeness, the Purchasing and Materials Management Department and Engineering and Stormwater Department prepare a bid tabulation noting all the pertinent data and exceptions. A recommendation for award is then made after all aspects, including the comment and recommendations of the using department, have been made. However, in the event that bids or proposal for any supplies or services are solicited and no bids or proposal are received at the time and place established by the applicable bid invitation, the City Council has the authority to authorize the Mayor or the director of Purchasing to negotiate directly with potential vendors and enter into a contract for the provision of such supplies or services within prescribed dollar limits as approved by the City Council. All documents for each bid are kept in a bid file in the Purchasing Department. The Mayor or the Director of Purchasing, unless all bids or proposals are rejected, accepts the bid or proposal which in the Mayor or directors judgement best serve the interest of the City. In evaluating bids or proposals, the Mayor or the Director of Purchasing have the right to, at the Mayor's discretion, waive irregularities in any bids or proposals, or accept items equal to those specified. In the event that tied bids or proposals are received, the following prioritized list of criteria is applied for award: (1) business located within City limits, with valid occupational license; (2) County based business; and (3) State based business.

If it is not possible to make the award on the above-mentioned criteria, awards are made by coin toss in the Purchasing Office by the Mayor or the Director

---

230 See *Laws of Florida*, (1931) Chapter 15505, 17(e); *City of St. Petersburg Ordinance No. 714-F*, 1, 1-19-84.

of Purchasing. In this event, the tied bidder is notified of the time and may be requested to have a representative attend.

In the event that a bid or proposal is awarded to a vendor who subsequently defaults on the contract, the Mayor or the Director of Purchasing, have the discretionary authority to award the contract to the second-lowest bidder or the next best offeror from the original solicitation process, providing that such bidder or offeror agrees to abide by the terms and conditions originally stated by such firm in its proposal.

In addition, the Mayor, the Director of Purchasing and Material Management Department or the Director of Engineering and Stormwater Department may utilize the contracts of other governmental entities, or solicit bids or proposals on behalf of (or to participate with) other government entities in a cooperative bid process, when to do so is in the best interest of the City, providing that such contract have been awarded on the basis of a public, competitive bid process. However, in the purchase of supplies or services with a value that exceed $50,000, such contract or proposal must be approved by the City Council.[231]

Progressive Payments

Any of the City of St. Petersburg's contracts may provide for progressive payment[232]. If progressive payments are provided, in most cases involving construction contracts, a ten percent retainage is held on all portions of the progressive payments made until 50 percent of the total job is complete. No additional retainage is withheld on the balance of the progressive payments until 100 percent completion. In addition, no payment is made under such progressive

---

[231] On February 26, 1998, the City Council amended the City's Procurement Code to increase City Council's approval threshold to $50,000.

[232] See *Laws of Florida*, (1931) Chapter 1105, 17(f); *Laws of Florida* (1951) Chapter 27873, 1; *City of St. Petersburg Ordinance No. 362-F*, 1, 6-21-79.

payment contract or any lump sum contract unless the payment has been approved by the proper department heads or the Mayor.

Contract Award Methods

The City of St. Petersburg uses seven methods to award contracts. The methods are: (a) competitive sealed bidding; (b) multi-step sealed bidding; (c) competitive sealed proposals; (d) sole source procurement; (e) emergency procurement; (f) alternative authorization; and (g) small purchases. With the exception of sole source procurement, emergency procurement and small purchases of $5,000 or less, all of these methods involve competitive solicitation[233]. Each of these contract award methods is described below.

Competitive Sealed Bidding

The competitive bidding process begins with the City issuing an invitation for bids which include specifications, and all contractual terms and conditions applicable to the procurement. A public notice of the invitation for bids is given for purchases that exceed $5,000 not less than five (5) calendar days prior to the date set forth in the notice for the opening of bids. The notice may be given either by mail or by publication in a subscription newspaper of general circulation in the City (including minority newspapers) stating the place, date and time of the opening. In issuing the public notice for invitation for bids, the City does not restrict the invitation to vendors within the City, but instead may request and receive bids from vendors outside the City. In addition, the City sends out notification to interested MBE firms.

Bids are opened publicly in the presence of one or more witnesses at the time and place designated in the public notice of invitation for bids. The amount of each

---

[233] A review of the City of St. Petersburg procurement data and interviews of City Purchasing staff revealed that during each fiscal year that approximately 90 percent of the total number or dollar value of the City's purchases are awarded using competitive bidding methods.

bid and other relevant information as deemed necessary by the Purchasing Agent, as well as the name of each bidder is recorded. Bids are unconditionally accepted without alteration or correction, except as authorized in the City's procurement code. Bids are evaluated based on the requirement set forth in the invitations for bids, which may include criteria to determine acceptability such as inspection, testing, quality workmanship, delivery, bonding, and suitability for a particular purpose. Those criteria that will affect the bid price, and be conditioned in evaluation for award, are objectively measured. The criteria may include: discounts, transportation costs, and total or life cycle costs. The invitation for bids sets forth the evaluation criteria to be used by the City. The basis of award, for most construction contracts, is spelled out in bid documents.

In rare instances, the City of St. Petersburg may permit correction or withdrawal of inadvertently erroneous bids before or after bid opening, or cancellation of awards or contracts based on such mistakes. Mistakes discovered before the bid opening may be modified or withdrawn by written or telephonic notice received in the City office designated in the invitation for bids prior to time set for the bid opening[234]. After bid opening, corrections in the bids are not permitted except the bidder can show by clear and convincing evidence that a mistake of a nonjudgmental character was made, the nature of the mistake, and the bid price actually intended[235]. In addition, after bid opening, the City does not allow changes in bid prices or other provisions of bids prejudicial to the interest of the City or fair competition. The mistake must be reported within 24 hours after bid opening, and not committed by an owner or senior member of the company. In lieu of bid correction, the City may permit a low bidder alleging a material mistake of fact to withdraw its bid provided either that the mistake is clearly evidence on the face of the

---

[234]Based upon an interview with the City's Purchasing Officials, these mistakes rarely occur.
[235] An interview with City Purchasing Officials revealed that these corrections rarely occur.

bid document but the intended correct bid is not similarly evident, or that the bidder submits evidence which clearly and convincingly demonstrated that a mistake was made. All decisions to permit the correction or withdrawal of bids, or to cancel awards or contracts based on bid mistakes, are supported by a written determination made by the Purchasing Agent and Engineering and Stormwater Department Director.

The City's procurement code specifies that contracts should be awarded with reasonable promptness by appropriate written notice to the lowest responsible and responsive bidder whose bid meets the requirement and criteria set forth in the invitation for bids. In the event that the low responsive and responsible bid for a construction project exceeds available funds or the engineer's estimate, the Mayor or his designated representative is authorized, when time or economic considerations preclude resolicitation of work of a reduced scope, to negotiate an adjustment of the bid price with the low responsive and responsible bidder, in order to bring the bid amount within the amount of available funds. Any such negotiated adjustment is based only upon eliminating independent deductive items specified in the invitations for bids. In the purchase of supplies or services of whatever nature or character, amounting in value to $10,000 or more, the Mayor or the Director of Purchasing makes a report and transmits the bids to the next regular session of City Council with a recommendation concerning accepting or rejection thereof, and the City Council thereupon approves or disapproves the recommendation of the Mayor or the Director of Purchasing. The City retains the right to reject all bids should negotiations fail.

Multi-step Sealed Bidding

This method involves a contracting situation when it is considered impractical to initially prepare a purchase description to support an award based on price. An invitation for bids may be issued requesting the submission of unpriced offers to be followed by an invitation for bids limited to those bidders whose offers have been determined to be technically acceptable under the criteria set forth in the first solicitation. In particular, under the multi-step sealed bidding method, an invitation for bids is issued requesting the submission of unpriced offer followed by an invitation for bids limited to those bidders whose offer have been determined to be technically acceptable under the criteria set forth in the first solicitation. In the first step, potential vendors are requested to submit unpriced technical proposals. Only those vendors who have submitted acceptable technical proposals are invited to submit competitive sealed bids in step two.

Multi-step sealed bidding may be used under the following circumstance: (1) when available specifications or purchase descriptions are not definite or complete; (2) when definite criteria exist for evaluating technical proposals; (3) when more than one technically qualified source is available; (4) when sufficient time will be available for using the two-step method; and (5) when a firm, fixed-price contract or a fixed price contract with economic adjustment will be used.

Competitive Sealed Proposals

The City of St. Petersburg uses competitive sealed proposals method to award a contract that exceed $10,000[236] when the Purchasing Manager determines in writing that the use of competitive sealed bidding is either not practicable or not advantageous to the City[237]. In general, the competitive sealed proposal method is used for contracts involving professional architectural, engineering, landscaping, architectural, and land surveying services. In this method, proposals are solicited

---

[236] On February 26, 1997, the St. Petersburg City Council amended the Procurement Code to increase the proposal threshold to $25,000. Since this amendment went into effect in the middle of the last of nine fiscal years analyzed, it was not used to delimit the units of analysis for this study. Hence, interpretation of the data for this period should be made with caution.

[237] A review of the City of St. Petersburg [purchasing data] and interview of the City's Purchasing Director indicate that a large majority (i.e. approximately 95 percent of contract dollars awarded) of the City's purchases are competitively bid, while all the other methods used to award contracts combined account for less than 5 percent of the City's purchases.

through a request for proposals. The City gives adequate public notice of the request for proposals in the same manner as for competitive sealed bidding (i.e. newspapers and Dodge)[238]. No proposal is opened until at the time designated in the public notice of the request for proposals. A register of proposals is prepared containing the name of each offeror, the number of modifications received, if any, and a description sufficient to identify the item offered.

The proposals are evaluated by a committee consisting of City Department heads, Purchasing Department staff and any other official designated by the City Mayor or City Manager, based on the relative importance of price, if appropriate, and other evaluation factors specified in the request for proposals. The City may conduct discussions with responsible offerors who submit proposals determined to be reasonably susceptible of being selected for award for the purpose of clarification to assure full understanding of, and conformance to, the solicitation requirements. Offerors are accorded fair and equal treatment with respect to any opportunity for discussion and revision of proposals. The revisions may be permitted after submissions and prior to award for the purpose of obtaining best and final offers.

The City of St. Petersburg makes an award to the responsible offeror whose proposal is determined in writing to be the most advantageous to the City, taking into consideration price and the evaluation factors set forth in the request for proposals. The City maintains a contract file containing the basis on which the award is made.

Sole Source Procurement

This method awards a contract without competition based on a determination in writing by the Purchasing Agent that there is only one source for the required

---

[238] The Public notice of the invitation for Proposals are given not less than five calendar days prior to the date set forth in the notice for the opening of proposals. Such notice may be given by publication in a subscription newspaper of general circulation including minority newspapers in the City. The notice states the due place, date, and time of proposal.

supply, service, or construction item. In awarding a sole source contract, the buyer, under the supervision of the Purchasing Manager, conducts negotiations, as appropriate, as to price, delivery, and terms. A record of sole source procurements is maintained as public record, listing each contractor's name, the amount and type of each contract, and the identification number of each contract file. For a sole source purchase exceeding $10,000, the Mayor or Purchasing Director shall prepare a written statement to the City Council certifying the conditions and circumstance. Upon receipt and approval of such statement, the City Council may authorize the purchase.

The City may negotiate with a sole source supplier under the following circumstances:

1. the needed supply or service is available from only one source;
2. the supply or service is wanted for experimental trial or testing;
3. the supply is purchase for resale; additional supplies or services are needed to complete an ongoing task; a supply or service is purchased from, or a sale is made to, another unit of government; the item is a component or replacement part for which there is no commercially available substitute and which can be purchased only from the manufacturer or distributor; and
4. the item is a used item which is subject to immediate sale.

Emergency Procurement

The City of St. Petersburg uses the emergency Procurement method to award a contract for the procurement of supplies, services, or construction items when there exists a threat to public health, welfare, or safety such as may arise by reason of hurricane, flood, equipment failure, or other disruption of essential service as may be declared by the City Manager or his designee. The procedure involves written determination of the basis for the emergency and for the selection of a particular contractor. As soon as practical, a record of each emergency procurement is made and set forth the contractor's name, the amount and type of the contract, the listing of the item(s) under the contract, and the identification number of the contract file.

Alternative Authorization

The alternative authorization method is used by the City of St. Petersburg to award a contract to purchase vehicles for the Police Department. The procedure for such purchases involves requesting proposals and quotations from potential vendors pursuant to the Florida Sheriff's Association's negotiated purchasing program for law enforcement vehicles. The City selects the proposal that is within five (5) percent of the lowest quotation available for similar vehicles from the latest State Purchasing Contract unless the Mayor or the Purchasing director determines in writing that there is no comparable vehicle price quote from the State contract. In this case, the Mayor or his designated representative undertakes an alternative means to verify that the price quotation is best available in the market.

Small Purchases

The City of St. Petersburg uses the small purchase procedure to award contracts that do not exceed $10,000.[239] Two types of small purchases are made: (a) small purchases in excess of $5,000; and (b) small purchases of $2,500 or less. For purchases in excess of $5000.00, the City solicits no less than three businesses to submit quotations from the City's vendor list, phone book or knowledge of purchasing staff. Award is made to the businesses offering the lowest acceptable

---

[239] The City of St. Petersburg prohibits the artificial division of purchases so as to constitute a small purchase. On February 1998, the City of St. Petersburg City Council amended the City's Procurement Code to provide unspecified higher limits for small purchases. This amendment was, however, not used to delimit the units of analysis for this study since it occurred during the last few months the nine fiscal years analyzed. However, interpretation of the results of data analysis for these last few months should be made with caution.

quotation. The names of the businesses submitting quotations, and the date and amount of each quotation is recorded and maintained as public record.

For small purchases of $5,000 or less, the Purchasing Manager obtains at least three (3) quotations for the supplies or services that are expected to exceed $1,000. A price check is made on expenditures less than 1,000 when purchasing unfamiliar supplies. The City uses two approaches to solicit quotes from potential vendors: (1) verbal quotations; and (2) written quotations. The verbal quotation approach is used to obtain quotes for purchase of standard or non-complex supplies with an estimated price less than $5,000. Prices are recorded on a telephone quotation form for documentation purposes. A purchase order is then prepared, signed by the City's Director of Purchasing and Materials Management, and issued to confirm the order. In the written quotation approach, the buyer prepares a request for quotations and a bidders' mailing list, and then issues the request for quotations to all vendors on the bidders mailing list. Upon receipt of all the quotations, the buyer, under the supervision of the Purchasing Manager, selects the lowest and best quotation and prepares a purchase order. The purchase order is then signed by the Director of Purchasing and Material Management and issued.

To confirm purchase orders under $1,000, the Director of the using department or a representative contacts the Purchasing department and requests a purchase order number. The representative, in exchange for the purchase order number, submits to Purchasing the following information: department name, name of the representative, requisition number, account number, vendor name, description of the purchase, and total amount of the purchase. The using department then makes the purchase. Meanwhile, purchases over $1,000 are confirmed only prior to a concurrent agreement between the director of the using department or a representative and the director or Manager of Purchasing.

Contracting Exceptions and Exemptions

The City of St. Petersburg generally uses the Competitive Sealed bids and competitive Proposals methods to award contracts, except for procurements designated by City as exemptions, such as: sole source and emergency procurement; purchases of groceries, foodstuff and alcoholic beverages, and expendable items of supplies used in connection with a restaurant or lounge business operated by the City; the purchase of merchandise for resale in City-operated retail shop; expert witness and other legal services procured through the City Attorney's Office in furtherance of anticipated or pending litigation; professional services[240] artistic services or works of art; asbestos abatement and removal bids under $20,000; demolition bids under $20,000; purchases of goods and services used in connection with the acquisition, demolition, new construction, rehabilitation, marketing and maintenance of properties identified in the neighborhood housing strategy. The City Council may authorize the contracts for legal, medical, and other professional services by negotiating with a lawyer or lawyers, medical doctor or doctors, and organizations selected or recommended by the Mayor or his designee on the basis of experience and skill.

With regard to exemptions, the City of St. Petersburg exempts from the provisions of the procurement code and ordinance 102-G, 1, purchases of supplies and services related to construction for adapting to a major sports tenant and/or operation of the multipurpose stadium being constructed in the portion of the In town Redevelopment Area known as the Gas Plant Area. Also exempt from the provisions of the City' Procurement ordinance are the following purchases: (a) supplies and

---

[240] Professional services refer to professional engineering, architectural, landscape architectural, registered land surveying, brokerage and financial investing, accounting, auditing and medical services. These services are covered by the *Consultant Competitive Negotiation Agreement* (Section 287.055, Florida Statute), 2004.

services related to the operation of the Bayfront Center; and (b) supplies and services related to the construction for tenant improvements and/or operation of the pier.

Cancellation of Invitations for Bids or Request for proposals

The City of St. Petersburg may cancel or reject in whole or in part as may be specified in the solicitation for bid an invitation for bids, a request for proposals, or other solicitations when it is for good cause and in the best interest of the City, and the reason made part of the contract file. When this occurs, a notice of cancellation is sent to all businesses solicited identifying the solicitation, explaining the reason for cancellation and, where appropriate, explaining that an opportunity will be given to compete on any resolicitation or future procurements of similar items.

Responsibility of Bidders and Offerors

The City of St. Petersburg requires bidders or offerors to submit information concerning their responsibility. If a bidder or offeror who otherwise would have been awarded a contract is found non-responsive, a written determination of non-responsibility, setting forth the basis of the finding, is prepared by the Purchasing Agent and sent to promptly to the non-responsive bidder or offeror. Grounds for a determination of non-responsibility may include, but not limited to, the unreasonable failure of a bidder or offeror to promptly supply information in connection with an inquiry with respect to responsibility.

A prospective contractor is required to submit cost or pricing data to the City when a contract is expected to exceed $100,000 and is to be awarded by competitive sealed proposal or by sole source procurement authority. However, the submission of cost or pricing data relating to the award of a contract is not required when: (a) the contract price is based on adequate price competition; (b) the contract price is based on established catalogue prices or market prices; (c) the contract price is set by law or regulation; or (d) it is determined in writing by the purchasing agent that the requirements of submitting a cost or pricing data may be waived, and the determination states the reason for such a waiver. Regarding submissions relating to change orders or contract modifications, a contractor is required to submit cost or pricing data prior to the pricing of any change order or modification, including adjustments to contracts awarded by competitive sealed bidding, whether cost or pricing data was required in connection with the initial pricing of the contract, especially when the change order or modification involves aggregator increases or aggregate decreases in cost plus applicable profits that are expected to exceed 10 percent of the initial contract. Exceptions to this provision include: (a) unrelated and separate priced adjustments for which cost pricing data would not be required are consolidated for administrative convenience; or (b) it is determined in writing that by the purchasing agent that the requirements of change order or contract modifications may be waived, and the determination states the reasons for such waiver. A prospective contractor is also required to certify that to the best of its knowledge and belief, the cost or pricing data submitted was accurate, complete, and current as of a mutually specified date prior to the award of the contract or the pricing of the change order or contract modification.

Finally the City requires any contract award, change order, or contract modification under which the submission and modification of cost or pricing data are required to contain a provision stating that the price to the City, including profit or fees, is adjusted to exclude any significant sums by which the City finds that such sum pricing was increased because the contractor-furnished cost or pricing data was inaccurate, incomplete, or not current.

Bid Performance and Payment Bonds on Supply, Construction or Service Contracts

The City of St. Petersburg also may requires prospective supply, construction and or service contractors to submit a bid, performance and payment bonds or other security as the City purchasing Agent or head of a using department deems advisable to protect the City's interest. Any such bonding requirements are set forth in the solicitation. However, bid performance or payment bonds cannot be used as a substitute for a determination of a bidder's or an offeror's responsibility.

Maximum Practicable Competition

The City's procurement code requires all soliciting departments to enforce the practice of maximum practicable competition. In particular, the code requires all City specifications to be drafted so as to promote the overall economy for the purpose intended and to encourage competition in satisfying the City's needs, and not to be unduly restrictive. This policy applies to all specifications, including, but not limited to those prepared for the City by architects, engineers, designers and draftsmen. To enforce this policy, the Purchasing Agent may develop a qualified product list that best satisfies the City's requirements when testing or examining supplies or construction items prior to issuance of solicitation. Prior to final approval of the proposed specifications for the qualified product list items, the Purchasing Agent should provide the using agency, and a reasonable number of manufacturers or suppliers, as deemed appropriate, an opportunity to comment on the draft of the proposed specifications.

When developing a qualified product list, a representative group of potential suppliers should be solicited in writing to submit products for testing and examination to determine acceptability for inclusion on a qualified product list. Any potential supplier, even though not solicited, may offer its product for consideration.

A qualified product list is included based on results of test or examination conducted in accordance with published requirements. The final approval of, and revisions to, and cancellation of qualified product list lists are made only upon approval of the Purchasing agent or the designee of the Purchasing Agent.

Capital Improvement Program

According to the City's administrative policy and procedure, capital improvement projects are purchases that meet the following screening criteria: (a) they must be related to an approved City service; (b) they involve the acquisition, construction, expansion or reconstruction of a structure or the acquisition of land for project-related or land banking purposes; (c) they require an expenditure of $50,000 or more; (d) they must have a minimum useful life expectancy of 10 years or more; and (e) they must involve fiscal requirements which may cross budget years.

The major categories of these capital projects include: (a) new or expanded facilities, infrastructure or land; (b) major maintenance; and (c) equipment purchases. The City's Department of Budget is responsible for determining which projects are to be considered "capital projects" and which expenditures are considered allowable expenditures under the provisions of the City's Administrative Policy and Procedure. A description of the City's administrative procedure and protocol for implementing for capital improvement program is presented below.

The expenditures allowable for a capital project may include the following: architectural, design, or engineering contracts; fees for special consultants, legal and court costs, building permits, environmental permits, and occupancy permits, and utilities; construction contracts; demolition contracts; leasing of equipment needed for construction; landscaping and irrigation, real estate acquisition and related costs; replatting, vacation of streets and zoning exception; reproduction cost for plans and blueprints; purchase of equipment and furnishings estimated to cost less than $5,000, if the item is determined to be necessary for the initial operation of the facility, purchases of equipment and furnishings estimated to cost more than $5,000; and other expenditures as approved by the Budget Department.

Expenditures and encumbrances for capital projects follow normal City procedures for request for payment, requisitions, and intergovernmental work order.[241] In addition, all requisitions, request for payment, and work orders must be initialized or signed by the Administrator for Public Works or the Department Director responsible for the project. Meanwhile, all encumbrances or expenditures for capital projects including all requisitions, request for payment, and work orders must be approved by the Budget Department.

Capital Improvement Policy Implementation

According to the City of St. Petersburg Administrative Policy and Procedure, all Capital Improvement Program (CIP) projects are required to have City Council approval and appropriation of adequate funds before project implementation. The City Administrator for Public Works is responsible for planning and implementing all CIP projects involving architectural and engineering design and construction. The Directors of other departments are responsible for planning and implementing projects which include only equipment and/or land purchases, and are not part of a construction project.

Capital improvement projects which may significantly affect residents or businesses of a particular area of the City are reviewed by the Mayor's Office before proceeding with project implementation. The projects must conform to all City Ordinances and codes and receive approval of all applicable boards, commissions, and regulatory agencies before construction. The department designated responsibility for a CIP project is required to control project schedules, expenditures,

---

[241] See City of St. Petersburg Administrative Policy and Procedure, Sections 6.03.02, 9.01.01, and 8.09.

and specification compliance, as well as obtain the necessary approvals for all change orders in advance and in accordance with established City policy.

During the implementation phase of a CIP project, the Budget Department coordinates the preparation of the CIP budget and five year CIP plan. Meanwhile, the Administrator for Public Works or his designee coordinates the design and construction of capital improvement projects. Other CIP projects not requiring design and/or inspection by the Engineering and Stormwater Department are coordinated similarly by the responsible department Director. Input from Maintenance and user Departments are solicited, and given due consideration.

For all CIP engineering or architectural design projects, the Administrator for Public Works determines whether efforts will be performed by the City Engineering and Stormwater Department or outside consultants. The selection of outside consultants is made in accordance with established City code, policies and procedures, and the State of Florida's Consultants' Competitive Negotiation Act (CCNA).[242]

To ensure effective implementation of the CIP program, the City's Administrator for Public Works performs the following tasks: (a) maintains an up-to-date budget and schedule; (b) signs and initialize all expenditure authorizations, Appropriation/budget Adjustments, requisitions, Request for Payment, and work orders; (c) is provided with a monthly Capital Project Ledger by Accounting; (d) reviews the Capital Project Ledger provided by the Accounting Department to verify that charges are proper and appropriate, and takes action to remove or terminate charges found to be improper; and (e) performs other project duties as required. The City's Director of Engineering and Stormwater or the department director responsible for project initiation is required to submit all the necessary Appropriation/Budget

[242] See City of St. Petersburg Administrative Policy and Procedure 8.04.01.

Adjustments to the Administration of Public Works. Appropriations not previously authorized in the CIP must be initiated by an Appropriation/Budget Adjustment and approved by City Council.

Upon approval of the CIP or supplemental appropriation, the Administrator of Public Works or the user department Director initiates action on, and assumes overall management of, the project involving coordination with consultants, contractors, and other City departments. Questions or inquiries concerning projects involving consultants, construction contractors or outside suppliers must be referred to the Administrator for Public Works or his designee, and not to outside parties.

Meanwhile, the Budget Department is responsible for monitoring all CIP projects information regarding budget, finance, and project status, as well as assisting the Administrator of Public Work or user department Director in this regard. Before seeking bids on any construction contracts, the Director of Engineering and Stormwater prepares a revised project budget and submits it to the Administrator for Public Works and Budget.

During the construction phase of CIPs, the Administrator for Public Works is responsible for coordinating all architectural and engineering design and construction project for the City. Meanwhile, the Director of Engineering and Stormwater Department is responsible for the preparation of design and engineering specifications for the construction of all public improvements, and for the coordination of all public improvements, and for the coordination of all related inspections whether performed by the City personnel or a consultant. During the planning, design, and construction of a project, the project is reviewed on a monthly basis jointly by the Administrator for Public Works, the Director of Engineering and Stormwater, the Director of the using Department, and the Budget Director.

All structural work normally requiring permits must have such permits issued by the Housing and Construction Service Department before the initiation of construction. Meanwhile, all contracts for construction of public improvements involving the expenditure of funds in excess of $2,500 must be obtained by written sealed bids solicited by legal advertisement, and contracts and change orders of more than $5,000 must be approved by City Council. The Mayor is authorized to execute all necessary change orders up to but not exceeding $5,000 per order, and not exceeding a cumulative total of $5,000 for all change orders on any contract. This authority is limited cumulatively to up to but not in excess of the monies appropriated by the City Council for the particular project.

Based on field inspection and initial coordination meeting, the Administrator for Public Works makes a determination whether a particular CIP project is to be designed by City agencies or by a consultant. If it is determined that the services of a consultant are required, the consultant is selected according to the City's standard administrative policy and procedure for selecting and contracting for architectural, engineering, or land surveying professional services discussed in the next section of this report[243].

The Director of Engineering and Stormwater Department prepares functional plans for the project, and hold review meetings to involving on-site inspection for both in-house and consultant-designed projects. The plans are revised and corrected as required and approved by all applicable parties. Once the functional plan is completed, a detailed plan, specification and estimate are prepared by the Engineering and Stormwater Department or the consultant under the direction of the Director of Engineering and Stormwater Department. A series of meeting are then held with all interested parties, including on-site inspections to familiarize all parties with the detailed plan.

---

243 Also see City of St. Petersburg Administrative Policy and Procedure Section 8.04.01.

Upon completion of the detailed plan, a solicitation for bids is issued. Bids for the CIP is received, tabulated, and reviewed by the Department of Engineering and Stormwater, and the Administrator for Public Works submits to the Mayor his or recommendation for awarding the contract. The Mayor then reviews the recommendation and, if approved, submits it to the City Council for action if required. The City Council may approve or disapprove awarding the contract to the recommended firm.

Following an award for the CIP, the project engineer holds a pre-construction conference with the contractor, all utilities, and the sponsoring agency represented to discuss project schedule, estimates and change orders. The estimates and change orders must be approved by the Director of Engineering and Stormwater and the Administrator for Public Works, and a notice to proceed is then issued.

During the construction phase, the Director of Engineering and Stormwater Department tests materials and conducts on-site inspection of the work in progress, as required. Meanwhile the project engineer keeps the sponsoring agency advised of the progress of the project and the anticipated dates of completion.

Upon completion of the project, the Director of Engineering and Stormwater prepares a plan of the project "as built" for the Department of Engineering and Stormwater files, and notify the Department of Budget of same so the project account may be closed. All current projects are reviewed at a monthly project management meeting composed of the following participants: the Administrator for Public works, the Director of Engineering and Stormwater, the Directors of all the departments sponsoring current projects, and the Director of the Department of Budget. The sponsoring department, assisted by the Administrator for Public Works or the Director of the responsible Department reports the Receipt of Fixed Assets.[244]

Purchase of Land for Public Housing

The City of St. Petersburg may also purchase parcel of land to be used as the location for constructing public housing. The purchase is made in accordance to Florida Statute involving the purchase of real estate[245]. Before such purchase occurs, the City Council holds public hearing on the proposed purchase. The City notifies all owners of real property, as listed in the current year ad valorem tax rolls of Pinellas County, that are within 200 feet of the land to be used as a location for constructing the public housing, not less than ten days before the schedule public hearing. The notification is made by either United States mail with a certificate of mailing returned to the Clerks of the City Council, or delivering to the owner and receipt thereof acknowledging by the signature of the owner. When the purchase involves a condominium or cooperative building, only the association, through its duly registered agent or officer, is notified. A sign is posted on the subject property by the City approximately one week before the public hearing.

Summary

In summation, the City of St. Petersburg has established formal procedures and protocol to be followed by City officials and prime contractors in the solicitation and awards of prime contracts and subcontracts. Contract can be awarded either through a competitively bid process or non-competitively bid process. In an interview with City officials and a review of the City's procurement records indicated

---

[244] See City of St. Petersburg Administrative Policy and Procedure, Section 6.05.01. It is important to note that the Administrator for Public Works or the department director responsible for project initiation may appoint Project coordinators to perform all the duties outlined in this section of the report.

[245] See Florida Statute 166.045.

that at least 80 percent of the total dollar value or number of the contract awarded by the City during each fiscal year is competitively bid. In addition, the two major departments (that is, Purchasing and Materials Management, and Engineering and Stormwater) responsible for administering the provisions of the City's procurement code and the City's Administrative Procedures related to procurement seem to be inconsistent in emphasis placed on the technical aspect of certain procurement provisions. However, during interviews with the City's procurement staff, it was revealed that these technical variations do not have a significant effect on the City's normal contracting process and law, although a number of procurement staff would prefer a more consistent operating procedure between the two departments.

Chapter Five

City of St. Petersburg Race Preference Policy and Program

This chapter provides a historical development of the City of St. Petersburg's race preference program and assesses its effectiveness in promoting minority participation in the city's contracting process.

The beginning of the commitment by the City of St. Petersburg to assist minority and woman-owned business enterprises (M/WBEs) with the awarding of City contracts can be traced back to 1982 with the passage of Ordinance 554-F. The Ordinance allocated 5 percent of all City goods and services contracts to M/WBEs. In 1984, the City made an assessment of the M/WBE program and found that the 5 percent goal was achieved[246]. This finding prompted the City Council to approve an increase of the M/WBE participation goal to 10 percent. In FY 1985, the City again assessed the performance of the M/WBE program and found that the 10 percent goal for the City's goods and services contracts has been achieved[247]. That same year the City adopted another race preference ordinance (Ordinance 814-F) for the City's construction services contracts.

In FY 1988, the City allowed Ordinance 554-F to sunset because of doubts about the constitutional (legal) justification of the M/WBE program. In FY 1989, the City voluntarily suspended Ordinance 1075-F after publication of the U.S. Supreme Court decision in *Croson*. That same year, as a result of the *Croson* decision, the City of St. Petersburg engaged the services of a consulting firm to develop evidence

---

[246] *City of St. Petersburg MBE Annual Report*, 1984, p. 1.
[247] *City of St. Petersburg MBE Annual Report*, 1985, p. 1.

of the nature and extent (if any) of discrimination against woman- and minority - owned business enterprises (M/WBEs)[248] in the relevant market area of the City, to determine if disparity existed between the availability and utilization of minority businesses, and to analyze the effect of race-neutral programs. The study findings presented in a report entitled *City of St. Petersburg Minority Business Enterprise Disparity Study,* dated June 1990 (and supplemental report dated November 9, 1990), found that a pattern of discrimination against black-owned business enterprises (BBEs) had resulted in significant statistical disparity between the availability of such businesses and their utilization in the City's construction contracting and procurement activities. In addition, the study found that the disparity exhibited by Hispanic-owned businesses (HBEs) and Woman-owned businesses (WBEs) were not statistically significant.

The City Council held hearings and resolved that the disparity study findings, along with anecdotal evidence of discrimination against black-owned business enterprises in construction services, provided sufficient evidence of compelling government interest in implementing race- and gender-based remedial initiatives to increase M/WBEs' participation in the City's construction contracting and procurement activities. Therefore, in 1990, the City re-enacted a race preference

---

[248] The City of St. Petersburg Ordinance No. 2023-F defines M/WBE as a Woman Business Enterprise as WBE), Black Business Enterprise as (BBE), or Hispanic Business Enterprise (HBE) certified by the City. WBE, BBE, and HBE mean a business which is at least fifty one (51) percent owned by a woman, a black, or a Hispanic person who also controls and operates the business. In the case of corporation, at least fifty one (51) present of the stock must be owned by a woman or women, Hispanic, or black individual(s), and the corporation must also be at least fifty one (51) percent controlled and operated by a woman or women, black, or Hispanic individual(s). This definition suggests that race and gender groups eligible to participate in the City's M/WBE program is limited to woman, black and Hispanic individuals only. This definition differs from the state and federal governments' definitions which also include Asian-American, Native Americans, the Eskimos, and Aleuts. Hence, since these other groups are not included in the City's program, the disparity study findings were applicable only to "defined minorities". This was likely done to comply with legal requirements that the ordinance be narrowly tailored to statistically significant groups.

ordinance (Ordinance No. 2023-F) establishing policies and procedures intended to provide black-, Hispanic- and woman-owned business enterprises with maximum opportunity to participate in the City's construction contracting and procurement activities.

The purpose of the race preference policy was "to establish procedures by which black, Hispanic and women business enterprises may be assured equal access to the City's construction contract program."[249]

The provisions of this re-enacted race preference ordinance called for an aggregate of 22 percent participation goal for M/WBEs on City construction contracts. Specifically, the law established mandatory participation goals of 8 percent for black-owned businesses and voluntary goals of seven 7 percent for Hispanic-owned firms and 7 percent for woman-owned businesses. In 1994, the City Council reviewed the performance of the M/WBE program and concluded that Hispanic- and woman-owned businesses in the City's relevant market area have been severely under-utilized in bid proposals for City contracts. As a result, the City ratified the race preference ordinance to include mandatory participation goals of seven 7 percent for Hispanic- and woman-owned businesses. Only certified M/WBEs were eligible to participate in the race preference program.[250]

In addition, the City Council established a *Sheltered Market Program* in which certain construction projects were reserved for bidding amongst minority-owned businesses only. As in the goals participation program, only certified minority business enterprises were eligible to participate in the shelter market program. The shelter market was utilized only where it was determined that there were sufficient

---

[249] City of St. Petersburg Administrative Policy and Procedure, section 2.177

[250] The City of St. Petersburg M/WBE certification enables firms to compete and bid on City construction projects as defined minority- and woman-owned and operated company. It is not an automatic guarantee that the contractor will be awarded a contract.

certified minority business enterprises to afford effective competition and it was necessary to assist in achievement of the annual Citywide goals for M/WBE participation. The City required that at least 50 percent of shelter market contracting effort, including the cost of materials, goods, and supplies be performed by M/WBE prime contractors or subcontractors with their own, organization and resources. Construction projects appropriate for the shelter market program were designated on a project-by-project basis. The City's Construction Committee was required to review projected projects and costs, and identify those projects which were appropriate for inclusion in the shelter market program. Projects may be sheltered to M/WBEs collectively or individually. The percentage of the total dollars placed in the shelter market program was to be reviewed each fiscal year by the Mayor, or a designee, to determine whether implementation of the sheltered market is still in the best interest of the City. Only certified M/WBEs were permitted to bid on those projects included in the shelter market program.

In effect, the City M/WBE law required soliciting departments and prime contractors to set aside a certain proportion (based upon established goals) of the City's construction contracts. The implementation of this set aside provision was to be based on availability of prime contractors and subcontractors in each category of black, Hispanic- and woman-owned business enterprise.[251] In effect, the City of St. Petersburg race preference program objectives suggested not only the City's intention to effectively create opportunities for participation through an active solicitation of available M/WBEs in the City's relevant market area, but also that such effort must

---

[251] The City M/WBE ordinance does not provide an operational definition of availability. However, based on recent court decisions on the subject matter, availability is operationally defined in this study as the proportion of the number or dollar value of competitively bid contracts (or subcontracts) by racial, ethnic or gender group per procurement category.

translate into the creation of wealth through government contracting for minorities and women.

Race Preference Program Administrative Structure

To achieve this objective of the City of St. Petersburg race preference policy, the City created a construction committee responsible for determining an annual M/WBE goal and individual black-, Hispanic- and woman-owned business enterprise participation percentages for each construction project, as well as administering the City's shelter market program. The membership of the Construction committee consisted of the Public Works Administrator, the Director of the Engineering and Stormwater Department, the Manager of Design of the Engineering and Stormwater Department, the Director of Community Affairs, and the Purchasing and Materials Management Director. The Director of Engineering and Stormwater Department served as Committee Chair. The participation percentages were based on availability of black-, Hispanic- and woman-owned business enterprise construction contractors on a contract-by-contract basis, and are included in all of the City's construction contract bid specifications and bid advertisements for all City construction contracts. However, not every contract had mandatory participation goals.

When goals were set, all construction prime contractors submitting bids to provide construction services to the City were required to achieve and maintain participation percentages for the duration of an awarded contract or document and demonstrate "good faith efforts" to comply with the established M/WBE goal. In particular, prime contractors bidding on construction contracts were required to submit with their bids, a list of the names of the certified black, Hispanic, or woman business enterprises to be utilized as subcontractors, a letter from each said black, Hispanic or woman business enterprise intending to perform as a subcontractor or serve as a material supplier, a description of the work to be performed by the black,

Hispanic or woman business enterprise subcontractor and the agreed upon dollar value for such work. This information was to be submitted on forms provided by the City administration and contained in the bid package.

The prime contractors were also required to obtain the City's approval of any proposed changes to a designated black, Hispanic or woman business enterprise subcontractor after the award of a contract. All substitutes for black, Hispanic, or woman business enterprise subcontractors required the approval by the Director of Economic Development and Property Management. The City approved the substitution only when: (a) the subcontractor requests to void its subcontract agreement with the prime contractor; (b) the subcontractor was unable to perform the work; and (c) or the subcontractor had consistently performed unacceptable work. Once an approval to substitute was granted, the prime contractor can replace a black, Hispanic or woman business enterprise with another certified M/WBE, unless the prime contractor can demonstrate that despite good faith efforts a comparable M/WBE was unavailable to participate on the project.

The M/WBE program staff was required to provide assistance in identifying black, Hispanic and woman business enterprise contractors. If a contractor was not able to achieve the required percentage goal, the contractor must demonstrate and document that every reasonable effort was made to achieve the goal.

The Mayor, or a designee, was required to provide City Council with an annual report in order to determine the efficacy of the City's M/WBE program[252]. If, as a result of this annual report, the City Council determined that parity has been achieved, the City Council was required to repeal or sunset the race preference program[253].

---

[252] *City of St. Petersburg Procurement Code*, Section 2-177, pp. CD 2:17 – CD 2:18.
[253] *Id* at CD 2:18.

Race Preference Contracting Goals

The City's contracting goals for particular contracts were established by a goal setting committee composed of representatives of the City administration. The criteria used by the Committee to set goals include: (1) a detailed description of the type of work required by the contract to be let; (2) the contracting and subcontracting opportunities for the M/WBEs, including normal support services to be let and construction suppliers opportunities and the number of certified M/WBEs available; (3) all past and current experience of the City in meeting its goals on projects of similar nature and the results and reasons therefore; and (4) special circumstances relating to the project, including, but not limited to scheduling constraints, constructability requirements and federal grant goal requirements.

Waiver Provisions

The City's M/WBE Ordinance and Procurement Code also had waiver provisions during pre-contract award and post bid award phases of the City's construction procurement process. Five types of pre-contract award waivers could be granted – emergency waiver; sole source waiver; construction of multipurpose stadium; construction of the Bayfront Medical Center; and the construction of the Pier[254]. An emergency waiver was to be granted by the Mayor or a designee on a partial or complete basis prior to the award of a contract or a purchase of goods and supplies in the event of an emergency[255]. Meanwhile, a sole source waiver was to be granted by the purchasing agent of the soliciting department in consultation with the

---

[254] Based on interviews with the City of St. Petersburg M/WBE program staff and the City's M/WBE Annual reports, MBE participation was encouraged and partially achieved on these three (3) exempt projects.

[255] See *City of St. Petersburg Procurement Code*, Sections 2-228, 2-229, 2-230, 2-231. However, based on interviews with City Procurement staff, in actuality, most of these construction projects were competitively bid.

M/WBE office.[256] A post-bid award waiver was granted in the event that an apparent successful bidder/proposer had demonstrated that it had exercised good faith effort in soliciting M/WBE participation, but had been unable to achieve the established project goal. In addition to the above waivers, the race preference ordinance also exempted construction contracts under $10,000.

Race Preference Policy Compliance

The contracts for projects with participation goals must comply with the M/WBE provisions in the City's race preference ordinance and all established procedures. Where it was determined that none of the bids met the M/WBE criteria set forth in the City's race preference ordinance and administrative regulations, the Mayor or a designee had the discretion to re-bid the contract or alternatively to select the bid which substantially complied with the M/WBE participation goals and was in the best interest of the City. If the latter option was selected, the Mayor, or his designee, was required to set forth in writing the basis of selection.

M/WBE Certification Process

As discussed above, a primary eligibility criterion to participate in the City of St. Petersburg's M/WBE program was that minority and woman-owned firms interested in receiving a preference when doing business with the City must undergo a certification process administered by the City's Minority Business Enterprise Office[257], or the Florida Minority Business Advocacy and Assistance Office of the

---

[256] See *City of St. Petersburg Procurement Code*, Section 2-226.

[257] During FY 1989 to FY 1992, the Minority Business Enterprise Office was under the auspice of the City's Public Works Administration. In FY 1992 to June 1996, the M/WBE Office was moved to the Human Relations Department (now known as the Community Affairs Department). In FY 1998, the Office was placed under the auspice of the City's Purchasing and Material Management Department. In February 1999, the Office was moved to the Department of Economic Development and Property Management, and renamed the City of St. Petersburg Business Development Center.

State Department of Labor. Florida State certified M/WBEs were required to register with the City's M/WBE Office. To be eligible for certification, the business must demonstrate that: (1) it was at least fifty one (51) percent owned and controlled by minorities or by women; (2) it was a business that operates in the appropriate market area for the type of goods or services provided; and (3) was an independent business[258]. All applicants wishing to be considered as certified businesses were required to complete an M/WBE Disclosure Affidavit and submit supporting documentation of the type of business ownership to the City's Minority Business Enterprise Office. Once an applicant submitted the application and supporting documentation and certification review completed, the firm was informed if its application for certification has been accepted or not.

Applicants denied certification were informed by certified mail, and informed of their rights to appeal the denial. An applicant denied certification may not reapply for certification for six (6) months from the denial of the certification. Any person or firm that believed it had been wrongly denied certification as an M/WBE may file an appeal in writing, signed and dated, with the Minority Business Enterprise Office. The appeal was to be filed no later than 10 days from the date of receipt of notice of denial of certification. The Minority Business Enterprise Office may extend the time for filing or waive the time limit in the interest of justice, specifying in writing the reason for so doing.

If an appeal is filed, an administrative hearing was to be conducted with the City's Economic Development and Property Management Director. The hearing was to be scheduled within 30 days of the filing of the request for appeal. The Economic Development and Property Management Director may grant a written request for extension of this hearing by an applicant in the interest of justice. During the

---

[258] See *City of St. Petersburg M/WBE Policy and Procedure* (1990) for procedures and documentation for validating these criteria.

hearing, the Director may consider any new information which was not available at the time of application. This hearing was the final step available in the City Administrative process for the denial of a certification application. The Director was required to provide written notice as to the outcome of the hearing within 10 working days of the date of the hearing. Any person who was a party to the proceeding before the Minority Business Enterprise Office may appeal to the Circuit Court of Pinellas County in accordance with applicable Florida Appellate Rules.

All certifications were effective for a period of one year from the date of notification of certification. Certified M/WBEs were required to submit an affidavit of their continued eligibility as an M/WBE 30 days before expiration of their certification. The Minority Business Enterprise Office may conduct site visits or review documents to ensure continued compliance as an M/WBE. If there was a change in ownership interest and/or control, the M/WBE must notify the Minority Business Enterprise Office within 30 days of the change. Supporting documents may be required for continued certification. A company that failed to submit its affidavit of continued eligibility or failed to submit documentation requested by the Minority Business Enterprise Office was no longer deemed certified or registered for purposes of participation as an M/WBE. The criteria for recertification were the same as for certification.

In case a firm was denied recertification, the applicant could request an appeal of denial of recertification within 15 days of receipt of notice of denial. The hearing was to be conducted in the same manner as for initial certification denial procedures discussed above.

Finally, the City may decertify a M/WBE if upon investigation the City found that: (1) the M/WBE could not be contacted at the last known address; (2) the M/WBE was no longer in business; (3) the M/WBE was no longer licensed for the type of business for which it was certified; (4) the M/WBE obtained its original certification and/or recertification through false representation or deceit; (5) the M/WBE had experienced such a substantial change in ownership or control that continued certification would be contrary to the policy of the City M/WBE program; and (6) the M/WBE had been disbarred or suspended as a vendor by the City Purchasing Agent. Once a decision was made to decertify a firm, the City was required to notify the M/WBE by certified mail of its recommendation. The M/WBE may request an appeal hearing of the decertification within 10 working days of receipt of the notice. A hearing is conducted and a notice of the outcome of the hearing is sent to the M/WBE within 10 working days of the hearing. This hearing was the final step in the administrative review of decertification.

In addition, false representation or making, or causing to be made, any willful misstatement, deception or fraud in the certification documents by any firm as an M/WBE for purpose of qualifying for certification as a minority and woman business enterprise was viewed as a misdemeanor of the second degree, and hence, punishable as provided in section 1-7 of the City of St. Petersburg code and Florida Statutes Chapter 775. In addition, any individual or company/corporation charged with or convicted of a violation of false representation or a conspiracy to falsely represent any entity could be disbarred from further bidding on City contracts for a minimum period of three years from the date of the conviction.

Preference Policy Law Enforcement

To ensure success of the race preference policy described above, the City of St. Petersburg developed specific administrative procedures and protocol that must be followed by the staff and contractors doing business with the City to monitor and track M/WBE participation. The Mayor had the overall responsibility for administering the provisions of the City's race preference ordinance.

However, the Minority Business Enterprise Office was responsible for developing, managing and implementing the race preference program on a day-to-day basis. In particular, the Mayor's administrative staff developed procedures consistent with City ordinance 127-G and any federal or state law, regulation or grant requirement. Participation in the City's preference program was intended, and designed to, assist these firms to overcome their economic disadvantage by providing such assistance as is necessary and appropriate to secure City contracts and strengthen their financial and managerial skills to compete in the private sector.

To ensure success of this initiative, the City of St. Petersburg committed itself to taking certain steps to ensure maximum opportunity for participation of minority and woman-owned businesses in the City's relevant market area. These steps included procedures targeted towards enhancing M/WBE competitiveness, and hence utilization, in the City's contracting process. The targeted initiatives were implemented by the City's M/WBE Office under the auspices of the Business Assistance Division. These targeted initiatives involve providing assistance in developing the technical, networking/outreaching, and financial capabilities of M/WBEs, as well as tracking and monitoring M/WBE participation in the City's contracting process.[259]

Technical Assistance

Technical assistance to M/WBEs was provided in the form of:

1. Employing sufficient staff with the authority and responsibility to implement an effective M/WBE program within the City of St. Petersburg.
2. Analyzing M/WBE availability to provide the construction related product or services identified for contracting.

---

[259] See *City of St. Petersburg M/WBE Annual Reports*, FY1989, FY1990, FY1991, FY1992, FY1993, FY1994, FY1995, FY1996, FY1997, and FY1998, Section VII, pp. 8-11.

3. Assisting the City of St. Petersburg M/WBE Construction Committee in the establishment of goals for construction contracting for M/WBE participation.
4. Encouraging the division of purchases and contracts into smaller units, areas or quantities, where feasible and likely to increase M/WBE participation without substantial adverse fiscal impact to the City of St. Petersburg.
5. Using services and assistance provided by the Small Business Administration and other agencies in locating available M/WBEs and encouraging the development of such businesses.
6. Providing M/WBEs with available information about plans, specifications and requirements of City contracts, and detailed instruction on project performance requirements.
7. Providing information and assistance on continued certification procedures, subcontracting practices and bonding requirements.
8. Ensuring that bid/proposals, specifications and plans were written or drawn so as not to prejudice or unreasonably limit M/WBE participation.
9. When appropriate, encouraging the limitation of the use of multi-year contracts and renewal provisions in contracts so as not to inhibit M/WBE participation.
10. Investigating race/gender neutral alternatives to lessen barriers to participation by any small business wishing to do business with the City.
11. Encouraging that reasonable time is provided for the submission of bids/proposals in order to facilitate the participation of M/WBEs.

Networking and Outreach

M/WBE Networking and outreach assistance was provided in the form of:

1. Identifying and notifying all contracting opportunities with the City.
2. Including certified M/WBEs on contract solicitation lists or vendor lists.

3. Promoting the City's M/WBE program both internally and externally.
4. Participating in pre-bid or pre-proposal meetings where appropriate, to inform potential contractors of M/WBE requirements and other bid/proposal requirements, and encouraging M/WBEs to attend the pre-bid meetings.
5. When appropriate, placing bid notices in M/WBE trade association newsletters, major local or regional newspaper and minority and women focused media. Also, placing plans and specifications for bids involving M/WBE goals in minority business development agencies (that is, ethnic chambers commerce, and so forth).
6. Planning and participating in training seminars for the purpose of informing potential bidders/proposers/vendors of the City's M/WBE program and the business opportunities available.
7. Creating and disseminating an M/WBE Enterprise Directory to contractors for use in identifying subcontractors and material suppliers.
8. Encouraging M/WBE financial capability assistance to M/WBEs and consideration to relax bonding requirements and/or providing assistance in obtaining bonding, lines of credit and insurance.

Tracking and Monitoring

Tracking and monitoring M/WBE participation was performed by:

(1) Monitoring and maintaining records sufficient for verification of steps taken and result achieved to maximize M/WBE participation.

(2) Maintaining a computerized listing of certified M/WBEs for planning and dissemination to interested parties.

(3) Requiring annual reports by the City's Minority Business Enterprise office to the City Council detailing the results of efforts to obtain M/WBE participation. This report was to include as a minimum, the total dollar amount of all procurement (including any change notices) during the fiscal year and the total dollars amount of contracts awarded (including any amendments or change orders), including

> subcontracts to M/WBEs during the fiscal year. If the report indicated that the City was behind in reaching the annual M/WBE participation goals, the report was to provide the reasons for the failure to meet the goals.

In addition to the directive and administrative procedures outlined above, the City of St. Petersburg requires all city departments and offices responsible for letting out contracts to analyze each project by identifying the various components of the project, and submit a report to the Minority Business Enterprise Office and the MBE Construction Committee outlining the potential contracting and subcontracting opportunities in the project or contract, and the estimated percentage that each subcontract component bears to the total project or contract. The report must include: (a) the scope of the anticipated work for each component to be subcontracted and the qualifications required of the subcontractor to do the work; and (b) an identification of specific requirements of the project or contract such as may be imposed by federal grant. The M/WBE Office, upon receipt of the report, was to review the certified list of M/WBEs and then determine the availability of M/WBE certified subcontractors qualified to do the work in each subcontract component, and submit a report to the MBE Construction Committee on the availability of M/WBEs certified to do the work.

The MBE Construction Committee, in turn, was to set the M/WBE project or contract goals based upon the availability of certified M/WBEs[260] or pursuant to any federal regulations applicable to the project or contract. In areas where goals were set, no project or contract goal was to exceed 50 percent M/WBE participation. If there were not at least three qualified M/WBE contractors available for the

[260] These goals are set in accordance with the City's annual goals as set forth in Section (e) of the City's M/WBE Ordinance No. 2023-F or pursuance to any federal regulations applicable to the project or contract. In areas where goals are set, no project or contract goal is allowed to exceed fifty (50) percent M/WBE participation.

contractible area, no goal was typically set in that area. The established goal was to be applied to the full monetary value of the base bid for the contract and be reflected in the full monetary portion spent on subcontracts for supplies, consulting, or construction services to be awarded to those M/WBEs meeting contract specifications.

In situations where an M/WBE was submitting a bid as a prime contractor, the M/WBE was to be credited with meeting the percentage of the project or contract goal that the M/WBE will be performing with its own work crew for their specific racial group plus the percentage of subcontracts awarded to other certified M/WBEs. Furthermore, a partnership consisting of an M/WBE and non-minority business, functioning as a prime contractor, was to be credited with M/WBE participation based on percentage of ownership, participation in the partnership, risk and profit by the M/WBE. With regards to subcontracting, the City was to give credit for M/WBE subcontracts for goal attainment only for subcontractors who were certified and licensed, if required, in the specific area of expertise for which credit was sought at the time of bid opening.

The City reserved the right to reject or disqualify a bidder who had previously failed to perform properly and who had done so by commission or omission of an act of such serious and compelling nature that the act indicated a serious lack of business integrity or honesty. These acts include:

1. Violating any applicable law, regulation, or contract provision relating to the performance of obligations incurred pursuant to an agreement with the recipient under a City contract.
2. Making, or procuring to make, any false statement or using deceit for purpose of influencing in any way any action of the City.
3. Making false representation as an M/WBE enterprise under a program that is designed to assist M/WBEs in the receipt of

contracts with the City for the provision of goods and services.

4. Misrepresentation and misconduct as it applies to fraud, deceit, or other actions indicating lack of business integrity or honesty with respect to the eligibility of firms to participate as M/WBEs, acts such as knowingly making use of a "front" company (that is, a firm) which was not in fact owned and controlled by minority individuals or women, but posed as such in order to participate as a M/WBE in City's program. Any contractor or firm which falsely represented to the City, pursuant to a City contract, that it was a M/WBE firm, or which represented that it would use the services or commodities of M/WBE firms and subsequently did not do so, without prior City approval, was to be considered in breach of contract. Upon determining that a breach of contract had occurred, the City was to invoke all available remedies for breach of contract, including forfeiting and recovering all the cash paid to the contractor or firm under the contract intended for the expenditure with the M/WBEs.[261]

Good Faith Effort

Contractors submitting bids or proposals to provide construction services to the City were required to comply with M/WBE participation goals as established in the race preference ordinance. However, in the event that the goals were not achieved, the contractor must include with the bid, evidence of "good faith effort" to achieve the goals. A bidder could still be awarded a contract if the bidder or contractor could prove, in writing with the bid or proposal documents submitted, that "good faith efforts" were made to obtain M/WBE goals. The provisions of "good faith effort" included, but are not limited to, the following guidelines for bidders on the city's contracts:[262]

---

[261] The City, at its sole discretion, may waive the breach and available remedies. However, waiver of the right under this provision does not constitute a waiver of rights for breach of any other provision of the contract.

[262] *See City of St. Petersburg Ordinance 127-G, Section (f)*, 1994.

(a) attending at pre-bid conference;
(b) publishing of advertisements concerning subcontracting opportunities, in area newspapers, trade association publications, and minority-oriented publications at least ten days before the bid opening date;
(c) giving written notification to a reasonable number of certified Minority Business Enterprises to solicit their interest in the project in sufficient time to allow the M/WBEs to participate;
(d) providing documentation of negotiations with M/WBE firms which include the following information: (1) the names, addresses, and telephone numbers of black, Hispanic, and woman business enterprise contacted, the date the negotiations took place and specifications for various subcontracting; and (2) a description of information provided to solicit black, Hispanic, and woman business enterprises subcontracting agreement;
(e) making efforts to assist firms contacted to obtain necessary bonding, insurance and financial assistance;
(f) utilizing services and resources of available minority community organizations; minority contractors group; local, state, and federal minority business assistance offices; and other agencies that provide assistance in the recruitment and placement of M/WBEs.
(g) providing evidence of actual M/WBE participation percentage achieved by the bidder; and
(h) submitting information bidder which demonstrate good faith effort or lack thereof.

In reviewing and analyzing the good faith effort, the City looked at not only the different kinds of efforts the contractor made, but also the quality, quantity, and intensity and timeliness of those efforts. The contractor was responsible for exercising this good faith effort, and hence, any act or omission by the City did not relieve the contractor of this responsibility. Where it was determined that none of the bids meets the M/WBE criteria set forth in the City's M/WBE Ordinance or Administrative Regulations, the Mayor or a designee was authorized to either award the contract to the bidder who substantially complied with the requirements or reject the bids in accordance with the city's race preference ordinance.

During the contract award phase of the City's procurement process, the contract was to be awarded to the lowest responsive and responsible bidders. The bidders were required to provide the City with documents regarding M/WBE participation and good faith effort as part of their bid documents or request for proposals. The documents were to include a list of all M/WBE subcontractors who will be used on the contract and the dollars amount of each M/WBE subcontract. If a contractor lists an M/WBE who has been decertified after submission of bids or proposals, but prior to the award of the contract, the City required the contractor, within a specified reasonable time frame, to attain the M/WBE goals with certified M/WBEs or make a showing of good faith efforts in an attempt to do so. The soliciting department was required to forward the bid documents relative to M/WBE participation of all bidders to the Minority Business Enterprise Office within three (3) business days of opening of the bids.

Once the contract was let, the Minority Business Enterprise Office was required to establish procedures for monitoring and evaluating contractor performance and compliance with the M/WBE requirements of the project. In principle, the City of St. Petersburg race preference ordinance specified that every contract let by the City for the performance of work, which had applicable M/WBE requirements must contain a provision requiring the prime contractor to certify in writing that all M/WBE subcontractors, subconsultants and suppliers have been utilized in accordance with the participation levels provided by the prime contractor at the time of contract award. In addition, the prime contractor was required to demonstrate that all M/WBE subcontractors have been paid for work and material from previous progress payments received, less any retainage, prior to receipt of any further progress payments. During the contract award, and upon completion of the contract, the City required documentation from the prime contractor to certify utilization and payment to M/WBE subcontractors, subconsultants or suppliers. Failure to utilize the M/WBEs or make payments to them within a reasonable time may result in the City withholding of payment to the prime contractor[263].

---

[263] This provision, however, in no way created any contractual relationship between any subcontractor, subconsultant or supplier and the City or any liability on the City for the contractor's failure to make timely payment to the subcontractor, subconsultant or supplier.

Chapter Six

City of St. Petersburg Anti-discrimination Laws and Public Contracting Laws

This Chapter is a review of anti-discrimination laws that could affect public contracting in the City of St. Petersburg. The review provides an assessment of the extent to which full enforcement of applicable local, state, or federal statutory non-discrimination provisions have been achieved. As a subdivision of the state of a state government (that is, the State of Florida) and recipient of funds from federal and other governments, the city of St. Petersburg contracting process, as any other local government, must comply with all federal, state, and local laws prohibiting unlawful discrimination practices. Therefore, any predicate study of the city's race preference program must include a review of anti-discrimination laws that could affect its contracting process. This review can be a useful gauge in validating the findings and conclusions of the predicate study.

While the State of Florida, Pinellas County, and the City of St. Petersburg have all adopted anti-discrimination laws in their respective statutes and codes,[264] those provisions primarily address discrimination in employment, housing and public accommodations. The most significant anti-discrimination laws that are likely to affect public contracting in St. Petersburg are (i) Executive Order No. 11246; (ii) the Rehabilitation Act of 1973, 29 U.S.C. § 701 *et seq.*; and (iii) the Vietnam Era Veterans Readjustment Assistance Act of 1974, 38 U.S.C. § 4212, *et seq.* Although

---

[264]*See generally* Chapter 760, *Florida Statutes*, § 112.042, *Florida Statutes*, Art. II, § 15-21, *et seq.*; *City of St. Petersburg Code*, Art. II, § 70-36, *et seq.*, *Pinellas County Code*, 1995.

these laws pertain primarily to the federal government, state and local governments that contract with the federal government are subject to these laws[265]. In addition, a number of federal agencies have promulgated anti-discrimination laws which could affect public contracting when the City of St. Petersburg is the recipient of a grant from one of those agencies. The agencies include: the Department of Transportation, the Department of Housing and Urban Development, Federal Aviation Authority, and the Environmental Protection Agency.

Federal Anti-discrimination Laws

The aforementioned three laws are administered by the Office of Federal Contract Compliance Programs in the United States Department of Labor. A comprehensive review of the provisions of Executive Order 11246, the Rehabilitation Act, and the Vietnam Era Veterans Readjustment Assistance Act is beyond the scope of this book. By way of example, there are over 300 pages of regulations implementing Executive Order 11246, the Rehabilitation Act, and the Vietnam Era Veterans Readjustment Assistance Act. By far, the most convoluted and well-chronicled of the three laws is Executive Order 11246. This summary will address the highlights of Executive Order 11246 and slightly touch on the significant provisions of the Rehabilitation Act and the Vietnam Era Veterans Readjustment Assistance Act.

Executive Order 11246

Generally speaking, Executive Order No. 11246 prohibits discrimination by contractors and subcontractors on the basis of race, color, religion, or national origin, and requires them to take "affirmative action" to prohibit discrimination against

---

[265]The President's power to impose fair employment conditions on government contractors in the context of federally-assisted state construction contracts was expressly recognized in *Contractors Association of Eastern Philadelphia v. Secretary of Labor*, 442 F.2d 159 (3d Cir. 1971).

individuals in those groups. As explained below, pursuant to Executive Order No. 11246, all contractors and subcontractors having a contract or subcontract of $10,000 or more in any 12-month period must incorporate an "equal opportunity clause" in each of their contracts and subcontracts[266]. In addition, a contractor or subcontractor with a series of federal contracts, which in the aggregate equal or exceed $10,000 during any 12-month period, must also include the equal opportunity clause in those contracts.[267] It is not uncommon for state, county and local governments to impose similar obligations upon contractors who do business with them and incorporate Executive Order 11246 into their own contracts.

Executive Order No. 11246 is implemented through the mandatory inclusion of what is known as an "equal opportunity clause" in all contracts that involve non-exempt "federally-assisted construction contracts." "Federally-assisted construction projects" are defined as:

> any agreement or modification thereof between any applicant and a person for construction work which is paid for in whole or in part with funds obtained from the [federal] Government or borrowed on the credit of the Government pursuant to any Federal program, involving a grant, contract, loan, insurance, or guarantee or undertaken pursuant to any Federal program involving such grant, contract, loan, insurance, or guarantee, or any application or modification thereof approved by the Government for a grant, contract, loan, insurance, or guarantee under which the applicant itself participates in the construction work.[268]

---

[266] 41 Code of Federal Regulations (Hereafter, C.F.R. § 60-1.5(a)(1)).
[267]For federally assisted construction contracts, or subcontracts thereunder, the amount of the contract or subcontract, rather than the amount of the federal financial assistance, governs whether the contract or subcontract exceeds the threshold amount. 41 C.F.R. § 60-1.5(a)(1).
[268] 41 C.F.R. § 60-1.3.

For federally assisted construction projects, each administering agency requires the inclusion of the following language as a condition of any grant, contract, loan, insurance, or guarantee involving federally assisted construction which is not otherwise exempt from the requirements of the equal opportunity clause:

> The applicant hereby agrees that it will incorporate or cause to be incorporated into any contract for construction work, or modification thereof, as defined in the regulations of the Secretary of Labor at 41 CFR Chapter 60, which is paid for in whole or in part with funds obtained from the Federal Government or borrowed on the credit of the Federal Government pursuant to a grant, contract, loan, insurance, or guarantee, or undertaken pursuant to any Federal program involving such grant, contract, loan, insurance, or guarantee, the following equal opportunity clause:
>
>> During the performance of his contract, the contractor agrees as follows:
>>
>> 1. The contractor will not discriminate against any employee or applicant for employment because of race, color, religion, sex, or national origin. The contractor will take affirmative action to ensure that applicants are employed, and that employees are treated during employment, without regard to their race, color, religion, sex or national origin. Such action shall include, but not be limited to the following: employment, upgrading, demotion, or transfer; recruitment or recruitment advertising; layoff or termination; rates of pay or other forms of compensation; and selection for training, including apprenticeship. The contractor agrees to post in conspicuous places, available to employees and applicants for employment, notices to be provided by the contracting officer setting forth the provisions of this non-discrimination clause.
>> 2. The contractor will, in all solicitations or advertisements for employees placed by or on behalf of the contractor, state that all qualified applicants will receive consideration for employment without regard to race, color, religion, sex or national origin.

3. The contractor will send to each labor union or representative of workers with which he has a collective bargaining agreement or other contract or understanding, a notice to be provided advising the labor union or workers' representatives of the contractor's commitments under this Section, and shall post copies of the notice in conspicuous places available to employees and applicants for employment.
4. The contractor will comply with all provisions of Executive Order No. 11246 of Sept. 24, 1965, and of the rules, regulations, and relevant orders of the Secretary of Labor.
5. The contractor will furnish all information and reports required by Executive Order No. 11246 of September 24, 1965, and by the rules, regulations, and orders of the Secretary of Labor, or pursuant thereto, and will permit access to his books, records, and accounts by the contracting agency and the Secretary of Labor for purposes of investigation to ascertain compliance with such rules, regulations, and orders.
6. In the event of the contractor's noncompliance with the nondiscrimination clauses of this contract or with any of the said rules, regulations, or orders, this contract may be canceled, terminated, or suspended in whole or in part and the contractor may be declared ineligible for further Government contracts or federally assisted construction contracts in accordance with procedures authorized in Executive Order 11246 of September 24, 1965, and such other sanctions may be imposed and remedies invoked as provided in Executive Order 11246 of September 24, 1965, or by rule, regulation, or order of the Secretary of Labor, or as otherwise provided by law.
7. The contractor will include the portion of the sentence immediately preceding paragraph (1) through (7) in every subcontract or purchase order unless exempted by rules, regulations, or orders of the Secretary of Labor issued pursuant to section 204 of Executive Order 11246 of September 24, 1995, so that such provisions will be binding upon each subcontractor or vendor. The contractor will take such action with respect to any

> subcontract or purchase order as the administering agency may direct as a means of enforcing such provisions, including sanctions for noncompliance: Provided, however, That in the event a contractor becomes involved in, or is threatened with, litigation with a subcontractor or vendor as a result of such direction by the administering agency the contractor may request the United States to enter into such litigation to protect the interests of the United States.[269]

Title 41, § 60-1.4(b) further provides that:

> The applicant further agrees that it will be bound by the above equal opportunity clause with respect to its own employment practices when it participates in federally assisted construction work: provided, that if the applicant so participating is a State or local government, the above equal opportunity clause is not applicable to any agency, instrumentality, or subdivision of such government which does not participate in work on or under the contract.[270]

Applicant as used in the preceding section "means an applicant for Federal assistance involving a construction contract, or other participant in a program involving a construction contract as determined by regulation of an administering agency. The term also includes such persons after they become recipients of such Federal assistance."[271]

In the case of municipalities involved in federally assisted construction projects, the municipality or other unit of local government must also agree that it will assist and "cooperate actively" with the administering agency and the Secretary of Labor in obtaining the compliance of contractors with the equal opportunity

---

[269] 41 C.F.R. § 60-1.4(B).
[270] *Id.*
[271] 41 C.F.R. § 60-1.3.

clause[272]. The municipality must further agree that it will refrain from entering into any contract or agreement subject to Executive Order 11246 "with a contractor debarred from, or who has not demonstrated eligibility for, federal government contracts or federally assisted government contracts."[273]

Executive Order 11246 also provides that contractors with 50 or more employees and a contract of $50,000 or more must develop and annually update a written Affirmative Action Plan ("AAP") for each of its establishments.[274] The regulations containing the contents of the Executive Order AAP are enumerated in 41 C.F.R. § 60-2. An AAP is a "set of specific and result-oriented procedures to which a contractor commits himself to apply every good faith effort."[275] An acceptable AAP must include an analysis of areas within which the contractor is deficient in the utilization of minorities and women and "further, goals and timetables to which the contractor's good faith efforts must be directed to correct the deficiencies and, thus, to achieve prompt and full utilization of minorities and women, at all levels and in all segments of its work force where deficiencies exist."[276]

Compliance with the provisions of Executive Order 11246 is supervised by the Office of Federal Contract Compliance Programs ("OFCCP"), whose review is initiated through either an investigation of complaints by individuals or compliance reviews. In the case of compliance reviews, if a contractor is deemed to be non-compliant, the OFCCP will attempt to negotiate a Letter of Commitment[277] or a Conciliation Agreement[278] with the contractor in order to rectify any deficiencies. If

---

[272] 41 C.F.R. § 60-1.4(b).
[273] *Id.*
[274] 41 C.F.R. § 60 - 1.40(a).
[275] 41 C.F.R. § 60-2.10.
[276] *Id.*
[277] *See* 41 C.F.R. § 60-1.20(b)
[278] *See* 41 C.F.R. § 60-1.33(a). Letters of commitment should be distinguished from conciliation agreements in that the former are more appropriate for resolving minor technical deficiencies.

voluntary compliance cannot be negotiated between the contractor and the OFCCP, the OFCCP may issue a 30-day "Show Cause" notice, during which 30-day period the contractor may show cause why it should not be held in non-compliance.[279] In the event enforcement proceedings become necessary, violations may be predicated upon any one of the following:[280]

1. The results of a complaint investigation;
2. The results of a compliance evaluation;
3. Analysis of an affirmative action program;
4. The results of an on-site review of the contractor's compliance with the [Executive] Order and its implementing regulations
5. A contractor's refusal to submit an affirmative action program;
6. A contractor's refusal to allow an on-site compliance evaluation to be conducted;
7. A contractor's refusal to provide data for off-site review or analysis as required by the regulations in this chapter;
8. A contractor's refusal to establish, maintain and supply records or other information as required by the regulations in this chapter or applicable construction industry requirements;
9. A contractor's alteration or falsification of records and information required to be maintained by the regulations in this chapter; or
10. Any substantial or material violation or the threat of a substantial or material violation of the contractual [sic] provisions of the Order, or of the rules or regulations in this chapter.

If the determination of non-compliance is sustained, the contractor may be subject to withholding of contract payments, cancellation of existing contracts, and debarment from receipt of future contracts.

---

[279] *See* 41 C.F.R. § 60-1.28.
[280] *See* 41 C.F.R. § 60-1.26.

Rehabilitation Act of 1973

State and local governments that contract with the federal government are also covered by the Rehabilitation Act of 1973. Section 503 of the Rehabilitation Act, 29 U.S.C. § 793, requires contractors to "take affirmative steps to employ and advance in employment qualified individuals with disabilities."[281] The applicable regulations implementing section 503 are contained in 41 C.F.R. Part 60-741. Similar to Executive Order 11246, an equal opportunity clause which commits the contractor to refrain from discriminating "in regard to any position for which the employee or applicant for employment is qualified" must be included in each applicable contract[282]. Additionally, contractors with 50 or more employees and a contract of $50,000 or more must prepare and maintain an affirmative action plan.[283]

Section 504 of the Rehabilitation Act, 29 U.S.C. § 794, further provides that:

> No otherwise qualified individual with a disability . . . shall, solely by reason of his or her disability be excluded from participation in, be denied the benefits of, or be subjected to discrimination under any program or activity receiving Federal financial assistance . . .[284]

Construing this provision, the court, in *Locascio v. City of St. Petersburg*, 731 F. Supp. 1522 (M.D. Fla. 1990), held that where federal urban renewal block grants and loan guarantees had been used in acquisition of a stadium site, the City of St. Petersburg's construction of the Florida Suncoast Dome was "part and parcel" of a federally funded project which was a "program or activity" subject to § 504 of the Rehabilitation Act, thereby requiring the City's compliance with federal standards

---

[281] *Id.*
[282] 41 C.F.R. § 60-741.5.
[283] 41 C.F.R. § 60-741.40.
[284] 29 U.S.C. § 794(a).

for handicapped accessibility in design and construction of the stadium.[285] *Accord Independent Housing Services of San Francisco v. Fillmore Center Associates, Inc.*, 840 F. Supp., 1328 (N.D. Ca. 1993) (holding that federal urban renewal block grants were within the definition of federal financial assistance for purposes of § 504 of the Rehabilitation Act).

Vietnam Era Veterans Readjustment Assistance Act of 1973

Section 402 of the Vietnam Era Veterans Readjustment Assistance Act of 1974, 38 U.S.C. § 4212, *et seq.* ("VEVRA") generally requires contractors "to take affirmative action to employ and advance in employment qualified disabled veterans and veterans of the Vietnam era."[286] The OFCCP regulations implementing Section 402 are contained in 41 C.F.R. § 60-250. The regulations apply to all government contracts and subcontracts of "$10,000 or more for the purchase, sale, or use of personal property or non-personal services (including construction)."[287] Each government contract under the regulations must contain an equal opportunity clause that "[t]he contractor will not discriminate against any employee or applicant for employment because he or she is a special disabled veteran or veteran of the Vietnam era in regard to any position for which the employee or applicant for employment is

---

[285] In reaching its decision, the court did not have to address the issue of whether the 1988 amendments to § 504 to the Rehabilitation Act were retroactive in application. In 1988, § 504 of the Rehabilitation Act was amended by the Civil Rights Restoration Act to add 29 U.S.C. § 794(b), which, in turn, defined the phrase "program or activity" under subsection (a) as:

> all of the operations of:
> (1)(A) a department, agency, special purpose district, or other instrumentality of a State or of a local government; or
> (1)(B) the entity of such State or local government that distributes such assistance and each such department or agency (and each other State or local government entity) to which the assistance is extended, in the case of assistance to a State of local government . . . .
> *Locascio*, 731 F. Supp. at 1522.

[286] *Id.*

[287] 41 C.F.R. § 60-250.1(b).

qualified."[288] Similar to the Rehabilitation Act and Executive Order 11246, contractors that have 50 or more employees and contracts of $50,000 or more must also, within 120 days of the commencement of the contract, submit an affirmative action program[289]. The required contents for the program, which must be reviewed and updated annually, are contained in 41 C.F.R. § 60-250.44.

Federal Agency Anti-discrimination Law

Following the passage of the laws discussed above, some federal agencies have established anti-discrimination regulations which could affect public contracting in the City of St. Petersburg when the City is the recipient of grants from these agencies. The federal agencies are the Department of Transportation ("DOT"), Department of Housing and Urban Development ("HUD"), Federal Aviation Authority ("FAA"), and Environmental Protection Agency ("EPA"). The sections below reviews the regulations promulgated by those agencies that could affect public contracting in St. Petersburg.[290]

Department of Transportation

The Secretary of Transportation has promulgated regulations at 49 C.F. R. Part 21, § 21.1 *et seq.*, entitled Nondiscrimination in Federally-Assisted Programs of The Department of Transportation. The purpose of the regulations is to effectuate the provisions of Title VI of the Civil Rights Act of 1964, which generally bars

---

288 41 C.F.R. § 60-250.5(a)(1)

289 41 C.F.R. § 60-250.40(a)-(b).

290 The reader should keep in mind that the discussion which follows addresses the agencies' umbrella regulations and that there could be other regulations which apply to specific programs and sub-agencies of the four agencies mentioned above. By way of example, the Federal Railroad Administration, which is a sub-agency of the Department of Transportation, has promulgated its own set of regulations which apply to contracts funded in whole or part through financial assistance provided under the auspices of the Railroad Revitalization and Regulatory Reform Act of 1976 or the Rail Passenger Service Act. A review of the program regulations for every sub-agency of the four agencies mentioned above is beyond the scope of this review.

discrimination in any program or activity receiving federal financial assistance. Section 21.5 of Part 21 tracks the language of Title VI and contains the general prohibition that:

> (a) No person in the United States shall, on the grounds of race, color, or national origin be excluded from participation in, be denied the benefits of, or otherwise be subjected to discrimination under, any program to which this part applies.

Subsection (b)(1) of Section 21.5 describes the specific acts of discrimination which are prohibited under Part 21. The prohibited acts include "deny[ing] a person an opportunity to participate in the program through the provision of services or otherwise afford[ing] him an opportunity to do so which is different from that afforded others under the program" and deny[ing] a person the opportunity to participate as a member of the planning, advisory, or similar body which is an integral part of the program."[291] Section 21.23 provides that "federal financial assistance" includes "grants and loans of federal funds." Subsection (f) provides that a "recipient" of federal financial assistance includes:

> any State, territory, possession, . . . or any political subdivision thereof, or instrumentality thereof, or any public or private agency institution, or organization . . . to whom federal financial assistance is extended, directly or through another recipient, for any program.[292]

Appendix A to Part 21 then lists several activities (federal programs) to which Part 21 applies, including, but not limited to, grants made in connection with the Highway

---

[291] See 49 C.F.R. § 21.5(b)(vi)-(vii).
[292] *Id.*

Safety Act, National Traffic and Motor Vehicle Safety Act, and the Federal Aid Airport Program.[293]

Section 21.7 provides for assurances to be given by any applicant for federal financial assistance that the applicant will comply with the provisions of Part 21. Section 21.7 provides, in relevant part, as follows:

> Every application for Federal financial assistance to carry out a program to which this part applies, . . . and every application for Federal financial assistance to provide a facility shall, as a condition to its approval and the extension of any Federal financial assistance, pursuant to the application, contain or be accompanied by, an assurance that the program will be conducted or the facility operated in compliance with the requirements imposed by or pursuant to this part . . . . In the case where the assurance is sought for the

---

293 The State of Florida's Highway Safety Traffic Program is the vehicle by which grant funds are received from the USDOT for implementation of the provisions set forth in the National Highway Safety Act of 1966. In accordance with § 14-98.007, *Florida Administrative Code*, which is a state regulation promulgated by the Florida DOT, all subgrantees (including units of local government to whom the Florida DOT awards a subgrant or contract) are required to include the following statement in all contracts and agreements which are financed, in whole or part, by federal funds:

> 1. Policy. It is the policy of the U.S Department of Transportation that disadvantaged business enterprises as defined in 49 C.F.R. Part 23 shall have the maximum opportunity to participate in the performance of contracts and subcontracts financed in whole or in part with Federal funds provided under this agreement. . . . [It important to note that Part 23 of 49 C.F.R. was recently (i.e. April 1999) replaced by Part 26. However, the provisions of Part 26 are not beyond to this review since its passage occurred after the study timeframe (i.e. FY 1989 to FY 1999).]
> 2. DBE Obligation. The recipient or its contractor agrees to ensure that disadvantaged business enterprises as defined in 49 C.F.R. Part 23 have the maximum opportunity to participate in the performance of contracts and subcontracts financed in whole or in part with Federal funds provided under this agreement. In this regard, all recipients or contractors shall take all necessary and reasonable steps in accordance with 49 C.F.R. Part 23 to ensure that recipients have the maximum opportunity to compete for and perform contracts. *Recipients and their contractors shall not discriminate on the basis of race, color, national origin, or sex in the award of and performance of U.S. DOT-assisted contracts.*

F.A.C. § 14-98.007(24) (emphasis added).

> construction of a facility or part of a facility[294], the assurance shall in any event extend to the entire facility and to facilities operated in connection therewith. The Secretary [of Transportation] shall specify the form of assurances for each program, and the extent to which like assurances will be required of subgrantees, contractors and subcontractors, transferees, successors in interest, and other participants in the program.[295]

Section 21.11 of Part 21 details the procedure whereby any person or group of persons who believes they have been subjected to discrimination may file a complaint with the Secretary of the Department of Transportation. The complaint must be filed within 180 days of the alleged discriminatory acts, unless the time is extended by the Secretary. The Secretary is then required to make a prompt investigation of the complaint and attempt to resolve the complaint through informal means. If the complaint cannot be resolved through informal means, Section 21.13 provides that the offending party's noncompliance can be effectuated through suspension, termination or refusal to continue Federal financial assistance or by any other means authorized by law, including, but not limited to, a referral to the Department of Justice that appropriate proceedings be brought to enforce any rights of the United States. In the event that a formal hearing becomes necessary, the particulars of the hearing format and procedures are described in Section 21.15.

With regard to the scope of Part 21, Section 21.21 expressly provides that nothing stated in Part 21 is intended to supersede Executive Order 11246 and the regulations promulgated thereunder or any other regulation to the extent that such other regulation prohibits discrimination on the basis of race, color, or national origin to which Part 21 may be inapplicable.

---

[294] A facility, as defined in section 21.23, includes "all or any part of structures, equipment, or other real or personal property or interests therein, and the provision of facilities includes the construction, expansion, renovation, remodeling, alteration, or acquisition of facilities."
[295] *Id.*

Department of Housing and Urban Development

The Secretary of the Department of Housing and Urban Development has promulgated regulations at 24 C.F. R. Part 1.1, *et seq.*, entitled Nondiscrimination in Federally-Assisted Programs of The Department of Housing and Urban Development. These regulations closely track the DOT's nondiscrimination regulations in terms of the prohibited discriminatory acts and contain analogous complaint and enforcement procedures.

Environmental Protection Agency

The Administrator of the Environmental Protection Agency has promulgated regulations at 40 C.F.R., Part 7, § 7.10, *et. seq.* entitled Nondiscrimination in Programs Receiving Federal Assistance from the Environmental Protection Agency. The purpose of these regulations is to implement Title VI of the Civil Rights Act of 1964; Section 504 of the Rehabilitation Act of 1973, and Section 13 of the Federal Water Pollution Control Act Amendments of 1972 and prohibit discrimination on the basis of race, color, national origin, sex, or handicap.[296]

The prohibited discriminatory acts under the EPA's regulations are similar to those contained in the HUD and DOT regulations referenced above.[297] The EPA Office of Civil Rights ("OCR") is responsible for developing and administering compliance with the EPA's programs under the various statutes mentioned above. Pursuant to § 7.95, local governments and other recipients of EPA assistance are required to post a notice in a prominent location that they do not discriminate on the basis of race, color, national origin, or handicap in any program receiving EPA assistance. The notice must be posted within thirty days of EPA assistance and continue for the duration of the EPA assistance.[298]

---

[296] *See* 40 C.F.R. §§ 7.35 and 7.50.
[297] *See* 40 C.F.R. § 7.35.
[298] 40 C.F.R. § 7.95.

Pursuant to § 7.115, the OCR may conduct periodic compliance reviews of any recipient's programs or activities receiving EPA assistance when the OCR has reason to believe that discrimination may be occurring in such programs or activities. The OCR may also launch an investigation following a complaint by any person or specific class of persons who believe they have been discriminated against in violation of the regulations[299]. If the OCR is unable to resolve the complaint informally, it must then follow the procedures established in § 7.115. If the OCR makes a preliminary determination that discrimination has occurred, it will issue preliminary findings to the recipient, following which the recipient may either accept the OCR's recommendations or engage in voluntary negotiations, where appropriate[300]. If the recipient fails to accept the OCR's recommendations or otherwise demonstrate that the preliminary findings are incorrect, the OCR will then issue a formal determination of noncompliance[301]. If the recipient fails to respond to the formal determination of noncompliance, the OCR may then initiate formal proceedings under 40 C.F.R. § 7.130. Penalties which may be imposed for a finding of noncompliance include termination or refusal to make an award or to continue assistance.[302]

Federal Aviation Administration

The Secretary of the Federal Aviation Administration has promulgated regulations at 14 C.F.R. Part 1.1, § 152.401, *et seq.*, entitled Nondiscrimination in Airport Aid Program. The purpose of the regulations is to implement section 30 of the Airport and Airway Development Act of 1930, which provides that:

---

[299] *See* 40 C.F.R. § 7.120.
[300] *Id.* at § (c)(i)-(iii).
[301] *Id.* at § (d)(1)-(2).
[302] *See* 40 C.F.R. § 7.130.

> The Secretary shall take affirmative action to assure that no person shall, on the grounds of race, creed, color, national origin, or sex, be excluded from participating in any activity conducted with funds received from any grant made under this title.

Subsection (b) of § 152.01 further provides that each grantee shall negotiate every contract or agreement to which the regulations apply to include any language necessary to effect compliance with Part 1.1.

Section 152.405 of Part 1.1 requires that in each application for financial assistance, the grantee must assure that it will adopt an affirmative action plan that no person, on the grounds of race, creed, color, national origin, or sex will be excluded from participating in any employment, contracting, or leasing activities. Section 152.405 likewise requires that the grantee assure that its sub-grantees will likewise comply with the provisions of that section. Section 152.407 describes the entities which are required to maintain affirmative action plans. Among the entities listed are "each state political subdivision, administering a grant under the [AADA] Airport and Airport Development Act to develop standards for airport development at general aviation airports, which employs 50 or more employees in its aviation workforce." Finally, section 152.411 provides that "[e]ach sponsor shall require each of its prime construction contractors with a contract or $10,000 or more to require each of its subcontractors on the airport to require each of the contractor's subcontractors to comply with the affirmative action steps [outlined in that section,] . . . unless the subcontractor is subject to an affirmative action plan, regulatory goals or timetables, or other mechanism which provides short and long-range goals for equal employment opportunity, or the subcontract is less than $10,000."[303] Pursuant to § 152.423, any person who believes that he or she has been subjected to

---

[303] *Id.*

discrimination in connection with a covered program may file a complaint with the Director of the Departmental Office of Civil Rights. The complaint must be filed within 180 days of the alleged discriminatory act(s). The same general regulations governing complaint procedures promulgated by the Department of Transportation (49 C.F.R., Part 21) discussed, *supra*, are generally applicable. Section 152.423(d) also empowers the Secretary of the Federal Aviation Administration to initiate investigations whenever it appears that investigation of a complaint may reveal a "pattern or practice of discrimination of noncompliance in the employment practices of the grantee or other covered organization." Finally, § 152.425 provides that nothing contained in the regulations supersedes the obligations imposed by Title VI or Executive Order 11246.

Summary

In summation, each of these state and federal anti-discrimination regulations have an impact on the City of St. Petersburg contracting when the City uses grants from these State and federal governments. For example, whenever the City contracts for supplies and services involving federal dollars, the City Procurement Code requires all using departments and prime contractors doing business with the City to comply with all applicable state and federal anti-discrimination laws. In effect, the existence of these requirements helps to ensure that the City of St. Petersburg will not discriminate on the basis on race, ethnicity, or gender in the award of contracts. A review of the City's contracting records where federal fund were used, and interviews with the City's legal staff, indicates that during the period studied (that is, FY 1989 to FY 1999), the City of St. Petersburg has never been subject to any federal complaints or enforcement action under any of the regulations outlined above.

Chapter Seven

Quantitative Analysis Findings

This chapter presents the results of the quantitative analysis of the City of St. Petersburg's procurement data. In particular, the chapter includes the results of analyses: (a) the city's particular goods and services procurement categories; (b) availability (actual and potential) of M/WBE and non-M/WBE firms in the city's relevant market area; (c) utilization of these firms; (d) contracting disparity; (e) bidding profile; and (f) race preference program structure and operation survey . The results provided the first insight into identifying and drawing conclusions about the existence (or non-existence) of some systematic effect in the city's contracting process which could be violative of the civil rights of particular racial groups to effectively compete under the Fourteenth Amendment of the United States Constitution.

Prime Contracts Particular Services

As discussed in Chapter Two, the *Croson* decision calls for measurement of disparities by particular services, so as to avoid results that are overly-inclusive and might mask underlying patterns. Table 1-1 displays the result of the analysis of particular services or products. The table indicates that during the time period covered by the study, St. Petersburg purchased in 103 different NIGP classes, but in many of these codes the number contracts or the amount of dollars purchased was too small to perform a meaningful statistical analysis. To make this data more manageable, related four digit NIGP classes were combined into two-digit NIGP codes. Tables 2-1 through 2-9 and 3-1 through 3-9 display this data.

Table 1-1
City of St. Petersburg
Contractual goods and services by National Industrial Government Purchasing (NIGP) Code

Description	Class Code	NIGP						
Agricultural Equipment, Implements, & Accessories	1	2000-2073	33500-33585	51500-51585	67500-67590	79000-79080	59500-59595	
Abrasives	2	500-584						
A/C, Heating and Ventilation Equipment, Air Compressors & Accessories	3	2500-2585	3100-3197					
Automotive Accessories, Supplies & Parts	4	5500-5595	6000-6097	6500-6595	7000-7095	7500-7597		
Belts: Conveyor, Elevator, Power Trans & Belts	5	11000-11095						
Boats, Motors and Marine & Wildlife supplies	6	12000-12097						
Builders Supplies	7	14500-14590	15000-15096	15500-15589	41500-41591	42000-42096	33000-33095	63000-63097
		54000-54097	65800-65895	65900-65997	67000-67093	72000-72090		
Clothing, Apparels, Uniforms & Accessories	8	20000-20084	73500-73560					
Office Machines, Equipment, Accessories	9	20400-20496	20600-20693	20800-20894	31000-31078	60000-60097	70300-80390	92800-92894
		70000-70088	20700-20789	20900-20995	39500-39580	64500-64590	96600-96695	
Equip. Maint. Reconditioning & Repair Services	10	93900-93994	93600-93695	93100-93188	92900-92985	80000-80088		

Table 1-1
City of St. Petersburg
Contractual goods and services by National Industrial Government Purchasing (NIGP) Code

Description	**Class Code**	**NIGP**						
Controllers, Measuring & monitoring & Record Supplies	11	22000-22087	78000-78095	28000-28090	28500-28595	28700-28796		
Elevators & Escalators building Type	12	29500-29570						
Engineering Equipment, Surveying Equip, Drawing	13	30500-30584						
Security, Fire, Safety & Emergency Services	14	34000-34094	99000-99090	34500-34594				
Construction Trade	15	91400-91488						
Foods: Staple Grocery & Grocery's Misc. Items	16	39300-39390						
Furniture: Cafeteria, Chapel, Dormitory, Household, School, clocks	17	19200-20000						
Hardware Tools & Machinery & Related items	18	24000-24096	44500-44591	54500-5490	57000-57095	45000-45093	54500-54590	
Janitorial Supplies, General Line	19	48500-48594						
Hospital, Lab & Surgical Equip., Instr. & Supplies	20	46500-46597	49000-49096	27000-27095	49300-49396			

Table 1-1
City of St. Petersburg
Contractual goods and services by National Industrial Government Purchasing (NIGP) Code

Description	Class Code	NIGP						
Material Handling & Storage Equip. & Allied Items	21	56000-56084						
Miscellaneous Products	22	57800-57894						
Paper & Plastic Products, Fiberglass, Construction, Forming, Lami	23	64000-64087	66500-66590					
Park, Playground, Recreation Area & Swimming Pool	24	65000-65080	98800-98889					
Photographic Equip. & Supplies (Not including Graphic)	25	65500-65592	57500-57576					
Police Equipment & Supplies	26	68000-68097						
Communications, TV and Media Related Services	27	72500-72595	73000-73096	91500-91590	84000-84086	88000-88088		
Road & Hwy Equip, Sign, Sign & Bldg. Materials	28	74500-74584	76500-76595	80100-80197	76000-76090	55000-55096	75000-75095	
Freight Cars, Locomotives, Rail Passenger & Specialized	29	55800-55885						

Table 1-1
City of St. Petersburg
Contractual goods and services by National Industrial Government Purchasing (NIGP) Code

Description	Class Code	NIGP						
Sporting & Athletic Goods	30	80500-80595						
Steam & Hot Water Boilers Steam Heating, Chemicals & Power	31	82000-82095	83000-83080	88500-88595	89000-89089			
Testing Apparatus & Instruments (Not For Electric)	32	84500-84597						
Professional Services	33	92000-92098	91800-91897	94118-94191	94800-94660	96100-96194	96200-98297	95800-95685
Bldg. Construction, Maintenance & Repairs Services	34	77000-77096	91000-91082	90600-90694	36000-36089	90900-90991		
General Construction Services	35	21002-1085	91200-91268	91300-91396	96800-96897			

Tables 2-1 through 2-9 show the distinctive NIGP codes which the City of St. Petersburg prime contracts were awarded and the proportion of business that went to those trade and services during fiscal years 1989, 1990, 1991, 1992, 1993, 1994, 1995, 1996, and 1997[304]. As indicated on the tables, the proportions are measured by the number of contracts and the dollar value of those contracts. From FY 1991 to FY 1992, the City made prime purchases in 10 major NIGP classes. The number of major NIGP classes where prime purchases were made increased to 35 from FY 1993 and FY 1997.

Table 2-1 shows the breakdown of prime contracts awarded by NIGP class during FY 1989. The data indicate that the City of St. Petersburg awarded a total of 18 prime contracts during FY 1989 for a total dollar value of $20,364,983. The smallest dollars value of contracts ($125,605) was awarded in the NIGP class entitled equipment maintenance reconditioning and repair services. The largest dollar amount of contracts (that is, 97.91 percent of total purchase value) was in general construction in the amount of $19,939,382. Meanwhile, the number of prime contracts awarded during this fiscal year ranged from a low of 3 in the NIGP class called equipment maintenance, reconditioning and repair services to a high of 10 (that is, 55.6 percent of total number of prime purchases) in general construction. Meanwhile, building construction services had 5 purchases with a proportion dollar value of less than 2 percent of total purchases.

---

[304] It is important to note that during FY 1989 to FY 1992 the procurement data used in this analysis was predominantly for construction and related services. During these fiscal years, the City's policy was to maintain this data for three fiscal years only. The data for the other major procurement classes which the City made purchases in were either not available or limited. Hence, during FY 1989 to FY 1992 it is possible that the City made more purchases in these procurement classes than presented in this report.

Table 2-1
City of St. Petersburg
Prime Contract Awards by Procurement Category
FY 89

NIGP Code	Procurement Category Descriptions	Awards			
		Dollars	Percent	Number	Percent
10	Equip. Maint. Reconditioning & Repair Services	$ 125,605	0.62%	3	16.67%
34	Building Construction, Maintenance	$ 299,996	1.47%	5	27.78%
35	General Construction Services	$19,838,382	97.91%	10	55.56%
	Total:	$20,364,983	100%	18	100%

Table 2-2 displays the distribution of prime contracts awarded by NIGP during FY 1990. During this fiscal year, the total number of prime contracts awarded was 42 for a total dollar amount of $30,812,808 in 5 NIGP classes. The range of the dollar value of contracts awarded by the City during this fiscal year was from a low of $5,700 in the NIGP class called controllers, measuring, monitoring and recording supplies to high of $27,160,569 in general construction. Meanwhile, the lowest number of prime contracts awarded was one (1) in the following two NIGP classes: controller, measuring, monitoring and recording supplies, and park, playground, recreational area and swimming pool. The largest number of prime contracts awarded by the City was 27 in general construction services.

A majority (64.3 percent) of the total proportion of the number of prime contract purchases was awarded in general construction services. The remaining 4 NIGP classes combined accounted for 35.7 percent of the City's total number of prime purchases. Meanwhile, a majority (88.2 percent) of the proportion of the City's prime contract dollars was awarded in building construction. The remaining 4 NIGP classes combined accounted for only 11.85 percent of the total prime contract dollars awarded by the City of St. Petersburg in FY1990.

Table 2-2 City of St. Petersburg Prime Contract Awards by Procurement Category FY 90					
NIGP Code	Procurement Category Descriptions	Awards			
		Dollars	Percent	Number	Percent
10	Equip. Maint. Reconditiong & Repair Services	$ 1,556,737	5.05%	5	11.90%
11	Controllers, Measuring & Monitoring	$ 5,700	0.02%	1	2.38%
24	Park, Playground, Recreational Area	$ 94,108	0.31%	1	2.38%
34	Building Construction, Maintenance	$ 1,995,694	6.48%	8	19.05%
35	General Construction Services	$27,160,569	88.15%	27	64.29%
	Total:	$30,812,808	100%	42	100%

Table 2-3 shows the distribution of the City of St. Petersburg competitively prime contracts awarded by NIGP classes during FY1991. The table indicates that the City awarded a total of 29 competitively bid prime contracts for a total dollar value of $11,256.035 in 7 different NIGP classes. The smallest dollar value of contracts (i.e. $12,400) was awarded in sporting and athletic goods, and the largest dollar value was $8,067,023 awarded in general construction services NIGP class. Meanwhile, the number of prime contracts awarded during this fiscal year ranged from a low of one (1) prime contract in NIGP classes entitled office machines, equipment, and accessories; and miscellaneous products, to a high of 17 in general construction services.

Approximately seventy nine (79 percent) of the total number of prime contracts were awarded in only three (3) NIGP classes. The NIGP classes are: general construction (58.6 percent); park, playground, recreational area and swimming (10.3 percent); and equipment maintenance reconditioning and repair services (10.3 percent). The remaining 4 NIGP classes combined accounted for only

20.7 percent of the total number of prime contracts awarded. Meanwhile, a large majority (97 percent) of the proportion of prime contract dollars was awarded in general construction; parks, playground, recreational area and swimming pool; and equipment, maintenance, reconditioning and repair services. The remaining 6 NIGP classes combined received only 3 percent of the total prime contract dollars awarded by the City during FY 1991.

Table 2-3
City of St. Petersburg
Prime Contract Awards by Procurement Category
FY 91

NIGP Code	Procurement Category Descriptions	Awards			
		Dollars	Percent	Number	Percent
9	Office Machines, Equipment, Accessories	$ 71,770	0.64%	1	3.45%
10	Equip. Maint. Reconditioning & Repair Services	$ 1,831,752	16.27%	3	10.34%
22	Miscellaneous Products	$ 80,000	0.71%	1	3.45%
24	Park, Playground, Recreational Area	$ 1,020,245	9.06%	3	10.34%
30	Sporting & Athletic Goods	$ 12,400	0.11%	2	6.90%
34	Building Construction, Maintenance	$ 172,845	1.54%	2	6.90%
35	General Construction Services	$ 8,067,023	71.67%	17	58.62%
	Total:	$11,256,035	100%	29	100%

Table 2-4 exhibits the output of the analysis of the City of St. Petersburg prime contracts awarded by NIGP class during FY1992. During this fiscal year, the City awarded a total of 33 competitively bid prime contracts for a total dollar amount of $7,679,372. The dollar value of the prime contracts awarded ranged from a low of $10 in miscellaneous products to a high of $6,232,395 in general construction. Meanwhile, the lowest number of prime contracts awarded was one (1) in four NIGP classes. The NIGP classes are: office machines, equipment, and accessories; hardware and related items; miscellaneous products; and professional services. The largest proportion of the number of prime contracts was 57.6 percent awarded in general construction. Four (4) NIGP classes accounted for 87.9 percent of the total number of prime contracts awarded during FY 1992. The NIGP classes are: equipment maintenance reconditioning and repair services (12.1 percent); park, playground, recreational area and swimming (9.1 percent); building construction, maintenance and repair services (9.1 percent); and general construction services (57.6 percent). The remaining 4 NIGP classes combined accounted for only 12.1 percent of the total number of prime contracts awarded. Meanwhile, general construction services accounted for a large majority (81.2 percent) of the dollar value of prime contract purchases made by the City of St. Petersburg during FY 1992. Each of the remaining 7 NIGP classes accounted for less than 8 percent of the total dollar value of purchases made during this fiscal year.

Table 2-4
City of St. Petersburg
Prime Contract Awards by Procurement Category
FY 92

NIGP Code	Procurement Category Descriptions	Awards			
		Dollars	Percent	Number	Percent
09	Office Machines, Equipment, Accessories	$ 6,268	0.08%	1	3.03%
10	Equip. Maint. Reconditioning & Repair Services	$ 546,340	7.11%	4	12.12%
18	Hardware & Related Items, Tools & Machinery Equip	$ 4,569	0.06%	1	3.03%
22	Miscellaneous Products	$ 10	0.00%	1	3.03%
24	Park, Playground, Recreational Area	$ 355,275	4.63%	3	9.09%
33	Professional Services	$ 21,000	0.27%	1	3.03%
34	Building Construction, Maintenance	$ 513,515	6.69%	3	9.09%
35	General Construction Services	$ 6,232,395	81.16%	19	57.58%
	Total:	$ 7,679,372	100%	33	100%

Table 2-5 shows the breakdown of the City of St. Petersburg prime contracts awarded during fiscal year 1993. The data indicate that during this fiscal year, the City awarded a total of 65 competitively bid prime contracts in 16 difference major NIGP classes for a total prime contract dollar value of $21,591,091. The smallest dollar amount of prime contract was $1,077 awarded in clothing, apparels, uniforms and accessories. The largest dollar value was $15,875,289 awarded in general construction services. The smallest number of prime contracts awarded was one (1) in: conveyor, elevator, power transmission belts; clothing apparels, uniforms and accessories; security, fire, safety and emergency services; park, playground, recreational area and swimming; road and highway equipment, signs and building materials; and professional services.

A large proportion (96.3 percent) of the total dollar amount of prime contracts awarded by the City during fiscal year 1993 went to only four (4) NIGP classes. The classes are: builders supplies (6.52 percent); equipment maintenance, reconditioning and repair services (10.4 percent); building construction, maintenance and repair services (5.70 percent); and general construction (73.7 percent). The remaining 12 NIGP classes combined accounted for only 3.70 percent of the total dollar value of prime contracts awarded during fiscal year 1993.

Meanwhile, 81.5 percent of the total number of prime contracts awarded during fiscal year 1993 went to 7 NIGP classes. The NIGP classes are: builder supplies (13.9 percent); equipment maintenance reconditioning and repair services (7.69 percent); controllers, measuring and monitoring equipment (7.69 percent); communications, TV and media related services (7.69 percent); building construction, maintenance and repair services (9.23 percent); sporting and athletic goods (6.15 percent); and general construction services (29.2 percent). The remaining 9 NIGP classes combined accounted for only 18.47 percent of the total number of prime contracts awarded by the City during fiscal year 1993.

Table 2-5
City of St. Petersburg
Prime Contract Awards by Procurement Category
FY 93

NIGP Code	Procurement Category Descriptions	Awards			
		Dollars	Percent	Number	Percent
05	Belts: Conveyor, Elevator, Power Transmission	$ 11,916	0.60%	1	1.54%
07	Builders Supplies	$ 1,405,199	6.52%	9	13.85%
08	Clothing, Apparel, Uniforms & Accessories	$ 1,077	0.00%	1	1.54%
10	Equip. Maint. Reconditioning & Repair Services	$ 2,243,111	10.41%	5	7.69%
11	Controllers, Measuring & Monitoring	$ 104,202	0.48%	5	7.69%
14	Security, Fire, Safety & Emergency services	$ 1,703	0.01%	1	1.54%
20	Hospital, Lab & Surgical Equipment, Instr & Supplies	$ 29,365	0.14%	2	3.08%
22	Miscellaneous Products	$ 3,406	0.02%	2	3.08%
23	Paper & Plastic Products, Fiberglass	$ 77,006	0.36%	2	3.08%
24	Part, Playground, Recreational Area	$ 476,560	2.21%	1	1.54%
27	Communications, TV & Media Related services	$ 17,677	0.08%	5	7.69%
28	Road & Hwy Equip, Sign & Bldg. Materials	$ 6,309	0.03%	1	1.54%
30	Sporting & Athletic Goods	$ 57,440	0.27%	4	6.15%
33	Professional Services	$ 10,984	0.05%	1	1.54%
34	Building Construction, Maint & Repairs	$ 1,228,310	5.70%	6	9.23%
35	General Construction Services	$15,875,289	73.67%	19	29.23%
	Total:	$21,549,554	100%	65	100%

Table 2-6 displays the proportion of purchases made by City of St. Petersburg during fiscal year 1994. During this year, the City awarded a total of 174 competitively bid prime contracts in 20 NIGP classes for a total dollar value of $21,278,724. The dollar value of purchases ranged from a low of $10,200 in A/C, heating and ventilation equipment, to a high of $7,280,614 in general construction services. Meanwhile, the smallest number of prime contracts (that is, one) was awarded in: A/C, heating and ventilation equipment; cafeteria, chapel and dormitory furniture; paper, fiberglass and plastic products; and professional services. The largest number of prime contracts was 32 awarded in the NIGP class called builders supplies.

Fifty eight (58 percent) of the total number of prime contracts awarded by the City during fiscal year 1994 went to five (5) major NIGP classes. The classes are: agricultural equipment, implements and supplies (15.5 percent); builders supplies (18.4 percent); hardware and related items, tools and machinery equipment (8.1 percent); communications, TV and media related services (6.9 percent); and general construction services (9.2 percent). The remaining 15 NIGP classes combined accounted for 42 percent of the City's total number of contracts awarded during fiscal year 1996.

With regard to dollar value of City's prime contracts awarded in FY1994, 90.34 percent of the total dollars was awarded in seven (7) NIGP classes. The classes include: agricultural equipment, implements and supplies (8.9 percent); builders supplies (6.28 percent); equipment maintenance, reconditioning and repair services (16.3 percent); hardware tools, machinery and related items (11.6 percent); park, playground, recreational area and swimming pool services (6.2 percent); building construction, maintenance and repair services (6.9 percent); and general construction (9.2 percent). electrical equipment and supplies (12.4 percent); architectural services (3.9 percent); The remaining 13 NIGP classes combined accounted for only 9.7 percent of the total dollar value of competitively bid prime contracts awarded.

Table 2-6 City of St. Petersburg Prime Contract Awards by Procurement Category FY 94					
NIGP Code	Procurement Category Descriptions	Awards			
		Dollars	Percent	Number	Percent
01	Agriculture Equipment, Implements	$ 1,896,032	8.91%	27	15.52%
03	A/C, Heating & Ventilation Equipment, air compressors & accessories	$ 10,200	0.05%	1	0.57%
04	Automotive Accessories, Supplies	$ 20,438	0.10%	2	1.15%
07	Builders Supplies	$ 1,336,460	6.28%	32	18.39%
08	Clothing, Apparel, Uniforms & Accessories	$ 149,066	0.70%	6	3.45%
09	Office Machines, Equipment, Accessories	$ 105,330	0.50%	7	4.02%
10	Equip. Maint. Reconditioning & Repair Services	$ 3,466,514	16.29%	6	3.45%
11	Controllers, Measuring & Monitoring	$ 70,926	0.33%	5	2.87%
14	Security, Fire, Safety & Emergency services	$ 103,962	0.49%	7	4.02%
17	Furniture: Cafeteria, Chapel, Dormitory	$ 12,452	0.06%	1	0.57%
18	Hardware Tools & machinery & related items	$ 2,477,374	11.64%	14	8.05%
20	Hospital, Lab & Surgical Equipment, Instruments	$ 472,943	2.22%	8	4.60%
22	Miscellaneous Products	$ 144,946	0.68%	8	4.60%
23	Paper & Plastic Products, Fiberglass	$ 27,271	0.13%	1	0.57%
24	Park, Playground, Recreational Area	$ 1,308,272	6.15%	8	4.60%
27	Communications, TV & Media Related services	$ 648,569	3.05%	12	6.90%
28	Road & Highway Equipment, Signs & Build	$ 277,420	1.30%	5	2.87%
33	Professionals Services	$ 12,460	0.06%	1	0.57%
34	Building Construction, Maint. & Repair	$ 1,457,475	6.85%	7	4.02%
35	General Construction Services	$ 7,280,614	34.22%	16	9.20%
	Total:	$ 21,278,724	100%	174	100%

Table 2-7 shows the breakdown of the City of St. Petersburg prime contracts awarded during fiscal year 1995. The data indicate that during this fiscal year, the City awarded a total of 159 competitively bid prime contracts in 19 different major NIGP classes for a total prime contract dollar value of $27,281,984. The smallest dollar amount of prime contract was $5,193 awarded in security, fire, safety and emergency services. The largest dollar value was $10,266,985 awarded in general construction services. The smallest number of prime contracts awarded was one (1) in: conveyor, elevator, power transmission belts; hospital, laboratory and surgical equipment and instruments; sporting and athletic goods; and professional services.

A large proportion (85 percent) of the total dollar amount of prime contracts awarded by the City during fiscal year 1995 went to only four (4) major NIGP classes. The classes are: general construction services (37.6 percent); building construction (11.5 percent); equipment maintenance, reconditioning and repair services (23.1 percent); and agricultural equipment, implements and supplies (12.7 percent). The remaining 15 NIGP classes combined accounted for only 15 percent of the total dollar value of competitively bid prime contracts awarded during fiscal year 1993.

Meanwhile, 73.6 percent of the total number of prime contracts awarded during fiscal year 1995 went to seven (7) NIGP classes. The NIGP classes are: agricultural equipment, implements and supplies (16.9 percent); builder supplies (13 percent); clothing, apparels, uniforms and accessories (6.29 percent); controllers, measuring and monitoring equipment (6.92 percent); communications, TV and media related services (6.92 percent); building construction, maintenance and repair services (10.7 percent); and general construction services (13.2 percent). The remaining 12 major NIGP classes combined accounted for only 26.4 percent of the total number of competitively bid prime contracts awarded by the City during fiscal year 1995.

Table 2-7 City of St. Petersburg Prime Contract Awards by Procurement Category FY 95					
NIGP Code	Procurement Category Descriptions	Awards			
		Dollars	Percent	Number	Percent
01	Agriculture Equipment, Implements	$ 3,470,624	12.72%	27	16.98%
04	Automotive Accessories, Supplies	$ 273,753	1.00%	3	1.89%
05	Belts: Conveyor, Elevator, Power Trans & Belts	$ 6,213	0.02%	1	0.63%
07	Builders Supplies	$ 413,908	1.52%	20	12.58%
08	Clothing, Apparel, Uniforms & Accessories	$ 282,016	1.03%	10	6.29%
09	Office Machines, Equipment, Accessories	$ 173,858	0.64%	6	3.77%
10	Equip. Maint. Reconditioning & Repair Services	$ 6,310,258	23.13%	7	4.40%
11	Controllers, Measuring & Monitoring	$ 653,861	2.40%	11	6.92%
14	Security, Fire, Safety & Emergency services	$ 5,193	0.02%	1	0.63%
18	Hardware, Tools & machinery & Related Items	$ 91,065	0.33%	6	3.77%
20	Hospital, Lab & Surgical Equipment, Instruments	$ 5,150	0.02%	1	0.63%
22	Miscellaneous Products	$ 213,639	0.78%	5	3.14%
24	Park, Playground, Recreational Area	$ 684,832	2.51%	7	4.40%
27	Communication, TV & Media Related services	$ 1,160,231	4.25%	11	6.92%
28	Road & Highway Equipment, Signs & Build	$ 106,275	0.39%	3	1.89%
30	Sporting & Athletic Goods	$ 8,970	0.03%	1	0.63%
33	Professional Services	$ 22,500	0.08%	1	0.63%
34	Building Construction, Maint & Repairs	$ 3,132,653	11.48%	17	10.69%
35	General Construction Services	$ 10,266,985	37.63%	21	13.21%
	Total:	$ 27,281,984	100%	159	100%

Table 2-8 shows the breakdown of the City of St. Petersburg prime contracts awarded during fiscal year 1996. The data indicate that during this fiscal year, the City awarded a total of 126 competitively bid prime contracts in 16 different major NIGP classes for a total prime contract dollar value of $29,643,546. The smallest dollar amount of prime contract was $16,650 awarded in miscellaneous products. The largest dollar value was $17,687,988. The smallest number of prime contracts awarded was one (1) in the following 3 NIGP classes: automotive accessories, supplies and parts; controllers, measuring, and monitoring equipment; and miscellaneous products.

A large proportion (95.3 percent) of the total dollar amount of prime contracts awarded by the City during fiscal year 1996 went to only five (5) major NIGP classes. The classes are: builders supplies (9 percent); equipment maintenance, reconditioning and repair services (10.4 percent); communication, TV and media related services (7.4 percent); building construction, maintenance and repair services (8.5 percent); and general construction (59.7 percent). The remaining 11 NIGP classes combined accounted for only 4.7 percent of the total dollar value of prime contracts awarded during fiscal year 1996.

Meanwhile, 72.2 percent of the total number of competitively bid prime contracts awarded during fiscal year 1996 went to five (5) NIGP classes. The NIGP classes are: builder supplies (24.6 percent); office machines, equipment and accessories (7.94 percent); communications, TV and media related services (7.1 percent); building construction, maintenance and repair services (12.7 percent); sporting and athletic goods (6.2 percent); and general construction services (19.8 percent). The remaining 11 major NIGP classes combined accounted for only 18.5 percent of the total number of competitively bid prime contracts awarded by the City during fiscal year 1996.

Table 2-8 City of St. Petersburg Prime Contract Awards by Procurement Category FY 96					
NIGP Code	Procurement Category Descriptions	Awards			
		Dollars	Percent	Number	Percent
01	Agriculture Equipment, Implements	$ 220,500	0.74%	3	2.38%
04	Automotive Accessories, Supplies	$ 55,367	0.19%	1	0.79%
05	Boats, Motors & Marine & Wildlife Supplies	$ 18,486	0.06%	1	0.79%
07	Builders Supplies	$ 2,654,876	8.96%	31	24.60%
09	Office Machines, Equipment, Accessories	$ 127,977	0.43%	10	7.94%
10	Equip. Maint. Reconditioning & Repair Services	$ 3,179,462	10.73%	5	3.97%
11	Controllers, Measuring & Monitoring	$ 19,900	0.07%	1	0.79%
14	Security, Fire, Safety & Emergency services	$ 106,780	0.36%	2	1.59%
18	Hardware, Tools & machinery & Related Items	$ 43,400	0.15%	4	3.17%
22	Miscellaneous Products	$ 16,650	0.06%	1	0.79%
23	Paper & Plastic Products, Fiberglass	$ 114,735	0.39%	4	3.17%
24	Park, Playground, Recreational Area	$ 168,500	0.57%	5	3.97%
27	Communictions, TV & Media Relatied services	$ 2,200,406	7.42%	9	7.14%
28	Road & Highway Equipment, Signs & Build	$ 156,392	0.53%	3	2.38%
30	Sporting & Athletic Goods	$ 347,985	1.17%	5	3.97%
34	Building Construction, Maint & Repairs	$ 2,524,142	8.51%	16	12.70%
35	General Construction Services	$ 17,687,988	59.67%	25	19.84%
	Total:	$ 29,643,546	100%	126	100%

Table 2-9 shows the distribution of the City of St. Petersburg competitively prime contracts awarded by NIGP classes during FY1997. The table indicates that the City awarded a total of 33 competitively bid prime contracts in 4 different NIGP classes for a total dollar value of $20,436,159. The smallest dollar value of contracts ($294,076) was awarded in security, fire, safety and emergency services. Meanwhile, the number of prime contracts awarded during this fiscal year ranged from a low of one prime contract in NIGP classes entitled equipment maintenance reconditioning and repair services, to a high of 25 in general construction services.

Approximately fifty-two (90.9 percent) of the total number of prime contracts were awarded in two (2) of the four NIGP classes. The NIGP classes are: general construction (75.8 percent); and building construction, maintenance and repair services (15.2 percent). The remaining 2 NIGP classes combined accounted for only 9.1 percent of the total number of competitively bid prime contracts awarded.

Meanwhile, a majority (86.9 percent) of the proportion of prime contract dollars was awarded in general construction. The remaining 3 major NIGP classes combined received only 11.1 percent of the total competitively bid prime contract dollars awarded by the City during FY 1997.

Table 2-9
City of St. Petersburg
Prime Contract Awards by Procurement Category
FY 97

NIGP Code	Procurement Category Descriptions	Awards			
		Dollars	Percent	Number	Percent
10	Equip. Maint. Reconditioning & Repair Services	$ 568,000	2.78%	1	3.03%
14	Security, Fire, Safety & Emergency services	$ 294,076	1.44%	2	6.06%
34	Building Construction, Maint & Repairs	$ 1,823,482	8.92%	5	15.15%
35	General Construction Services	$ 17,750,601	86.86%	25	75.76%
	Total:	$ 20,436,159	100%	33	100%

Procurement Categories with more than 5 Percent Prime Contract Purchases

Tables 3-1 through 3-9 show the breakdown by fiscal year of NIGP classes exhibiting more than 5 percent of the total number or dollar amount of prime contracts awarded by the City of St. Petersburg. The tables display the data in either number or dollars awarded for each NIGP class. In particular, during the nine (9) fiscal years under study the City awarded 5 percent or more number of contracts in a total of thirteen (13) major NIGP classes. Each of the 13 NIGP classes had more than 5 percent of total dollar value of competitively bid prime contracts awarded by the City during the study time frame. The NIGP classes include: agricultural equipment, implements and accessories (FY1994 and FY1995); builders supplies (FY1993, FY1994 and FY1996); equipment maintenance, reconditioning and repair services (FY1990 - FY1996); hardware, tools, machinery and related items (FY1994); parks, playground, recreational area and swimming pool (FY1991, FY1994, and FY1996); building construction, maintenance and repair services (FY1990 - FY1997); general construction services (FY1989 – FY1997); and residual supplies and services (FY1994).

Meanwhile, the NIGP classes with more than 5 percent of the total number of contracts awarded were: agricultural equipment, implements and accessories (FY1994 and FY1995); builder supplies (FY1993, FY1994, FY1995, and FY1996); clothing, apparels, uniforms and accessories (FY1995); office machine, equipment and accessories (FY1996); equipment maintenance, reconditioning and repair services (FY1989 – FY 1994); controllers, measuring, monitoring and recording supplies (FY1993 and FY 1995); hardware, tools, machinery and related items (FY1994); parks, playground, recreational area (FY1991, FY1992); communication, TV and media relations (FY1993, FY1994, FY1995 and FY1996); sporting and athletic goods (FY1991 and FY1993); building construction, maintenance and repair services (FY1989, FY1990, FY1991, FY1992, FY1993, FY1995, FY1996 and

FY1997); general construction services (FY1989 – FY1997) and residual NIGP category (FY 1991 – FY 1996).

In summation, 13 procurement categories exceeded 5 percent either the number or the dollar value of total prime contracts awarded by the City of St. Petersburg through competitive bidding during each fiscal year. The thirteen procurement categories are: agricultural equipment, implements and accessories; builder supplies; clothing, apparels, uniforms and accessories; office machine, equipment and accessories; equipment maintenance, reconditioning and repair services; controllers, measuring, monitoring and recording supplies; hardware, tools, machinery and related items; parks, playground, recreational area; communication, TV and media relations; sporting and athletic goods; building construction, maintenance and repair services; general construction services; and residual NIGP category.

Subsequent statistical analyses were performed on these procurement categories only. These NIGP classes varied in the method and the frequency of competitive solicitation used by the City of St. Petersburg to award contracts. This variation has major implications on the volume and type of data appropriate for the analysis of availability and utilization, and subsequent analysis of patterns of disparity in the City's procurement system.

Table 3-1 City of St. Petersburg Procurement categories above 5% for either Dollar or Number percentage of prime contract awards FY 89					
NIGP Code	Procurement Category Descriptions	Awards			
		Dollars	Percent	Number	Percent
10	Equip. Maint. Reconditioning & Repair Services	$ 125,605	0.62%	3	16.67%
34	Building Construction, Maintenance	$ 299,996	1.47%	5	27.78%
35	General Construction Services	$ 19,939,382	97.91%	10	55.56%
	Total:	$ 20,374,982	100%	18	100%

Table 3-2 City of St. Petersburg Procurement categories above 5% for either Dollar or Number percentage of prime contract awards FY 90					
NIGP Code	Procurement Category Descriptions	Awards			
		Dollars	Percent	Number	Percent
10	Equip. Maint. Recond & Repair Services	$ 1,556,737	5.05%	5	11.90%
34	Building Construction, Maintenance	$ 1,995,694	6.48%	8	19.05%
35	General Construction Services	$ 27,160,569	88.15%	27	64.29%
Mics. NIGP	Residual NIGP Services*	99,808	0.32%	2	4.76%
	Total:	$ 30,812,808	100%	42	100%

Table 3-3
City of St. Petersburg
Procurement categories above 5% for
either Dollar or Number percentage of prime contract awards
FY 91

NIGP Code	Procurement Category Descriptions	Awards			
		Dollars	Percent	Number	Percent
10	Equip. Maint. Recond & Repair Services	$ 1,831,752	16.27%	3	10.34%
24	Park, Playground, Recreational Area	$ 1,020,245	9.06%	3	10.34%
30	Sporting & Athletic Goods	$ 12,400	0.11%	2	6.90%
34	Building Construction, Maintenance	$ 172,845	1.54%	2	6.90%
35	General Construction Services	$ 8,067,023	71.67%	17	58.62%
Mics. NIGP	Residual NIGP Services*	$ 151,770	1.35%	2	6.90%
	Total:	$ 11,256,035	100%	29	100%

Table 3-4
City of St. Petersburg
Procurement categories above 5% for
either Dollar or Number percentage of prime contract awards
FY 92

NIGP Code	Procurement Category Descriptions	Awards			
		Dollars	Percent	Number	Percent
10	Equip. Maint. Recond & Repair Services	$ 546,340	7.11%	4	12.12%
24	Park, Playground, Recreational Area	$ 355,275	4.63%	3	9.09%
34	Building Construction, Maintenance	$ 513,515	6.69%	3	9.09%
35	General Construction Services	$ 6,232,395	81.16%	19	57.58%
Mics. NIGP	Residual NIGP Services*	$ 31,847	0.41%	4	12.12%
	Total:	$ 7,679,372	100%	33	100%

Table 3-5 City of St. Petersburg Procurement categories above 5% for either Dollar or Number percentage of prime contract awards FY 93					
NIGP Code	Procurement Category Descriptions	Awards			
		Dollars	Percent	Number	Percent
07	Builders Supplies	$ 1,405,199	6.52%	9	13.85%
10	Equip. Maint. Recond & Repair Services	$ 2,243,111	10.41%	5	7.69%
11	Controllers, Measuring & Monitoring	$ 104,202	0.48%	5	7.69%
27	Communications, TV & Media Related services	$ 17,677	0.08%	5	7.69%
30	Sporting & Athletic Goods	$ 57,440	0.27%	4	6.15%
34	Building Construction, Maintenance	$ 1,228,310	5.70%	6	9.23%
35	General Construction Services	$ 15,875,289	73.67%	19	29.23%
Mics. NIGP	Residual NIGP Services*	$ 618,326	2.87%	12	18.46%
	Total:	$21,549,554	100%	65	100%

Table 3-6 City of St. Petersburg Procurement categories above 5% for either Dollar or Number percentage of prime contract awards FY 94					
NIGP Code	Procurement Category Descriptions	Awards			
		Dollars	Percent	Number	Percent
01	Agriculture Equipment, Implements	$ 1,896,032	8.91%	27	15.52%
07	Builders Supplies	$ 1,336,460	6.28%	32	18.39%
10	Equip. Maint. Reconditioning & Repair Services	$ 3,466,514	16.29%	6	3.45%
18	Hardware Items, Tools & mahinery & Related	$ 2,477,374	11.64%	14	8.05%
24	Park, Playground, Recreational Area	$ 1,308,272	6.15%	8	4.60%
27	Communications, TV & Media Related se	$ 648,569	3.05%	12	6.90%
34	Building Construction, Maintenance	$ 1,457,475	6.85%	7	4.02%
35	General Construction Services	$ 7,280,614	34.22%	16	9.20%
Mics. NIGP	Residual NIGP Services*	$ 1,407,414	6.61%	52	29.89%
	Total:	$21,278,724	100%	174	100%

Table 3-7 City of St. Petersburg Procurement categories above 5% for either Dollar or Number percentage of prime contract awards FY 95					
NIGP Code	Procurement Category Descriptions	Awards			
		Dollars	Percent	Number	Percent
01	Agriculture Equipment, Implements	$ 3,470,624	12.72%	27	16.98%
07	Builders Supplies	$ 413,908	1.52%	20	12.58%
8	Clothing, Apparel, Uniforms & Accessories	$ 282,016	1.03%	10	6.29%
10	Equip. Maint. Reconditioning & Repair Services	$ 6,310,258	23.13%	7	4.40%
11	Controllers, Measuring & Monitoring	$ 653,861	2.40%	11	6.92%
27	Communications, TV & Media Related Services	$ 1,160,231	4.25%	11	6.92%
34	Building Construction, Maintenance	$ 3,132,653	11.48%	17	10.69%
35	General Construction Services	$ 10,266,985	37.63%	21	13.21%
Mics. NIGP	Residual NIGP Services*	$ 1,591,448	5.83%	35	22.01%
	Total:	$ 27,281,984	100%	159	100%

Table 3-8 City of St. Petersburg Procurement categories above 5% for either Dollar or Number percentage of prime contract awards FY 96					
NIGP Code	Procurement Category Descriptions	Awards			
		Dollars	Percent	Number	Percent
07	Builders Supplies	$ 2,654,876	8.96%	31	24.60%
09	Office Machines, Equipment, Accessories	$ 127,977	0.43%	10	7.94%
10	Equip. Maint. Reconditioning & Repair Services	$ 3,179,462	10.73%	5	3.97%
27	Communications, TV & Media Related Services	$ 2,200,406	7.42%	9	7.14%
34	Building Construction, Maintenance	$ 2,524,142	8.51%	16	12.70%
35	General Construction Services	$ 17,687,988	59.67%	25	19.84%
Mics. NIGP	Residual NIGP Services*	$ 1,268,695	4.28%	30	23.81%
	Total:	$ 29,643,546	100%	126	100%

Table 3-9 City of St. Petersburg Procurement categories above 5% for either Dollar or Number percentage of prime contract awards FY 97					
NIGP Code	Procurement Category Descriptions	Awards			
			Percent	Number	Percent
14	Security, Fire, Safety & Emergency Services	$ 294,076	1.44%	2	6.06%
34	Building Construction, Maintenance	$ 1,823,482	8.92%	5	15.15%
35	General Construction Services	$ 17,750,601	86.86%	25	75.76%
Mics. NIGP	Residual NIGP Services*	$ 568,000	2.78%	1	3.03%
	Total:	$ 20,436,159	100%	33	100%

Prime Contract Availability

As discussed in Chapter Two, availability is conceptually defined as the proportion of contractors in each race, ethnic or gender group within a particular NIGP class that are qualified, capable, and willing to compete for the City contracts during the study time frame (FY 1989 – FY 1997). The study used two concepts of availability – actual and potential. Operationally, actual available firms for prime contracts are firms that are actively bidding, or submitting quotes to the City during the study's relevant time frame (FY 1989 – FY1997). Actual available firms for subcontracting are firms that have provided quotes to prime contractors during the study time frame. Potentially available firms are defined as all the firms that have the qualifications and capacity to bid on prime contracts or submit subcontracting quotes to prime contractors, but have not done so. As mentioned above, availability was estimated only for each distinctive trade or service NIGP class that constituted 5 percent or more of the City's competitively bid purchases.[305] The estimates were made for the number and dollar value of bids or quotes separately for each relevant NIGP class.

Number of Prime Contract bids

Tables 4-1 to 4-12 presents the proportion of the number of prime contract bids by racial, ethnic, and gender categories for each distinctive NIGP class with more than 5 percent of the City's purchases during fiscal years (FY) 1989 – 1997. The tables indicate that twelve (12) distinctive NIGP classes exhibited 5 percent or more of the number of City's competitively bid prime purchases.

Table 4-1 displays the breakdown of the proportion of the number of prime contract bids by racial, ethnic and gender categories for agricultural equipment, implements and accessories. The City of St. Petersburg awarded these prime contracts competitively through solicitation of verbal quotes from qualified vendors during each of the fiscal years studied[306]. The data indicate that in this NIGP class, with the exception of FY1997 where there were no competitive bids, the City's purchases were more than 5 percent during each of the fiscal years analyzed.

---

[305] The City of St. Petersburgh uses four (4) methods to make competitive purchases. These methods are: competitive sealed bids, competitive sealed proposals, written quotes, and verbal quotes. Since the operational definition of actual availability is the proportion of the dollar or number of competitive purchases, the units of analysis of availability are all competitively bid and quoted contracts.

[306] No data was available during FY1989 to FY 1993. Hence analysis was performed for FY1994 to FY1997 only.

Table 4-1
City of St. Petersburg
Number of Prime contract Bids By Racial, Ethnic, and Gender Groups
Agricultural Equipment, Implements and Accessories (NIGP #1)
FY 89-97

Fiscal Year	Total # of Contracts	Total # of Bids	Non-minority		Women		Black		Hispanic		Other		Total M/WBE	
			#	%	#	%	#	%	#	%	#	%	#	%
1989 to 1993	No data available for these fiscal years.													
1994	27	55	54	98.18	0	0	1	1.82	0	0	0	0	1	1.82
1995	27	45	43	95.56	1	2.22	1	2.22	0	0	0	0	2	4.44
1996	3	11	11	100	0	0	0	0	0	0	0	0	0	0
1997	0	0	0	0	0	0	0	0	0	0	0	0	0	0
Total	57	111	108	97.30	1	0.9	2	1.80	0	0	0	0	3	2.70

During this time frame, a total of 108 prime contract bids were submitted in this NIGP class by contractors in the City's relevant market area. Of this total, non-minority firms submitted a large proportion (97.3 percent) of the number of the bids. Meanwhile, all the M/WBE groups combined submitted only 2.7 percent of the total number of agricultural equipment, implements and accessories bids. When the data was disaggregated by ethnic, racial or gender subgroup per fiscal year, the analysis indicates that non-minority-owned firms consistently submitted over 95 percent of the bids in this NIGP class. Meanwhile, each of the M/WBE subgroups submitted less than 2.5 percent of the total agricultural implements and accessories bids per fiscal year. Woman and black firms were the only minority-owned firms that submitted bid in this procurement class during the study period.

Table 4-2 displays the proportion of the number of prime contract bids for builders supplies. The data indicate that the City solicited competitive bids in this NIGP class during FY1993 to FY1996. During this study period a total of 238 prime contract bid were submitted in this NIGP class. Of this total, non-minority firms submitted a large proportion (97.5 percent) of the number of the bids. Meanwhile, all the M/WBE groups combined submitted only 2.46 percent of the total number of builders supplies bids. When the data was disaggregated by ethnic, racial or gender subgroup per fiscal year, the analysis indicate that non-minority-owned firms consistently submitted over 92 percent of the bids in this NIGP class. Meanwhile, each of the M/WBE subgroups submitted less than 7 percent of the total builders supplies bids per fiscal year. Women and Hispanic firms were the only minority-owned firms that submitted bid in this procurement class during the study period.

Table 4-2
City of St. Petersburg
Number of Prime contract Bids By Racial, Ethnic, and Gender Groups
Agricultural Equipment, Implements and Accessories (NIGP #7)
FY 89-97

Fiscal Year	Total # of Contracts	Total # of Bids	Non-minority		Women		Black		Hispanic		Other		Total M/WBE	
			#	%	#	%	#	%	#	%	#	%	#	%
1989 to 1992	No data available for these fiscal years.													
1993	9	13	12	92.31	1	7.69	0	0	0	0	0	0	1	7.69
1994	32	101	99	98.02	2	1.98	0	0	0	0	0	0	1	1.98
1995	20	40	40	100	0	0	0	0	0	0	0	0	0	0
1996	31	90	87	96.67	2	2.22	0	0	1	1.11	0	0	3	3.33
1997	0	0	0	0	0	0	0	0	0	0	0	0	0	0
Total	92	244	238	97.54	5	2.05	0	0	1	0.41	0	0	6	2.46

Table 4-3 presents the distribution of the proportion of number of prime contract bids for clothing, apparel, uniforms and accessories. Similar to builders supplies, the data indicate that the City solicited competitive bids in this NIGP class during FY 1993 to FY 1996. During this study period a total of 60 prime contract bids were submitted in this NIGP class. Of this total, non-minority firms submitted a large proportion (98.3 percent) of the number of the bids. Meanwhile, all the M/WBE groups combined submitted less than 2 percent of the total number of clothing, apparels, uniforms and accessories bids. When the data was disaggregated by ethnic, racial or gender subgroup per fiscal year, the analysis indicate that non-minority-owned firms consistently submitted a large majority (over 96 percent) of the bids in this NIGP class during each fiscal year analyzed. Meanwhile, each of the

M/WBE subgroups submitted less than 3.50 percent of the total clothing, apparels, uniforms and accessories prime contract bids per fiscal year analyzed. Hispanic firms were the only minority-owned firms that submitted bid in this procurement class during the study period.

Table 4-3
City of St. Petersburg
Number of Prime contract Bids By Racial, Ethnic, and Gender Groups
Agricultural Equipment, Implements and Accessories (NIGP #8)
FY 89-97

Fiscal Year	Total # of Contracts	Total # of Bids	Non-minority		Women		Black		Hispanic		Other		Total M/WBE	
			#	%	#	%	#	%	#	%	#	%	#	%
1989 to 1992	No data available for these fiscal years.													
1993	1	6	6	100	0	0	0	0	0	0	0	0	0	0
1994	6	21	21	100	0	0	0	0	0	0	0	0	0	0
1995	10	33	32	96.97	0	0	0	0	1	3.03	0	0	1	3.03
1996	0	0	0	0	0	0	0	0	0	0	0	0	0	0
1997	0	0	0	0	0	0	0	0	0	0	0	0	0	0
Total	17	60	60	98.33	0	0	0	0	1	1.67	0	0	1	1.67

Table 4-4 displays the proportion of the number of prime contract bids by racial, ethnic, or gender group for office machines, equipment and accessories. The data indicate that the City of St. Petersburg solicited competitively bid prime contracts in this procurement class during FY1991 to FY1997. During this study period, contractors in the City's relevant market area submitted a total of 194 prime contract bids in this NIGP class. Of this total, non-minority firms submitted a large proportion (99.5 percent) of the number of the prime bids. Meanwhile, all the non-minority groups combined submitted less than 1 percent of the total number office machines, equipment and accessories bids. When the data was disaggregated by ethnic, racial or gender subgroup per fiscal year, the analysis indicates that non-minority-owned firms consistently submitted a large majority (over 98 percent) of the bids in this NIGP class during each fiscal year analyzed. Meanwhile, each of the M/WBE subgroups submitted less than 1.00 percent of the total clothing, apparels, uniforms and accessories prime contract bids per fiscal year analyzed. Black firms were the only minority-owned firms that submitted bid in this procurement class during the study period.

Table 4-4
City of St. Petersburg
Number of Prime contract Bids By Racial, Ethnic, and Gender Groups
Agricultural Equipment, Implements and Accessories (NIGP #9)
FY 89-97

Fiscal Year	Total # of Contracts	Total # of Bids	Non-minority		Women		Black		Hispanic		Other		Total M/WBE	
			#	%	#	%	#	%	#	%	#	%	#	%
1989 to 1990	No data available for these fiscal years.													
1991	1	5	5	100	0	0	0	0	0	0	0	0	0	0
1992	1	26	26	100	0	0	0	0	0	0	0	0	0	0
1993	0	0	0	0	0	0	0	0	0	0	0	0	0	0
1994	7	57	56	98.25	0	0	1	2.75	0	0	0	0	1	1.76
1995	6	25	25	100	0	0	0	0	0	0	0	0	1	0
1996	10	81	81	100	0	0	0	0	0	0	0	0	0	0
1997	0	0	0	0	0	0	0	0	0	0	0	0	0	0
Total	25	194	193	00.48	0	0	1	0.52	0	0	0	0	1	0.52

Table 4-5 shows the distribution of the proportion of the number of equipment maintenance, reconditioning and repair services prime contract bids by racial, ethnic, or gender category. All the contracts in this NIGP class are competitively bid each fiscal year. The City of St. Petersburg solicited sealed bid, written quotes and verbal quotes from vendors in this NIGP class during each of the fiscal years studied.

During this study period, contractors in the City's relevant market area submitted a total of 175 prime contract bids in this NIGP class. Of this total, non-minority firms submitted a large proportion (94.3 percent) of the total number of the prime bids. Meanwhile, all the M/WBE groups combined submitted less than 6 percent of the total number equipment maintenance, reconditioning and repair services bids. When the data was disaggregated by ethnic, racial or gender subgroup per fiscal year, the analysis indicate that non-minority-owned firms consistently submitted a large majority (over 83 percent) of the bids in this NIGP class during each fiscal year analyzed. Meanwhile, each of the M/WBE subgroups submitted less than 17 percent of the total equipment maintenance, reconditioning and repair services prime contract bids per fiscal year analyzed.

Women and Hispanic firms were the only minority-owned firms that submitted bid in this procurement class during the study period. The proportion of bids submitted by woman-owned firms steadily declined from 9.1 percent in FY 1989 to 0 percent in FY1997. Meanwhile, the trend was opposite for Hispanic-owned firms which exhibited a steady improvement from 0 percent of total number of equipment maintenance, reconditioning and repair services prime contract bids in FY 1989 to 16.7 percent in FY 1997.

Table 4-5 City of St. Petersburg Number of Prime contract Bids By Racial, Ethnic, and Gender Groups Agricultural Equipment, Implements and Accessories (NIGP #10) FY 89-97														
Fiscal Year	Total # of Contracts	Total # of Bids	Non-minority		Women		Black		Hispanic		Other		Total M/WBE	
			#	%	#	%	#	%	#	%	#	%	#	%
1989	3	11	10	90.91	1	9.09	0	0	0	0	0	0	1	9
1990	5	23	22	95.65	0	0	0	0	1	4.35	0	0	1	9
1991	3	18	18	100	0	0	0	0	0	0	0	0	0	0
1992	4	16	15	93.75	1	6.25	0	0	0	0	0	0	1	6.25
1993	5	22	21	95	0	0	0	0	1	5	0	0	0	0
1994	6	35	33	94.29	2	5.71	0	0	0	0	0	0	2	5.71
1995	7	18	16	88.89	1	5.56	0	0	1	5.56	0	0	1	11.11
1996	5	26	25	96.15	0	0	0	0	1	3.85	0	0	1	3.85
1997	1	6	5	83.33	0	0	0	0	1	16.67	0	0	1	16.67
Total	25	194	193	00.48	0	0	1	0.52	0	0	0	0	1	0.52

Table 4-6 displays the proportion of the number of controllers, measuring, monitoring and recording supplies prime contract bids by racial, gender, or ethnic category. Similar to equipment maintenance, reconditioning and repair services, the contracts in this NIGP class are competitively bid by the City each fiscal year through sealed bids, written quotes or verbal quotes.

During the study period, the City received a total of 66 controllers, measuring, monitoring and recording supplies bids and quotes. Of this total, non-minority firms submitted a large proportion (89.4 percent) of the total number of the prime bids. Meanwhile, all the non-minority groups combined submitted less than 10 percent of the total number of controller, measuring, monitoring and recording supplies bids.

When the data was disaggregated by ethnic, racial or gender subgroup per fiscal year, non-minority, the analysis indicates that non-minority-owned firms consistently submitted a large majority (over 81 percent) of the bids in this NIGP class during each fiscal year. Meanwhile, each of the M/WBE subgroups submitted less than 12 percent of the total controllers, measuring, monitoring and recording supplies prime contract bids per fiscal year analyzed.

Women and Hispanic firms were the only minority-owned firms that submitted bid in this procurement class during the study period. Woman-owned firms submitted bids in this NIGP class in FY 1994 and FY 1995, while Hispanic-owned firms submitted bids in this NIGP class from FY 1993 to FY 1995 only.

The trend indicate that the proportion of the number of controller, measuring, monitoring and recording supplies bids for both woman- and Hispanic-owned firms steadily declined during the study period.

Table 4-6
City of St. Petersburg
Number of Prime contract Bids By Racial, Ethnic, and Gender Groups
Agricultural Equipment, Implements and Accessories (NIGP #11)
FY 89-97

Fiscal Year	Total # of Contracts	Total # of Bids	Non-minority		Women		Black		Hispanic		Other		Total M/WBE	
			#	%	#	%	#	%	#	%	#	%	#	%
1989	0	0	0	0	0	0	0	0	0	0	0	0	0	0
1990	1	3	3	100	0	0	0	0	0	0	0	0	0	0
1991	0	0	0	0	0	0	0	0	0	0	0	0	0	0
1992	0	0	0	0	0	0	0	0	0	0	0	0	0	0
1993	5	14	13	92.86	0	0	0	0	1	7.14	0	0	1	7.14
1994	5	16	13	82.25	2	12.50	0	0	1	6.25	0	0	3	18.75
1995	11	30	27	90.00	2	6.67	0	0	1	3.33	0	0	3	10.00
1996	1	3	3	100	0	0	0	0	0	0	0	0	0	0
1997	0	0	0	0	0	0	0	0	0	0	0	0	0	0
Total	23	66	59	89.39	4	6.06	0	0	3	4.55	0	0	7	10.61

Table 4-7 presents the proportion of the number of prime contract bids for hardware, tools, machinery and related items by racial, ethnic, or gender group. The data indicate that during the six fiscal years studied the City of St. Petersburg bid prime contracts in this NIGP class during FY 1992, FY 1994, FY 1995, and FY 1996 only.

During this period, the City received a total of 59 bids. Non-minority-owned firms submitted the largest proportion (96.6 percent) of the total number of bids in this NIGP class. Meanwhile, all the M/WBE groups combined submitted less than 4.00 percent of the total hardware, tools, machinery and related prime contract bids during the fiscal years analyzed.

When the data was disaggregated by racial, ethnic or gender group, the trend in non-minority firm bid submittal showed a steady increase from 67 percent in FY 1992 to 100 percent in FY 1996. Meanwhile, the trend was opposite for the two M/WBE groups (woman- and black-owned firms) that submitted bids in this NIGP class. In particular, the trend for both groups declined during the time frame studied. As discussed earlier in this report, this procurement class includes the NIGP classes with less than 5 percent of the City's total purchases during each fiscal year.

Table 4-7
City of St. Petersburg
Number of Prime contract Bids By Racial, Ethnic, and Gender Groups
Agricultural Equipment, Implements and Accessories (NIGP #18)
FY 89-97

Fiscal Year	Total # of Contracts	Total # of Bids	Non-minority		Women		Black		Hispanic		Other		Total M/WBE	
			#	%	#	%	#	%	#	%	#	%	#	%
1989 to 1991	No data available for these fiscal years.													
1992	1	3	2	67	1	33.33	0	0	0	0	0	0	1	33.33
1993	0	0	0	0	0	0	0	0	0	0	0	0	0	0
1994	14	31	30	97	0	0	1	3.23	0	0	0	0	1	3.23
1995	6	13	13	100	0	0	0	0	0	0	0	0	0	0
1996	4	12	12	100	0	0	0	0	0	0	0	0	0	0
1997	0	0	0	0	0	0	0	0	0	0	0	0	0	0
Total	25	59	57	96.61	1	1.72	1	1.69	0	0	0	0	2	3.39

Table 4-8 displays the proportion of the number of park, playground, and recreational area and swimming pool prime contract bids by racial, gender, or ethnic category. Similar to equipment maintenance, reconditioning and repair services, the contracts in this NIGP class are competitively bid by the City each fiscal year through sealed bids, written quotes or verbal quotes.

During the study period, the City received a total of 96 bids or quotes in this NIGP class. Of this total, non-minority firms submitted a large proportion (89.6 percent) of the total number of the prime bids. Meanwhile, all the M/WBE groups combined submitted less than 10 percent of the total number park, playground, recreational area and swimming pool bids.

When the data was disaggregated by ethnic, racial or gender subgroup per fiscal year, the analysis indicates that non-minority-owned firms consistently submitted a majority (over 71 percent) of the bids in this NIGP class during each fiscal year that the City put the contract out for bid. Meanwhile, the trend of the proportion of the dollar value for black-owned firms improved from 0 percent in FY 1989 to 28.6 in FY 1992, and then declined to 0 percent in subsequent fiscal years analyzed. The trend for Hispanic-owned firms was similar to black-owned firms in that it increased from 0 percent in FY 1989 to 8 percent in FY 1994, and then declined steadily to 0 percent in FY 1997. Woman-owned firms bid only once (that is, FY 1994) during the period studied, while the other M/WBE group did not submit bids in this NIGP class.

Table 4-8 City of St. Petersburg Number of Prime contract Bids By Racial, Ethnic, and Gender Groups Agricultural Equipment, Implements and Accessories (NIGP #24) FY 89-97															
Fiscal Year	Total # of Contracts	Total # of Bids	Non-minority		Women		Black		Hispanic		Other		Total M/WBE	
			#	%	#	%	#	%	#	%	#	%	#	%
1989	0	0	0	0	0	0	0	0	0	0	0	0	0	0
1990	1	3	3	100	0	0	0	0	0	0	0	0	0	0
1991	3	10	8	80.00	0	0	2	20.00	0	0	0	0	2	20.00
1992	3	7	5	71.43	0	0	2	28.57	0	0	0	0	2	28.57
1993	1	2	2	100	0	0	0	0	0	0	0	0	0	0
1994	8	25	21	84.00	1	4.00	0	0	3	12.00	0	0	3	12.00
1995	7	26	25	96.15	0	0	0	0	1	3.85	0	0	1	3.85
1996	5	23	22	95.65	0	0	0	0	1	4.35	0	0	1	4.35
1997	0	0	0	0	0	0	0	0	0	0	0	0	0	0
Total	27	96	86	89.58	1	1.04	4	4.17	5	5.21	0	0	9	9.38

Table 4-9 shows the distribution of the proportion of the number of communication, TV and media related services bids by racial, ethnic, or gender category. All the contracts in this NIGP class are competitively bid each fiscal year.

During the fiscal year studied, the City of St. Petersburg solicited sealed bid, written quotes and verbal quotes from vendors in this NIGP class in FY 1993 through FY 1996 only. During this study period, contractors in the City's relevant market area submitted a total of 106 prime contract bids in this NIGP class. Of this total, non-minority firms submitted a large proportion (98.1 percent) of the total number of the prime bids. Meanwhile, all the M/WBE groups combined submitted less than 2 percent of the total number of communication, TV and media related services bids.

When the data was disaggregated by ethnic, racial or gender subgroup per fiscal year, the analysis indicates that non-minority-owned firms consistently submitted a large majority (over 94 percent) of the bids in this NIGP class during each fiscal year analyzed. Meanwhile, the only M/WBE subgroup (black-owned firms) that bid in this NIGP during the period analyzed submitted less than 6 percent of the total number of bids in each fiscal year.

Table 4-9
City of St. Petersburg
Number of Prime contract Bids By Racial, Ethnic, and Gender Groups
Agricultural Equipment, Implements and Accessories (NIGP #27)
FY 89-97

Fiscal Year	Total # of Contracts	Total # of Bids	Non-minority		Women		Black		Hispanic		Other		Total M/WBE	
			#	%	#	%	#	%	#	%	#	%	#	%
1989 to 1992	No data available for these fiscal years.													
1993	5	18	17	94.44	0	0	1	5.56	0	0	0	0	1	5.56
1994	12	27	26	96.30	0	0	1	3.70	0	0	0	0	1	3.70
1995	11	31	31	100	0	0	0	0	0	0	0	0	0	0
1996	10	30	30	100	0	0	0	0	0	0	0	0	0	0
1997	0	0	0	0	0	0	0	0	0	0	0	0	0	0
Total	38	106	104	98.11	0	0	2	1.89	0	0	0	0	1	1.89

Table 4-10 displays the proportion of the number of prime contract bids for sporting and athletic goods. The data indicate that the City solicited competitive bids in this NIGP class during FY 1991, FY 1993 and FY 1996. During this study period, a total of 23 prime contract bids were submitted in this NIGP class. Non-minority firms submitted all the bids in this NIGP class.

Table 4-11 shows the distribution of the proportion of the number of building construction, maintenance and repair services prime contract bids by racial, ethnic, or gender category. All the contracts in this NIGP class are competitively bid each fiscal year. The City of St. Petersburg solicited sealed bid from vendors in this NIGP class during each of the fiscal years studied.

During this study period, contractors in the City's relevant market area submitted a total of 283 prime contract bids in this NIGP class. Of this total, non-minority firms submitted a large proportion (82.3 percent) of the total number of the prime bids. Meanwhile, all the M/WBE groups combined submitted only 17.7 percent of the total number building construction, maintenance and repair services bids. When the data was disaggregated by ethnic, racial or gender subgroup per fiscal year, the analysis indicates that non-minority-owned firms consistently submitted a large majority (over 71 percent) of the bids in this NIGP class during each fiscal year analyzed. Meanwhile, each of the M/WBE subgroups submitted less than 16 percent of the total prime contract bids in this NIGP class per fiscal year analyzed. Each of M/WBE groups submitted bids in this procurement class during the study period. Hispanic-owned firms submitted the largest proportion of the number of M/WBE bids, followed by woman-owned firms, then black-owned firm, and the least were other minority-owned firms. The proportion of the number of bids submitted by black-owned firms steadily declined from 11.1 percent in FY1989 to 4.8 percent in FY 1997. Meanwhile, the trend was opposite for Hispanic-owned firms which exhibited a steady improvement from 0 percent of total number building construction, maintenance and repair services prime contract bids in FY1989 to 13.64 percent in FY 1996, and then decreasing to 4.7 percent in FY 1997. The trend was mixed for woman-owned firms. The other minority-owned firms bid only once during the period studied.

Table 4-10
City of St. Petersburg
Number of Prime contract Bids By Racial, Ethnic, and Gender Groups
Agricultural Equipment, Implements and Accessories (NIGP #30)
FY 89-97

Fiscal Year	Total # of Contracts	Total # of Bids	Non-minority		Women		Black		Hispanic		Other		Total M/WBE	
			#	%	#	%	#	%	#	%	#	%	#	%
1989 to 1990	No data available for these fiscal years.													
1991	2	5	5	100	0	0	0	0	0	0	0	0	0	0
1992	0	0	0	0	0	0	0	0	0	0	0	0	0	0
1993	4	8	8	100	0	0	0	0	0	0	0	0	0	0
1994	0	0	0	0	0	0	0	0	0	0	0	0	0	0
1995	0	0	0	0	0	0	0	0	0	0	0	0	0	0
1996	5	10	10	100	0	0	0	0	0	0	0	0	0	0
1997	0	0	0	0	0	0	0	0	0	0	0	0	0	0
Total	11	23	23	100	0	0	0	0	0	0	0	0	0	0

Table 4-11
City of St. Petersburg
Number of Prime contract Bids By Racial, Ethnic, and Gender Groups
Agricultural Equipment, Implements and Accessories (NIGP #34)
FY 89-97

Fiscal	Total # of Contracts	Total # of Bids	Non-minority		Women		Black		Hispanic		Other		Total M/WBE	
			#	%	#	%	#	%	#	%	#	%	#	%
1989	5	27	23	85.19	1	3.70	3	11.11	0	0	0	0	4	14.81
1990	8	29	25	86.21	1	3.45	1	3.47	1	3.45	1	3.45	4	13.79
1991	2	10	10	100	0	0	0	0	0	0	0	0	0	0
1992	3	13	10	76.92	0	0	1	7.69	2	15.38	0	0	3	23.08
1993	6	31	27	87.10	1	3.23	3	9.68	0	0	0	0	4	12.90
1994	7	29	28	96.55	0	0	0	0	1	3.45	0	0	1	3.45
1995	17	57	41	71.93	9	15.7 9	2	3.51	5	8.77	0	0	16	18.07
1996	16	66	50	75.76	4	6.06	3	4.55	9	13.64	0	0	16	24.34
1997	5	21	19	90.48	0	0	1	4.76	1	4.76	0	0	2	9.52
Total	69	283	233	82.23	16	6.00	14	4.95	19	6.71	1	3.45	50	17.67

Table 4-12 shows the distribution of the proportion of the number of general construction services prime contract bids by racial, ethnic, or gender category. Similar to building construction, maintenance and repair services, all the contracts in this NIGP class are competitively bid each fiscal year. The City of St. Petersburg solicited sealed bid from contractors in this NIGP class during each of the fiscal years studied.

During this study period, contractors in the City's relevant market area submitted a total of 848 prime contract bids in this NIGP class. Of this total, non-minority firms submitted a large proportion (87 percent) of the total number of the prime bids. Meanwhile, all the M/WBE groups combined submitted only 13 percent of the total number of general construction services bids. When the data was disaggregated by ethnic, racial or gender subgroup per fiscal year, the analysis indicates that non-minority-owned firms consistently submitted a large majority (over 69 percent) of the bids in this NIGP class during each fiscal year analyzed. Meanwhile, each of the M/WBE subgroups submitted less than 19 percent of the total general construction services prime contract bids per fiscal year analyzed. Woman, black and Hispanic firms were the only minority-owned firms that submitted bid in this procurement class during the study period. The trend of the proportion of bids submitted by non-minority firms shows a steady decline from FY 1989 to FY 1997. Meanwhile, trend for each of the M/WBE subgroups generally improved during the study period.

Table 4-12
City of St. Petersburg
Number of Prime contract Bids By Racial, Ethnic, and Gender Groups
Agricultural Equipment, Implements and Accessories (NIGP #35)
FY 89-97

Fiscal	Total # of Contracts	Total # of Bids	Non-minority		Women		Black		Hispanic		Other		Total M/WBE	
			#	%	#	%	#	%	#	%	#	%	#	%
1989	10	64	62	96.9	1	1.56	1	1.56	0	0	0	0	2	3.13
1990	27	172	169	98.3	2	1.16	0	0	1	0.58	0	0	3	1.74
1991	17	85	79	92.9	1	1.18	4	4.71	1	1.18	0	0	6	7.06
1992	19	93	88	94.6	0	0	0	0	5	5.38	0	0	5	5.38
1993	19	78	70	89.7	1	1.28	0	0	7	8.97	0	0	8	10.26
1994	16	53	37	69.8	6	11.32	0	0	10	18.87	0	0	16	30.19
1995	21	76	58	76.3	4	5.26	1	1.32	13	17.11	0	0	18	30.19
1996	25	101	78	77.2	8	7.92	2	1.98	13	12.87	0	0	23	22.77
1997	25	126	97	77.0	11	9.00	8	6.35	10	7.94	0	0	29	23.02
Total	179	848	748	87.0	34	4.01	16	1.89	60	7.08	0	0	110	121.97

Dollar Value of Prime Contract Bids

Tables 5-1 to 5-12 present the distribution of the proportion of the dollar amount of prime contract bids for NIGP classes with more than 5 percent of the total dollars of the City of St. Petersburg prime contract purchases during FY 1991 to FY 1996. Table 4.1 shows the proportion of the dollar amount of prime contract bids by racial, ethnic, or gender category for agricultural equipment, implements and accessories. Similar to the number of bids discussed above, the City of St. Petersburg awards these prime contracts competitively through solicitation of sealed bid and verbal quotes from qualified vendors during each of the fiscal years studied.

The data indicate that in this NIGP class, with the exception of FY 1997 where there were no competitive bids, the City's purchases were more than 5 percent during each of the fiscal years analyzed. In particular, during the period analyzed a total dollar amount of $12,079,782 prime contract bid were submitted in this NIGP class. Of this total, non-minority firms submitted a large proportion (99.3 percent) of the dollar value of the bids. Meanwhile, all the M/WBE groups combined submitted only 0.75 percent of the total dollar amount of agricultural equipment, implements and accessories bids. When the data was disaggregated by ethnic, racial or gender subgroup per fiscal year, the analysis indicates that non-minority-owned firms consistently submitted over 98 percent of the bids in this NIGP class. Meanwhile, each of the M/WBE subgroups submitted less than one percent of the total agricultural implements and accessories bids per fiscal year. Women and black firms were the only minority-owned firms that submitted bid in this procurement class during the period analyzed.

Table 5-1
City of St. Petersburg
Dollar Amount of Prime Contract Bids by Racial, Ethnic, and Gender Groups
Agricultural Equipment, Implements and Accessories (NIGP #1)
FY 89-97

Fiscal Year	Total # of Contracts	Total $ of Bids	Non-minority		Women		Black		Hispanic		Other		Total M/WBE	
			$	%	$	%	$	%	$	%	$	%	$	%
89	No data available for these fiscal years.													
90														
91														
92														
93														
94	27	$ 6,600,127	$ 6,563,515	99.45	$0	0	$ 36,612	0.55	$0	0	$0	0	$ 36,612	0.55
95	27	$ 4,761,972	$ 4,707,767	98.86	$34,295	0.72	$ 19,910	0.42	$0	0	$0	0	$ 54,205	1.14
96	3	$ 808,500	$ 808,500	100	$0	0	$ 0	0	$0	0	$0	0	$ 0	0
97	0	$ 0	$ 0	0	$0	0	$ 0	0	$0	0	$0	0	$ 0	0
Total	57	$ 12,170,599	$ 12,079,782	99.25	$34,295	0.28	0.46	0.46	$0	0	$0	0	$ 90,817	0.75

Table 5-2 displays the proportion of the dollar amount of prime contract bids for builders supplies. The data indicate that the City solicited competitive bids in this NIGP class during FY 1993 to FY 1996. During this study period a total dollar value of $13,720,495 prime contract bid were submitted in this NIGP class. Of this total, non-minority firms submitted a large proportion (96.5 percent) of the number of the bids. Meanwhile, all the M/WBE groups combined submitted only 3.6 percent of the total number of builders supplies bids.

When the data was disaggregated by ethnic, racial or gender subgroup per fiscal year, the analysis indicates that owned firms consistently submitted over 89 percent of the bids in this NIGP class. Meanwhile, each of the M/WBE subgroups submitted less than 10.2 percent of the total builder supplies bids per fiscal year. Women and Hispanic firms were the only minority-owned firms that submitted bid in this procurement class during the study period.

Table 5-2
City of St. Petersburg
Dollar Amount of Prime Contract Bids by Racial, Ethnic, and Gender Groups
Agricultural Equipment, Implements and Accessories (NIGP #7)
FY 89-97

Fiscal Year	Total # of Contracts	Total $ of Bids	Non-minority		Women		Black		Hispanic		Other		Total M/WBE	
			$	%	$	%	$	%	$	%	$	%	$	%
89	No data available for these fiscal years.													
90														
91														
92														
93	9	$ 1,679,861	$ 1,508,516	89.09	$ 171,345	10.20	$0	0	$0	0	$0	0	$ 171,345	10.20
94	32	$ 3,632,928	$ 3,537,565	97.38	$ 95,363	2.62	$0	0	$0	0	$0	0	$ 95,363	2.62
95	13	$ 2,212,621	$ 2,212,621	100	$ 0	0.00	$0	0	$0	0	$0	0	$ 0	0
96	31	$ 6,195,085	$ 5,974,411	96.44	$ 216,078	3.49	$0	0	$ 4,596	0.07	$0	0	$ 220,674	3.56
97	0	$ 0	$ 0	0	$ 0	0.00	$0	0	$0	0	$0	0	$ 0	0
Total	85	$ 13,720,495	$ 13,233,113	96.45	$ 482,786	0.3.52	$0	0	$4,596	0.03	$0	0	$ 487,382	3.55

Table 5-3 presents the distribution of the proportion of dollar value of prime contract bids for clothing, apparel, uniforms and accessories. Similar to builders supplies, the data indicate that the City solicited competitive bids in this NIGP class during FY 1993 to FY 1996. During this study period a total dollar value of $1,329,086 prime contract bids were submitted in this NIGP class. Of this total, non-minority firms submitted a large proportion (98.6 percent) of the dollar amount of the bids. Meanwhile, all the non-minority groups combined submitted less than 2 percent of the total dollar value of clothing, apparels, uniforms and accessories bids. When the data was disaggregated by ethnic, racial or gender subgroup per fiscal year, the analysis indicates that non-minority-owned firms consistently submitted a large majority (over 97 percent) of the dollar value of bids in this NIGP class during each fiscal year analyzed. Meanwhile, each of the M/WBE subgroups submitted less than 3 percent of the total clothing, apparels, uniforms and accessories prime contract bids per fiscal year analyzed. Hispanic firms were the only minority-owned firms that submitted bid in this procurement class during the study period.

Table 5-3
City of St. Petersburg
Dollar Amount of Prime Contract Bids by Racial, Ethnic, and Gender Groups
Clothing, Apparels, Uniforms and Accessories (NIGP #8)
FY 89-97

Fiscal Year	Total # of Contracts	Total $ of Bids	Non-minority		Women		Black		Hispanic		Other		Total M/WBE	
			$	%	$	%	$	%	$	%	$	%	$	%
89	No data available for these fiscal years.													
90														
91														
92														
93	1	$ 6,462	$ 6,462	100	$ 0	0	$0	0	$0	0	$0	0	$ 0	0
94	6	$ 475,031	$ 475,031	100	$ 0	0	$0	0	$0	0	$0	0	$ 0	0
95	10	$ 847,593	$ 828,314	97.73	$ 0	0	$0	0	$19,279	2.27	$0	0	$19,279	2.27
96	0	$ 0	$ 0	0	$ 0	0	$0	0	$ 0	0	$0	0	$ 0	0
97	0	$ 0	$ 0	0	$ 0	0	$0	0	$0	0	$0	0	$ 0	0
Total	17	$ 1,329,086	$ 1,309,807	98.55	$ 0	0	$0	0	$19,279	1.45	$0	0	$ 19,279	1.45

Table 5-4 displays the proportion of the dollar value of prime contract bids by racial, ethnic, or gender group for office machines, equipment and accessories. The data indicates that the City of St. Petersburg solicit competitively bid prime contracts in this procurement class during FY 1991 to FY 1997. During this study period, contractors in the City relevant market area submitted a total of dollar amount of $2,835,867 prime contract bids in this NIGP class. Of this total, non-minority firms submitted a large proportion (99.5 percent) of the dollar value of the prime bids. Meanwhile, all the non-minority groups combined submitted less than 1 percent of the total dollar value office machines, equipment and accessories bids. When the data was disaggregated by ethnic, racial or gender subgroup per fiscal year, the analysis indicates that non-minority-owned firms consistently submitted a large majority (over 97 percent) of the dollar amount of bids in this NIGP class during each fiscal year analyzed. Meanwhile, each of the M/WBE subgroups submitted less than 2 percent of the total office machines, equipment and accessories prime contract bids per fiscal year analyzed. Black firms were the only minority-owned firms that submitted bids in this procurement class during the study period.

Table 5-4
City of St. Petersburg
Dollar Amount of Prime Contract Bids by Racial, Ethnic, and Gender Groups
Office Machines, Equipment and Accessories (NIGP #9)
FY 89-97

Fiscal Year	Total # of Contracts	Total $ of Bids	Non-minority		Women		Black		Hispanic		Other		Total M/WBE	
			$	%	$	%	$	%	$	%	$	%	$	%
89	No data available for these fiscal years.													
90														
91	1	$ 71,770	$ 71,770	100	$ 0	0	$0	0	$0	0	$0	0	$0	0
92	1	$ 162,968	$ 162,968	100	$ 0	0	$0	0	$0	0	$0	0	$0	0
93	0	$ 0	$ 0	0.0	$ 0	0	$0	0	$0	0	$0	0	$ 0	0
94	7	$ 655,527	$ 641,425	97.85	$ 0	0	$ 14,102	2.15	$0	0	$0	0	$ 14,102	2.15
95	6	$ 652,367	$ 652,267	100	$ 0	0	$0	0	$0	0	$0	0	$ 0	0
96	10	$ 1,292,867	$ 1,292,867	100	$ 0	0	$0	0	$0	0	$0	0	$ 0	0
97	0	$ 0	$ 0	0	$ 0	0	$0	0	$0	0	$0	0	$ 0	0
Total	25	$ 2,835,499	$ 2,821,397	99.50	$ 0	0	$14,102	0.50	$0	0	$0	0	$ 14,102	0.50

Table 5-5 shows the distribution of the proportion of the dollar amount of equipment maintenance, reconditioning and repair services prime contract bids by racial, ethnic, or gender category. All the contracts in this NIGP class are competitively bid each fiscal year. The City of St. Petersburg solicited sealed bid, written quotes and verbal quotes from vendors in this NIGP class during each of the fiscal years studied. During this study period, contractors in the City relevant market area submitted a total dollar value of $93,582,779 prime contract bids in this NIGP class. Of this total, non-minority firms submitted a large proportion (96.8 percent) of the total dollar amount of the prime bids. Meanwhile, all the M/WBE groups combined submitted less than 4 percent of the total dollar value of equipment maintenance, reconditioning and repair services bids.

When the data was disaggregated by ethnic, racial or gender subgroup per fiscal year, the analysis indicates that non-minority-owned firms consistently submitted a large majority (over 83 percent) of the bids in this NIGP class during each fiscal year analyzed. Meanwhile, each of the M/WBE subgroups submitted less than 17 percent of the total dollar amount of equipment maintenance, reconditioning and repair services prime contract bids per fiscal year analyzed. Woman- and Hispanic-owned firms were the only minority-owned firms that submitted bids in this procurement class during the study period. The trend indicates that the proportion of the dollar value of bids submitted by woman-owned firms steadily declined from 6 percent in FY 1989 to 0 percent in FY 1997. Meanwhile, the trend was opposite for Hispanic-owned firms which exhibited a steady improvement from 0 percent of total dollar value of equipment maintenance, reconditioning and repair services prime contract bids in FY 1989 to 16.7 percent in FY 1997.

Table 5-5
City of St. Petersburg
Dollar Amount of Prime Contract Bids by Racial, Ethnic, and Gender Groups
Equipment Maintenance, Reconditioning and Repair Services (NIGP #10)
FY 89-97

Fiscal Year	Total # of Contracts	Total $ of Bids	Non-minority		Women		Black		Hispanic		Other		Total M/WBE	
			$	%	$	%	$	%	$	%	$	%	$	%
89	3	$481,298	$452,269	93.97	$29,029	6.03	$0	0	$0	0	$0	0	$29,029	6.03
90	5	$10,232,920	$10,015,695	97.88	$0	0	$0	0	$217,225	2.12	$0	0	$217,225	2.12
91	3	$14,343,636	$14,343,636	100	$0	0	$0	0	$0	0	$0	0	$0	0
92	4	$1,862,173	$1,574,872	84.57	$287,301	15.43	$0	0	$0	0	$0	0	$287,301	15.43
93	5	$5,240,948	$5,113,306	98	$0	0	$0	0	$127,642	2	$0	0	$ 127,642	2
94	6	$22,996,248	$22,836,390	99.30	$159,858	0.70	$0	0	$0	0	$0	0	$ 159,858	0.70
95	7	$20,011,666	$18,443,209	92.16	$21,643	0.11	$0	0	$1,546,814	7.73	$0	0	$ 1,568,457	7.84
96	5	$15,005,890	$14,972,290	99.78	$0	0	$0	0	$ 33,600	0.22	$0	0	$ 33,600	0.22
97	1	$3,408,000	$2,840,000	83.33	$0	0	$0	0	$568,000	16.67	$0	0	$ 568,000	16.67
Total	39	$93,582,779	$90,591,667	96.80	$497,831	0.53	$0	0	$42,493,281	2.66	$0	0	$ 2,991,112	3.20

Table 5-6 displays the proportion of the dollar value of controllers, measuring, monitoring and recording supplies prime contract bids by racial, gender, or ethnic category. Similar to equipment maintenance, reconditioning and repair services, contracts in this NIGP class are competitively bid by the City each fiscal year through sealed bids, written quotes or verbal quotes.

During the study period, the City received a total dollar value of $1,875,771 of controllers, measuring, monitoring and recording supplies bids and quotes. Of this total, non-minority firms submitted a large proportion (92.4 percent) of the total dollar amount of the prime bids. Meanwhile, all the M/WBE groups combined submitted less than 7 percent of the total dollar amount of controllers, measuring, monitoring and recording supplies bids.

When the data was disaggregated by ethnic, racial or gender subgroup per fiscal year, the analysis indicates that non-minority-owned firms consistently submitted a large majority (over 81 percent) of the dollar value of bids in this NIGP class during each fiscal year that the City put out for competitive bidding. Meanwhile, each of the M/WBE subgroups submitted less than 14 percent of the total dollar value of controllers, measuring, monitoring and recording supplies prime contract bids per fiscal year analyzed.

Women and Hispanic firms were the only minority-owned firms that submitted bid in this procurement class during the study period. Woman-owned firms submitted bids in this NIGP class in FY1994 and FY 1995, while Hispanic-owned firms submitted bids in this NIGP class from FY1993 to FY 1995 only.

The trend indicates that the proportion of the dollar amount of controller, measuring, monitoring and recording supplies bids for both woman- and Hispanic-owned firms steadily declined during the study period.

Table 5-6
City of St. Petersburg
Dollar Amount of Prime Contract Bids by Racial, Ethnic, and Gender Groups
Controllers, Measuring, Monitoring and Recording Supplies (NIGP #11)
FY 89-97

Fiscal Year	Total # of Contracts	Total $ of Bids	Non-minority		Women		Black		Hispanic		Other		Total M/WBE	
			$	%	$	%	$	%	$	%	$	%	$	%
89	0	$0	$0	0	$0	0	$0	0	$0	0	$0	0	$0	0
90	1	$17,100	$17,100	100	$0	0	$0	0	$0	0	$0	0	$0	0
91	0	$0	$0	0	$0	0	$0	0	$0	0	$0	0	$0	0
92	0	$0	$0	0	$0	0	$0	0	$0	0	$0	0	$0	0
93	5	$334,967	$318,054	94.95	$0	0	$0	0	$16,913	5.05	$0	0	$ 16,913	5.05
94	5	$271,585	$221,852	81.69	$38,434	14.15	$0	0	$11,299	4.16	$0	0	$ 49,733	18.31
95	11	$1,192,419	$1,116,176	93.61	$65,381	5.48	$0	0	$10,862	0.91	$0	0	$ 76,243	6.39
96	1	$59,700	$59,700	100	$0	0	$0	0	$ 0	0	$0	0	$ 0	0
97	0	$0	$0	0	$0	0	$0	0	$0	0	$0	0	$ 0	0
Total	23	$1,875,771	$1,732,882	92.38	$103,815	5.53	$0	0	$39,074	2.08	$0	0	$ 142,889	7.62

Table 5-7 presents the proportion of the dollar amount of prime contract bids for hardware, tools, machinery and related items by racial, ethnic, or gender group. The data indicate that during the six fiscal years studied, the City of St. Petersburg bid prime contract in this NIGP class during FY 1992, FY 1994, FY 1995, and FY 1996 only.

During this period, the City received a total dollar amount of $6,023,494 bids. Non-minority-owned firms submitted the largest proportion (87.1 percent) of the total dollar value of prime contract bids. Meanwhile, all the M/WBE groups combined submitted less than 12 percent of the total dollar value of hardware, tools, machinery and related prime contract bids during the fiscal years analyzed.

When the data was disaggregated by racial, ethnic or gender group, the trend in non-minority firm bid submittal showed a steady increase in the proportion of dollar amount of prime bids submitted from 66.7 percent in FY 1992 to 100 percent in FY 1996. Meanwhile, the trend was opposite for the two M/WBE groups (woman- and black-owned firms) that submitted bids in this NIGP class. In particular, trend for both groups declined during the time frame studied. As discussed earlier in this report, this procurement class includes the NIGP classes with less than 5 percent of the City's total purchases during each fiscal year.

Table 5-7
City of St. Petersburg
Dollar Amount of Prime Contract Bids by Racial, Ethnic, and Gender Groups
Hardware and Related items, Tools, Machinery (NIGP #18)
FY 89-97

Fiscal Year	Total # of Contracts	Total # of Bids	Non-minority		Women		Black		Hispanic		Other		Total M/WBE	
			$	%	$	%	$	%	$	%	$	%	$	%
89	No data available for these fiscal years.													
90														
91														
92	1	$13,707	$9,138	66.67	$4,569	33.33	$0	0	$0	0	$0	0	$4,569	33.33
93	0	$0	$0	0	$0	0	$0	0	$0	0	$0	0	$ 0	0
94	14	$5,681,663	$4,908,222	86.39	$0	0	$773,441	13.61	$0	0	$0	0	$ 773,441	13.61
95	6	$197,924	$197,924	100	$0	0	$0	0	$0	0	$0	0	$ 0	0
96	4	$130,200	$130,200	100	$0	0	$0	0	$ 0	0	$0	0	$ 0	0
97	0	$0	$0	0	$0	0	$0	0	$0	0	$0	0	$ 0	0
Total	25	$6,023,494	$5,245,484	87.08	$4,569	0.08	$773,441	12.84	$0	0	$0	0	$ 778,010	12.92

Table 5-8 displays the proportion of the dollar amount of park, playground, recreational area, and swimming pool prime contract bids by racial, gender, or ethnic category. Similar to equipment maintenance, reconditioning and repair services, the contracts in this NIGP class are competitively bid by the City each fiscal year through sealed bids, written quotes or verbal quotes.

During the study period, the City received a total dollar value of $13,700,795 prime contract bids or quotes in this NIGP class. Of this total, non-minority firms submitted a large proportion (82.6 percent) of the total dollar amount of the prime bids or quotes. Meanwhile, all the M/WBE groups combined submitted only 17.4 percent of the total dollar value of park, playground, recreational area and swimming pool bids.

When the data was disaggregated by ethnic, racial or gender subgroup per fiscal year, the analysis indicates that non-minority-owned firms consistently submitted a majority (over 55 percent) of the dollar value of bids in this NIGP class during each fiscal year that the City put the contract out for bid. Meanwhile, the trend of the proportion of the dollar value for black-owned firms improved from 0 percent in FY1989 to 44.4 percent in FY 1992, and then declined to 0 percent in subsequent fiscal years analyzed. The trend for Hispanic-owned firms was similar to black-owned firms in that it increased from 0 percent in FY 1989 to 26.4 percent in FY 1994, and then steadily declined steadily to 0 percent in FY 1997. Woman-owned firms bid only once (that is, FY 1994) during the period studied, while the other M/WBE group did not submit bids in this NIGP class.

Table 5-8
City of St. Petersburg
Dollar Amount of Prime Contract Bids by Racial, Ethnic, and Gender Groups
For Park, Playground, Recreational Area (NIGP #24)
FY 89-97

Fiscal Year	Total # of Contracts	Total $ of Bids	Non-minority		Women		Black		Hispanic		Other		Total M/WBE	
			$	%	$	%	$	%	$	%	$	%	$	%
89	0	$0	$0	0	$0	0	$0	0	$0	0	$0	0	$0	0
90	1	$282,324	$282,324	100	$0	0	$0	0	$0	0	$0	0	$0	0
91	3	$3,641,771	$3,066,585	84.21	$0	0	$575,186	15.79	$0	0	$0	0	$575,186	15.79
92	3	$738,025	$410,225	55.58	$0	0	$327,800	44.42	$0	0	$0	0	$327,800	44.42
93	1	$953,120	$953,120	100	$0	0	$0	0	$0	0	$0	0	$ 0	0
94	8	$5,219,202	$3,817,062	73.13	$27,002	0.52	$0	0	$1,375,818	26.36	$0	0	$ 1,402,820	26.87
95	6	$2,254,470	$2,204,207	97.77	$0	0	$0	0	$50,263	2.23	$0	0	$ 50,263	2.23
96	5	$611,183	$586,183	95.91	$0	0	$0	0	$ 25,000	4.09	$0	0	$ 25,000	4.09
97	0	$0	$0	0	$0	0	$0	0	$0	0	$0	0	$ 0	0
Total	27	$13,700,795	$11,319,706	82.62	$27,002	0.20	$902,986	6.59	$1,451,081	10.49	$0	0	$ 2,381,069	17.38

Table 5-9 shows the distribution of the proportion of the dollar value of communication, TV and media related services bids by racial, ethnic, or gender category. All the contracts in this NIGP class are competitively bid each fiscal year. During the fiscal years analyzed, the City of St. Petersburg solicited sealed bid, written quotes and verbal quotes from vendors in this NIGP class in FY 1993 through FY 1996 only.

During this study period, contractors in the City relevant market area submitted a total dollar value of $9,407,763 prime contract bids in this NIGP class. Of this total, non-minority firms submitted a large proportion (96 percent) of the total dollar amount of the prime bids. Meanwhile, all the M/WBE groups combined submitted less than 4 percent of the total dollar value of communication, TV and media related services bids.

When the data was disaggregated by ethnic, racial or gender subgroup per fiscal year, the analysis indicates that non-minority-owned firms consistently submitted a large majority (over 90 percent) of the total dollar value of bids in this NIGP class during each fiscal year analyzed. Meanwhile, the only M/WBE subgroup (black-owned firms) that bid in this NIGP during the period analyzed submitted less than 4 percent of the total dollar value of bids in each fiscal year.

Table 5-9
City of St. Petersburg
Dollar Amount of Prime Contract Bids by Racial, Ethnic, and Gender Groups
Communications, TV and Media Related Services (NIGP #27)
FY 89-97

Fiscal Year	Total # of Contracts	Total $ of Bids	Non-minority		Women		Black		Hispanic		Other		Total M/WBE	
			$	%	$	%	$	%	$	%	$	%	$	%
89	No data available for these fiscal years.													
90														
91														
92														
93	5	$1,070,593	$1,060,603	99.1	$0	0	$9,990	0.93	$0	0	$0	0	$9,990	0.93
94	14	$3,830,935	$3,474,654	90.7	$0	0	$356,281	9.30	$0	0	$0	0	$ 356,281	9.30
95	11	$2,305,829	$2,305,829	100	$0	0	$0	0	$0	0	$0	0	$ 0	0
96	9	$2,200,406	$2,200,406	100	$0	0	$0	0	$ 0	0	$0	0	$ 0	0
97	0	$0	$0	0	$0	0	$0	0	$0	0	$0	0	$ 0	0
Total	39	$9,407,763	$9,041,492	96	$0	0	$366,271	3.89	$0	0	$0	0	$ 366,271	3.89

Table 5-10 displays the proportion of the dollar amount of prime contract bids for sporting and athletic goods. The data indicate that the City solicited competitive bids in this NIGP class during FY 1991, FY 1993 and FY 1996 only. During this study period, a total dollar value of $841,870 prime contract bids were submitted in this NIGP class. Non-minority firms submitted all the bids in this NIGP class.

Table 5-11 shows the distribution of the proportion of the dollar amount of building construction, maintenance and repair services prime contract bids by racial, ethnic, or gender category. All the contracts in this NIGP class are competitively bid each fiscal year. The City of St. Petersburg solicited sealed bid from vendors in this NIGP class during each of the fiscal years studied.

During this study period, contractors in the City relevant market area submitted a total dollar value of $60,839,925 prime contract bids in this NIGP class. Of this total, non-minority firms submitted a large proportion (86.4 percent) of the total dollar amount of the prime bids. Meanwhile, all the M/WBE groups combined submitted only 13.6 percent of the total number building construction, maintenance and repair services bids.

When the data was disaggregated by ethnic, racial or gender subgroup per fiscal year, the analysis indicates that non-minority-owned firms consistently submitted a majority (over 73 percent) of the bids in this NIGP class during each fiscal year analyzed. Meanwhile, each of the M/WBE subgroups submitted less than 21 percent of the total prime contract bids in this NIGP class per fiscal year analyzed. Each of M/WBE groups submitted bids in this procurement class during the study period. Hispanic-owned firms submitted the largest proportion of the total dollar amount of M/WBE bids (6.5 percent), followed by woman-owned firms (4 percent), then black-owned firms (3.5 percent), and the least were other minority-owned firms.

Table 5-10
City of St. Petersburg
Dollar Amount of Prime Contract Bids by Racial, Ethnic, and Gender Groups
Sporting and Athletic Goods (NIGP #30)
FY 89-97

Fiscal Year	Total # of Contracts	Total $ of Bids	Non-minority		Women		Black		Hispanic		Other		Total M/WBE	
			$	%	$	%	$	%	$	%	$	%	$	%
89	No data available for these fiscal years.													
90														
91	2	$31,000	$31,000	100	$0	0	$0	0	$0	0	$0	0	$0	0
92	0	$0	$0	0	$0	0	$0	0	$0	0	$0	0	$0	0
93	4	$114,880	$114,880	100	$0	0	$0	0	$0	0	$0	0	$0	0
94	0	$0	$0	0	$0	0	$0	0	$0	0	$0	0	$0	0
95	0	$0	$0	0	$0	0	$0	0	$0	0	$0	0	$0	0
96	5	$695,970	$695,970	100	$0	0	$0	0	$0	0	$0	0	$0	0
97	0	$0	$0	0	$0	0	$0	0	$0	0	$0	0	$0	0
Total	11	$841,850	$841,850	100	$0	0	$0	0	$0	0	$0	0	$0	0

Table 5-11
City of St. Petersburg
Dollar Amount of Prime Contract Bids by Racial, Ethnic, and Gender Groups
Building Construction, Maintenance & Repair Services (NIGP #34)
FY 89-97

Fiscal Year	Total # of Contracts	Total $ of Bids	Non-minority		Women		Black		Hispanic		Other		Total M/WBE	
			$	%	$	%	$	%	$	%	$	%	$	%
89	5	$1,306,736	$1,023,140	78.30	$15,200	1.16	$268,396	20.54	$0	0	$0	0	$283,596	21.70
90	8	$7,881,742	$7,570,967	96.06	$54,925	0.70	$146,000	1.85	$54,925	0.70	$54,925	0.70	$310,775	3.94
91	2	$864,225	$864,225	100	$0	0	$0	0	$0	0	$0	0	$0	0
92	3	$3,005,500	$2,194,765	73.02	$0	0	$357,000	11.88	$453,735	15.10	$0	0	$810,735	26.98
93	6	$4,036,572	$3,924,706	97.23	$26,222	0.65	$85,644	2.12	$0	0	$0	0	$ 111,866	2.77
94	7	$7,369,453	$6,518.513	88.45	$0	0	$0	0	$877,940	11.91	$0	0	$ 877,940	11.91
95	17	$10,642,721	$8,829.981	82.97	$710,007	6.67	$34,490	0.32	$1,068,243	10.04	$0	0	$ 1,812,740	17.03
96	16	$14,057,312	$11,565,501	82.27	$1,391,596	9.90	$452,052	3.22	$ 648,163	4.61	$0	0	$ 2,491,811	17.73
97	5	$11,675,664	$10,088,964	86.41	$0	0	$768,000	6.58	$818,700	7.01	$0	0	$ 1,586,700	13.59
Total	69	$60,839,925	$52,580,762	86.42	$2,197,950	4	$2,111,582	3.47	$3,921,706	6.45	$54.925	0	$ 8,286,163	13.62

The proportion of the dollar value of bids submitted by black-owned firms declined from 20.5 percent in FY 1989 to 6.6 percent in FY 1997. Meanwhile, the trend was opposite for Hispanic-owned firms which exhibited a steady improvement from 0.00 percent of total dollar amount of building construction, maintenance and repair services prime contract bids in FY 1989 to 11.9 percent in FY 1994, and then decreased to 7 percent in FY 1997. The trend was mixed for woman-owned firms. The other minority-owned firms bid only once (FY 1990) during the period studied.

Table 5-12 shows the distribution of the proportion of the dollar amount of general construction services prime contract bids by racial, ethnic, or gender category. Similar to building construction, maintenance and repair services, all the contracts in this NIGP class are competitively bid each fiscal year. The City of St. Petersburg solicited sealed bids from contractors in this NIGP class during each of the fiscal years studied.

During this study period, contractors in the City relevant market area submitted a total dollar value of $654,989,664 prime contract bids in this NIGP class. Of this total, non-minority firms submitted a large proportion (93.7 percent) of the total dollar value of the prime bids. Meanwhile, all the non-minority groups combined submitted only 13.6 percent of the total dollar amount of general construction services bids.

When the data was disaggregated by ethnic, racial or gender subgroup per fiscal year, the analysis indicates that non-minority-owned firms consistently submitted a majority (over 73 percent) of the dollar value of bids in this NIGP class during each fiscal year analyzed. Meanwhile, each of the M/WBE subgroups submitted less than 21 percent of the total dollar value of general construction services prime contract bids per fiscal year analyzed. Woman, black and Hispanic firms were the only minority-owned firms that submitted bid in this procurement class during the study period.

The trend in the proportion of the dollar value of bids submitted by non-minority firms stayed consistent at over 73 percent from FY 1989 to FY 1997. Meanwhile, with the exception of black-owned firms with a mixed trend, the trend in the proportion of the dollar amount of general construction services bids for each of the M/WBE subgroups generally improved during the study period.

Table 5-12
City of St. Petersburg
Dollar Amount of Prime Contract Bids by Racial, Ethnic, and Gender Groups
General Construction Services (NIGP #35)
FY 89-97

Fiscal Year	Total # of Contracts	Total $ of Bids	Non-minority		Women		Black		Hispanic		Other		Total M/WBE	
			$	%	$	%	$	%	$	%	$	%	$	%
89	10	$107,394,205	$101,423,505	99.44	$2,847,212	2.65	$3,123,487	2.91	$0	$0	$0	0	$5,970,699	5.56
90	27	$193,187,777	$191,424,982	99.09	$1,528,035	0.79	$0	0	$	$234,760	$0	0	$1,762,795	0.91
91	17	$52,480,245	$51,617,269	98.36	$34,100	0.06	$577,146	1.10	$0	$251,730	$0	0	$862,976	1.64
92	19	$30,948,146	$30,303,197	97.92	$0	0	$0	0	$0	$644,949	$0	0	$644,949	2.08
93	19	$53,917,161	$52,009,629	96.46	$197,658	0.37	$0	0	$	$1,709,874	$0	0	$1,907,532	3.54
94	16	$22,695,721	$16,654,790	73.38	$3,791,982	16.71	$0	0	$0	$2,248,949	$0	0	$ 6,040,931	26.62
95	21	$42,755,305	$35,892,915	83.95	$1,756,368	4.11	$67,363	0.16	$	$5,038,658	$0	0	$ 6,862,389	16.05
96	25	$84,558,546	$73,307,428	86.69	$6,339,504	7.50	$40,412	0.95	$	$4,871,202	$0	0	$ 11,251,118	13.31
97	25	$67,052,558	$61,292,929	91.41	$2,070,930	3.09	$1,291,487	1.93	$	$2,397,212	$0	0	$5,759,629	8.59
Total	179	$654,989,664	$613,926,644	93.73	$18,565,789	2.83	$5,099,895	0.78	$	$17,397,334	$0	0	$41,063,018	6.27

Prime Contract Utilization Analysis

Tables 6-1 through 6-12 exhibit the City of St. Petersburg prime contract utilization analysis output for NIGP classes with more than 5 percent of the City's purchases from FY 1989 to FY 1997. As discussed in the methodology chapter of this report, utilization is the proportion of contracts awarded by racial, ethnic, and gender group for each distinctive NIGP class. This study measures utilization of firms in each group for each NIGP class by: (1) the number of contracts awarded,[307] and (2) the amount of dollars awarded.

Number of Prime Contract awards

Tables 6-1 through 6-12 present the proportion of the number of prime contract awards by racial, ethnic, and gender categories for each distinctive NIGP class with more than 5 percent of the City's purchases during fiscal years (FY) 1989 – 1997. The tables indicate that 12 distinctive NIGP classes exhibited 5 percent or more of the number of City's competitively bid prime purchases.

Table 6-1 displays the breakdown of the proportion of the number of prime contract awards by racial, ethnic and gender categories for agricultural equipment, implements and accessories. The City of St. Petersburg awarded these prime contracts competitively through solicitation of verbal quotes from qualified vendors during each of the fiscal years studied. The data indicate that in this NIGP class, with the exception of FY1997 where there were no competitive bids, the City's purchases were more than 5 percent during each of the fiscal years analyzed.

---

[307] An interview with the City of St. Petersburg Purchasing Director and staff, and a review of the City's competitive bid and award data, revealed that quite frequently a bid will generate more than one award. Hence, it is not unusual to have more number of awards than number of bids, especially in commodities.

During the study period, a total of 57 prime contract awards were made in this NIGP class. Of this total, non-minority firms received a large proportion (94.7 percent) of the number of the bids. Meanwhile, all the non-minority groups combined received only 5.3 percent of the total number of agricultural equipment, implements and accessories awards.

When the data was disaggregated by ethnic, racial or gender subgroup per fiscal year, non-minority, the analysis indicates that owned firms consistently were awarded over 92 percent of the contracts in this NIGP class. Meanwhile, each of the M/WBE subgroups were awarded less than 6 percent of the total agricultural implements and accessories contracts per fiscal year. Woman and black firms were the only minority-owned firms that were awarded contracts in this procurement class during the study period.

Table 6-1
City of St. Petersburg
Number of Prime Contract Awards by Racial, Ethnic, and Gender Groups
Agricultural Equipment, Implements and Accessories (NIGP #35)
FY 89-97

Fiscal Year	Total # of Contracts	Total # of Awards	Non-minority		Women		Black		Hispanic		Other		Total M/WBE	
			#	%	#	%	#	%	#	%	#	%	#	%
89	No data available for these fiscal years													
90														
91														
92														
93														
94	27	27	26	96.30	0	0	1	3.70	0	0	0	0	1	3.70
95	27	27	25	92.59	1	3.70	1	3.70	0	0	0	0	2	7.41
96	3	3	3	100	0	0	0	0	0	0	0	0	0	0
97	0	0	0	0	0	0	0	0	0	0	0	0	0	0
Total	57	57	54	94.74	1	1.75	2	3.51	0	0	0	0	3	5.26

Table 6-2 displays the proportion of the number of prime contract awards for builders supplies. The data indicate that the City awarded competitively bid contracts in this NIGP class during FY 1993 to FY 1996.

Table 6-2
City of St. Petersburg
Number of Prime Contract Awards by Racial, Ethnic, and Gender Groups
Builders Supplies (NIGP #7)
FY 89-97

Fiscal Year	Total # of Contracts	Total # of Awards	Non-minority		Women		Black		Hispanic		Other		Total M/WBE	
			#	%	#	%	#	%	#	%	#	%	#	%
89	No data available for these fiscal years.													
90														
91														
92														
93	9	9	8	88.89	1	11.11	0	0	0	0	0	0	1	11.11
94	32	32	32	100	0	0	0	0	0	0	0	0	0	0
95	20	20	20	100	0	0	0	0	0	0	0	0	0	0
96	31	31	31	100	0	0	0	0	0	0	0	0	0	0
97	0	0	0	0	0	0	0	0	0	0	0	0	0	0
Total	92	92	91	98.91	1	1.09	0	0	0	0	0	0	1	1.09

During this study period a total of 92 prime contract awards were made by the City in this NIGP class. Of this total, non-minority firms were awarded a large proportion (98.9 percent) of the number of the contracts. Meanwhile, all the non-minority groups combined were awarded only 1 percent of the total number of builders supplies bids.

When the data was disaggregated by ethnic, racial or gender subgroup per fiscal year, the analysis indicates that non-minority-owned firms consistently were awarded over 88 percent of the bids in this NIGP class. Meanwhile, the only

M/WBE subgroup that was awarded a prime contract in this NIGP class was woman-owned firms with a proportion of the total number of awards of 11 percent.

Table 6-3 presents the distribution of the proportion of number of prime contract awards for clothing, apparel, uniforms and accessories. Similar to builders supplies, the data indicate that the City awarded competitively contracts in this NIGP class during FY1993 to FY1996.

Table 6-3
City of St. Petersburg
Number of Prime Contract Awards by Racial, Ethnic, and Gender Groups
Clothing, Apparels, Uniforms and Accessories (NIGP #8)
FY 89-97

Fiscal Year	Total # of Contracts	Total # of Awards	Non-minority		Women		Black		Hispanic		Other		Total M/WBE	
			#	%	#	%	#	%	#	%	#	%	#	%
89	No data available for these fiscal years.													
90														
91														
92														
93	1	1	1	100	0	0	0	0	0	0	0	0	0	0
94	6	6	6	100	0	0	0	0	0	0	0	0	0	0
95	10	10	9	90.00	0	0	0	0	1	10.00	0	0	1	10
96	0	0	0	0	0	0	0	0	0	0	0	0	0	0
97	0	0	0	0	0	0	0	0	0	0	0	0	0	0
Total	17	17	16	94.12	0	0	0	0	1	5.88	0	0	1	5.88

During this study period, a total of 17 prime contract awards were made in this NIGP class. Of this total, non-minority firms were awarded a large proportion (94 percent) of the number of the bids. Meanwhile, all the non-minority groups combined were awarded less than 6 percent of the total number of clothing, apparels, uniforms and accessories contracts.

When the data was disaggregated by ethnic, racial or gender subgroup per fiscal year, non-minority, the analysis indicates that non-minority-owned firms consistently submitted a large majority (over 96 percent) of the bids in this NIGP class during each fiscal year analyzed. Meanwhile, the only M/WBE subgroup that was awarded a contract in this NIGP class was Hispanic-owned firms with 10.00 percent of the number of awards in FY 1995.

Table 6-4 displays the proportion of the number of prime contract awards by racial, ethnic, or gender group for office machines, equipment and accessories. The data indicate that the City of St. Petersburg solicit competitively bid prime contracts in this procurement class during FY1991 to FY1997. During this study period, contractors in the City's relevant market area were awarded a total of 25 prime contracts in this NIGP class. All the contracts were awarded to non-minority firms.

Table 6-4
City of St. Petersburg
Number of Prime Contract Awards by Racial, Ethnic, and Gender Groups
Office Machines, Equipment and Accessories (NIGP #9)
FY 89-97

Fiscal Year	Total # of Contracts	Total # of Awards	Non-minority		Women		Black		Hispanic		Other		Total M/WBE	
			#	%	#	%	#	%	#	%	#	%	#	%
89	No data available for these fiscal years.													
90														
91	1	1	1	100	0	0	0	0	0	0	0	0	0	0
92	1	1	1	100	0	0	0	0	0	0	0	0	0	0
93	0	0	0	0	0	0	0	0	0	0	0	0	0	0
94	7	7	7	100	0	0	0	0	0	0	0	0	0	0
95	6	6	6	100	0	0	0	0	0	0	0	0	0	0
96	10	10	10	100	0	0	0	0	0	0	0	0	0	0
97	0	0	0	0	0	0	0	0	0	0	0	0	0	0
Total	25	25	25	100	0	0	0	0	0	0	0	0	0	0

Table 6-5 shows the distribution of the proportion of the number of equipment maintenance, reconditioning and repair services prime contract awards by racial, ethnic, or gender category. All the contracts in this NIGP class are competitively bid each fiscal year. The City of St. Petersburg solicited sealed bid, written quotes and verbal quotes from vendors in this NIGP class during each of the fiscal years studied.

Table 6-5
City of St. Petersburg
Number of Prime Contract Awards by Racial, Ethnic, and Gender Groups
Equipment Maintenance, Recondition and Repair Services (NIGP #10)
FY 89-97

Fiscal Year	Total # of Contracts	Total # of Awards	Non-minority		Women		Black		Hispanic		Other		Total M/WBE	
			#	%	#	%	#	%	#	%	#	%	#	%
89	3	3	2	66.7	1	33.33	0	0	0	0	0	0	1	33.33
90	5	5	4	80.0	0	0	0	0	1	20.00	0	0	1	20.00
91	3	3	3	100	0	0	0	0	0	0	0	0	0	0
92	4	4	3	75.0	1	25.00	0	0	0	0	0	0	1	25.00
93	5	5	4	80	0	0	0	0	1	20	0	0	0	0
94	6	6	5	83.3	1	16.67	0	0	0	0	0	0	1	16.67
95	7	7	7	100	0	0	0	0	0	0	0	0	0	0
96	5	5	4	80.0	0	0	0	0	1	20.00	0	0	1	20.00
97	1	1	1	100	0	0	0	0	0	0	0	0	0	0
Total	39	39	33	84.62	3	7.69	0	0	3	7.69	0	0	5	12.82

During this study period, contractors in the City's relevant market area were awarded a total of 39 prime contract contracts in this NIGP class. Of this total, non-minority firms received a larger proportion (84.62 percent) of the total number of the prime contract awards. Meanwhile, all the M/WBE groups combined were awarded only 12.82 percent of the total number equipment maintenance, reconditioning and repair services contracts.

When the data was disaggregated by ethnic, racial or gender subgroup per fiscal year, the analysis indicates that non-minority-owned firms consistently were awarded a majority (over 66.00 percent) of the City's contracts in this NIGP class during each fiscal year analyzed. Meanwhile, each of the M/WBE subgroups were awarded less than 33.00 percent of the total equipment maintenance, reconditioning and repair services prime contracts per fiscal year analyzed.

Women and Hispanic firms were the only minority-owned firms that were awarded City contracts in this procurement class during the study period. The proportion of the number of awards made to woman-owned firms-owned firms steadily declined from 33.33 percent in FY1989 to 0.00 percent in FY1997. Meanwhile, the trend was opposite for Hispanic-owned firms which exhibited a steady improvement from 0.00 percent of total number of equipment maintenance, reconditioning and repair services prime contract bids in FY1989 to 20.00 percent in FY1996.

Table 6-6 displays the proportion of the number of controllers, measuring, monitoring and recording supplies prime contract awards by racial, gender, or ethnic category. Similar to equipment maintenance, reconditioning and repair services, the contracts in this NIGP class are competitively bid by the City each fiscal year through sealed bids, written quotes or verbal quotes.

During the study period, the City awarded a total of 23 controllers, measuring, monitoring and recording supplies prime contracts. Of this total, non-minority firms were awarded a large proportion (i.e. 91.30 percent) of the total number of the prime contracts. Meanwhile, all the M/WBE groups combined were awarded less than 8.70 percent of the total controller, measuring, monitoring and recording supplies prime contracts.

Table 6-6
City of St. Petersburg
Number of Prime Contract Awards by Racial, Ethnic, and Gender Groups
Controllers, Measuring, Monitoring and Recording Supplies (NIGP #11)
FY 89-97

Fiscal Year	Total # of Contracts	Total # of Awards	Non-minority		Women		Black		Hispanic		Other		Total M/WBE	
			#	%	#	%	#	%	#	%	#	%	#	%
89	No data available for this fiscal year.													
90	1	1	1	100	0	0	0	0	0	0	0	0	0	0
91	0	0	0	0	0	0	0	0	0	0	0	0	0	0
92	0	0	0	0	0	0	0	0	0	0	0	0	0	0
93	5	5	5	100	0	0	0	0	0	0	0	0	0	0
94	5	5	4	80.00	0	0	0	0	1	20.00	0	0	1	20.00
95	11	11	10	90.91	1	9.09	0	0	0	0	0	0	1	9.09
96	1	1	1	100	0	0	0	0	0	0	0	0	0	0
97	0	0	0	0	0	0	0	0	0	0	0	0	0	0
Total	23	23	21	91.30	1	4.35	0	0	1	4.35	0	0	2	8.70

When the data was disaggregated by ethnic, racial or gender subgroup per fiscal year, the analysis indicates that non-minority-owned firms consistently were awarded a large majority (over 80 percent) of the contracts in this NIGP class during each fiscal year. Meanwhile, each of the M/WBE subgroups were awarded less than 21 percent of the total controllers, measuring, monitoring and recording supplies prime contracts per fiscal year analyzed.

Women and Hispanic firms were the only minority-owned firms that were awarded competitively bid prime contracts in this procurement class during the study period. Woman-owned firms were awarded contract in this NIGP class in FY1995 only, while Hispanic-owned firms were awarded prime contracts in this NIGP class in FY1994 only.

Table 6-7 presents the proportion of the number of competitively bid prime contract awards for hardware, tools, machinery and related items by racial, ethnic, or gender group. The data indicate that during the six fiscal years studied the City of St. Petersburg awarded prime contracts in this NIGP class during FY1992, FY1994, FY1995, and FY1996 only. During this period, the City awarded a total of 59 contracts. Non-minority-owned firms were awarded all the City's hardwarc, tools, machinery and related prime contracts.

Table 6-7
City of St. Petersburg
Number of Prime Contract Awards by Racial, Ethnic, and Gender Groups
Hardware and Related items, Tools, Machinery (NIGP #18)
FY 89-97

Fiscal Year	Total # of Contracts	Total # of Awards	Non-minority		Women		Black		Hispanic		Other		Total M/WBE	
			#	%	#	%	#	%	#	%	#	%	#	%
89	No data available for these fiscal years.													
90														
91														
92	1	1	1	100	0	0	0	0	0	0	0	0	0	0
93	0	0	0	0	0	0	0	0	0	0	0	0	0	0
94	14	14	14	100	0	0	0	0	0	0	0	0	0	0
95	6	6	6	100	0	0	0	0	0	0	0	0	0	0
96	4	4	4	100	0	0	0	0	0	0	0	0	0	0
97	0	0	0	0	0	0	0	0	0	0	0	0	0	0
Total	25	25	25	100	0	0	0	0	0	0	0	0	0	0

Table 6-8 displays the proportion of the number of park, playground, recreational area and swimming pool prime contract awards by racial, gender, or ethnic category. Similar to equipment maintenance, reconditioning and repair services, contracts in this NIGP class are competitively bid by the City each fiscal year through sealed bids, written quotes or verbal quotes.

During the study period, the City awarded a total of 28 contracts in this NIGP class. Of this total, non-minority firms were awarded a large proportion (89.3 percent) of the total number of the prime contracts. Meanwhile, all the M/WBE groups combined were awarded only 10.7 percent of the total number park, playground, recreational area and swimming pool contracts.

When the data was disaggregated by ethnic, racial or gender subgroup per fiscal year, the output indicates that non-minority-owned firms consistently were awarded a majority (over 66 percent) of the contracts in this NIGP class during each fiscal year that the City analyzed. Meanwhile, the black- and Hispanic-owned firms were awarded all the M/WBE share of the contracts in this NIGP class.

Table 6-8
City of St. Petersburg
Number of Prime Contract Awards by Racial, Ethnic, and Gender Groups
Park, Playground, Recreational Area and Swimming Pool (NIGP #24)
FY 89-97

Fiscal Year	Total # of Contracts	Total # of Awards	Non-minority		Women		Black		Hispanic		Other		Total M/WBE	
			#	%	#	%	#	%	#	%	#	%	#	%
89	No data available for this fiscal year.													
90	1	1	1	100	0	0	0	0	0	0	0	0	0	0
91	3	3	2	66.7	0	0	1	33.33	0	0	0	0	1	33.33
92	3	3	2	66.7	0	0	1	33.33	0	0	0	0	1	33.33
93	1	1	1	100	0	0	0	0	0	0	0	0	0	0
94	8	8	7	87.5	0	0	0	0	1	12.50	0	0	1	12.50
95	7	7	7	100	0	0	0	0	0	0	0	0	0	0
96	5	5	5	100	0	0	0	0	0	0	0	0	0	0
97	0	0	0	0	0	0	0	0	0	0	0	0	0	0
Total	28	28	25	89.29	0	0	2	7.14	1	3.57	0	0	3	10.71

Table 6-9 shows the distribution of the proportion of the number of communication, TV and media related services awards by racial, ethnic, or gender category. All the contracts in this NIGP class are competitively bid each fiscal year.

During the fiscal year studied, the City of St. Petersburg solicited sealed bid, written quotes and verbal quotes from vendors in this NIGP class in FY1993 through FY 1996 only. During this study period, contractors in the City's relevant market area were awarded a total of 38 prime contracts in this NIGP class. Non-minority firms were awarded all of the communication, TV and media related services competitively bid prime contracts.

Table 6-9
City of St. Petersburg
Number of Prime Contract Awards by Racial, Ethnic, and Gender Groups
Communications, TV and Media Related Services (NIGP #27)
FY 89-97

Fiscal Year	Total # of Contracts	Total # of Awards	Non-minority		Women		Black		Hispanic		Other		Total M/WBE	
			#	%	#	%	#	%	#	%	#	%	#	%
89	No data available for these fiscal years.													
90														
91														
92														
93	5	5	5	100	0	0	0	0	0	0	0	0	0	0
94	12	12	12	100	0	0	0	0	0	0	0	0	0	0
95	11	11	11	100	0	0	0	0	0	0	0	0	0	0
96	10	10	10	100	0	0	0	0	0	0	0	0	0	0
97	0	0	0	0	0	0	0	0	0	0	0	0	0	0
Total	38	38	38	100	0	0	0	0	0	0	0	0	0	0

Table 6-10 displays the proportion of the number of prime contract awards for sporting and athletic goods. The data indicate that the City solicited competitive bids in this NIGP class during FY1991, FY1993 and FY1996. During this study period, the City of St. Petersburg awarded a total of 11 competitively bid prime contract in this NIGP class. All the awards were made to Non-minority-owned firms.

Table 6-10
City of St. Petersburg
Number of Prime Contract Awards by Racial, Ethnic, and Gender Groups
Sporting and Athletic Goods (NIGP #30)
FY 89-97

Fiscal Year	Total # of Contracts	Total # of Awards	Non-minority		Women		Black		Hispanic		Other		Total M/WBE	
			#	%	#	%	#	%	#	%	#	%	#	%
89	No data available for these fiscal years.													
90														
91	2	2	2	100	0	0	0	0	0	0	0	0	0	0
92	0	0	0	0	0	0	0	0	0	0	0	0	0	0
93	4	4	4	100	0	0	0	0	0	0	0	0	0	0
94	0	0	0	0	0	0	0	0	1	2	0	0	0	0
95	0	0	0	0	0	0	0	0	0	0	0	0	0	0
96	5	5	5	100	0	0	0	0	0	0	0	0	0	0
97	0	0	0	0	0	0	0	0	0	0	0	0	0	0
Total	11	11	11	100	0	0	0	0	0	0	0	0	0	0

Table 6-11 shows the distribution of the proportion of the number of building construction, maintenance and repair services prime contract awards by racial, ethnic, or gender category. All the contracts in this NIGP class are competitively bid each fiscal year. The City of St. Petersburg solicited sealed bid from vendors in this NIGP class during each of the fiscal years studied. .

During this study period, contractors in the City relevant market area were awarded a total of 69 prime contracts in this NIGP class. Of this total, non-minority firms were awarded a larger proportion (79.7 percent) of the total number of the prime contracts. Meanwhile, all the M/WBE groups combined were awarded only 20.3 percent of the total number building construction, maintenance and repair services bids.

Table 6-11
City of St. Petersburg
Number of Prime Contract Awards by Racial, Ethnic, and Gender Groups
Building Construction, Maintenance & Repair Services (NIGP #34)
FY 89-97

Fiscal Year	Total # of Contracts	Total # of Awards	Non-minority		Women		Black		Hispanic		Other		Total M/WBE	
			#	%	#	%	#	%	#	%	#	%	#	%
89	5	5	4	80.00	0	0	1	20.00	0	0	0	0	1	20.00
90	8	8	7	87.50	0	0	1	12.50	0	0	0	0	1	12.50
91	2	2	2	100	0	0	0	0	0	0	0	0	0	0
92	3	3	2	67	0	0	0	0	1	33	0	0	1	33
93	6	6	5	83.33	2	16.67	0	0	0	0	0	0	1	16.67
94	7	7	66	85.71	0	0	0	0	1	14.29	0	0	1	14.29
95	17	17	11	64.71	3	17.65	0	0	3	17.65	0	0	6	35.29
96	16	16	14	87.50	0	0	1	6.25	1	6.25	0	0	2	12.50
97	5	5	4	80.00	0	0	1	209.00	0	0	0	0	1	20.00
Tota6l	69	69	55	79.71	4	5.80	4	5.80	6	8.70	0	0	14	20.29

When the data was disaggregated by ethnic, racial or gender subgroup per fiscal year, the output indicate that non-minority-owned firms consistently were awarded a majority (over 64 percent) of the total contracts in this NIGP class during each fiscal year analyzed. Meanwhile, each of the M/WBE subgroups received less than 34 percent of the total prime contract awards in this NIGP class per fiscal year analyzed. With the exception of the other minority group, each of M/WBE groups were awarded contracts in this procurement class during the study period. Hispanic-owned firms were awarded the largest proportion of the number of M/WBE contracts with 8.7 percent of the total contracts awarded, followed by woman-owned firms and black-owned firms with 5.8 percent each, and the least were other minority-owned firms with no awards.

The trend in the proportion of number of contracts awarded to each M/WBE group generally improved during the time frame studied.

Table 6-12 shows the distribution of the proportion of the number of general construction services prime contract awards by racial, ethnic, or gender category. Similar to building construction, maintenance and repair services, all the contracts in this NIGP class are competitively bid each fiscal year. The City of St. Petersburg solicited sealed bid from contractors in this NIGP class during each of the fiscal years studied. .

Table 6-12
City of St. Petersburg
Number of Prime Contract Awards by Racial, Ethnic, and Gender Groups
General Construction Services (NIGP #35)
FY 89-97

Fiscal Year	Total # of Contracts	Total # of Awards	Non-minority		Women		Black		Hispanic		Other		Total M/WBE	
			#	%	#	%	#	%	#	%	#	%	#	%
89	10	10	10	100	0	0	0	0	0	0	0	0	0	0
90	27	27	26	96.30	1	3.70	0	0	0	0	0	0	1	3.70
91	17	17	17	100	0	0	0	0	0	0	0	0	0	0
92	19	19	18	94.7	0	0	0	0	1	5.26	0	0	1	5.26
93	19	19	17	89.5	0	0	0	0	2	10.53	0	0	2	10.53
94	16	16	13	81.3	0	0	0	0	3	18.75	0	0	3	18.75
95	21	21	14	66.7	2	9.52	1	4.76	4	19.05	0	0	7	33.33
96	25	25	19	76.0	3	12.00	1	4.00	2	8.00	0	0	6	24.00
97	25	25	19	76.0	2	8.00	3	12.00	1	4.00	0	0	6	24.00
Total	179	179	153	85.47	8	4.47	5	2.79	13	7.26	0	0	26	14.53

During this study period, contractors in the City relevant market area were awarded a total of 179 prime contracts in this NIGP class. Of this total, non-minority firms were awarded a larger proportion (85.5 percent) of the total number of the prime bids. Meanwhile, all the M/WBE groups combined were awarded only 14.5 percent of the total number of general construction services contracts.

When the data was disaggregated by ethnic, racial or gender subgroup per fiscal year, the analysis indicates that non-minority-owned firms consistently were awarded a majority (over 66 percent) of the contracts in this NIGP class during each fiscal year analyzed. Meanwhile, each of the M/WBE subgroups received less than 20 percent of the total general construction services prime contract awards per fiscal year analyzed.

Woman, black and Hispanic firms were the only minority-owned firms that were awarded prime contracts in this procurement class during the study period. The trend of the proportion of contract awards to non-minority firms shows a mixed pattern from FY 1989 to FY 1997. Meanwhile, trend for each of the M/WBE subgroups generally improved during the study period.

Dollar Value of Prime Contract Awards

Table 7-1 to 7-12 present the distribution of the proportion of the dollar amount of competitively bid prime contract awards for NIGP classes with more than 5 percent of the total dollars of the City of St. Petersburg prime contract purchases during FY 1991 to FY 1996.

Table 7-1 shows the proportion of the dollar amount of prime contract awards by racial, ethnic, or gender category for agricultural equipment, implements and accessories. Similar to the number of bids discussed above, the City of St. Petersburg awarded these prime contracts competitively through solicitation of sealed bid, written quotes and verbal quotes from qualified vendors during each of the fiscal years studied.

The data indicate that in this NIGP class, with the exception of FY 1997 where there were no competitive bids, the City's purchases were more than 5 percent during each of the fiscal years analyzed. In particular, during the period analyzed a total dollar amount of $5,587,156 prime contracts were awarded in this NIGP class. Of this total, non-minority firms were awarded a large proportion (97 percent) of the dollar value of the contracts. Meanwhile, all the M/WBE groups combined were awarded only 2.95 percent of the total dollar amount of agricultural equipment, implements and accessories prime contracts.

When the data was disaggregated by ethnic, racial or gender subgroup per fiscal year, non-minority, the analysis indicates that non-minority-owned firms consistently were awarded over 98 percent of the prime contracts in this NIGP class. Meanwhile, each of the M/WBE subgroups received less than 1 percent of the total agricultural implements and accessories prime contracts per fiscal year.

Woman and black firms were the only minority-owned firms that were awarded prime contracts in this procurement class during the period analyzed.

Table 7-2 displays the proportion of the dollar amount of competitively bid prime contract awards for builders supplies. The data indicate that the City awarded competitively bid prime contracts in this NIGP class during FY 1993 to FY 1996.

During this study period, a total dollar value of $5,810,443 prime contracts was awarded in this NIGP class. Of this total, non-minority firms received a large proportion (97 percent) of the total number of awards. Meanwhile, all the M/WBE groups combined were awarded only 2.95 percent of the total number of builders supplies contracts.

When the data was disaggregated by ethnic, racial or gender subgroup per fiscal year, the analysis indicates that owned firms consistently were awarded over 87 percent of the bids in this NIGP class. Meanwhile, each of the M/WBE subgroups were awarded less than 12 percent of the total builder supplies bids per fiscal year. Women firms were the only minority-owned firms that were awarded prime contracts in this procurement class during the study period.

Table 7-1
City of St. Petersburg
Dollar Amount of Prime Contract Bids by Racial, Ethnic, and Gender Groups
Agricultural Equipment, Implements and Accessories (NIGP #1)
FY 89-97

Fiscal Year	Total # of Contracts	Total Amount of Awards	Non-minority		Women		Black		Hispanic		Other		Total M/WBE	
			$	%	$	%	$	%	$	%	$	%	$	%
89	No data available for these fiscal years.													
90														
91														
92														
93														
94	27	$1,896,032	$1,898,87	99.68	$0	0	$6,160	0.32	$0	0	$0	0	$6,160	0.32
95	27	$3,470,624	$3,416,419	98.44	$34,295	0.99	$19,910	0.57	$0	0	$0	0	$54,205	1.56
96	3	$220,500	$220,500	100	$0	0	$0	0	$0	0	$0	0	$0	0
97	0	$0	$0	0	$0	0	$0	0	$0	0	$0	0	$0	0
Total	57	$5,587,156	$5,526,791	98.92	$34,295	0.61	$26,060	0.47	$0	0	$0	0	$60,365	1.08

Table 7-2
City of St. Petersburg
Dollar Amount of Prime Contract Bids by Racial, Ethnic, and Gender Groups
Builders Supplies (NIGP #7)
FY 89-97

Fiscal Year	Total # of Contracts	Total Amount of Awards	Non-minority		Women		Black		Hispanic		Other		Total M/WBE	
			$	%	$	%	$	%	$	%	$	%	$	%
89	No data available for these fiscal years.													
90														
91														
92														
93	9	$1,405,199	$1,233,854	87.81	$171,345	12.19	$0	0	$0	0	$0	0	$171,345	12.19
94	32	$1,336,460	$1,336,460	100	$0	0	$0	0	$0	0	$0	0	$0	0
95	20	$413,908	$413,908	100	$0	0	$0	0	$0	0	$0	0	$0	0
96	31	$2,654,876	$2,654,876	100	$0	0	$0	0	$0	0	$0	0	$0	0
97	0	$0	$0	0	$0	0	$0	0	$0	0	$0	0	$0	0
Total	92	$5,810,443	$5,639,098	97.05	$171,345	2.95	$0	0	$0	0	$0	0	$171,345	2.95

Table 7-3 presents the distribution of the proportion of dollar value of prime contracts awarded for clothing, apparel, uniforms and accessories. Similar to builders supplies, the data indicate that the City solicited competitive bids in this NIGP class during FY 1993 to FY 1996.

During this study period, a total dollar value of $432,159 prime contract was awarded in this NIGP class. Of this total, non-minority firms were awarded a large proportion (95.5 percent) of the dollar amount of the contracts. Meanwhile, all the M/WBE groups combined were awarded less than 5 percent of the total dollar value of clothing, apparels, uniforms and accessories contracts.

When the data was disaggregated by ethnic, racial or gender subgroup per fiscal year, the analysis indicates that non-minority-owned firms consistently were awarded a large proportion (over 93 percent) of the dollar value of contracts in this NIGP class during each fiscal year analyzed. Meanwhile, each of the M/WBE subgroups were awarded less than 6 percent of the total clothing, apparels, uniforms and accessories prime contracts per fiscal year analyzed.

Hispanic firms were the only minority-owned firms that were awarded prime contracts in this procurement class during the study period.

Table 7-3
City of St. Petersburg
Dollar Amount of Prime Contract Bids by Racial, Ethnic, and Gender Groups
Clothing, Apparels, Uniforms and Accessories (NIGP #8)
FY 89-97

Fiscal Year	Total # of Contracts	Total Amount of Awards	Non-minority		Women		Black		Hispanic		Other		Total M/WBE	
			$	%	$	%	$	%	$	%	$	%	$	%
89	No data available for these fiscal years.													
90														
91														
92														
93	1	$1,077	$1,077	100	$0	0	$0	0	$0	0	$0	0	$0	0
94	6	$149,066	$149,066	100	$0	0	$0	0	$0	0	$0	0	$0	0
95	10	$282,016	$262,737	93.16	$0	0	$0	0	$19,279	6.84	$0	0	$19,279	6.84
96	0	$0	$0	0	$0	0	$0	0	$0	0	$0	0	$0	0
97	0	$0	$0	0	$0	0	$0	0	$0	0	$0	0	$0	0
Total	17	$432,159	412,880	95.54	$0	0	$0	0	$19,279	4.46	$0	0	$19,279	4.46

Table 7-4 displays the proportion of the dollar value of prime contracts awarded by racial, ethnic, or gender group for office machines, equipment and accessories. The data indicates that the City of St. Petersburg solicit competitively bid prime contracts in this procurement class during FY1991 to FY1997.

During this study period, contractors in the City relevant market area were awarded a total dollar amount of $485,203 prime contracts in this NIGP class. Non-minority-owned firms were awarded all the competitively bid prime contracts in this NIGP class during the time frame analyzed.

Table 7-5 shows the distribution of the proportion of the dollar amount of equipment maintenance, reconditioning and repair services prime contract bids by racial, ethnic, or gender category. All the contracts in this NIGP class are competitively bid each fiscal year. The City of St. Petersburg solicited sealed bid, written quotes and verbal quotes from vendors in this NIGP class during each of the fiscal years studied. .

During this study period, contractors in the City relevant market area were awarded a total dollar value of $19,319,579 prime contracts in this NIGP class. Of this total, non-minority firms received a large proportion (96 percent) of the total dollar amount of the prime contracts. Meanwhile, all the M/WBE groups combined were awarded only 3.91 percent of the total dollar value of equipment maintenance, reconditioning and repair services prime contracts.

When the data was disaggregated by ethnic, racial or gender subgroup per fiscal year, the analysis indicates that, with the exception of FY 1992, non-minority-owned firms consistently were awarded a majority (over 76 percent) of the prime contracts in this NIGP class during each fiscal year analyzed. Meanwhile, except for woman-owned firms in FY 1992 with 52.6 percent of the total dollar value of contract awards, each of the M/WBE subgroups were awarded less than 24 percent

Table 7-4
City of St. Petersburg
Dollar Amount of Prime Contract Bids by Racial, Ethnic, and Gender Groups
Office Machines, Equipment and Accessories (NIGP #9)
FY 89-97

Fiscal Year	Total # of Contracts	Total Amount of Awards	Non-minority		Women		Black		Hispanic		Other		Total M/WBE	
			$	%	$	%	$	%	$	%	$	%	$	%
89	No data available for these fiscal years.													
90														
91	1	$71,770	$71,770	100	$0	0	$0	0	$0	0	$0	0	$0	0
92	1	$6,268	$6,268	100	$0	0	$0	0	$0	0	$0	0	$0	0
93	0	$0	$0	0	$0	0	$0	0	$0	0	$0	0	$0	0
94	7	$105,330	$105,330	100	$0	0	$0	0	$0	0	$0	0	$0	0
95	6	$173,858	$173,858	100	$0	0	$0	0	$0	0	$0	0	$0	0
96	10	$127,977	$127,977	100	$0	0	$0	0	$0	0	$0	0	$0	0
97	0	$0	$0	0	$0	0	$0	0	$0	0	$0	0	$0	0
Total	25	$485,203	$485,203	100	$0	0	$0	0	$0	0	$0	0	$0	2.95

Table 7-5
City of St. Petersburg
Dollar Amount of Prime Contract Bids by Racial, Ethnic, and Gender Groups
Equipment Maintenance, Reconditioning and Repair Services (NIGP #10)
FY 89-97

Fiscal Year	Total # of Contracts	Total Amount of Awards	Non-minority		Women		Black		Hispanic		Other		Total M/WBE	
			$	%	$	%	$	%	$	%	$	%	$	%
89	3	$125,605	$96,576	76.89	$29,029	23.11	$0	0	$0	0	$0	0	$29,029	323.11
90	5	$1,556,737	$1,339,512	86.05	$0	0	$0	0	$217,225	13.95	$0	0	$217,225	13.95
91	3	$1,831,752	$1,831,752	100	$0	0	$0	0	$0	0	$0	0	$0	0
92	4	$546,340	$259,039	47.41	$287,301	52.59	$0	0	$0	0	$0	0	$287,301	53
93	5	$2,243,111	$2,115,469	94	$0	0	$0	0	$127,642	6	$0	0	$127,642	6
94	6	$3,466,514	$3,386,585	97.69	$76,929	2.22	$0	0	$0	0	$0	0	$76,929	2.22
95	7	$6,310,258	$6,310,258	100	$0	0	$0	0	$0	0	$0	0	$0	0
96	5	$3,179,462	$3,162,662	99.47	$0	0	$0	0	$16,800	0.53	$0	0	$16,800	0.53
97	1	$56,800	$56,800	100	$0	0	$0	0	$0	0	$0	0	$0	0
Total	39	$19,316,579	$18,558,653	96.08	$393,259	2.04	$0	0	$361,667	1.87	$0	0	$754,926	3.91

of the total dollar amount of equipment maintenance, reconditioning and repair services prime contract per fiscal year analyzed.

Women and Hispanic firms were the only minority-owned firms that were awarded competitively bid prime contracts in this procurement class during the study period.

The trend indicates that the proportion of the dollar value of awards made to both woman- and Hispanic-owned firms steadily declined.

Table 7-6 displays the proportion of the dollar value of controllers, measuring, monitoring and recording supplies prime contract awards by racial, gender, or ethnic category. Similar to equipment maintenance, reconditioning and repair services, the contracts in this NIGP class are competitively bid by the City each fiscal year through sealed bids, written quotes or verbal quotes.

During the study period, the City awarded a total dollar value of $854,589 controllers, measuring, monitoring and recording supplies competitively bid prime contracts. Of this total, non-minority firms were awarded a large proportion (92.9 percent) of the total dollar amount of the prime contracts. Meanwhile, all the M/WBE groups combined received less than 7 percent of the total dollar amount of controllers, measuring, monitoring and recording supplies contracts.

When the data was disaggregated by ethnic, racial or gender subgroup per fiscal year, the analysis indicates that non-minority-owned firms consistently were awarded a large majority (over 84 percent) of the dollar value of prime contracts in this NIGP class during each fiscal year that the City put the contract out for competitive bidding. Meanwhile, each of the M/WBE subgroups were awarded less than 16 percent of the total dollar value of controllers, measuring, monitoring and recording supplies prime contracts per fiscal year analyzed.

Women and Hispanic firms were the only minority-owned firms that were awarded prime contracts in this procurement class during the study period. Woman-

Table 7-6
City of St. Petersburg
Dollar Amount of Prime Contract Bids by Racial, Ethnic, and Gender Groups
Controllers, Measuring, Monitoring and Recording Supplies (NIGP #11)
FY 89-97

Fiscal Year	Total # of Contracts	Total Amount of Awards	Non-minority		Women		Black		Hispanic		Other		Total M/WBE	
			$	%	$	%	$	%	$	%	$	%	$	%
89	No data available for these fiscal years.													
90	1	$5,700	$5,700	100	$0	0	$0	0	$0	0	$0	0	$0	0
91	0	$0	$0	0	$0	0	$0	0	$0	0	$0	0	$0	0
92	0	$0	$0	0	$0	0	$0	0	$0	0	$0	0	$0	0
93	5	$104,202	$104,202	100	$0	0	$0	0	$0	0	$0	0	$0	0
94	5	$70,926	$59,627	84.07	$0	0	$0	0	$11,299	15.93	$0	0	$11,299	15.93
95	11	$653,861	$604,281	92.42	$92.42	7.58	$0	0	$0	0	$0	0	$49,580	7.58
96	1	$19,900	$19,900	100	100	0	$0	0	$0	0	$0	0	$0	0
97	0	$0	$0	0	0	0	$0	0	$0	0	$0	0	$0	0
Total	23	$854,589	$793,710	92.88	$92.88	5.80	$0	0	$11,299	1.32	$0	0	$60,879	7.12

Table 7-7
City of St. Petersburg
Dollar Amount of Prime Contract Bids by Racial, Ethnic, and Gender Groups
Hardware and Related Items, Tools, Machinery (NIGP #18)
FY 89-97

Fiscal Year	Total # of Contracts	Total Amount of Awards	Non-minority		Women		Black		Hispanic		Other		Total M/WBE	
			$	%	$	%	$	%	$	%	$	%	$	%
89	No data available for these fiscal years.													
90														
91														
92	1	$4,569	$4,569	100	$0	0	$0	0	$0	0	$0	0	0	0
93	0	$0	$0	0	$0	0	$0	0	$0	0	$0	0	0	0
94	14	$2,477,374	$2,477,374	100	$0	0	$0	0	$0	0	$0	0	0	0
95	6	$91,065	$91,065	100	$0	0	$0	0	$0	0	$0	0	0	0
96	4	$43,400	$43,400	100	$0	0	$0	0	$0	0	$0	0	0	0
97	0	$0	$0	0	$0	0	$0	0	$0	0	$0	0	0	0
Total	25	$2,616,408	$2,616,408	100	$0	0	$0	0	$0	0	$0	0	0	0

owned firms received 7.6 percent of the total dollar value of prime contracts in this NIGP class in FY1995, while Hispanic-owned firms received 15.9 percent of the total dollar amount of contracts in this NIGP class from FY1994.

Table 7-7 presents the proportion of the dollar amount of prime contract awards for hardwarc, tools, machinery and related items by racial, ethnic, or gender group. The data indicate that during the six fiscal years studied, the City of St. Petersburg bid prime contract in this NIGP class during FY 1992, FY 1994, FY 1995, and FY 1996 only. During this period, the City awarded a total dollar amount of $4,107,792 competitively bid prime contracts. Non-minority-owned firms were awarded all the competitively bid prime contracts in this NIGP class during the study time frame.

Table 7-8 displays the proportion of the dollar amount of park, playground, recreational area and swimming pool prime contract awards by racial, gender, or ethnic category. Similar to equipment maintenance, reconditioning and repair services, contracts in this NIGP class are competitively bid by the City each fiscal year through sealed bids, written quotes or verbal quotes.

During the study period, the City awarded a total dollar value of $4,107,792 prime contracts in this NIGP class. Of this total, non-minority firms were awarded a major proportion (72.5 percent) of the total dollar amount of the prime contracts. Meanwhile, all the M/WBE groups combined received less than 28 percent of the total dollar value of park, playground, rccreational area and swimming pool contracts.

When the data was disaggregated by ethnic, racial or gender subgroup per fiscal year, the analysis indicates that with the exception of FY 1994 when Hispanic-owned firms received 63.9 percent of the total dollar value of prime contracts, non-minority-owned firms consistently were awarded a majority (over 71 percent) of the dollar value of contracts in this NIGP class during each fiscal year that the City put the contract out for bid. Black-owned firms were the only other M/WBE firms that

Table 7-8
City of St. Petersburg
Dollar Amount of Prime Contract Bids by Racial, Ethnic, and Gender Groups
For Park, Playground, Recreational Area (NIGP #24)
FY 89-97

Fiscal Year	Total # of Contracts	Total Amount of Awards	Non-minority		Women		Black		Hispanic		Other		Total M/WBE	
			$	%	$	%	$	%	$	%	$	%	$	%
89	0	$0	$0	0	$0	0	$0	0	$0	0	$0	0	$0	0
90	1	$94,108	$94,108	100	$0	0	$0	0	$0	0	$0	0	$0	0
91	3	$1,020,245	$725,489	71.11	$0	0	$294,756	28.89	$0	0	$0	0	$294,756	28.89
92	3	$355,275	$355,275	100	$0	0	$0	0	$0	0	$0	0	$0	0
93	1	$476,560	$476,560	100	$0	0	$0	0	$0	0	$0	0	$0	0
94	8	$1,308,272	$471,874	36.07	$0	0	$0	0	$836,398	63.93	$0	0	$836,398	63.93
95	7	$684,832	$684,832	100	$0	0	$0	0	$0	0	$0	0	$0	0
96	5	$168,500	$168,500	100	$0	0	$0	0	$0	0	$0	0	$0	0
97	0	$0	$0	0	$0	0	$0	0	$0	0	$0	0	$0	0
Total	28	$4,107,792	$2,976,638	72.46	$0	0	$294,756	7.18	$836,398	20.36	$0	0	$1,131,154	27.54

Table 7-9
City of St. Petersburg
Dollar Amount of Prime Contract Bids by Racial, Ethnic, and Gender Groups
Communications, TV and Media Related Services (NIGP #27)
FY 89-97

Fiscal Year	Total # of Contracts	Total Amount of Awards	Non-minority		Women		Black		Hispanic		Other		Total M/WBE	
			$	%	$	%	$	%	$	%	$	%	$	%
89	No data available for these fiscal years.													
90														
91														
92														
93	5	$17,677	$17,677	100	$0	0	$0	0	$0	0	$0	0	$0	0
94	12	$648,569	$648,569	100	$0	0	$0	0	$0	0	$0	0	$0	0
95	11	$1,160,231	$1,160,231	100	$0	0	$0	0	$0	0	$0	0	$0	0
96	10	$240,444	$240,444	100	$0	0	$0	0	$0	0	$0	0	$0	0
97	0	$0	$0	0	$0	0	$0	0	$0	0	$0	0	$0	0
Total	38	$2,066,921	$2,066,921	100	$0	0	$0	0	$0	0	$0	0	$0	2.95

were awarded competitively bid prime contracts in this NIGP class with 28.9 percent of the total awards made by the City in FY 1991.

Table 7-9 shows the distribution of the proportion of the dollar value of communication, TV and media related services prime contract awards by racial, ethnic, or gender category. All the contracts in this NIGP class are competitively bid each fiscal year. During the fiscal years analyzed, the City of St. Petersburg solicited sealed bid, written quotes and verbal quotes from vendors in this NIGP class in FY 1993 through FY 1996 only.

During this study period, contractors in the City relevant market area were awarded a total dollar value of $2,066,921 prime contracts in this NIGP class. All the competitively bid prime contracts in this NIGP class were awarded to non-minority-owned firms during the time frame studied.

Table 7-10 displays the proportion of the dollar amount of prime contract awards for sporting and athletic goods. The data indicate that the City awarded competitively bid contracts in this NIGP class during FY 1991, FY 1993 and FY 1996 only. During this study period a total dollar value of $417,825 prime contract bids were awarded in this NIGP class. Non-minority firms were awarded all the contracts in this NIGP class.

Table 7-11 shows the distribution of the proportion of the dollar amount of building construction, maintenance and repair services prime contract awards by racial, ethnic, or gender category. All the contracts in this NIGP class are competitively bid each fiscal year. The City of St. Petersburg solicited sealed bid from vendors in this NIGP class during each of the fiscal years studied.

During this study period, contractors in the City relevant market area were awarded a total dollar value of $13,148,112 prime contracts in this NIGP class. Of this total, non-minority firms received a large proportion (80.6 percent) of the total dollar amount of the prime awards. Meanwhile, all the M/WBE groups combined

Table 7-10
City of St. Petersburg
Dollar Amount of Prime Contract Bids by Racial, Ethnic, and Gender Groups
Sporting and Athletic Goods (NIGP #30)
FY 89-97

Fiscal Year	Total # of Contracts	Total Amount of Awards	Non-minority		Women		Black		Hispanic		Other		Total M/WBE	
			$	%	$	%	$	%	$	%	$	%	$	%
89	No data available for these fiscal years.													
90														
91	2	$12,400	$12,400	100	$0	0	$0	0	$0	0	$0	0	$0	0
92	0	$0	$0	0	$0	0	$0	0	$0	0	$0	0	$0	0
93	4	$57,440	$57,440	100	$0	0	$0	0	$0	0	$0	0	$0	0
94	0	$0	$0	0	$0	0	$0	0	$0	0	$0	0	$0	0
95	0	$0	$0	0	$0	0	$0	0	$0	0	$0	0	$0	0
96	5	$347,985	$347,985	100	$0	0	$0	0	$0	0	$0	0	$0	0
97	0	$0	$0	0	$0	0	$0	0	$0	0	$0	0	$0	0
Total	11	$417,825	$417,825	100	$0	0	$0	0	$0	0	$0	0	$0	0

Table 7-11
City of St. Petersburg
Dollar Amount of Prime Contract Bids by Racial, Ethnic, and Gender Groups
Building Construction, Maintenance & Repair Services (NIGP #34)
FY 89-97

Fiscal Year	Total # of Contracts	Total Amount of Awards	Non-minority		Women		Black		Hispanic		Other		Total M/WBE	
			$	%	$	%	$	%	$	%	$	%	$	%
89	5	$299,996	$253,196	84.40	$0	0	$46,800	15.60	$0	0	$0	0	$46,800	15.60
90	8	$1,995,694	$1,849,694	92.68	$0	0	$146,000	7.32	$0	0	$0	0	$146,000	7.32
91	2	$172,845	$172,845	100	$0	0	$0	0	$0	0	$0	0	$0	0
92	3	$513,514	$416,780	81	$0	0	$0	0	$96,735	0	$0	0	$0	0
93	6	$1,228,310	$1,202,088	97.87	$26,222	2.13	$0	0	$0	0	$0	0	$26,222	2.13
94	7	$1,457,475	$579,535	39.76	$0	0	$0	0	$877,940	60.24	$0	0	$877,940	60,24
95	17	$3,132,653	$2,625,290	83.80	$376,245	12.01	$0	0	$131,118	4.19	$0	0	$507,363	16.20
96	16	$2,524,142	$2,446,694	96.93	$0	0	$65,448	2.59	$12,000	0.48	$0	0	$77,448	3.07
97	5	$1,823,482	$1,055,482	57.88	$0	0	$768,000	42.12	$0	0	$0	0	$768,000	42.12
Total	69	$13,148,112	$10,601,604	80.63	$402,467	3.06	$1,026,248	7.81	$1,117,793	8.50	$0	0	$2,449,773	18.63

were awarded only 18.6 percent of the total number building construction, maintenance and repair services contracts.

When the data was disaggregated by ethnic, racial or gender subgroup per fiscal year, the analysis indicates that, with the exception of FY 1994 when Hispanic-owned firm received 60.3 percent of the total dollar value of contracts, non-minority-owned firms consistently were awarded a majority (over 57 percent) of the dollar value of contracts in this NIGP class during each fiscal year analyzed. Meanwhile, with the exception of Hispanic-owned firms in FY 1994, each of the M/WBE subgroups received less than 43 percent of the City's total dollar value of prime contract awards in this NIGP class per fiscal year analyzed. With the exception of the other M/WBE group, each of M/WBE groups were awarded prime contract in this procurement class during the study period. Hispanic-owned firms were awarded the largest proportion of the total dollar amount of M/WBE contracts (8.5 percent), followed by black-owned firms (7.8 percent), the least were woman-owned firms (3.1 percent).

The trend in the proportion of the dollar value of contracts awarded to black-owned firms declined from 15.6 percent in FY 1989 to 0 percent in FY 1995, and then steadily improved to 42.1 percent in FY 1997. Meanwhile, the trend was opposite for Hispanic-owned firms which exhibited an improvement from 0 percent of total dollar amount of building construction, maintenance and repair services prime contract bids in FY 1989 to 60.3 percent in FY 1994, and then decreased sharply and steadily to 0 percent in FY 1997. The trend was mixed for woman-owned firms.

Table 7-12 shows the distribution of the proportion of the dollar amount of general construction services prime contract bids by racial, ethnic, or gender category. Similar to building construction, maintenance and repair services, all the contracts in this NIGP class are competitively bid each fiscal year. The City of St.

Petersburg solicited sealed bid from contractors in this NIGP class during each of the fiscal years studied.

During this study period, contractors in the City relevant market area were awarded a total dollar value of $130,260,846 prime contracts in this NIGP class. Of this total, non-minority firms were awarded a large proportion (94.2 percent) of the total dollar value of the prime contracts. Meanwhile, all the M/WBE groups combined were awarded only 5.8 percent of the total dollar amount of general construction services prime contracts.

When the data was disaggregated by ethnic, racial or gender subgroup per fiscal year, the analysis indicate that non-minority-owned firms consistently were awarded a majority (over 59 percent) of the dollar value of contracts in this NIGP class during each fiscal year analyzed. Meanwhile, each of the M/WBE subgroups received less than 25 percent of the total dollar value of general construction services prime contract awards per fiscal year analyzed. Woman, black and Hispanic firms were the only minority-owned firms that were awarded contracts in this procurement class during the study period.

With the exception of FY 1995, the trend in the proportion of the dollar value of contract awarded to non-minority firms stayed consistently above 94 percent total awards during each of the fiscal years analyzed. The trend for black-owned firms gradually improved from 0 percent in FY 1989 to 2.9 percent in FY. Meanwhile, the trend for woman- and Hispanic-owned firms improved from FY 1989 to FY 1995, and then declined sharply during FY 1996 and FY 1997.

Table 7-12
City of St. Petersburg
Dollar Amount of Prime Contract Bids by Racial, Ethnic, and Gender Groups
General Construction Services (NIGP #35)
FY 89-97

Fiscal Year	Total # of Contracts	Total Amount of Awards	Non-minority		Women		Black		Hispanic		Other		Total M/WBE	
			$	%	$	%	$	%	$	%	$	%	$	%
89	10	$19,939,382	$19,939,382	100	$0	0	$0	0	$0	0	$0	0	$0	0
90	27	$27,160,569	$25,937,385	95.50	$1,223,184	4.50	$0	0	$0	0	$0	0	$1,223,184	4.50
91	17	$8,067,023	$8,067,023	100	$0	0	$0	0	$0	0	$0	0	$0	0
92	19	$6,232,395	$6,152,839	98.72	$0	0	$0	0	$79,556	1.28	$0	0	$79,556	1.28
93	19	$15,875,289	$15.518,357	97.75	$0	0	$0	0	$356,932	2.25	$0	0	4356,932	2.25
94	16	$7,280,614	$6,844,219	94.01	$0	0	$0	0	$436,395	5.99	$0	0	$436,395	5.99
95	21	$10,266,985	$6.159,551	59.99	$1,569,558	15.29	$67,363	0.66	$2,470,513	24.06	$0	0	$4,107,434	40.01
96	25	$17,687,988	$17,322,971	97.94	$307,617	1.74	$16,988	0.10	$40,412	0.23	$0	0	$365,017	2.06
97	25	$17,750,601	$15,792,268	94.60	$402,560	2.27	$519,921	2.93	$35,852	0.20	$0	0	$958,333	5.40
Total	179	$130,260,846	$122,733,995	94.22	$3,502,919	2.69	$604,272	0.46	$3,419,660	2.63	$0	0	$7,526,851	5.78

Prime Contract Disparity Analysis Results

The results of the City of St. Petersburg's prime contracting t-test analysis are presented in Tables 8-1 through 9-12 for each distinctive NIGP class with more than 5 percent of the City's purchases during the nine (9) fiscal years analyzed.

Number of Prime Contracts Disparity Analysis Results

Tables 8-1 to 9-12 display the t-test results for the number of prime contracts during FY 1989 – FY 1997.

Table 8-1 shows the output of the disparity analysis of the number of agricultural equipment, implements and accessories prime contracts during FY 1994 to FY 1997. The data indicate that during this period, non-minority-owned firms were under-utilized, but the t-test statistic indicates that the observed under-utilization was not significant. Meanwhile, the t-test result for all the M/WBE groups combined shows that M/WBEs in this procurement category were over-utilized, but the observed over-utilization was not statistically significant.

When the data was disaggregated by M/WBE group, the result indicates that woman- and black-owned firms were the only two M/WBE groups that participated in the City's prime contracting within this NIGP class during the time frame analyzed. The t-test results indicate that each of these groups was over-utilized, but the over-utilization was not statistically significant.

Hence, it can be concluded that no statistically significant disparity in awarding contracts to M/WBE firms was observed in the City of St. Petersburg's number of agricultural equipment, implements, and accessories competitively bid prime contracting during the FY 1994 to FY 1996.

Table 8-1
City of St. Petersburg
Disparity Analysis of Number of Prime Contracts by Racial, Ethnic, and Gender Groups
Agricultural Equipment, Implements and Accessories (NIGP #1)
FY 89-97

Fiscal Year	Non-minority			Women			Black			Hispanic			Other			Total M/WBE		
	% Avail	% Util	T-Test *	% Avail	% Util	T-Test *	% Avail	% Util	T-Test *	% Avail	% Util	T-Test *	% Avail	% Util	T-Test *	% Avail	% Util	T-Test *
89	No data available for these fiscal years.																	
90																		
91																		
92																		
93																		
94	98.18	96.3	-0.7	0	0	0	1.82	3.7	+0.114	0	0	0	0	0	0	1.82	3.7	+0.114
95	95.56	92.59	-0.71	2.22	3.7	+0.084	2.22	3.7	+0.084	0	0	0	0	0	0	4.44	7.41	+0.144
96	100	100	0	0	0	0	0	0	0	0	0	0	0	0	0	0	0	0
97	0	0	0	0	0	0	0	0	0	0	0	0	0	0	0	0	0	0
Total	97.3	94.74	-1.15	0.9	1.75	+0.062	1.8	3.51	+0.129	0	0	0	0	0	0	2.7	5.26	+0.223

Table 8-2 shows the output of the disparity analysis of the number of builders supplies prime contracts during FY 1993 to FY 1997. The data indicate that during this period, non-minority-owned firms were over-utilized, but the t-test statistic indicates that the observed over-utilization was not significant. Meanwhile the t-test result for all the M/WBE groups combined shows that M/WBEs in this procurement category were under-utilized, but the observed under-utilization was not statistically significant.

When the data was disaggregated by M/WBE group, the result indicates that woman- and Hispanic-owned firms were the only two M/WBE groups that participated in the City's prime contracting within this NIGP class during the time frame analyzed. The t-test results indicate that each of these groups was under-utilized, but the under-utilization was not statistically significant.

Hence, it can be concluded that no "gross" pattern of disparity in awarding contracts to M/WBE firms was observed in the City of St. Petersburg's number of builders supplies competitively bid prime contracting during the FY 1993 to FY 1996.

Table 8-2
City of St. Petersburg
Disparity Analysis of Number of Prime Contracts by Racial, Ethnic, and Gender Groups
Builders Supplies (NIGP #7)
FY 89-97

Fiscal Year	Non-minority				Women				Black				Hispanic				Other				Total M/WBE			
	% Avail	% Util	T-Test	*	% Avail	% Util	T-Test	*	% Avail	% Util	T-Test	*	% Avail	% Util	T-Test	*	% Avail	% Util	T-Test	*	% Avail	% Util	T-Test	*
89	No data available for these fiscal years.																							
90																								
91																								
92																								
93	92.31	88.89	-0.34		7.69	11.11	+0.121		0	0	0		0	0	0		0	0	0		7.69	11.11	+0.121	
94	98.02	100	+0.791		1.98	0	-0.1		0	0	0		0	0	0		0	0	0		1.98	0	-0.1	
95	100	100	0		0	0	0		0	0	0		0	0	0		0	0	0		0	0	0	
96	96.67	100	+1.015		2.22	0	-0.11		0	0	0		1.11	0	-0.06		0	0	0		3.33	0	-0.15	
97	0	0	0		0	0	0		0	0	0		0	0	0		0	0	0		0	0	0	
Total	97.54	98.91	+0.839		2.05	1.09	-0.06		0	0	0		0.41	0	-0.03		0	0	0		2.46	1.09	-0.07	

Table 8-3 shows the output of the disparity analysis of the number of clothing, apparels, uniforms and accessories prime contracts during FY 1993 to FY 1997. The data indicate that during this period, non-minority-owned firms were under-utilized, but the t-test statistic indicates that the observed under-utilization was not statistically significant. Meanwhile, the t-test result for all the M/WBE groups combined shows that M/WBEs in this procurement category were over-utilized, but the observed over-utilization was not statistically significant. When the data was disaggregated by M/WBE group, the result indicates that Hispanic-owned firms were the only M/WBE group that participated in the City's prime contracting within this NIGP class during the time frame analyzed.

Hence, it can be concluded that no statistically significant pattern of disparity in awarding contracts to M/WBE firms was observed in the City of St. Petersburg's number of clothing, apparels, uniforms and accessories competitively bid prime contracting during the FY 1993 to FY 1997.

Table 8-4 shows the output of the disparity analysis of the number of office machines, equipment and accessories prime contracts during FY 1991 to FY 1997. The data indicate that during this period, non-minority-owned firms were over-utilized, but the t-test statistic indicates that the observed over-utilization was not significant. Meanwhile, the t-test result for all the M/WBE groups combined shows that M/WBEs in this procurement category were under-utilized, but the observed under-utilization was not statistically significant. When the data was disaggregated by M/WBE group, the result indicates that black-owned firms was the only M/WBE group that participated in the City's prime contracting within this NIGP class during the time frame analyzed.

Table 8-3
City of St. Petersburg
Disparity Analysis of Number of Prime Contracts by Racial, Ethnic, and Gender Groups
Clothing, Apparels, Uniforms and Accessories (NIGP #8)
FY 89-97

Fiscal Year	Non-minority				Women				Black				Hispanic				Other				Total M/WBE			
	% Avail	% Util	T-Test	*	% Avail	% Util	T-Test	*	% Avail	% Util	T-Test	*	% Avail	% Util	T-Test	*	% Avail	% Util	T-Test	*	% Avail	% Util	T-Test	*
89	No data available for these fiscal years.																							
90																								
91																								
92																								
93	100	100	0		0	0	0		0	0	0		0	0	0		0	0	0		0	0	0	
94	100	100	0		0	0	0		0	0	0		0	0	0		0	0	0		0	0	0	
95	96.97	90	-1.15		0	0	0		0	0	0		3.3	10	+0.299		0	0	0		3.3	10	+0.299	
96	0	0	0		0	0	0		0	0	0		0	0	0		0	0	0		0	0	0	
97	0	0	0		0	0	0		0	0	0		0	0	0		0	0	0		0	0	0	
Total	98.33	94.12	-1.27		0	0	0		0	0	0		1.67	5.88	+0.261		0	0	0		1.67	5.88	+0.261	

Table 8-4
City of St. Petersburg
Disparity Analysis of Number of Prime Contracts by Racial, Ethnic, and Gender Groups
Office Machines, Equipment and Accessories (NIGP #9)
FY 89-97

Fiscal Year	Non-minority				Women				Black				Hispanic				Other				Total M/WBE			
	% Avail	% Util	T-Test	*	% Avail	% Util	T-Test	*	% Avail	% Util	T-Test	*	% Avail	% Util	T-Test	*	% Avail		T-Test	*		% Util	T-Test	*
89	No data available for these fiscal years.																							
90																								
91	100	100	0		0	0	0		0	0	0		0	0	0		0	0	0		0	0	0	
92	100	100	0		0	0	0		0	0	0		0	0	0		0	0	0		0	0	0	
93	0	0	0		0	0	0		0	0	0		0	0	0		0	0	0		0	0	0	
94	98.25	100	+0.327		0	0	0		1.75	0	-0.09		0	0	0		0	0	0		0	0	0	
95	100	100	0		0	0	0		0	0	0		0	0	0		0	0	0		0	0	0	
96	100	100	0		0	0	0		0	0	0		0	0	0		0	0	0		0	0	0	
97	0	0	0		0	0	0		0	0	0		0	0	0		0	0	0		0	0	0	
Total	99.48	100	+0.354		0	0	0		0.52	0	-0.03		0	0	0		0	0	0		0	0	0	

Hence, it can be concluded that no statistically significant pattern of disparity in awarding contracts to M/WBE firms was observed in the City of St. Petersburg's number of office machines, equipment and accessories competitively bid prime contracting during the FY 1991 to FY 1997.

Table 8-5 shows the output of the disparity analysis of the number of equipment maintenance, reconditioning and repair services prime contracts during FY 1989 to FY 1997. The data indicate that during this period, non-minority-owned firms were significantly under-utilized. Meanwhile, the t-test result for all the M/WBE groups combined shows that M/WBEs in this procurement category were over-utilized, but the observed over-utilization was not statistically significant. When the data was disaggregated by M/WBE group, the result indicates that woman- and Hispanic-owned firms were the only two M/WBE groups that participated in the City's prime contracting within this NIGP class during the time frame analyzed. The t-test results indicate that each of these groups was over-utilized, but the over-utilization was not statistically significant.

Hence, it can be concluded that no "gross" pattern of disparity in awarding contracts to M/WBE firms was observed in the City of St. Petersburg's number of equipment maintenance, reconditioning and repair services competitively bid prime contracting during the FY 1989 to FY 1997. Meanwhile, a statistically significant pattern of disparity of non-minority-owned firms was observed in this NIGP class.

Table 8-5
City of St. Petersburg
Disparity Analysis of Number of Prime Contracts by Racial, Ethnic, and Gender Groups
Equipment Maintenance, Reconditioning and Repair Services (NIGP #10)
FY 89-97

Fiscal Year	Non-minority				Women				Black				Hispanic				Other				Total M/WBE			
	% Avail	% Util	T-Test	*	% Avail	% Util	T-Test	*	% Avail	% Util	T-Test	*	% Avail	% Util	T-Test	*	% Avail	% Util	T-Test	*	% Avail	% Util	T-Test	*
89	90.91	66.7	-0.84		9.09	33.33	+0.805		0	0	0		0	0	0		0	0	0		9.09	33.33	+0.805	
90	96.65	80	-1.33		0	0	0		0	0	0		4.35	20	+0.695		0	0	0		4.35	20	+0.695	
91	100	100	0		0	0	0		0	0	0		0	0	0		0	0	0		0	0	0	
92	93.75	75	-1.1		6.25	25	+0.723		0	0	0		0	0	0		0	0	0		6.25	25	+0.723	
93	95	80	0		0	0	0		0	0	0		5	20	0		0	0	0		5	20	0	
94	94.29	83.3	-0.95		5.71	16.67	+0.438		0	0	0		0	0	0		0	0	0		5.71	16.67	+0.438	
95	88.29	100	+0.866		5.56	0	-0.21		0	0	0		5.56	0	-0.21		0	0	0		11.11	0	-0.33	
96	96.15	80	-1.45		0	0	0		0	0	0		3.85	20	+0.752		0	0	0		3.85	20	+0.752	
97	83.33	100	0		0	0	0		0	0	0		16.67	0	-0.43		0	0	0		16.67	0	-0.43	
Total	94.86	87.18	-2		2.86	7.69	+0.410		0	0	0		2.29	5.13	+0.190		0	0	0		5.14	12.82	+0.696	

Table 8-6 shows the output of the disparity analysis of the number of controller, measuring, monitoring and recording supplies prime contracts during FY 1990 to FY 1997. The data indicate that during this period, non-minority-owned firms were over-utilized, but the t-test statistic indicates that the observed under-utilization was not significant. Meanwhile, the t-test result for all the M/WBE groups combined shows that M/WBEs in this procurement category were also under-utilized, but the observed under-utilization was not statistically significant. When the data was disaggregated by M/WBE group, the result indicates that woman- and Hispanic-owned firms were the only two M/WBE groups that participated in the City's prime contracting within this NIGP class during the time frame analyzed. The t-test results indicate that each of these groups was under-utilized, but the under-utilization was not statistically significant.

Hence, it can be concluded that no statistically significant pattern of disparity in awarding contracts to M/WBE firms was observed in the City of St. Petersburg's number of controller, measuring, monitoring and recording supplies competitively bid prime contracting during the FY 1990 to FY 1997.

Table 8-7 shows the output of the disparity analysis of the number of hardware, tools, machinery and related items prime contracts during FY 1992 to FY 1997. The data indicate that during this period, non-minority-owned firms were over-utilized, but the t-test statistic indicates that the observed over-utilization was not significant. Meanwhile, the t-test result for all the M/WBE groups combined shows that M/WBEs in this procurement category were under-utilized, but the observed under-utilization was not statistically significant. When the data was disaggregated by M/WBE group, the result indicates that woman- and black-owned firms were the only two M/WBE groups that participated in the City's prime contracting within this NIGP class during the time frame analyzed. The t-test results

Table 8-6
City of St. Petersburg
Disparity Analysis of Number of Prime Contracts by Racial, Ethnic, and Gender Groups
Controllers, Measuring, Monitoring and Recording Supplies (NIGP #11)
FY 89-97

Fiscal Year	Non-minority				Women				Black				Hispanic				Other				Total M/WBE			
	% Avail	% Util	T-Test	*	% Avail	% Util	T-Test	*	% Avail	% Util	T-Test	*	% Avail	% Util	T-Test	*	% Avail	% Util	T-Test	*	% Avail	% Util	T-Test	*
89	No data for this fiscal year.																							
90	100	100	0		0	0	0		0	0	0		0	0	0		0	0	0		0	0	0	
91	0	0	0		0	0	0		0	0	0		0	0	0		0	0	0		0	0	0	
92	0	0	0		0	0	0		0	0	0		0	0	0		0	0	0		0	0	0	
93	92.86	100	+0.555		0	0	0		0	0	0		7.14	0	-0.25		0	0	0		7.14	0	-0.25	
94	81.25	80	-0.06		12.5	0	-0.36		0	0	0		6.25	20	+0.530		0	0	0		18.75	20	+0.031	
95	90	90.91	+0.091		6.67	9.09	+0.091		0	0	0		0	0	0		0	0	0		6.67	9.09	+0.091	
96	100	100	0		0	0	0		0	0	0		0	0	0		0	0	0		0	0	0	
97	0	0	0		0	0	0		0	0	0		0	0	0		0	0	0		0	0	0	
Total	89.39	91.3	+0.277		6.06	4.35	-0.07		0	0	0		4.55	4.35	-0.01		0	0	0		10.61	8.7	-0.06	

Table 8-7
City of St. Petersburg
Disparity Analysis of Number of Prime Contracts by Racial, Ethnic, and Gender Groups
Hardware and Related Items, Tools Machinery (NIGP #18)
FY 89-97

Fiscal Year	Non-minority				Women				Black				Hispanic				Other				Total M/WBE			
	% Avail	% Util	T-Test	*	% Avail	% Util	T-Test	*	% Avail	% Util	T-Test	*	% Avail	% Util	T-Test	*	% Avail	% Util	T-Test	*	% Avail	% Util	T-Test	*
89	No data available for these fiscal years.																							
90																								
91																								
92	66.67	100	+0.713		33.33	0	-0.7		0	0	0		0	0	0		0	0	0		33.33	0	-0.7	
93	0	0	0		0	0	0		0	0	0		0	0	0		0	0	0		0	0	0	
94	96.77	100	+0.659		3.23	0	-0.15		3.23	0	-0.16		0	0	0		0	0	0		3.23	0	- 0.15	
95	100	100	0		0	0	0		0	0	0		0	0	0		0	0	0		0	0	0	
96	100	100	0		0	0	0		0	0	0		0	0	0		0	0	0		0	0	0	
97	0	0	0		0	0	0		0	0	0		0	0	0		0	0	0		C	0	0	
Total	96.61	100	+0.918		1.69	0	-0.09		1.69	0	-0.09		0	0	0		0	0	0		3.39	0	- 0.19	

indicate that each of these groups was under-utilized, but the under-utilization was not statistically significant.

Hence, it can be concluded that no "gross" pattern of disparity in awarding contracts to M/WBE firms was observed in the City of St. Petersburg's number hardware, tools, machinery and related items competitively bid prime contracting during the FY 1992 to FY 1997.

Table 8.8 shows the output of the disparity analysis of the number of parks, playground, recreational area and swimming pool prime contracts during FY 1990 to FY 1997. The data indicate that during this period, non-minority-owned firms were under-utilized, but the t-test statistic indicates that the observed under-utilization was not significant. Meanwhile, the t-test result for all the M/WBE groups combined shows that M/WBEs in this procurement category were over-utilized, but the observed over-utilization was not statistically significant. When the data was disaggregated by M/WBE group, the result indicates that woman- Hispanic- and black-owned firms were the only M/WBE groups that participated in the City's prime contracting within this NIGP class during the time frame analyzed. The t-test results indicate that woman- and Hispanic-owned firms were under-utilized, but the under-utilization was not statistically significant. Meanwhile, black-owned firms were over-utilized, but the over-utilized was not statistically significant.

Hence, it can be concluded that no "gross" pattern of disparity in awarding contracts to M/WBE firms was observed in the City of St. Petersburg's number of park, playground, recreational area and swimming pool competitively bid prime contracting during the FY 1990 to FY 1997.

Table 8-8
City of St. Petersburg
Disparity Analysis of Number of Prime Contracts by Racial, Ethnic, and Gender Groups
Park, Playground, Recreational Area and Swimming Pool (NIGP #24)
FY 89-97

Fiscal Year	Non-minority				Women				Black				Hispanic				Other				Total M/WBE			
	% Avail	% Util	T-Test	*	% Avail	% Util	T-Test	*	% Avail	% Util	T-Test	*	% Avail	% Util	T-Test	*	% Avail	% Util	T-Test	*	% Avail	% Util	T-Test	*
89	No data available for this fiscal year.																							
90	100	100	0		0	0	0		0	0	0		0	0	0		0	0	0		0	0	0	
91	80	66.7	-0.33		0	0	0		20	33.3	+0.327		0	0	0		0	0	0		20	33.3	+0.327	
92	71.43	66.7	-0.1		0	0	0		28.57	33.33	+0.104		0	0	0		0	0	0		28.57	33.33	+0.104	
93	100	100	0		0	0	0		0	0	0		0	0	0		0	0	0		0	0	0	
94	84	87.5	+0.234		4	0	-0.17		0	0	0		12	12.5	+0.015		0	0	0		16	12.5	-0.09	
95	96.15	100	+0.490		0	0	0		0	0	0		3.85	0	-0.16		0	0	0		3.85	0	-0.16	
96	95.65	100	+0.427		0	0	0		0	0	0		4.35	0	-0.18		0	0	0		4.35	0	-0.18	
97	0	0	0		0	0	0		0	0	0		0	0	0		0	0	0		0	0	0	
Total	90.63	89.29	-0.23		1.04	0	-0.06		4.17	7.14	+0.149		4.17	3.57	-0.03		0	0	0		9.38	10.71	+0.065	

Table 8-9 shows the output of the disparity analysis of the number of communications, TV and media related services prime contracts during FY 1993 to FY 1997. The data indicate that during this period, non-minority-owned firms were over-utilized, but the t-test statistic indicates that the observed over-utilization was not significant. Meanwhile, the t-test result for all the M/WBE groups combined shows that M/WBEs in this procurement category were under-utilized, but the observed under-utilization was not statistically significant. When the data was disaggregated by M/WBE group, the result indicates that black-owned firms were the only M/WBE group that participated in the City's prime contracting within this NIGP class during the time frame analyzed.

Hence, it can be concluded that no 'gross" pattern of disparity in awarding contracts to M/WBE firms was observed in the City of St. Petersburg's number of communications, TV and media related services competitively bid prime contracting during the FY 1992 to FY 1997.

Table 8-10 shows the output of the disparity analysis of the number of sporting and athletic goods prime contracts during FY 1991 to FY 1997. The data indicate that during this period, all the non-minority-owned firms that bid were utilized. None of the M/WBE groups participated in competitively bid prime contracting in this NIGP class during the fiscal years studied. Hence, it can be concluded that no "gross" pattern of disparity in awarding contracts to M/WBE firms was observed in the City of St. Petersburg's number of sporting and athletic goods competitively bid prime contracting during the FY 1991 to FY 1996.

Table 8-9
City of St. Petersburg
Disparity Analysis of Number of Prime Contracts by Racial, Ethnic, and Gender Groups
Communications, TV and Media Related Service (NIGP #27)
FY 89-97

Fiscal Year	Non-minority				Women				Black				Hispanic				Other				Total M/WBE			
	% Avail	% Util	T-Test	*	% Avail	% Util	T-Test	*	% Avail	% Util	T-Test	*	% Avail	% Util	T-Test	*	% Avail	% Util	T-Test	*	% Avail	% Util	T-Test	*
89	No data available for these fiscal years.																							
90																								
91																								
92																								
93	94.44	100	+0.485		0	0	0		5.56	0	-0.21		0	0	0		0	0	0		5.56	0	-0.21	
94	96.3	100	+0.650		0	0	0		3.7	0	-0.16		0	0	0		0	0	0		3.7	0	-0.16	
95	100	100	0		0	0	0		0	0	0		0	0	0		0	0	0		0	0	0	
96	100	100	0		0	0	0		0	0	0		0	0	0		0	0	0		0	0	0	
97	0	0	0		0	0	0		0	0	0		0	0	0		0	0	0		0	0	0	
Total	98.11	100	+0.844		0	0	0		1.89	0	-0.1		0	0	0		0	0	0		1.89	0	-0.1	

Table 8-10
City of St. Petersburg
Disparity Analysis of Number of Prime Contracts by Racial, Ethnic, and Gender Groups
Sporting and Athletic Goods (NIGP #30)
FY 89-97

Fiscal Year	Non-minority				Women				Black				Hispanic				Other				Total M/WBE			
	% Avail	% Util	T-Test	*	% Avail	% Util	T-Test	*	% Avail	% Util	T-Test	*	% Avail	% Util	T-Test	*	% Avail	% Util	T-Test	*	% Avail	% Util	T-Test	*
89	No data available for these fiscal years.																							
90																								
91	100	100	0		0	0	0		0	0	0		0	0	0		0	0	0		0	0	0	
92	0	0	0		0	0	0		0	0	0		0	0	0		0	0	0		0	0	0	
93	100	100	0		0	0	0		0	0	0		0	0	0		0	0	0		0	0	0	
94	0	0	0		0	0	0		0	0	0		0	0	0		0	0	0		0	0	0	
95	0	0	0		0	0	0		0	0	0		0	0	0		0	0	0		0	0	0	
96	100	100	0		0	0	0		0	0	0		0	0	0		0	0	0		0	0	0	
97	0	0	0		0	0	0		0	0	0		0	0	0		0	0	0		0	0	0	
Total	100	100	0		0	0	0		0	0	0		0	0	0		0	0	0		0	0	0	

Table 8-11 shows the output of the disparity analysis of the number of building construction, maintenance and repair services prime contracts during FY 1989 to FY 1997. The data indicate that during this period, non-minority-owned firms were under-utilized, but the t-test statistic indicates that the observed under-utilization was not significant. Meanwhile, the t-test result for all the M/WBE groups combined shows that M/WBEs in this procurement category were over-utilized, but the observed over-utilization was not statistically significant. When the data was disaggregated by M/WBE group, the result indicates that all the M/WBE groups participated in the City's prime contracting within this NIGP class during the time frame analyzed. The t-test results indicate that Hispanic- and black-owned firms were over-utilized, while woman-owned firms were under-utilized, but the utilization pattern was not statistically significant. The other M/WBE group firms' utilization was at parity compared to their availability.

Hence, it can be concluded that no "gross" pattern of disparity in awarding contracts to M/WBE firms was observed in the City of St. Petersburg's number of building construction, maintenance and repair services competitively bid prime contracting during the FY 1989 to FY 1997.

Table 8-11
City of St. Petersburg
Disparity Analysis of Number of Prime Contracts by Racial, Ethnic, and Gender Groups
Building Construction, Maintenance & Repair Services (NIGP #34)
FY 89-97

Fiscal Year	Non-minority				Women				Black				Hispanic				Other				Total M/WBE			
	% Avail	% Util	T-Test	*	% Avail	% Util	T-Test	*	% Avail	% Util	T-Test	*	% Avail	% Util	T-Test	*	% Avail	% Util	T-Test	*	% Avail	% Util	T-Test	*
89	85.19	80	-0.25		3.7	0	-0.16		11.11	20	+0.272		0	0	0		0	0	0		14.81	20	+0.142	
90	86.21	87.5	+0.092		3.45	0	-0.15		3.45	12.5	+0.439		3.45	0	-0.15		3.45	0	-0.15		13.79	12.5	-0.04	
91	100	100	0		0	0	0		0	0	0		0	0	0		0	0	0		0	0	0	
92	76.92	67	-0.24		0	0	0		7.69	0	-0.26		15.38	33	+0.476		0	0	0		23.07	33	+0.324	
93	87.1	83.33	-0.22		3.23	16.67	+0.668		9.68	0	-0.3		0	0	0		0	0	0		12.9	16.67	+0.109	
94	96.55	85.71	-1.33		0	0	0		0	0	0		3.45	14.29	+0.526		0	0	0		3.45	14.29	+0.526	
95	71.93	64.71	-0.51		15.79	17.65	+0.072		3.51	0	0		8.77	17.65	+0.444		0	0	0		28.07	35.29	+0.359	
96	75.76	87.5	+0.988		6.06	0	-0.22		4.55	6.25	+0.074		13.64	6.25	-0.21		0	0	0		24.24	12.5	-0.27	
97	90.48	80	-0.62		0	0	0		4.76	20	+0.654		4.76	0	-0.19		0	0	0		9.52	20	+0.342	
Total	82.69	81.15	-0.3		6	5.8	-0.01		4.95	5.8	+0.068		6.36	7.25	+0.073		0	0	0		17.31	18.84	+0.140	

Table 8-12 shows the output of the disparity analysis of the number of general construction services prime contracts during FY 1989 to FY 1997. The data indicate that during this period, non-minority-owned firms were under-utilized, but the t-test statistic indicates that the observed under-utilization was not significant. Meanwhile, the t-test result for all the M/WBE groups combined shows that M/WBEs in this procurement category were over-utilized, but the observed over-utilization was not statistically significant.

When the data was disaggregated by M/WBE group, the result indicates that woman- and black- and Hispanic-owned firms were the only three M/WBE groups that participated in the City's prime contracting within this NIGP class during the time frame analyzed. The t-test results indicate that woman- and black-owned firms were over-utilized, while Hispanic-owned firms were under-utilized. However, the pattern of the observed utilization for each of these M/WBE groups was not statistically significant.

Hence, it can be concluded that no "gross" pattern of disparity in awarding contracts to M/WBE firms was observed in the City of St. Petersburg's number of general construction services competitively bid prime contracting during the FY 1989 to FY 1997.

Table 8-12
City of St. Petersburg
Disparity Analysis of Number of Prime Contracts by Racial, Ethnic, and Gender Groups
General Construction Services (NIGP #35)
FY 89-97

Fiscal Year	Non-minority				Women				Black				Hispanic				Other			Total M/WBE				
	% Avail	% Util	T-Test	*	% Avail	% Util	T-Test	*	% Avail	% Util	T-Test	*	% Avail	% Util	T-Test	*	% Avail	% Util	T-Test	*	% Avail	% Util	T-Test	*
89	96.88	100	+0.538		1.56	0	-0.08		1.56	0	-0.08		0	0	0		0	0	0		3.13	0	-0.14	
90	98.26	96.3	-0.75		1.16	3.7	+0.175		0	0	0		0.58	0	-0.04		0	0	0		1.74	3.7	+0.120	
91	92.9	100	+1.106		1.18	0	-0.07		4.71	0	-0.19		1.18	0	-0.07		0	0	0		7.06	0	-0.25	
92	94.6	94.7	+0.018		0	0	0		0	0	0		5.38	5.26	-0		0	0	0		5.38	5.26	-0	
93	89.7	89.5	-0.03		1.28	0	-0.07		0	0	0		8.97	10.53	+0.074		0	0	0		10.26	10.53	+0.012	
94	69.8	81.3	+0.868		11.32	0	-0.33		0	0	0		18.87	18.75	-0.01		0	0	0		10.53	18.75	-0.43	
95	76.3	66.7	-0.81		5.26	9.52	+0.191		1.32	4.76	+0.229		17.11	19.05	+0.089		0	0	0		18.75	33.33	+0.555	
96	77.2	76	-0.12		7.92	12	+0.214		1.98	4	+0.119		12.9	8	-0.15		0	0	0		33.33	24	+0.064	
97	77	76	-0.1		9	8	-0.03		6.35	12	+0..328		7.94	4	-0.14		0	0	0		24	24	+0.052	
Total	88.09	87.15	-0.36		4.01	4.74	+0.098		1.89	2.79	+0.132		6.01	5.03	-0.12		0	0	0		24	12.29	+0.054	

Dollar Amount of Prime Contracts Disparity Analysis Results

The result of the disparity analysis of the dollar value of competitively bid prime contracts is presented in Tables 9-1 through 9-12. The NIGP classes analyzed are: electrical equipment and supplies; hardware and related items; office supplies; water supply and sewage treatment equipment; building construction services; general construction services; miscellaneous professional services; and residual services and supplies.

Table 9-1 shows the output of the disparity analysis of the dollar amount of agricultural equipment, implements and accessories prime contracts during FY 1994 to FY 1997. The data indicate that during this period, non-minority-owned firms were under-utilized, but the t-test statistic indicates that the observed under-utilization was not significant. Meanwhile the t-test result for all the M/WBE groups combined shows that M/WBEs in this procurement category were under-utilized, but the observed under-utilization was not statistically significant. When the data was disaggregated by M/WBE group, the result indicates that woman- and black-owned firms were the only two M/WBE groups that participated in the City's prime contracting within this NIGP class during the time frame analyzed. The t-test results indicate that woman-owned firms were under-utilized, while black-owned firms were over-utilized. However, the utilization pattern for each of these two groups was not statistically significant.

Hence, it can be concluded that no statistically significant pattern of disparity in awarding contracts to M/WBE firms was observed in the City of St. Petersburg's dollar value of agricultural equipment, implements and accessories competitively bid prime contracting during the FY 1994 to FY 1996.

Table 9-1
City of St. Petersburg
Disparity Analysis of $ Amount of Prime Contracts by Racial, Ethnic, and Gender Groups
Agricultural Equipment, Implements and Accessories (NIGP #1)
FY 89-97

Fiscal Year	Non-minority				Women				Black				Hispanic				Other				Total M/WBE			
	% Avail	% Util	T-Test	*	% Avail	% Util	T-Test	*	% Avail	% Util	T-Test	*	% Avail	% Util	T-Test	*	% Avail	% Util	T-Test	*	% Avail	% Util	T-Test	*
89	No data available for these fiscal years.																							
90																								
91																								
92																								
93																								
94	99.45	99.68	+0.155		0	0	0		0.55	0.32	-0.02		0	0	0		0	0	0		0.55	0.32	-0.02	
95	98.86	98.44	-0.19		0.72	0.99	+0.021		0.42	0.57	+0.013		0	0	0		0	0	0		1.14	1.56	+0.040	
96	100	100	+0.000		0	0	0		0	0	0		0	0	0		0	0	0		0	0	0	
97	0	0	0		0	0	0		0	0	0		0	0	0		0	0	0		0	0	0	
Total	99.25	98.92	-0.28		3.25	0.61	-0.13		0.46	0.47	+0.001		0	0	0		0	0	0		3.55	1.08	-0.19	

Table 9-2 shows the output of the disparity analysis of the dollar value of builders supplies prime contracts during FY 1993 to FY 1997. The data indicate that during this period, non-minority-owned firms were over-utilized, but the t-test statistic indicates that the observed under-utilization was not significant. Meanwhile, the t-test result for all the M/WBE groups combined shows that M/WBEs in this procurement category were under-utilized, but the observed under-utilization was not statistically significant. When the data was disaggregated by M/WBE group, the result indicates that woman- and Hispanic-owned firms were the only two M/WBE groups that participated in the City's prime contracting within this NIGP class during the time frame analyzed. The t-test results indicate that each of these groups was under-utilized, but the under-utilization was not statistically significant.

Hence, it can be concluded that no "gross" pattern of disparity in awarding contracts to M/WBE firms was observed in the City of St. Petersburg's dollar value of builder supplies competitively bid prime contracting during the FY 1993 to FY 1996.

Table 9-3 shows the output of the disparity analysis of the dollar amount of clothing, apparels, uniforms and accessories prime contracts during FY 1993 to FY 1997. The data indicate that during this period, non-minority-owned firms were under-utilized, but the t-test statistic indicates that the observed under-utilization was not significant. Meanwhile, the t-test result for all the M/WBE groups combined shows that M/WBEs in this procurement category were over-utilized, but the observed over-utilization was not statistically significant. When the data was disaggregated by M/WBE group, the result indicates that Hispanic-owned firms were the only M/WBE group that participated in the City's prime contracting within this NIGP class during the time frame analyzed.

Table 9-2
City of St. Petersburg
Disparity Analysis of $ Amount of Prime Contracts by Racial, Ethnic, and Gender Groups
Builders Supplies (NIGP #7)
FY 89-97

Fiscal Year	Non-minority				Women				Black				Hispanic				Other				Total M/WBE			
	% Avail	% Util	T-Test	*	% Avail	% Util	T-Test	*	% Avail	% Util	T-Test	*	% Avail	% Util	T-Test	*	% Avail	% Util	T-Test	*	% Avail	% Util	T-Test	*
89	No data available for these fiscal years.																							
90																								
91																								
92																								
93	89.8	87.81	-0.17		10.2	12.19	+0.063		0	0	0		0	0	0		0	0	0		10.2	12.19	+0.063	
94	97.38	100	+0.913		2.62	0	-0.12		0	0	0		0	0	0		0	0	0		0	0	0	
95	100	100	+0.000		0	0	0		0	0	0		0	0	0		0	0	0		0	0	0	
96	96.44	100	+1.052		3.49	0	-0.15		0	0	0		0.07	0	0		0	0	0		3.49	0	-0.15	
97	0	0	0		0	0	0		0	0	0		0	0	0		0	0	0		0	0	0	
Total	96.45	97.05	+0.308		3.52	2.95	-0.03		0	0	0		0.03	0	0		0	0	0		3.55	2.95	-0.03	

Table 9-3
City of St. Petersburg
Disparity Analysis of $ Amount of Prime Contracts by Racial, Ethnic, and Gender Groups
Clothing, Apparels, Uniforms and Accessories (NIGP #8)
FY 89-97

Fiscal Year	Non-minority				Women				Black				Hispanic				Other				Total M/WBE			
	% Avail	% Util	T-Test	*	% Avail	% Util	T-Test	*	% Avail	% Util	T-Test	*	% Avail	% Util	T-Test	*	% Avail	% Util	T-Test	*	% Avail	% Util	T-Test	*
89	No data available for these fiscal years.																							
90																								
91																								
92																								
93	100	100	+0.000		0	0	0		0	0	0		0	0	0		0	0	0		0	0	0	
94	100	100	+0.000		0	0	0		0	0	0		0	0	0		0	0	0		0	0	0	
95	97.73	93.16	-0.87		0	0	0		0	0	0		2.27	6.84	+0.257		0	0	0		2.27	6.84	+0.257	
96	0	0	0		0	0	0		0	0	0		0	0	0		0	0	0		0	0	0	
97	0	0	0		0	0	0		0	0	0		0	0	0		0	0	0		0	0	0	
Total	98.55	95.54	-0.98		0	0	0		0	0	0		1.45	4.46	+0.195		0	0	0		1.45	4.46	+0.195	

Hence, it can be concluded that no "gross" pattern of disparity in awarding contracts to M/WBE firms was observed in the City of St. Petersburg's dollar amount of clothing, apparels, uniforms and accessories competitively bid prime contracting during the FY 1993 to FY 1997.

Table 9-4 shows the output of the disparity analysis of the dollar value of office machines, equipment and accessories prime contracts during FY 1991 to FY 1997. The data indicate that during this period, non-minority-owned firms were over-utilized, but the t-test statistic indicates that the observed over-utilization was not significant. Meanwhile the t-test result for all the M/WBE groups combined shows that M/WBEs in this procurement category were under-utilized, but the observed under-utilization was not statistically significant. When the data was disaggregated by M/WBE group, the result indicates that black-owned firms was the only M/WBE group that participated in the City's prime contracting within this NIGP class during the time frame analyzed.

Hence, it can be concluded that no "gross" pattern of disparity in awarding contracts to M/WBE firms was observed in the City of St. Petersburg's dollar value of office machines, equipment and accessories competitively bid prime contracting during the FY 1991 to FY 1997.

Table 9-4
City of St. Petersburg
Disparity Analysis of $ Amount of Prime Contracts by Racial, Ethnic, and Gender Groups
Office Machines, Equipment and Accessories (NIGP #9)
FY 89-97

Fiscal Year	Non-minority				Women				Black				Hispanic				Other				Total M/WBE			
	% Avail	% Util	T-Test	*	% Avail	% Util	T-Test	*	% Avail	% Util	T-Test	*	% Avail	% Util	T-Test	*	% Avail	% Util	T-Test	*	% Avail	% Util	T-Test	*
89	No data available for these fiscal years.																							
90																								
91	100	100	+0.000		0	0	0		0	0	0		0	0	0		0	0	0		0	0	0	
92	100	100	+0.000		0	0	0		0	0	0		0	0	0		0	0	0		0	0	0	
93	0	0	0		0	0	0		0	0	0		0	0	0		0	0	0		0	0	0	
94	97.85	100	+0.363		0	0	0		2.15	0	-0.11		0	0	0		0	0	0		0	0	0	
95	100	100	+0.000		0	0	0		0	0	0		0	0	0		0	0	0		0	0	0	
96	100	100	+0.000		0	0	0		0	0	0		0	0	0		0	0	0		0	0	0	
97	0	0	0		0	0	0		0	0	0		0	0	0		0	0	0		0	0	0	
Total	99.5	100	+0.347		0	0	0		0.5	0	-0.03		0	0	0		0	0	0		0.5	0	-0.03	

Table 9-5 shows the output of the disparity analysis of the dollar value of equipment maintenance, reconditioning and repair services prime contracts during FY 1989 to FY 1997. The data indicate that during this period, non-minority-owned firms were over-utilized, but the over-utilization was not statistically significant. Meanwhile, the t-test result for all the M/WBE groups combined shows that M/WBEs in this procurement category were under-utilized, but the observed under-utilization was not statistically significant. When the data was disaggregated by M/WBE group, the result indicates that woman- and Hispanic-owned firms were the only two M/WBE groups that participated in the City's prime contracting within this NIGP class during the time frame analyzed. The t-test results indicate that woman-owned firms were over-utilized, while Hispanic-owned firms were under-utilized. However, the pattern of utilization for each of these two groups was not statistically significant.

Hence, it can be concluded that no "gross" pattern of disparity in awarding contracts to M/WBE firms was observed in the City of St. Petersburg's dollar amount of equipment maintenance, reconditioning and repair services competitively bid prime contracting during the FY 1989 to FY 1997.

Table 9-6 shows the output of the disparity analysis of the dollar amount of controller, measuring, monitoring and recording supplies prime contracts during FY 1990 to FY 1997. The data indicate that during this period, non-minority-owned firms were over-utilized, but the t-test statistic indicates that the observed under-utilization was not significant. Meanwhile the t-test result for all the M/WBE groups combined shows that M/WBEs in this procurement category were also under-utilized, but the observed under-utilization was not statistically significant. When the data was disaggregated by M/WBE group, the result indicates that woman- and Hispanic-owned firms were the only two M/WBE groups that participated in the City's prime contracting within this NIGP class during the time frame analyzed. The t-test results

Table 9-5
City of St. Petersburg
Disparity Analysis of $ Amount of Prime Contracts by Racial, Ethnic, and Gender Groups
Equipment Maintenance, Reconditioning and Repair Services (NIGP #10)
FY 89-97

Fiscal Year	Non-minority				Women				Black				Hispanic				Other				Total M/WBE			
	% Avail	% Util	T-Test	*	% Avail	% Util	T-Test	*	% Avail	% Util	T-Test	*	% Avail	% Util	T-Test	*	% Avail	% Util	T-Test	*	% Avail	% Util	T-Test	*
89	93.97	76.89	-0.72		6.03	23.11	+0.668		0	0	0		0	0	0		0	0	0		6.03	23.11	+0.668	
90	97.88	86.05	-1.42		0	0	0		0	0	0		2.12	13.95	+0.680		0	0	0		2.12	13.95	+0.680	
91	100	100	0		0	0	0		0	0	0		0	0	0		0	0	0		0	0	0	
92	84.57	47.41	-1.45		15.43	0	-0.42		0	0	0		0	0	0		0	0	0		15.43	0	-0.42	
93	100	100	0		0	0	0		0	0	0		0	0	0		0	0	0		0	0	0	
94	99.3	97.69	-0.39		0.7	2.22	+0.118		0	0	0		0	0	0		0	0	0		0.7	2.22	+0.118	
95	92.16	100	+0.714		0.11	0	-0.01		0	0	0		7.73	0	-0.26		0	0	0		7.84	0	-0.26	
96	99.78	99.47	-0.11		0	0	0		0	0	0		0.22	0.53	+0.028		0	0	0		0.22	0.53	+0.028	
97	83.33	100	+0.459		0	0	0		0	0	0		16.67	0	-0.43		0	0	0		16.67	0	-0.43	
Total	96.94	98.22	+0.427		0.53	0.55	+0.002		0	0	0		2.53	1.21	-0.08		0	0	0		3.06	1.76	-0.11	

Table 9-6
City of St. Petersburg
Disparity Analysis of $ Amount of Prime Contracts by Racial, Ethnic, and Gender Groups
Controllers, Measuring, Monitoring and Recording Supplies(NIGP #11)
FY 89-97

Fiscal Year	Non-minority				Women				Black				Hispanic				Other				Total M/WBE			
	% Avail	% Util	T-Test	*	% Avail	% Util	T-Test	*	% Avail	% Util	T-Test	*	% Avail	% Util	T-Test	*	% Avail	% Util	T-Test	*	% Avail	% Util	T-Test	*
89	No data available for this fiscal year.																							
90	100	100	0		0	0	0		0	0	0		0	0	0		0	0	0		0	0	0	
91	0	0	0		0	0	0		0	0	0		0	0	0		0	0	0		0	0	0	
92	0	0	0		0	0	0		0	0	0		0	0	0		0	0	0		0	0	0	
93	94.95	100	+0.461		0	0	0		0	0	0		5.05	0	-0.2		0	0	0		5.05	0	-0.2	
94	81.69	84.07	+0.107		14.15	0	-0.38		0	0	0		4.16	15.93	+0.532		0	0	0		18.31	15.93	-0.06	
95	93.61	92.42	-0.15		5.48	7.58	+0.085		0	0	0		0.91	0	-0.05		0	0	0		6.39	7.58	+0.045	
96	100	100	0		0	0	0		0	0	0		0	0	0		0	0	0		0	0	0	
97	0	0	0		0	0	0		0	0	0		0	0	0		0	0	0		0	0	0	
Total	92.38	92.88	+0.084		5.53	5.8	+0.011		0	0	0		2.08	1.32	-0.04		0	0	0		7.62	7.12	-0.02	

indicate that woman-owned firms were over-utilized, while Hispanic-owned firms were under-utilized. However, the observed utilization pattern for each of these M/WBE groups was not statistically significant.

Hence, it can be concluded that no "gross" pattern of disparity in awarding contracts to M/WBE firms was observed in the City of St. Petersburg's dollar amount of controller, measuring, monitoring and recording supplies competitively bid prime contracting during the FY 1990 to FY 1997.

Table 9-7 shows the output of the disparity analysis of the dollar value of hardware, tools, machinery and related items prime contracts during FY 1992 to FY 1997. The data indicate that during this period, non-minority-owned firms were significantly over-utilized. Meanwhile, the t-test result for all the M/WBE groups combined shows that M/WBEs in this procurement category were under-utilized, but the observed under-utilization was not statistically significant. When the data was disaggregated by M/WBE group, the result indicates that woman- and black-owned firms were the only two M/WBE groups that participated in the City's prime contracting within this NIGP class during the time frame analyzed. The t-test results indicate that each of these groups was under-utilized, but the under-utilization was not statistically significant.

Hence, it can be concluded that no "gross" pattern of disparity in awarding contracts to M/WBE firms was observed in the City of St. Petersburg's dollar value of hardware, tools, machinery and related items competitively bid prime contracting during the FY 1992 to FY 1997.

Table 9-7
City of St. Petersburg
Disparity Analysis of $ Amount of Prime Contracts by Racial, Ethnic, and Gender Groups
Hardware and Related Items, Tool Machinery (NIGP #18)
FY 89-97

Fiscal Year	Non-minority				Women				Black				Hispanic				Other				Total M/WBE			
	% Avail	% Util	T-Test	*	% Avail	% Util	T-Test	*	% Avail	% Util	T-Test	*	% Avail	% Util	T-Test	*	% Avail	% Util	T-Test	*	% Avail	% Util	T-Test	*
89	No data for these fiscal years.																							
90																								
91																								
92	66.67	100	+0.713		33.33	0	-0.7		0	0	0		0	0	0		0	0	0		33.33	0	-0.7	
93	0	0	0		0	0	0		0	0	0		0	0	0		0	0	0		0	0	0	
94	86.39	100	+1.431		0	0	0		13.61	0	-0.37		0	0	0		0	0	0		13.61	0	-0.37	
95	100	100	+0.000		0	0	0		0	0	0		0	0	0		0	0	0		0	0	0	
96	100	100	+0.000		0	0	0		0	0	0		0	0	0		0	0	0		0	0	0	
97	0	0	0		0	0	0		0	0	0		0	0	0		0	0	0		0	0	0	
Total	87.08	100	+1.887		0.08	0	-0.01		12.84	0	-0.36		0	0	0		0	0	0		12.92	0	-0.36	

Table 9-8 shows the output of the disparity analysis of the dollar amount of parks, playground, recreational area and swimming pool prime contracts during FY 1990 to FY 1997. The data indicate that during this period, non-minority-owned firms were under-utilized, but the t-test statistic indicates that the observed under-utilization was not significant. Meanwhile, the t-test result for all the M/WBE groups combined shows that M/WBEs in this procurement category were over-utilized, but the observed over-utilization was not statistically significant. When the data was disaggregated by M/WBE group, the result indicates that woman-, Hispanic- and black-owned firms were the only M/WBE groups that participated in the City's prime contracting within this NIGP class during the time frame analyzed. The t-test results indicate that black- and Hispanic-owned firms were over-utilized, but the over-utilization was not statistically significant. Meanwhile, woman-owned firms were under-utilized, but the under-utilized was not statistically significant.

Hence, it can be concluded that no "gross" pattern of disparity in awarding contracts to M/WBE firms was observed in the City of St. Petersburg's dollar value of park, playground, recreational area and swimming pool competitively bid prime contracting during the FY 1990 to FY 1997.

Table 9-9 shows the output of the disparity analysis of the dollar value of communications, TV and media related services prime contracts during FY 1993 to FY 1997. The data indicate that during this period, non-minority-owned firms were over-utilized, but the t-test statistic indicates that the observed over-utilization was not significant. Meanwhile, the t-test result for all the M/WBE groups combined shows that M/WBEs in this procurement category were under-utilized, but the observed under-utilization was not statistically significant. When the data was disaggregated by M/WBE group, the result indicates that black-owned firms were the only M/WBE group that participated in the City's prime contracting within this NIGP class during the time frame analyzed.

Table 9-8
City of St. Petersburg
Disparity Analysis of $ Amount of Prime Contracts by Racial, Ethnic, and Gender Groups
For Park, Playground, Recreational Area (NIGP #24)
FY 89-97

Fiscal Year	Non-minority				Women				Black				Hispanic				Other				Total M/WBE			
	% Avail	% Util	T-Test	*	% Avail	% Util	T-Test	*	% Avail	% Util	T-Test	*	% Avail	% Util	T-Test	*	% Avail	% Util	T-Test	*	% Avail	% Util	T-Test	*
89	0	0	0		0	0	0		0	0	0		0	0	0		0	0	0		0	0	0	
90	100	1090	0		0	0	0		0	0	0		0	0	0		0	0	0		0	0	0	
91	84.21	71.11	-0.36		0	0	0		15.79	7.18	-0.23		0	0	0		0	0	0		15.79	7.18	-0.23	
92	55.58	100	+0.894		0	0	0		44.42	0	-0.89		0	0	0		0	0	0		44.42	0	-0.89	
93	100	100	+0.000		0	0	0		0	0	0		0	0	0		0	0	0		0	0	0	
94	78.29	36.07	-2.51		0.52	0	-0.03		0	0	0		21.19	63.93	+1.029		0	0	0		21.71	63.93	+1.404	
95	97.77	100	+0.370		0	0	0		0	0	0		2.23	0	-0.13		0	0	0		2.23	0	-0.13	
96	95.91	100	+0.413		0	0	0		0	0	0		4.09	0	-0.17		0	0	0		4.09	0	-0.17	
97	0	0	0		0	0	0		0	0	0		0	0	0		0	0	0		0	0	0	
Total	84.59	72.46	-1.65		0.2	0	0		6.59	7.18	+0.024		8.62	20.36	+0.398		0	0	0		15.41	27.54	+0.475	

Table 9-9
City of St. Petersburg
Disparity Analysis of $ Amount of Prime Contracts by Racial, Ethnic, and Gender Groups
Communicaticns, TV and Media Related Services (NIGP #27)
FY 89-97

Fiscal Year	Non-minority				Women				Black				Hispanic				Other				Total M/WBE			
	% Avail	% Util	T-Test	*	% Avail	% Util	T-Test	*	% Avail	% Util	T-Test	*	% Avail	% Util	T-Test	*	% Avail	% Util	T-Test	*	% Avail	% Util	T-Test	*
89	No data available for these fiscal years.																							
90																								
91																								
92																								
93	99.1	100	+0.191		0	0	0		0.93	0	-0.06		0	0	0		0	0	0		0.93	0	-0.06	
94	90.7	100	+1.062		0	0	0		9.3	0	-0.29		0	0	0		0	0	0		9.3	0	-0.29	
95	100	100	0		0	0	0		0	0	0		0	0	0		0	0	0		0	0	0	
96	100	100	0		0	0	0		0	0	0		0	0	0		0	0	0		0	0	0	
97	0	0	0		0	0	0		0	0	0		0	0	0		0	0	0		0	0	0	
Total	96	100	+1.242		0	0	0		3.89	0	-0.17		0	0	0		0	0	0		3.89	0	-0.17	

Hence, it can be concluded that no "gross" pattern of disparity in awarding contracts to M/WBE firms was observed in the City of St. Petersburg's dollar amount of communications, TV and media related services competitively bid prime contracting during the FY 1992 to FY 1997.

Table 9-10 shows the output of the disparity analysis of the dollar value of sporting and athletic goods prime contracts during FY 1991 to FY 1997. The data indicate that during this period, all the non-minority-owned firms that bid were utilized. None of the M/WBE groups participated in competitively bid prime contracting in this NIGP class during the fiscal years studied.

Hence, it can be concluded that no "gross" pattern of disparity in awarding contracts to M/WBE firms was observed in the City of St. Petersburg's dollar amount of sporting and athletic goods competitively bid prime contracting during the FY 1991 to FY 1996.

Table 9-11 shows the output of the disparity analysis of the dollar amount of building construction, maintenance and repair services prime contracts during FY 1989 to FY 1997. The data indicate that during this period, non-minority-owned firms were under-utilized, but the t-test statistic indicates that the observed under-utilization was not significant. Meanwhile, the t-test result for all the M/WBE groups combined shows that M/WBEs in this procurement category were over-utilized, but the observed over-utilization was not statistically significant. When the data was disaggregated by M/WBE group, the result indicates that all the M/WBE groups participated in the City's prime contracting within this NIGP class during the time frame analyzed. The t-test results indicate that black- and Hispanic-owned firms were over-utilized, while woman-owned firms and the other M/WBE groups were under-utilized, but these utilization patterns were not statistically significant.

Table 9-10
City of St. Petersburg
Disparity Analysis of $ Amount of Prime Contracts by Racial, Ethnic, and Gender Groups
Sporting and Athletic Goods (NIGP #30)
FY 89-97

Fiscal Year	Non-minority				Women				Black				Hispanic				Other				Total M/WBE			
	% Avail	% Util	T-Test	*	% Avail	% Util	T-Test	*	% Avail	% Util	T-Test	*	% Avail	% Util	T-Test	*	% Avail	% Util	T-Test	*	% Avail	% Util	T-Test	*
89	No data available for these fiscal years.																							
90																								
91	100	100	0		0	0	0		0	0	0		0	0	0		0	0	0		0	0	0	
92	0	0	0		0	0	0		0	0	0		0	0	0		0	0	0		0	0	0	
93	100	100	+0.000		0	0	0		0	0	0		0	0	0		0	0	0		0	0	0	
94	0	0	0		0	0	0		0	0	0		0	0	0		0	0	0		0	0	0	
95	0	0	0		0	0	0		0	0	0		0	0	0		0	0	0		0	0	0	
96	100	100	+0.000		0	0	0		0	0	0		0	0	0		0	0	0		0	0	0	
97	0	0	0		0	0	0		0	0	0		0	0	0		0	0	0		0	0	0	
Total	100	100	+0.000		0	0	0		0	0	0		0	0	0		0	0	0		0	0	0	

Table 9-11
City of St. Petersburg
Disparity Analysis of $ Amount of Prime Contracts by Racial, Ethnic, and Gender Groups
Building Construction, Maintenance & Repair Services (NIGP #34)
FY 89-97

Fiscal Year	Non-minority				Women				Black				Hispanic				Other				Total M/WBE			
	% Avail	% Util	T-Test	*	% Avail	% Util	T-Test	*	% Avail	% Util	T-Test	*	% Avail	% Util	T-Test	*	% Avail	% Util	T-Test	*	% Avail	% Util	T-Test	*
89	78.3	84.4	+0.256		1.16	0	-0.07		20.54	15.6	-0.12		0	0	0		0	0	0		21.7	15.6	-0.15	
90	96.06	92.68	-0.43		0.7	0	-0.04		1.85	7.32	+0.329		0.7	0	-0.04		0.7	0	-0.043		3.94	7.32	+0.156	
91	100	100	+0.000		0	0	0		0	0	0		0	0	0		0	0	0		0	0		
92	76.24	100	+0.789		0	0	0		11.88	0	-0.34		11.88	0	-0.34		0	0	0		23.76	0	-0.54	
93	97.23	97.87	+0.078		0.65	2.13	+0.116		2.12	0	-0.11		0	0	0		0	0	0		2.77	2.13	-0.03	
94	88.45	39.76	-3.41	*	0	0	0		0	0	0		11.91	60.24	+1.441		0	0	0		11.91	60.24	+1.441	
95	82.97	83.8	+0.070		6.67	12.01	+0.303		0.32	0	-0.02		1.04	4.19	+0.439		0	0	0		17.03	16.2	-0.05	
96	82.27	96.93	+1.384		9.9	2	-0.29		3.22	2.59	-0.03		4.61	0.48	-0.18		0	0	0		17.73	3.07	-0.38	
97	86.41	57.88	-1.44		0	0	0		6.58	42.12	+1.343		7.01	0	-0.24		0	0	0		13.59	42.12	+0.808	
Total	86.58	81.37	-1.13		3.66	3.06	-0.06		3.47	7.81	+0.411		6.29	7.77	+0.122		0.001	0	0		13.46	18.63	+0.525	

Hence, it can be concluded that no "gross" pattern of disparity in awarding contracts to M/WBE firms was observed in the City of St. Petersburg's dollar value of building construction, maintenance and repair services competitively bid prime contracting during the FY 1989 to FY 1997.

Table 9-12 shows the output of the disparity analysis of the number of general construction services prime contracts during FY 1989 to FY 1997. The data indicate that during this period, non-minority-owned firms were under-utilized, but the t-test statistic indicates that the observed under-utilization was not significant. Meanwhile, the t-test result for all the M/WBE groups combined shows that M/WBEs in this procurement category were over-utilized, but the observed over-utilization was not statistically significant. When the data was disaggregated by M/WBE group, the result indicates that woman- and black- and Hispanic-owned firms were the only three M/WBE groups that participated in the City's prime contracting within this NIGP class during the time frame analyzed. The t-test results indicate that each of the M/WBE groups was under-utilized. However, the pattern of the observed utilization for each of these M/WBE groups was not statistically significant.

Hence, it can be concluded that no "gross" pattern of disparity in awarding contracts to M/WBE firms was observed in the City of St. Petersburg's dollar value of general construction services competitively bid prime contracting during the FY 1989 to FY 1997.

Table 9-12
City of St. Petersburg
Disparity Analysis of $ Amount of Prime Contracts by Racial, Ethnic, and Gender Groups
General Construction Services (NIGP #35)
FY 89-97

Fiscal Year	Non-minority				Women				Black				Hispanic				Other				Total M/WBE			
	% Avail	% Util	T-Test	*	% Avail	% Util	T-Test	*	% Avail	% Util	T-Test	*	% Avail	% Util	T-Test	*	% Avail	% Util	T-Test	*	% Avail	% Util	T-Test	*
89	94.44	100	+0.728		2.65	0	-0.13		2.91	0	-0.13		0	0	0		0	0	0		5.56	0	-0.21	
90	99.09	95.5	-1.89	*	0.79	4.5	+0.280		0	0	0		0.12	0			0	0	0		0.91	4.5	+0.262	
91	98.36	100	+0.517		0.06	0	-0		1.1	0	-0.06		0.48	0	-0.03		0	0	0		1.64	0	-0.09	
92	97.92	98.72	+0.231		0	0	0		0	0	0		2.08	1.28	-0.05		0	0	0		2.08	1.28	-0.05	
93	96.46	97.75	+0.279		0.37	0	-0.02		0	0	0		3.17	2.25	-0.07		0	0	0		3.54	2.25	-0.09	
94	76.21	94.31	+1.533		16.35	0	-0.42		0	0	0		7.43	5.69	-0.06		0	0	0		23.79	5.69	-0.42	
95	85.44	65.62	-2.1	*	4.11	15.29	+0.563		0.16	0.66	+0.047		10.29	18.43	+0.3 79		0	0	0		14.56	34.38	+1.257	
96	88.85	97.94	+1.225		7.5	1.74	-0.31		0.05	0.1	+0.005		3.61	0.23	-0.18		0	0	0		11.15	2.06	-0.65	
97	91.41	94.6	+0.483		3.09	2.27	-0.05		1.93	2.93	+0.103		3.58	0.2	-0.16		0	0	0		8.59	5.4	-0.25	
Total	94.25	94.82	+0.305		2.82	2.69	-0.02		0.78	0.46	-0.07		2.14	2.03	-0.02		0	0	0		5.73	5.18	-0.11	

Bidding Analysis Results

This section presents the results of the analysis of bidding in the City of St. Petersburg contracting process. The results of the bidding analysis include: (1) a frequency distribution of potential availability and actual availability; (2) a comparison of potential availability to actual availability; and (3) a summary of major reasons why potentially available firms have not bid; and (4) dollar value of bidding analysis by racial, ethnic and gender group. The result are displayed in Tables 10-1 through 10-5.

Table 10-1 presents the frequency distribution of potential availability and actual availability by racial, gender or ethnic group. The data indicate that the City of St. Petersburg had a total of 399 potentially available contractors during the nine fiscal years studied. Of this total number of potentially available contractors, a majority (62.6 percent) were non-minority-owned firms. Meanwhile, all the M/WBE groups combined accounted for 37.4 percent of the total potentially available firms in the City's relevant market area. Disaggregating the data by M/WBE subgroup indicate that woman-owned firms had the largest share (19.5 percent) of M/WBE potential availability, followed by black owned firms with 8.95 percent, third is Hispanic-owned firms with 8.63 percent, and the least was the other minority-owned firms with 0.31 percent. Meanwhile, the City of St. Petersburg had a total of 672 actually available contractors. Of this total number of actually available contractors, 95.7 percent were non-minority-owned firms. The M/WBE groups combined accounted for only 4.27 percent of the total number of actually available contractors. Disaggregating the data by M/WBE subgroup indicates that woman-owned firms had the largest proportion of actually available contractors (1.85 percent), followed by black- and Hispanic-owned firms with 1.42 percent and 1 percent respectively, and with the least was the other minority-owned firms with only 0 percent of total number of actually available firms.

Table 10-1
City of St. Petersburg
Frequency Distribution of Potential Availability and actual Availability*
Fiscal Year 1991-1996

Available Contractor	Total Number	Non-Minority		Women		Black		Hispanic		Other		Total M/WBE	
		#	%	#	%	#	%	#	%	#	%	#	%
Potential	1339	1071	79.99	137	10.23	67	5.00	62	4.63	2	0.15	268	20.01
Actual	702	672	95.73	13	1.85	10	1.42	7	1.00	0	0.00	30	4.27

*Potential available firms are firms that are on the City's vendors list. Actual available firm are firms that bid.

Table 10-2 displays the comparison of potential availability to actual availability by racial, ethnic or gender group. The comparison was performed using the student t-test described in Chapter Two. The test results indicate that non-minority-owned firms significantly over-bid relative to their potential availability in the City's relevant market area. Meanwhile, all the M/WBE groups combined significantly under-bid. When the data was desegregated by M/WBE group, disparity in bidding by each of M/WBE group was apparent. For example, each of the M/WBE groups under-bid relative to their potential availability, with the under-bidding significant among woman-, black- and Hispanic-owned firms. Hence, it can be inferred that the City's data of potentially available and actually available firms exhibit disparity in bidding by woman-, black-, and Hispanic-owned firms. These findings indicate that minority-owned firms that are registered to do business with the City of St. Petersburg (that is, potentially available) are not actively participating in the city's contracting process as expected. Meanwhile, the level of participation of non-minority-owned firms in the city's contracting process far exceeds expectation.

Table 10-2
City of St. Petersburg
Comparison of Potential Availability to Actual Availability by Racial, Ethnic,
Fiscal Year 1991-1996

Race	% on Vendor List	% of Actual Bidders	T-Score	Significant Disparity
Non-Minority	79.99	95.73	10.191*	Yes
Women	10.23	1.85	-0.958	No
Black	5	1.42	-0.493	No
Hispanic	4.63	1.0	-0.423	No
Other	0.15	0	-0.01	No
Total	20.01	4.27	-2.119	Yes

Positive T-Score indicates an overbid situation
Negative T-Score indicates and underbid situation
*Significant at X = 0.05 level

Table 10-3 displays the frequency distribution of major reasons provided by the City's potentially available firms for not bidding on the City of St. Petersburg's prime contracts. Based on telephone interviews and survey of 101 potentially available contractors in the City's relevant market area, the following reasons for not bidding on prime contracts were given. A majority (32.7 percent) of the contractors indicated that the reason they have not bid on prime contracts was because they were in specialized field that either provided supportive services and/or products to prime contractors or was not purchased by the City. The next most common reason why potential contractors provided for not bidding on prime contracts was other reasons such as: they were located out the Tampa/St. Petersburg area, they just moved into the area, or their chances of winning a prime contract was better elsewhere than participating in the City of St. Petersburg prime contracting process. The third most common reason cited for not bidding on prime contracts was lack of information. Discrimination ranked forth as the most common reason why the potentially available contractors did not bid on the City's prime contracts. The fifth major reason provided by the contractors for not bidding on prime contracts was that the City's procurement system was too cumbersome. Meanwhile, only 10.90 percent of all the potentially available contractors cited discrimination as a reason for not bidding on the City's prime contracts.

When the data was disaggregated by racial, gender or ethnic group, a mixed reason provided for not bidding on the City's prime contracts was apparent. For example, a majority (66.7 percent) of non-M/WBEs cited a lack of information for not bidding on the City's prime contracts. Most black- and woman-owned firms cited specialized field and other reasons (such as, located outside the Tampa/St. Petersburg area) as reasons for not bidding on the City's prime contracts. A majority (52.6 percent) of Hispanic-owned firms said they did not bid on the City's prime contracts because they were in specialized fields, while less than 16 percent of these

Table 10-3
City of St. Petersburg
Reasons For Not Biding On Prime Contracts
Fiscal Year 1991-1996

Reasons for Not Biding On Prime Contracts	M/WBE													
	N-MBE		Woman		Black		Hispanic		Other		Total MBE		All	
	#	%	#	%	#	%	#	%	#	%	#	%	#	%
Cumbersome Procurement System	3	12.50	1	3.23	2	7.69	2	10.53	1	100.00	6	7.79	9	8.91
Lack of Technical Skills	0	0.00	0	0.00	0	0.00	0	0.00	0	0.00	0	0.00	0	0.00
High Bonding & Insurance	0	0.00	0	0.00	1	3.85	0	0.00	0	0.00	1	1.30	1	0.99
Discriminatory Contracting System	1	4.17	2	6.45	5	19.23	3	15.79	0	0.00	10	12.99	11	10.89
Lack of Information	16	66.67	2	6.45	2	7.69	0	0.00	0	0.00	4	5.19	20	19.80
Specialized Field	3	12.50	13	41.94	7	26.92	10	52.63	0	0.00	30	38.96	33	32.67
Small Business Size	0	0.00	0	0.00	0	0.00	1	5.26	0	0.00	1	1.30	1	0.99
Choose to Bid as Sub	1	4.17	2	6.45	1	3.85	0	0.00	0	0.00	3	3.90	4	3.96
Other	0	0.00	11	35.48	8	30.77	3	15.79	0	0.00	22	28.57	22	21.78
Total	24	100%	31	100%	26	100%	19	100%	1	100%	77	100%	101	100%

firms cited discrimination and other reasons for not bidding on prime contracts. The other M/WBE subgroup viewed the City prime contracting system as too cumbersome for them to participate. Meanwhile, less than 20.00 percent of potentially available contractors in each of the racial, gender or ethnic group cited discrimination as a reason for not bidding on the City's prime contracts.

Table 10-4 exhibits the frequency distribution of major reasons provided by the City's potentially available firms for not bidding on the City of St. Petersburg's subcontracts. A majority (44.7 percent) of the contractors indicated that the reason they have not bid on prime contracts was because of lack of information on subcontracting opportunities. The next most common reason why potential contractors provided for not bidding on subcontracts was because they were in specialized fields that basically provided supportive services and supplies to prime contractors. Discrimination ranked third as the most common reason cited by all the contractors for not bidding on the City's subcontracts. And the fourth most cited reason provided by the contractors for not bidding on the City's subcontracts was other reasons such as: they were located out the Tampa/St. Petersburg area, they just moved into the area, or their chances of winning a prime contract was better elsewhere than participating in the City of St. Petersburg prime contracting process. The third most common reason cited for not bidding on prime contracts was lack of information. Discrimination ranked forth as the most common reason why the potentially available contractors did not bid on the City's prime contracts. The fifth major reason provided by the contractors for not bidding on prime contracts was that the City's procurement system was too cumbersome. Meanwhile, a majority of all the M/WBE groups combined cited a lack of information on subcontracting opportunities as a reason for not participating in the City's subcontracting process.

Table 10-4
City of St. Petersburg
Reasons For Not Biding On Sub Contracts
Fiscal Year 1991-1996

Reasons for Not Biding On Prime Contracts	M/WBE													
	N-MBE		Woman		Black		Hispanic		Other		Total MBE		All	
	#	%	#	%	#	%	#	%	#	%	#	%	#	%
Cumbersome Procurement System	1	5.26	0	0.00	1	11.11	1	25.00	1	100.0	3	15.79	4	10.53
Lack of Technical Skills	0	0.00	0	0.00	0	0.00	0	0.00	0	0.00	0	0.00	0	0.00
High Bonding & Insurance	0	0.00	0	0.00	2	22.22	0	0.00	0	0.00	2	10.53	2	5.26
Discriminatory Contracting System	1	5.26	1	20.00	1	11.11	2	50.00	0	0.00	4	21.05	5	13.16
Lack of Information	12	63.16	2	40.00	3	33.33	0	0.00	0	0.00	5	26.32	17	44.74
Specialized Field	4	21.05	1	20.00	0	0.00	1	25.00	0	0.00	2	10.53	6	15.79
Small Business Size	0	0.00	0	0.00	0	0.00	0	0.00	0	0.00	0	0.00	0	0.00
Other	1	5.26	1	20.00	2	22.22	0	0.00	0	0.00	3	15.79	4	10.53
Total	19	100%	5	100%	9	100%	4	100%	1	100%	19	100%	38	100%

When the data was disaggregated by racial, gender or ethnic group, a mixed reason provided for not bidding on the City's prime contracts was apparent. For example, a majority of non-minority-, woman-, black-owned firms cited a lack of information as reason for not bidding on the City's prime contracts. Meanwhile, a majority of Hispanic-owned firms cited discrimination as a reason why they have not participated in the City's subcontracting process.

Table 10-5 displays the frequency distribution of the dollar level of bids submitted by racial, ethnic or gender group. The levels are: \$0 to \$25,000; \$25,001 to \$100,000; \$100,001 to \$500,000; \$500,001 to \$1,000,000; and over \$1,000,000. The data indicate that contractors in the City's relevant market area submitted a total of 269 prime contract bids during the nine fiscal years studied. Of this total, non-minority firms submitted a large majority (91.9 percent) of the prime contract bids, followed by Hispanic-owned firms with 3.89 percent of the total bids, third place was woman-owned firms with 2.61 percent of the total number of bids, fourth were black-owned firms with 1.60 percent of the total bids, and the least were the other M/WBE group with 0.04 percent of the total bids submitted during FY 1989 to FY 1997.

When the data was disaggregated by the level of dollar value of bids submitted by each racial, ethnic or racial group, a mixed pattern immerged. For example, non-minority firms consistently submitted over 88 percent of the total number of bids at each of the dollar levels of bids analyzed. Meanwhile, all the M/WBE groups combined tended to bid low on extremely low and extremely high ticket contracts, and highest on contracts with dollars values ranging from \$50,000 to \$500,000.

Table 10-5
City of St. Petersburg
Dollar Level of Prime Contract bids by Racial, Ethnic, and Gender Groups
FY 89-97

Amount	Total	Non-minority		Woman		Black		Hispanic		Other		Total MBE	
		#	%	#	%	#	%	#	%	#	%	#	%
0 – 25,000	845	807	95.50	10	1.18	8	0.95	20	2.37	0	0	38	4.50
25,001 – 50,000	335	310	92.54	12	3.58	7	2.09	6	1.79	0	0	25	7.46
50,001 – 100,000	305	269	88.2	15	4.92	5	1.64	15	4.92	1	0.33	36	11.80
100,001 – 500,000	696	612	87.9	23	3.30	18	2.59	43	6.18	0	0	84	12.07
500,001 – 1,000,000	186	172	92.5	0	0.00	2	1.08	12	6.45	0	0	14	7.53
> 1,000,000	202	190	94.1	7	3.47	1	0.50	4	1.98	0	0	12	5.94
Grand Totals	2569	2360	91.86	67	2.61	41	1.60	100	3.89	1	0.04	209	8.14

When the data was disaggregated by M/WBE subgroup, again a mixed bidding pattern was apparent. For instance, woman-owned firms bid low on contracts with dollar value ranges from $0 to $25,000 and contracts with dollar value within the range of $500,00 to $1,000,000 dollar value, and higher in all the other dollar value levels analyzed. Black-owned firms consistently bid less than 3.00 percent in each of the dollar levels analyzed, with the lowest proportion of number of bids submitted occurring at the extremely low ($0 to $25,000) and extremely high range (i.e. over $1000,000). Meanwhile, Hispanic-owned firms, with the exception of the over $1000,000 range, bid more on large dollar value contracts and less on small dollar value contracts. The other M/WBE group bid only once (that is, at the $50,000 to $100,000 level) during the nine fiscal years analyzed.

In summation, with the exception of the other M/WBE group, all the M/WBE groups bid less often than they were represented on the City's vendors list. The major reasons provided by the contractors for not bidding on the City's prime contracts are: (a) specialized field; (b) lack of information; and (c) other reasons. Meanwhile, majors reason cited by the City's potentially available contractors for not bidding on subcontracts were: (a) lack of information; (b) specialized field; (c) discrimination; and (d) other reasons. The bid analysis indicated that non-minority firms consistently bid high in each of the dollar value levels analyzed, while all the M/WBE groups combined bid low on extremely low and extremely high dollar value contracts. Hispanic-owned firms generally bid more on large dollar value contracts, while black-owned and the other M/WBE firms bid low in each the dollar value level of contracts. The bidding pattern for woman-owned firms is mixed, but generally steady at each of the dollar value levels analyzed.

Summary

The results of the disparity analysis of the City of St. Petersburg's contracting data indicate that during FY 1989 to FY 1999 no "gross" disparity between availability and utilization of M/WBEs in 12 major procurement categories analyzed. Altogether during the period studied (FY 1989 to FY 1999) M/WBEs supplied 8.83 percent of the total number of bids and received 9.12 percent of the total number of contracts awarded by the City of St. Petersburg. Meanwhile, M/WBEs submitted 6.50 percent of the total dollar value of bids and received 6.58 percent of the total dollars awarded by the City. Therefore, when M/WBE bid on the City of St. Petersburg's contracts, the outcomes are proportional. The problem is that M/WBEs in the City of St. Petersburg's relevant market area do not bid very often. The question becomes, why? The next chapter provides the findings of a survey of a random sample of potentially available M/WBEs who had not bid on the city's contracts, as well as the results of interviews with city officials. The purpose of the survey and interview was to substantiate the findings (and identify other barriers) of the bidding analysis which indicated that minority-owned firms were not participating in the city's contracting process as expected due predominantly to lack of information, specialized fields and other reasons.

Chapter Eight

Qualitative Analysis Findings

This chapter presents the verified and corroborated findings of qualitative analysis of personal experience of M/WBEs and survey of contractors (M/WBEs and non-M/WBEs) who either have contracted with the City of St. Petersburg or are still doing business with the City, as well as representatives of community organizations in the City's relevant market area. The chapter also present the results of a survey of and interviews of city officials. The survey and interview results were used to further corroborate the anecdotes of unfair or disparate treatment of contractors in the city's relevant market area.

Incidence of Discrimination Anecdotes

This section presents specific incidences of alleged discrimination or disparate treatment provided by M/WBEs interviewed and conclusion drawn from verification and corroboration of these anecdotes.

Response Time Problem with Prime Contractor

A non-minority prime contractor who was bidding on a City of St. Petersburg contract contacted a black WBE. The project involved the construction of a golf course. The non-minority prime contractor requested that the black WBE owner submit a bid if interested, since the City required an M/WBE participation goal on the project. The WBE was also informed that plans and specifications for the project were available for her perusal at the non-minority prime contractor's main office located about 30 miles away, and at all Dodge and CMD rooms. The prime contractor also faxed a "Letter of Intent" to the WBE to be completed, signed and returned to the prime contractor's office if the WBE planned to bid on this project. If the WBE was not going to bid on the project, she was instructed to just write "NO BID" on the Letter of Intent and fax it back to the prime contractor.

The WBE had approximately less than 10 days only to respond to the prime contractor's notice to bid. However, upon review of the plan, the WBE estimated that it would normally take at least 21 days or more to complete and submit the bid package to the prime contractor. Hence, she decided not to submit a bid to the prime contractor. The WBE felt that the prime contractor deliberately sent her the notice too close to the deadline in order to make it virtually impossible for her to submit a bid, and hence classifying the WBE as non-responsive. The WBE also felt that the non-minority contractor wanted her to return a "NO BID" Letter of Intent so that the prime contractor can used it as an indication of "good faith effort" to solicit M/WBE participation. When asked if she filed a protest with the City of express her concerns, the WBE said no. She believes that a small business shelter program may prevent these types of problems from occurring in the future.

Upon verification, I found that the prime contractor did indeed send a solicitation letter and a "Letter of Intent" to the black WBE less than ten days to the deadline of the bid. However, an interview of City Officials and a review of City bid records on the project in question, revealed that the prime contractor in question was not awarded the contract, but was the third lowest bidder. The City found the first lowest bidder responsive with a total M/WBE participation of 16.1 percent. The City's procurement staff recommended this lowest responsive bidder for award of this contract at the next City Council meeting which was scheduled for October 7, 1999. The City established M/WBE participation goals of 8 percent for BBE, 7 percent for HBE, and 7 percent for WBE for a total M/WBE participation goal of 22 percent. The lowest responsive bidder who was recommended by City staff achieved a goal of 5.6 percent for BBE, 5.3 percent for HBE and 5.2 percent for WBE for a total M/WBE participation goal of 16.1 percent.

An interview with the accused prime contractor and a review of the prime contractor records on the project indicated that the prime contractor sent out the "Letter of Intent" to 30 M/WBEs in the City's relevant market area. These letters were sent on the same date as that sent to the WBE in question. Over 60 percent of the M/WBEs solicited responded to the prime contractor's solicitation before the bid deadline. The prime contractor selected the most qualified M/WBEs from this pool of respondents to meet (and even exceed) his M/WBE participation goal of 8 percent BBE, 4.9 percent HBE and 14.5 percent WBE.

Hence, it can be concluded that the WBE's claim of unfair treatment for not being informed on time to respond to the prime contractor's solicitation is *not substantiated.*

Price Problem with Manufacturer and Supplier

A black MBE received a solicitation for bid on a City of St. Petersburg contract. The contract involved the supply of electrical equipment and accessories. The contractor has been in the electrical business for 40 years. He is also certified with the City of St. Petersburg. He went to a non-minority electrical supplies and accessories manufacturer for a price quote on items being solicited by the City. The manufacturer informed the black MBE that he does not do business directly with independent retailers, and advised him to contact one of the wholesale distributors in the area. The black MBE took the manufacturer's advice and contacted one of the major wholesale electrical distributors in the area. The distributor provided the black MBE with prices for the items being bid by the City of St. Petersburg. When the black MBE submitted his bid to the City, he found not only that his bid ranked highest of all the bids submitted, but also that the wholesale distributor had also submitted a bid which was lower than that submitted by the black MBE for the same contract. The black electrical contractor believes that the wholesaler deliberately gave him higher prices to the item being solicited by the City in order to gain a competitive edge based on price to win the contract. When asked if he was unfairly quoted higher prices by the wholesaler because of his race, the black MBE contractor was not too sure. He was also not sure if the wholesaler in question was the successful bidder on this particular contract. However, after a couple of unsuccessful bids with the City of St. Petersburg and other local governments in the area, and experiencing the same price problem with wholesalers, he decided to stop bidding with the City, and instead do business with the private sector.

The black MBE believes that the establishment by the City of a small business shelter program, which allows only firms of comparable size to competitively bid on City contracts, may prevent problems like this from occurring in the future.

Upon verification, the City MBE officials contend that they made several attempts to get the BBE to recertify with the City, but they received no response from the BBE. In addition, the City officials were uncertain which contracts that the BBE allegedly bid on. Hence, verification of this anecdote *is inconclusive.*

Problem with Prerequisite to bid on City Contract

A black WBE received a notice to participate on a major City of St. Petersburg project. The project involved supplying furniture to the City's dome stadium (Tropicana Field), which was under construction. The managers of the project informed the black WBE that a prerequisite to participate in the contracting process was to purchase season tickets worth $1,200. She went ahead and purchased the tickets, and in return her name was submitted to the successful prime contractor working on the project. The prime contractor sent her a solicitation for quotes to supply furniture for the dome. She completed the bid package and sent it to the prime contractors. However, the prime contractor never contacted her to let her know if she won the contract or not.

Upon verification, it was revealed by the City staff that the purchase of furniture was done by the Tampa Bay Devil Rays baseball organization (a private corporation), and not by the City of St. Petersburg. The City asserts that it was rumored that the Devil Rays required *all* vendors and suppliers to be "season ticket holders." According to the City, if this rumor was, in fact, the case, (as alleged by the black WBE), it was a requirement that was not requested, nor endorsed, by the City of St. Petersburg. The City's staff could not attest to whether this was a prerequisite, nor whether all vendors or suppliers did purchase the season tickets. We made several telephone calls to the Devil Rays baseball team organization, but could not reach the team officials for comments on the sale of "season tickets" to potential contractors. Hence, verification of this *anecdote is inconclusive*.

Problem with City funding of Community Development Corporation

Officials of a Community Development Corporation (CDC) contend that the City has been providing funding to the organization for small minority business loans. This funding has been provided for over 15 years, however the organization recently received a notice from the City expressing the City's intention to discontinue the program at the end of fiscal year 1998. The organization contends that the City gave no explanation for discontinuing the program and that this action by the City will adversely effect small minority businesses in the relevant market area who cannot qualify for regular traditional financing.

Upon verification of this claim with the City officials charged with managing the loan program, we found that the funds were indeed discontinued. However, the City Officials contend that they had already informed the organization that the reason for discontinuing funds was because of poor performance. In particular, the City contends that the organization has not been making enough loans to small minority businesses in the area to justify continued funding. In addition, City Officials contend that the community organization did apply for funding for FY 2000. However, a 14-person committee, which included three citizens from the housing Roundtable, reviewed the applications for funding, and ranked the community organization 19th out a total of twenty-one applicants. The City is currently providing funding to two community organizations for a micro-loan program and a working capital Peer-to-Peer loan program for all small businesses in the City's relevant market area. The City believes that these two loan programs will more effectively target financial assistance to small minority businesses in the local area than under the previous arrangement with the community organization in question, especially since the recipient community organizations have a proven record of assisting local small businesses in getting loans. Hence, it can be concluded that the CDC contention that the City provided no explanation for discontinuing the funding for the micro-loan program and that this action will adversely affect small minority businesses in the area is *not substantiated.*

Pricing and Technology problems with competitors

A black MBE received a solicitation to bid on a City of St. Petersburg contract. This was a long-term contract awarded every two years to provide printing and copying services to the City. The MBE has been in business since 1989, and has a net worth of approximately $500,000. The contract amount was in the range of sixty to seventy thousand dollars. The first time that the black MBE contractor submitted a bid was in 1989. He was competing with two other non-minority firms who traditionally have been awarded the contract by the City in the previous years. The MBE's bid was not considered the first two times he competed for the contract due to technicalities involving submission of the appropriate bid documents or papers.

On the third attempt he lost to one of his competitors because his bid price was too high. On the fourth attempt the black MBE submitted the price that was quoted two years earlier, and again his bid price came out higher than that of his competitors. When asked what he attributed the constant high pricing to, he said that his competitors were larger companies who have the capability of purchasing paper stock and other printing supplies in bulk. According to the black MBE, in their industry such purchasing strategies are rewarded by discounts for items purchased. Since he is a small company, he cannot afford to make these bulk purchases of supplies in order to take advantage of these discounts being afforded by either the manufactures or the wholesaler. Furthermore, as a small company he does not have the financial capital to purchase the type of machines owned by his competitors. These factors have placed him in a competitive disadvantage when setting his price for City bids.

When asked if his race had any influence on the City's decision to deny him the contracts, he said he was not too sure but would like some level of policing of the City's contracting process to ensure that contracts are awarded not on the basis of who you know, but on the objective criteria of bidding established by the City. He also was in support of a race neutral procurement policy based on business size. He also was very critical of City Officials advising him to go through the certification process only to be told that certification is only good for participation in construction related projects. He believed that an across the board small business shelter program based on size may afford small businesses like his better opportunity to effectively compete on City contracts than available in the City's current M/WBE program. However, he cautioned that the effectiveness of the shelter program will be determined, for the most part, by the threshold definition of a small business established by the City.

Upon verification, I found that the black MBE did indeed submit bids for the printing contract to the City and lost because his bid was too high. In addition, City's Procurement Officials explained that printing contracts are not a part of the M/WBE set-aside and shelter programs, and are awarded through the normal sealed competitive bidding process.

Hence, it can be concluded that *the black WBE may not have been a victim of discrimination or disparate treatment in the award of a contract by the City of St. Petersburg, but a victim of lack of financial capital in a highly competitive marekt (that is, the printing industry).*

No Response Problem

A black MBE (BBE) contractor received a notice to bid from a non-minority prime contractor as subcontractor. The project involved producing fuel for construction of a sports complex. The BBE contractor responded to the request for quotes by the prime, and also submitted a letter of intent to perform as a certified Black Business Enterprise (BBE). However, the prime contractor never called or wrote the BBE to inform him whether or not his bid was accepted. The BBE feels that he was unfairly treated by the prime by subjecting him to spend business time putting together and submitting the bid packet and not getting a courtesy response from the prime. The BBE did not know if the prime contractor ever submitted his name to the City to meet his minority participation goal. Neither did he know if the prime contractor ever met his minority participation goal requirements. We contacted the contractor and city to corrobate this claim, and it was revealed that the prime contractor selected what he considered to be the most qualified M/WBEs to do the work. The records indicated the prime contractor did meet his M/WBE goal on this particular project. Hence, it can be concluded that the BBEs claim of unfiar treatment was *not substantiated.*

Pricing Problems with Suppliers

A black MBE received a solicitation for bid from the City. The contractor has been in business since 1986, but has been certified to do business with the City since 1989. The contract for which bids were being solicited involved the sale of fuel/oil for a City co-operative contract. This was a 3-year contract. The BBE contacted the supplier to obtain price quotes for the required volume of oil being solicited by the City. His five other non-minority competitors also contacted the same supplier to obtain price quotes. After submitting his bids to the City he was informed that one of the non-minority competitors was the lowest bidder and, hence, was awarded the contract. Meanwhile, his price was the highest of all the bid prices submitted.

The MBE believes that he was unfairly treated by the supplier who engaged in what the BBE said is commonly referred to in this industry as "Predatory Pricing" (i.e. antitrust law violation pricing). He also felt that the City has continued to directly or indirectly allow this unfair practice to continue, despite numerous complaints that he has filed with the City's purchasing officials.

Upon verification, we found out that indeed the price submitted by the non-minority winner of the contract was lower than that of the BBE. In addition, it was revealed that the winner of the contract obtained his price from the same oil supplier as the BBE. The price quoted to the BBE by the supplier was the daily "OPIS" price. However, the lower price given to the non-minority firm that won the contract was a discounted price (that is, less than the OPIS Daily Pricing). Hence, the non-minority was able to under bid the BBE based on price. Based on the facts obtained from verification, it can be concluded that the black BBE claim of unfair treatment by the oil supplier has been substantiated and corroborated. Hence, it can be concluded that in this particular incident the City of St. Petersburg was *a "passive participant" in a discriminatory pricing system.*

Co-operative Bidding Problem

A black MBE complained that the City of St. Petersburg engaged in co-operative purchasing practices with other municipalities when soliciting bids for the purchase of fuel, gasoline and diesel. This is a long-term (that is, three years) contract involving the purchase of a large volume of these products at once. The black MBE contends that in this industry, it is common practice for the major suppliers to discount the price for these products when the distributor is a buyer of large volumes of fuel, gasoline or diesel. The BBE feels that such practices favor the larger companies not the small ones like his. Hence, he feels that the City indirectly discriminated against him and other small businesses like his by continuously engaging in such co-operative purchasing arrangements. The black MBE believes that a small business shelter program based on business size may prevent problems like these from occurring in the future.

Upon verification, I found that the primary reasons that the City of St. Petersburg engages in co-operative bidding are: (a) to obtain better prices due to larger volume of purchases by participating public entities; (b) better quality of product or services purchased due to improved competitive specifications; and (c) savings in time since only one facilitating public entity prepares and issues "Invitations for Bids" for each item purchased through the joint bid program. The City of St. Petersburg has the option of not participating in such joint bid purchase if doing so would be disadvantageous in terms of price or otherwise.

In preparing the requirements for the co-operative purchase the facilitating public agency: (a) prepares draft specifications; (b) obtains estimates of requirements from all public entities interested in participating in the proposed purchase;[308] (c)

---

[308] It is not necessary for all member entities to participate in every purchase. However, once a bid is awarded, each participant is expected to honor its commitment.

develops the invitation for bid format; and (d) prepares a list of suggested suppliers to whom invitations for bids will be mailed. After the service or product specifications, invitations for bids and a list of suppliers are drafted, the City of St. Petersburg and other participants reviews the specifications of invitation for bid format and a list of potential suppliers, and recommend changes as they see fit.

The facilitating public agency solicits bids using the agreed upon specifications, invitation for bid format, and a list of potential suppliers. The procedures followed are no different from those used when soliciting bids on items required by facilitating agency's own entities. The City of St. Petersburg ensures that the facilitating agencies comply with the city's requirements for legal advertising (that is, solicitation notice to bidders are as regular as the City's). Based on the facilitators determination, the representatives of the City in the co-op recommends contract award to the City Council.

All unresolved controversies relating to specifications, other provision of the invitations for bids, evaluation of bids, or subsequent contractual matters, including failure to comply with deliveries or specifications, are reported to the facilitating agency.

Any other controversies for which the facilitating agency has no control, for example violation of contractual conditions, including late payment on the part of other participating entities, are resolved with that public entity and the vendor.

Hence, it can be concluded that *the City's cooperative purchasing process seem to conform to standard competitive bidding process with emphasis on awarding contracts to the lowest bidder. However, although a long term cooperative purchase may place a small competitor at a competitive disadvantage, the City's participation in such procurement arrangement does not seem to intentionally discriminate against small businesses. However, the city of St. Petersburg can be viewed as "a passive participant in discriminatory procurement system."*

Termination without Payment Problem

A white WBE was awarded a subcontract by a black MBE to provide pipeline demolition and underground utilities services for the construction of a golf course. The WBE completed the first half of the work and waited for six months to be invited by the black prime to complete the second half of the work. Upon checking with the black prime contractor about her status on the project, the WBE was informed that the BBE had replaced her with another sub contractor to do the second half of the work. When the WBE asked the prime BBE the reason for his decision, the BBE said his decision was based on poor performance by the WBE. The WBE contacted the City to find out if the prime contractor has filed any documents accusing her of poor performance on the project. The City did not provide such documentation, nor made a concerted effort to investigate the black prime contractor's reason for substituting her with another subcontractor. She believes that she was unfairly treated or discriminated against by both the prime contractor and the City because of her gender. When asked why she believes that she was unfairly treated because of her gender, she said she does not truly believe that the City would have treated a male contractor the same way. When we contacted the city to find out if the WBE's claim was valid, the city officials said their procurement policy does not allow them to get into disputes between prime contractors and subcontractors unless the relationship was adversely affecting the progress of the project. According to the city officials, this particular project progressed normally from start to finish. Hence, it can be concluded that based on verification *this anecdote can be concluded that the city was a passive participant in an unfair treatment of subcontractor by a prime contractor.*

Non-payment Problem

A white WBE was awarded a subcontract by a black prime contractor on a City project involving laying pipelines. After the WBE started working on the job, the prime contractor withdrew her from the project and paid for her truck rental, but not for the work already done. The WBE filed a complaint with the City, but the City took no action to rectify the payment problem. She believes that both the City and the prime contractor unfairly treated her because of her gender. When asked why she believes her that she was unfairly treated because of her gender, the WBE said she simply cannot believe the male contractors are treated the same way.

Upon verification, I found that the white WBE did indeed work on the pipeline project. However, City officials contend that the WBE making the claim of unfair treatment was the not M/WBE on record. The officials found out that this particular WBE was working on this project only during an onsite visit conducted on June 9, 1998. In September 9, 1998, the City's MBE Office received a letter via fax from the principal of the WBE requesting the City to advise her of the proper procedure to follow to collect her payment from the black contractor. To provide a response to her request, the City's MBE Office asked the City's Legal Department for an opinion. According to the Legal Department officials, the MBE Office can informally ask parties in a dispute to resolve their issues, but once that is done, the MBE Office does not have authorization or responsibility to provide assistance in the resolution of collection issues which may arise between prime contractors and subcontractors. Furthermore, the legal department suggested that the WBE was advised to contact the user department (that is, Engineering and Stormwater) to determine if any provisions existed in the City's contract with the black prime contractor which may help the WBE in her collection efforts. The Legal Department also suggested that the WBE was informed to seek the advise of a private legal counsel to enforce her rights under her contract with the black prime contractor.

On September 15, 1998, the Engineering Department sent a letter to the black prime contractor stating that according to "City Contract Standards Article G-28, Subcontractors," the City is authorized to withhold further payment on the contract until such time that the prime contractor can provide an explanation to the City of why payments have not been made to the WBE. The black prime contractor did contact the city and explained that the WBE was not paid for her services because of poor performance. According to city officials, the black contractor said he did not feel obligated to pay the WBE for a poorly performed work. Therefore, he had no choice but to replace the WBE with another subcontractor to complete the work. The "new' contractor did complete the work and was paid in full for his services. Hence, it can be concluded that *the WBE's allegation of unfair or disparate treatment was not substantiated.*

Termination due to alleged poor performance

A black BBE was awarded a subcontract by a Hispanic HBE. The project involved the building of the City of St. Petersburg North Branch Library. When the project began, the BBE realized that the prime contractor spent very little time on the project. He also discovered that the design of the roof and other aspects of the project were wrong. This caused a delay in completing the project. The HBE blamed the BBE for the mistakes and delay. The BBE filed a complaint with the City, and invited the City to come and inspect the work. The City sent a MBE Official who was not an expert in construction to do the inspection. To the black subcontractor's surprise, after the BBE walked the Official through the project and showed her all the design and delay problems caused by the prime HBE, the City Official decided to take sides with the prime and accused the BBE of incompetence. This decision resulted in the BBE loosing the subcontract. The BBE feels that he was unfairly treated by both the prime HBE and the City of St. Petersburg. Specifically, the BBE views the City's MBE Program as lacking in an effective mechanism for monitoring MBE participation, and insuring that MBEs stay on the job and are fairly treated by prime contractors.

Upon verification, I found that the prime HBE had sent a letter to the BBE on October 10, 1998 informing the BBE of his dissatisfaction with work performed by the BBE. A review of the city's records of this particular contract revealed that another black construction company was the BBE listed in on City records as the MBE participant on the project, not the BBE that is complaining about unfair treatment. Apparently, there was another tier of subcontracting which involved the complaining BBE. The City did verify the claim of unsatisfactory performance made by the prime HBE. In particular, city records showed that officials of the City's Capital Improvement Division of the Leisure Service Department and the MBE Office met with the principal of the BBE and the HBE on October 10, 1989 to discuss the status of the project and verify the claims made by both parties. The City's MBE officials asserted that they did not inspect the work because: (a) this was not their responsibility; and (b) they had no expertise in this area. The City MBE staff explained that the inspection of construction work for the City is normally handled by either City personnel who have specific knowledge and experience in this area, or by consultants that the City hires to serve in this capacity. The MBE staff's role is one of mediation, when appropriate.

In this particular contract dispute situation, the MBE staff listened to all the parties involved, including the architect's opinion and that of the project manager. Letters were subsequently sent by the HBE prime contractor to the BBE to correct the problem and bring the project up to the standard specified in the contract documents. The prime contractor further stated in a letter to the BBE that failure to do so may result in the BBE being removed from the project and replaced by another subcontractor. According the staff of the MBE Office, the BBE never responded to the letter, and was subsequently found in breach of his contract by the prime contractor. MBE Office records indicate that the other BBE was allegedly out of the area when the mistakes were made by the BBE claiming unfair treatment. Therefore, the City MBE staff asserted, the prime contractor was left no choice but to terminate the contract with the BBE. After terminating the BBE, the prime contractor hired another firm to complete the job. The MBE staff contends that the prime contractor was particularly concerned about the completion date for the project, and wanted to avoid liquidation damages of $400 a day.

With regards to the BBE's claim that he was misguided by a project design mistake caused by the prime contractor, the City's project manager provided the following two explanation based on his observation during a visit to the site and discussions with the prime contractor and the BBE. First, there was notification filed by the BBE of nonpayment in excess of $4,000. The BBE then took the matter to the bonding company and the bonding company did not accept his claim. The manager believes that the BBE apparently did not have enough back up to support his claim, although the manager could not substantiate his belief.

Second, the east of the building wall was built slightly higher than in the work specification plan, which led to the steel beam being of the wrong slope. The manager asserted that this was not BBE fault, but a lack of proper handling of the job by the steel contractor. Specifically, the manager said that the steel contractor knew that the slope was inconsistent and how it is supposed to look but they went ahead and kept working because they were doing what the plans said. The result was the construction of a high wall which caused the beam to be installed improperly by the BBE. Moverover, the City Manager did not believe that the BBE caused the error since he (the BBE) was simply following the architectural plan provided to him by the HBE. The Manager, however, faulted the BBE for knowing that the beam was not laying correctly, and not notifying HBE so that it may be corrected early on. The

City manager contends that this is not good practice, and that if the job were properly manned, a supervisor would have notified the HBE prime contractor.

Third, the City manager asserted that although the BBE was only at fault for not communication to the contractor, another installation was also incorrectly installed. This second installation was not to the high wall. Rather, the framing angle for the fascia and soffit was installed incorrectly, and other outlookers were installed out of plumb. Finally, the manager said that the HBE prime contractor, concerned that these problems would delay the project, had called the BBE on several occasions to correct the problem, but the BBE neither responded nor came out to the site to correct the outlookers. The manager informed the HBE prime contractor that the City's concern was for the project to be completed on time even if it required someone else to complete the job. Furthermore, the Manager reminded the HBE that the City has a contract with him, the prime contractor, and not the subcontractors that he hired. Therefore, the prime contractor would be liable for nonperformance and not the BBE. The Manager said the prime contractor responded by contracting with another steel contractor to complete the work after a three weeks delay.

The city manager was not sure if the two parties continued to disagree, but he found no fault in the BBE installation of the beams at the incorrect slope. The contractor did agree that full responsibility for effective completion rest on him, and not on the BBE. Hence, based upon verification, it can be concluded that *the BBE was unfairly treated by the HBE prime contractor.*

Imposition of Unwritten Clause Problem; Overriding a Bonding Agency's Choice of Subcontractor Problem

A black MBE stated that he won a contract to do construction work at a dome stadium project after bidding the lowest amount out of several competitors. The contract consisted of installing concrete sidewalks, and driveways. After being awarded the contract, the City of St. Peterburg informed the BBE that he must subcontract with other minority businesses, a requirement that was not stated in his contract. He contended that the City habitually imposed unwritten clauses on contractors during project execution. By way of example, he said that in this contracting situation the records would show that the City counted both the amount of his contract and the amount he paid to the subcontractor as minority participation despite the fact that only one contract was involved. A list of firms was included in the bid information. The subcontractors must have a bond of twenty thousand dollars, which took him about three to four weeks to find a subcontractor that met the qualifications. One of the subcontractors on the city's list that he was to use had already been terminated from a previous job for lack of qualification. The City refused to pay the BBE because he did not have minority participation for subcontracting. They terminated the contract. The BBE says that it is unconstitutional for the City to award him a contract and make him subcontract out portions of it. The contract was then given to the bonding company to complete. The bonding company hired the same BBE to go back out to the work site to complete the job after the City initially fired them. After the City sent someone out to the work site to check on the progress of the project and discovered that the original BBE was back on the job site, they informed him that they were terminated. The City later wrote a letter stating that the bonding company must send a company that they approve of. The BBE stated that there has never been an instance where the City would over-ride the bonding company's choice of contractors, except in this case. He said that this creates a ripple effect where the bonding company does not want to hire Minority contractors.

The BBE said that the City also has a strategy of delaying contract completion which in turn causes contractors not to meet deadlines set by the City, which causes them to be fired from projects. An example of this in his case is that other projects on the same job site must be completed before he can even begin to start his job. He says that there are major conflicts of what is supposed to happen and when it should happen.

The BBE also stated that after receiving his contract, he was forced to wait on another company whose job was to install special glass glazing around a baseball dome stadium project. They could not complete their sidewalks because cranes had to be used to get the glass installed. The sidewalks could not hold the weight of the cranes, which was another delay. With all the project delays and complications, the City paid contractors extra money in excess of one million dollars to complete the project jobs early. The BBE believes that situations like this do not happen to non-minorities at all. He says that this creates a ripple effect where the bonding company does not want to hire minority contractors.

After this incident, the BBE said that the City would not renew his MBE Certification and refused to respond to why he would not be recertified. The BBE also stated that the City of St. Petersburg is very biased and discriminatory against minority businesses. He feels that the contracts are to the detriment of minority businesses. The BBE feels that the City has failed to develop minority businesses, yet they encourage larger firms. He also feels that the City has a major problem with their implementation process.

Problems with delay of project by Prime Contractor

A black BBE was awarded a subcontract by a Hispanic HBE. The project involved the building of the City of St. Petersburg North Branch Library. When the project began the BBE was given six weeks to finish, when the project was half way completed the HBE prime contractor reduced the BBE's time of completion to four weeks due to the HBE's delay on the front end of the project. The BBE was faced with either hiring more people to meet the deadline or pay liquidated damages for the delay of the project imposed by the City. The BBE requested a change order, which the prime refused to provide. This prompted the BBE to withdraw from the project. The City never intervened in support of the MBE's subcontractor's cause. The BBE believes that the prime contractor unfairly treated him. When asked if this unfair treatment could be attributed to his race, the BBE was not sure. However, he does not believe that the HBE would have treated a white or Hispanic subcontractor the way he was treated.

Upon verification, I found that the BBE did not voluntarily withdraw from the project, but was actually terminated by the prime HBE allegedly due to poor performance. The BBE's claim that the prime HBE delayed the project in the front end could not be substantiated, and hence the *BBE's claim of unfair treatment was not substantiated.*

Summary

In summation, of the 13 anecdotes of unfair or disparate treatment of minoritites by the city of St. Petersburg in the award of contracts that were verified, a large majority (9 out of 13 or 68 percent) were found to be either inconclusive or unsubstantiated; 23 percent found the city to be a "passive participant" in a discriminatory subcontracting process; and 8 percent found minorities to be victims of aggressive market competitive factors.

Anecdotes from Community Organizations

This section presents the anecdotal comments from interviews with community organizations. As discussed above, a total of 12 community organization representatives were selected to be interviewed. Of this total number of representatives, six were actually interviewed. However, only three of these representatives provided anecdotal comments that were worth reporting in this book because they seemed to corroborate the findings and conclusions derived from the verified anecdotes presented above. The remaining nine anecdotes from representatives of community organizations could not be corroborated upon verification. The comments are as follows:

1. A black community leader who served on City Council for several years commented that a major problem with most minority businesses is that they are not licensed or do not have formal training in various trades and procurement areas that are bid by the City of St. Petersburg. In addition, he views the City's race-conscious construction program as limiting several minority businesses' chance of doing business with the City. He also feels that it is extremely difficult, if not impossible, to effectively monitor and document "good faith effort" made by prime contractors to use M/WBEs. He feels that most of the problems encountered by M/WBE in the City's relevant market area can be resolved by establishing a citywide Small Business Shelter Program which allows all small businesses to bid on certain City contracts irrespective of race, gender or ethnicity of the owner. The small business program should be expanded into all the City's procurement areas, not just construction. He also recommends that the City should be involved in sponsoring a small business academy that provides small business owners in the area with basic training in business management and government contracting. Finally, he strongly recommended that the City immediately cease to sponsor community organizations that directly or indirectly provide loan packaging assistance to businesses based on race, gender or ethnicity, and instead channel the funds to organizations that provide micro-loans to small businesses irrespective of the owners' race, gender or ethnicity.
2. A female representative of a non-minority financial institution feels that major problems encountered by M/WBEs applying for business loans are (a) no training or background experience in business management; and (2) poor personal credit. She contends that sponsoring organizations that assist in loan packaging may be inefficient and ineffective in that the banks ultimately evaluate these loan packages using standard competitive market criteria. Instead, she recommends that the City may get more return for its

investment if it encourages M/WBEs to participate in existing business management classes being offered by a local business academy.

3. A representative of a black business organization feels that affirmative action and the City's M/WBE program is detrimental to black business development. In particular, he feels that these programs create an unnecessary tension between the various racial and ethnic groups in the local community. Hence, he recommends that the City may be well served by instituting and supporting a small business initiative irrespective of race, gender or ethnic background of the business owners.

Contracting Discrimination Survey Results

This section presents the result of a survey of a random sample of 89 contractors and vendors in the City of St. Petersburg relevant market area. The results of the survey corroborated the findings of anecdotal evidence of unfair treatment or discrimination outlined above. Of the total number of contractors and vendors surveyed, 44.9 percent were non-minority businesses, while 55.1 percent were M/WBEs. Disaggregating the data by racial, ethnic and gender group, the data indicate that 44.9 percent of the total respondents were non-minority contractors or vendors, 9.0 percent were black contractors or vendors, 13.5 percent were Hispanic contractors or vendors, 24. 7 percent were women contractors or vendors, and 7.0 percent were other minority contractors or vendors.

Tables 11-1 to 11-9 present the results of the contractors' or vendors' (M/WBE and non-M/WBEs) experience with discrimination in the City of St. Petersburg's contracting process. Table 11-1 presents the result of the respondents' opinion regarding denial of contracting opportunity because of their race or gender. The result indicates that a large majority (87.8 percent) of the contractors indicated that they have seldom to never been denied contracting opportunity because of their race or gender.

Table 11-1
Rating of contracts opportunity denial due to race, gender or ethnic group
by race, gender or ethnic group
City of St. Petersburg

Rating	M/WBE													
	Non-minority		Woman		Black		Hispanic		Other		Total M/WBE		All Races	
	#	%	#	%	#	%	#	%	#	%	#	%	#	%
Never	27	87.10	15	78.95	4	66.67	12	100.00	5	83.33	36	83.72	63	85.14
Seldom	0	0.00	2	10.53	0	0.00	0	0.00	0	0.00	2	4.65	2	2.70
Sometimes	1	3.23	1	5.26	0	0.00	0	0.00	0	0.00	1	2.33	2	2.70
Often	2	6.45	1	5.26	1	16.67	0	0.00	0	0.00	2	4.65	4	5.41
Always	1	3.23	0	0.00	1	16.67	0	0.00	1	16.67	2	4.65	3	4.05
Total	31	100	19	100	6	100	12	100	6	100	43	100	74	100

Table 11-2
Importance of race, gender or ethnic group as determining factor in prime contract award by race, gender or ethnic group
City of St. Petersburg

Rating	M/WBE													
	Non-minority		Woman		Black		Hispanic		Other		Total M/WBE		All Races	
	#	%	#	%	#	%	#	%	#	%	#	%	#	%
Not Important	41	56.16	9	47.37	2	28.57	5	45.45	3	60.00	19	45.24	60	52.17
Somewhat Important	10	13.70	3	15.79	1	14.29	3	27.27	0	0.00	7	16.67	17	14.78
Important	8	10.96	3	15.79	2	28.57	1	9.09	0	0.00	6	14.29	14	12.17
Very Important	7	9.59	1	5.26	0	0.00	2	18.18	2	40.00	5	11.90	12	10.43
Extremely important	7	9.59	3	15.79	2	28.57	0	0.00	0	0.00	5	11.90	12	10.43
Total	73	100	19	100	7	100	11	100	5	100	42	100	115	100

When the data was disaggregated by M/WBEs and non-M/WBEs, the result was consistent with the overall finding in that a large majority of M/WBEs and non-M/WBEs indicated that they have seldom to never been denied contracting opportunities by the City of St. Petersburg because of their race, ethnicity, or gender. A majority (over 66 percent) of each of the M/WBE group also indicated that they have seldom to never been denied contracting opportunities because of their race or gender.

Furthermore, a majority (52.2 percent) of the respondents viewed race or gender as not an important factor in determining contract award by the City (see Table 11-2). However, when the data was disaggregated by racial, ethnic or gender group, a mixed opinion was apparent. For example, a majority (56.2 percent) of non-M/WBEs viewed race and gender as not an important determining factor in the award of prime contracts. Amongst the M/WBE groups, black respondents constituted the largest proportion of M/WBEs who view race, ethnicity or gender as a determining factor in the award of prime contracts by the City, followed by woman- and Hispanic-owned firms, and the least were the other W/MBE group.

With regard to subcontracting (see Table 11-3), a majority (51.3 percent) of all the contractors surveyed viewed race, gender or ethnicity as not an important factor in the award of subcontracts by prime contractors. However, when the data was disaggregated by racial, gender, or ethnic group, a contrasting opinion between non-M/WBEs and M/WBEs was apparent. For example, as in prime contracting, majority M/WBEs (55.4 percent) viewed race as a somewhat to extremely determining factor in the award of subcontracts by prime contractors in the City's relevant market area. In contrast, a majority (55.4 percent) of non-M/WBEs viewed race, gender or ethnicity as *not* determining factor in the award of subcontracts by the prime contractors. (see Table 11-3). A majority of black-, Hispanic-, and woman-owned businesses contractors viewed race, gender or ethnicity as a somewhat to

Table 11-3
Importance of race ethnicity or gender as a determining factor in subcontract awards by race, gender or ethnic group
City of St. Petersburg

Rating	M/WBE													
	Non-minority		Woman		Black		Hispanic		Other		Total M/WBE		All Races	
	#	%	#	%	#	%	#	%	#	%	#	%	#	%
Not Important	41	55.41	8	40.00	3	42.86	5	45.45	3	60.00	19	44.19	60	51.28
Somewhat Important	8	10.81	2	10.00	0	0.00	3	27.27	0	0.00	5	11.63	13	11.11
Important	7	9.46	4	20.00	2	28.57	0	0.00	0	0.00	6	13.95	13	11.11
Very Important	9	12.16	1	5.00	0	0.00	3	27.27	2	40.00	6	13.95	15	12.82
Extremely important	9	12.16	5	25.00	2	28.57	0	0.00	0	0.00	7	16.28	16	13.68
Total	74	100	20	100	7	100	11	100	5	100	43	100	117	100

Table 11-4
Importance of race ethnicity or gender as a determining factor in sub-contractors by primes by race, gender or ethnic group
City of St. Petersburg

Rating	M/WBE													
	Non-minority		Woman		Black		Hispanic		Other		Total M/WBE		All Races	
	#	%	#	%	#	%	#	%	#	%	#	%	#	%
Not Important	19	65 52	7	36.84	3	50.00	6	54.55	2	40.00	18	43.90	37	52.86
Somewhat Important	3	10.34	2	10.53	0	0.00	3	27.27	1	20.00	6	14.63	9	12.86
Important	2	6.90	2	10.53	1	16.67	1	9.09	0	0.00	4	9.76	6	8.57
Very Important	3	10.34	3	15.79	1	16.67	1	9.09	2	40.00	7	17.07	10	14.29
Extremely important	2	6.90	5	26.32	1	16.67	0	0.00	0	0.00	6	14.63	8	11.43
Total	29	100	19	100	6	100	11	100	5	100	41	100	70	100

extremely important factor in the award of subcontracts by prime contractors in the City of St. Petersburg's relevant market area.

When asked if race, gender or ethnicity was a determining factor in the selection of subcontractors by prime contractors, a majority (52.9 percent) of the respondents viewed race, ethnicity or gender as not important in the selection of subcontractors by prime contractors. (see Table 11-4). However, when the data was disaggregated by racial, ethnic or gender group, a contrast of opinion was apparent between non-M/WBEs and M/WBEs. For example, only 34.5 percent of non-M/WBE contractors viewed race, gender or ethnicity as a somewhat to extremely important factor in the selection of subcontractors by prime contractors. Meanwhile, a majority (56.1 percent) of M/WBE respondents viewed race, gender or ethnicity as a determining factor in the selection of subcontractors by prime contractors. A majority of woman- and other minority-owned business contractors viewed race, gender or ethnicity as a somewhat to extremely important factor in the selection of subcontractors by prime contractors.

With regard to technical assistance, a large majority (84.3 percent) of the respondent contractors said the City has never denied providing them with technical assistance because of their race, ethnicity or gender (see Table 11-5). When the data was disaggregated by racial, ethnicity or gender group, the result was consistent with the overall finding in that a majority of each of the group was of the opinion that the City has never denied providing them with technical assistance because of their race, ethnicity or gender.

Table 11-5
Rating of technical assistance not provided due to race, gender or ethnic group
by race, gender or ethnic group
City of St. Petersburg

Rating	M/WBE													
	Non-minority		Woman		Black		Hispanic		Other		Total M/WBE		All Races	
	#	%	#	%	#	%	#	%	#	%	#	%	#	%
Never	29	93.55	12	75.00	5	71.43	9	81.82	4	80.00	30	76.92	59	84.29
Seldom	0	0.00	2	12.50	2	28.57	2	18.18	0	0.00	6	15.38	6	8.57
Sometimes	1	3.23	1	6.25	0	0.00	0	0.00	0	0.00	1	2.56	2	2.86
Often	0	0.00	1	6.25	0	0.00	0	0.00	0	0.00	1	2.56	1	1.43
Always	1	3.23	0	0.00	0	0.00	0	0.00	1	20.00	1	2.56	2	2.86
Total	31	100	16	100	7	100	11	100	5	100	39	100	70	100

Table 11-6
Rating of City delaying payment due to race, gender or ethnic group by race, gender or ethnic group
City of St. Petersburg

Rating	M/WBE													
	Non-minority		Woman		Black		Hispanic		Other		Total M/WBE		All Races	
	#	%	#	%	#	%	#	%	#	%	#	%	#	%
Never	22	91.67	10	83.33	5	100.00	4	57.14	4	80.00	23	79.31	45	84.91
Seldom	0	0.00	2	16.67	0	0.00	3	42.86	1	20.00	6	20.69	6	11.32
Sometimes	1	4.17	0	0.00	0	0.00	0	0.00	0	0.00	0	0.00	1	1.89
Often	1	4.17	0	0.00	0	0.00	0	0.00	0	0.00	0	0.00	1	1.89
Always	0	0.00	0	0.00	0	0.00	0	0.00	0	0.00	0	0.00	0	0.00
Total	24	100	12	100	5	100	7	100	5	100	29	100	53	100

Table 11-7
Frequency of primes delaying payment of sub-contractors due to race, gender or ethnic group
City of St. Petersburg

Rating	M/WBE													
	Non-minority		Woman		Black		Hispanic		Other		Total M/WBE		All Races	
	#	%	#	%	#	%	#	%	#	%	#	%	#	%
Never	20	95.24	7	77.78	4	66.67	6	75.00	1	100.00	18	75.00	38	84.44
Seldom	0	0.00	1	11.11	1	16.67	0	0.00	0	0.00	2	8.33	2	4.44
Sometimes	0	0.00	0	0.00	0	0.00	0	0.00	0	0.00	0	0.00	0	0.00
Often	0	0.00	1	11.11	1	16.67	2	25.00	0	0.00	4	16.67	4	8.89
Always	1	4.76	0	0.00	0	0.00	0	0.00	0	0.00	0	0.00	1	2.22
Total	21	100	9	100	6	100	8	100	1	100	24	100	45	100

With regard to prompt payment, a large majority (over 88.5 percent) of the respondent contractors said the City and the prime contractors doing business with the City have seldom to never delayed paying them for services provided because of their race or gender. (see Tables 11-6 and 11-7). When the data was disaggregated by racial, ethnicity or gender group, the result was consistent with the overall finding in that a majority of each of the group was of the opinion that the City has seldom to never delayed paying them for services provided because of their race, gender or ethnicity.

The M/WBEs' opinion regarding not being informed of contracting opportunities because of their race, gender or ethnicity was consistent with the other findings outlined above in this section (see Table 11-8). For example, a large majority of the respondent contractors (96.3 percent) were of the opinion that the City has seldom to never not informed them of contracting opportunities because of their race, ender or ethnicity. When the data was disaggregated by racial, ethnicity or gender group, the result was consistent with the overall finding in that a majority of each of the groups was of the opinion that the City has seldom to never not informed them of contracting.

Finally, when asked how frequent they have been treated unfairly by the City of St. Petersburg because of their race or gender, a large majority (92.1 percent) said seldom to never. (see Table 11-9). When the data was disaggregated by racial, ethnicity or gender group, the result was consistent with the overall finding in that a majority of each of the groups was of the opinion that the City has seldom to never treated them unfairly because of their race, gender or ethnicity.

Table 11-8
Frequency of primes delaying payment of sub-contractors due to race, gender or ethnic group
City of St. Petersburg

Rating	M/WBE													
	Non-minority		Woman		Black		Hispanic		Other		Total M/WBE		All Races	
	#	%	#	%	#	%	#	%	#	%	#	%	#	%
Never	27	90.00	8	61.54	4	66.67	10	83.33	2	66.67	24	70.59	51	79.69
Seldom	1	3.33	5	38.46	2	33.33	2	16.67	0	0.00	9	26.47	10	15.63
Sometimes	0	0.00	0	0.00	0	0.00	0	0.00	0	0.00	0	0.00	0	0.00
Often	1	3.33	0	0.00	0	0.00	0	0.00	1	33.33	1	2.94	2	3.13
Always	1	3.33	0	0.00	0	0.00	0	0.00	0	0.00	0	0.00	1	1.56
Total	30	100	13	100	6	100	12	100	3	100	34	100	64	100

Table 11-9
Rating of unfair treatment by City on other issues due to race, gender or ethnic group by race, gender or ethnic group
City of St. Petersburg

Rating	M/WBE													
	Non-minority		Woman		Black		Hispanic		Other		Total M/WBE		All Races	
	#	%	#	%	#	%	#	%	#	%	#	%	#	%
Very Poor	33	94.29	12	70.59	5	71.43	8	72.73	4	66.67	29	70.73	62	81.58
Poor	0	0.00	3	17.65	2	28.57	2	18.18	1	16.67	8	19.51	8	10.53
Fair	1	2.86	1	5.88	0	0.00	0	0.00	0	0.00	1	2.44	2	2.63
Good	0	0.00	1	5.88	0	0.00	1	9.09	0	0.00	2	4.88	2	2.63
Excellent	1	2.86	0	0.00	0	0.00	0	0.00	1	16.67	1	2.44	2	2.63
Total	35	100	17	100	7	100	11	100	6	100	41	100	76	100

Based on the survey results above, it can be concluded that:

(1) A majority of the contractors and vendors surveyed in the City of St. Petersburg's relevant market area contend that they have seldom to never been denied contracting opportunities because of their race, gender or ethnicity.

(2) A majority of contractors and vendors in the City of St. Petersburg's relevant market area surveyed view race or gender as not a determining factor in the award of prime contracts by the City, and the award of subcontracts by prime contractors. However, most black contractors surveyed view race, ethnicity or gender as a determining factor in the award of prime contracts by the City. Meanwhile, a majority of M/WBEs surveyed view race, ethnicity and gender as a determining factor in the award of subcontracts by prime contractors.

(3) A majority of contractors and vendors surveyed in the City of St. Petersburg's relevant market area view race, gender or ethnicity as not an important factor in the award of subcontracts by the City. However, this majority opinion is not shared by a majority of black-, Hispanic- and woman-owned business contractors and vendors who view race, gender, or ethnicity as a somewhat to extremely important factor in the award of subcontracts by prime contractors in the City's relevant market area.

(4) A majority of contractors and vendors in the City of St. Petersburg's relevant market area do not view race, gender or ethnicity as a determining factor in the selection of subcontractors by prime contractors. However, a majority of M/WBE respondents, especially woman- and other minority-owned contractors, view race, gender or ethnicity as a determining factor in the selection of subcontractors by prime contractors.

(5) A majority of contractors and vendors in the City of St. Petersburg's relevant market area view race, gender or ethnicity as not a determining factor in the selection of contractors and subcontractors, the provision of technical assistance to effectively compete for the City's contracts, fair

treatment by the City, and being informed of contracting opportunities.

City Officials Interview Results

This section presents the findings of interviews of city officials which were conducted to determine the extent of progress made by the City's race preference program in ensuring parity in the city's contracting process. In particular, this section reports the findings of interviews conducted with the political leaderships and senior staff of major departments in the City of St. Petersburg that procure and award construction contracts. The senior staff interviewed included: the Mayor, the City Administrator, the City's Chief of Staff, the Administrator for Economic Development, the Administrator for Public Works Department, the Director and staff of the Purchasing and Materials Management Department, the Director and staff of the Engineering and Stormwater Department, and the Director and staff of the Economic Development and Material Management Department. The section also include responses from the Manager and staff of the M/WBE program Office and seven community organizations and individuals that provide assistance to M/WBEs in the City's relevant market area.

The interview addressed issues related to M/WBE program operations, tracking, monitoring, and reporting. These issues include: (1) the departments' and political leadership's understanding, knowledge and implementation efforts of the City's M/WBE policy and program; and (2) a determination of the extent to which cooperation and/or conflict exist between the departments, the City officials and political leadership, and community organizations in implementing the M/WBE ordinance, and how these implementation characteristics affect M/WBE utilization in the City's procurement of goods and services.

The questions used for the interview were divided into five major areas: (1) M/WBE Policy; (2) type of good faith efforts; (3) procurement organizational structure; (4) reporting and monitoring of M/WBE participation; and (5) payment and bonding requirements. A total of 36 members of community organizations, and senior staff and political leaders of the City were identified to be surveyed or interviewed. Of this total, 29 individuals were actually surveyed or interviewed, representing a response rate of 80 percent. The remaining 20 percent could not be reached to schedule an interview despite several telephone calls to do so by the author of this book.

Race Preference Policy Awareness

All but three City officials and political leaders indicated that they were aware of the City of St. Petersburg's race preference policy that is designed to afford M/WBEs maximum opportunity to participate in the City's procurement and contracting process. All the members of City Council interviewed, and a majority (55 percent) City officials and staff, knew and understood the M/WBE policy as set forth in the City's race preference ordinance. All the City officials interviewed, except five, provided examples of the objectives of policies they use to maximize M/WBE participation including increase in M/WBE participation in City construction contracting commensurate with availability, informing M/WBEs of construction contracting opportunities in the departments, ensuring M/WBE involvement in the bidding process, and givimg M/WBE vendors an equal chance to earn City construction dollars. A large majority (that is, 80 percent) of the City officials interviewed were aware of state and federal legislations and guidelines that govern race preference operations and decision-making.

Coordination of Race Preference Operations

Regarding coordination of race preference operations, a majority (80 percent) of the department officials interviewed indicated having individuals within their department who serve as an official or unofficial M/WBE liaison to the MBE Construction (Goal Setting) Committee or M/WBE office; while the other departments rely solely on the M/WBE Office and the MBE Construction (Goal Setting) Committee to coordinate M/WBE operations. All the department officials interviewed provided examples of the responsibilities of the M/WBE coordinator and the construction committee which include: (1) ensuring that the M/WBE ordinance is enforced; (2) ensuring that appropriate M/WBE participation goals are set in construction; (3) determining which projects should be sheltered and which should be goal-oriented; (4) certifying and decertifying of firms; (5) maintaining a listing of certified minority and women-owned; (6) providing M/WBE Committee with percent of available M/WBEs; (7) promoting M/WBE opportunities and participation; (8) providing the construction committee with all available W/MBEs for different scopes of work required on projects; (9) establishing M/WBE goals according to availability; (10) evaluating prime contractors' compliance prior to contract award; (11) ensuring that M/WBE is responsible for at least 50 percent of the contract amount of shelter projects; (12) managing the Business Assistance Division; and (12) reporting to the Mayor and City Council on M/WBE participation. Hence, it can be concluded that the officials and political leaders of the City of St. Petersburg are generally aware of the City's M/WBE policy, and its coordination and implementation structure.

M/WBE Awareness and Tracking

When asked who handles M/WBE awareness and tracking, the opinion of the City officials was consistent with the M/WBE ordinance and the City Administrative Code. For example, with the exception of two City officials, all the officials interviewed viewed M/WBE awareness and tracking as the responsibility of the M/WBE office and the Construction committee, not the departments. However, during the period studied, the Department of Engineering and Stormwater and the Purchasing and Material Management Department monitored and tracked M/WBE participation. Hence, it can be concluded that the City of St. Petersburg's M/WBE awareness and tracking system is generally well organized and consistent with the provisions of the City's M/WBE ordinance.

Race Preference Program Coordination Effectiveness

A majority (63.2 percent) of City officials interviewed had no problem with the existing race preference program coordination efforts, and was aware of annual purchasing and tracking reports of M/WBE contracting. Some members of community organizations, however, expressed concern about the continuous shifting of the M/WBE Office from the auspices of one City department to another during the last nine years. In particular, these members viewed the continual shifts as making it difficult for them to have a consistent and stable working relationship with City on M/WBE issues. However, over 90 percent of the interviewees (that is, city officials and community organizations alike) view the recent establishment and placement of the Business Development Center under the Economic Development and Property Management Department as a positive step in facilitating and enhancing the implementation of the City's race preference policy. Some community groups and City officials, however, expressed concern about the location of the new Business Development Center as inappropriate for catering to all M/WBE groups' concerns[309]. Finally, a majority of the interviewees preferred not only that the race preference program be extended to other commodity areas, but also that the program be targeted towards all small businesses irrespective of race, gender or ethnicity of the owners. Hence, it can be concluded that the City officials and community organizations interviewed are, for the most part, satisfied with the existing coordination (and

---

309 The center was located in a predominantly African American neighborhood with less than 1 percent of the businesses owned and operated by other minority groups.

implementation) structure of the City M/WBE program. In addition, most of the interviewees view the recently established Business Development Center under the Economic Development and Property Management Department as a positive step in facilitating and enhancing an effective implementation (and coordination) of the City's race preference policy. These findings are consistent with those derived from verified anecdotes presented above.

M/WBE Certification

All the officials viewed M/WBE certification, recertification, decertification and verification as the function of the M/WBE Office.

Race Preference Program Staffing

Regarding staffing of the City's race preference program, all the City departments indicated that they do not have enough staff to handle the M/WBE workload as specified in the M/WBE Ordinance, but rather rely on the M/WBE office staff (and the Construction Committee) to effectively implement the M/WBE policy.

Based on these findings, it can be concluded that the City of St. Petersburg departments' awareness, coordination and tracking of W/MBE are generally organized and consistent with the provisions specified in the City's M/WBE ordinance and Administrative Code. In addition, most of the City officials do seem to understand their role regarding tracking, coordinating and promoting M/WBE awareness as specified in the City's race preference ordinance. However, staffing within departments for M/WBE operations as specified in the M/WBE Ordinance and Administrative Code is limited.

Good Faith and Outreach Efforts

A majority of the officials indicated that they were not familiar with the process of prime contractors making good faith and outreach efforts to inform M/WBEs of contracting/procurement opportunities. For those officials who were familiar with the process, they indicated that several types of outreach efforts are utilized including sending pre-bid and bid notices about shelter projects to all appropriate certified M/WBEs, and advertising in local newspapers, the Dodge Report, and minority-oriented newspapers. In addition, prime contractors bidding on construction contracts with M/WBE participation goals are encouraged to demonstrate good faith efforts by sending (and documenting) "Intent to Bid" letters and subcontracting bid notices to available M/WBEs in the City's relevant market area.

With regards to enforcing good faith efforts made by prime contractors, the Engineering and Stormwater Department and the Purchasing and Material Management Department indicated that ever since the M/WBE ordinance was enacted, all the prime contractors bidding on construction projects requiring M/WBE participation have been encouraged to make good faith efforts as specified in Section (f) of the City's race preference ordinance.

These findings suggest that the City departments (Engineering and Stormwater, and Purchasing and Material Management) responsible for implementing Section (f) of the City's race preference ordinance have made some attempt to enforce the City's M/WBE Ordinance provisions of "good faith effort".

Race Preference Program Organizational Structure and Administration Effectiveness Results

This section provides the findings of the level of effectiveness of the City of St. Petersburg race preference program in providing technical assistance, networking and outreach assistance, tracking and monitoring M/WBE participation in the city's contracting process, and bonding and payment requirements. The section concludes with some suggestions made by city officials and community leaders on how to improve the city's race preference program operations.

Technical Assistance Effectiveness

As discussed earlier, the City's race preference ordinance required soliciting departments to provide targeted technical assistance to M/WBEs in order to enhance their chances of competing for the City's construction contracts. Most of the City officials and community organizations interviewed indicated that they would like to see this effort extended to other commodity areas such as goods and professional services, not only construction.

With regards to employing sufficient staff to implement an effective race preference program within the City, all contracting department officials in the City government indicated that they have a staff person within the department assigned to track, monitor and report M/WBE operations, and serve as a liaison with the race preference program staff. The M/WBE Office indicated that they could use additional staff to effectively implement the City's race preference ordinance.

Depending on the product or services to be purchased by the City, the departments interviewed admitted to having implemented the provision of dividing purchases and contracts into smaller units, areas, or quantities where feasible and likely to increase M/WBE participation. Some departments, however, expressed a conflict between this provision and contracting provisions of the City procurement code.

With regards to the use of community organizations to locate and assist M/WBEs to take advantage of the City's contracting opportunities, with the exception of one organization, all the organizations interviewed indicated that they have established a strong and positive horizontal linkage with the City. The one organization expressed concern about the City terminating its funding for an M/WBE loan program after 15 years. As discussed earlier, in an interview with City staff, it was revealed that the particular funding was withdrawn because of lack of performance by the community organization.

Concerning the provision of ensuring that bid/proposals, specifications and plans are written or drawn so as not to prejudice or unreasonably limit M/WBE participation, all the City departments interviewed admitted to having implemented this provision, except in contracting situations involving multi-year contracts, renewals, and exemptions.

Based on the above findings, it can be concluded that the City of St. Petersburg departments, have effectively implemented the targeted technical assistance provisions as specified in the City's race preference ordinance and the City's Administrative Code. Also, the City has established a sound working relationship with community organizations to assist M/WBEs in the City's relevant market area to participate in the City's contracting process.

M/WBE Networking and Outreach Assistance Effectiveness

The departments responsible for implementing the City's race preference policy were of the opinion that the City has made considerable effort to implement all the provisions for M/WBE networking and outreach assistance provisions as specified in the race preference ordinance and the City Administrative Code. Most of these efforts were made by the City's M/WBE office. A verification of the office's records, documents, database and reports indicated that during the study time frame (that is, from FY 1989 to FY 1997) the City of St. Petersburg has either sponsored or organized several M/WBE networking and outreach assistance activities. These activities include: (a) distribution of certification application and M/WBE program flyers at trades fairs, meetings and conferences such as, the Annual Small Business Government Contracting Trade Fair, the Annual National Minority Supplier Development Council Conference, the Equal Employment Opportunity/contract Compliance Conference, the Annual Minority Business Matchmaker, American Public Works Association Conference, the Florida Association of Minority Business Enterprise Organizations conference, and the

Minority Business Enterprise Development Week; and (b) sponsoring, organizing and attending workshops and seminars to inform M/WBEs of the City's race preference program such as "Minority Enterprise and Education for Tomorrow" workshop, Hispanic Business Institute Workshop, and the City of St. Petersburg Chamber of Commerce Business Retention Mentor/Protégé Program and the South Central Council workshop.

Despite these efforts, however, an analysis of surveys administered to M/WBEs in the City's relevant market area indicated that a lack of information was the most cited reason for them not bidding on the City's prime contracts and subcontract[310]. Therefore, it can be concluded that the result of an assessment of the City of St. Petersburg efforts in providing networking and outreach assistance to M/WBEs is inclusive.

Tracking and Monitoring M/WBE Participation

The two departments primarily responsible for implementing the City's M/WBE policy (that is, Engineering and Stormwater, and Purchasing and Material Management) and the M/WBE office indicated that they monitor M/WBE participation on construction prime contracts and subcontracts. However, most of the departments' officials interviewed viewed this function as the responsibility of the M/WBE Office. A review of the City's race preference program activity records indicates that the M/WBE Office does have prepared forms used to track and monitor M/WBE subcontracting participation.

Furthermore, the two departments and the M/WBE Office have procedures in place to monitor whether the prime contractors are utilizing M/WBEs on construction. These procedures include: (a) requiring contractors to provide a list of M/WBEs on the job; (b) an agreement by prime contractors to maintain M/WBE

---

[310] See Tables 10-3 and 10-4 of this report.

subcontractors; (c) site visits to monitor M/WBE utilization on projects; (d) review of invoices for consistency; (e) requiring prime contractors to submit letters of intent to use M/WBEs before contract award is made; (f) requiring prime contractors to get approval before taking an M/WBE off a project; (g) identifying payments made to M/WBEs on the "Contractor Utilization" form; and (h) verifying final payment made to M/WBEs.

With regards to challenging "good faith effort" by prime contractors and compliance monitoring of M/WBE participation, most of the City's department officials and political leaders interviewed view these activities as the responsibility of the M/WBE Office.

With regards to delineation of responsibility between departments to monitor compliance, a majority (68 percent) of the City departments indicated that there was no clear delineation of responsibility between the departments on how to monitor and enforce M/WBE compliance. However, most of the respondents viewed this task as the responsibility of the M/WBE office and the Legal department.

All the departments indicated that the City has a computerize database of M/WBE subcontractors, but not the amount paid to them.

Based on the above findings, it can be concluded that with a few exceptions, the City of St. Petersburg departments' tracking and monitoring of M/WBE participation in the City's contracting and subcontracting activities are well coordinated, organized and consistent with the provisions of the City's race preference ordinance. In addition, the two departments and the M/WBE office responsible for implementing the City's M/WBE policy seem to understand their role in tracking and monitoring M/WBE participation as specified in the City's M/WBE ordinance.

Payment and Bonding requirements

Most departments indicated that they were aware of the City's prompt payment policy. Three departments indicated that this was the responsibility of the Finance department. Three departments reported that payments usually take five to seven days. Two departments reported that it takes two weeks, while three said it takes 30 days. Two of the City officials interviewed indicated that they have on occasion received complaints from M/WBEs about delay in payment by prime contractors for work or services provided to the City. A majority of the departments reported that they do have a bond waiver provision for M/WBEs.

Hence, the following conclusions can be made concerning the City of St. Petersburg's the effective implementation of payment and bonding provisions of city's race preference program. Although the city departments have different time frames for paying contractors doing business with the city, the departments have generally been effective in enforcing the city's prompt payment provision as specified in the City's M/WBE ordinance. Meanwhile, most of the city departments do have a bond waiver provision for M/WBEs.

M/WBE Program Improvement Suggestions

The respondent department officials and political leaders of the City of St. Petersburg made some suggestions for improving the M/WBEs participation in the City's contracting process. The suggestions are as follows:

M/WBE Capacity Building

A City Council member suggested that the emphasis in M/WBE development should be in assisting minority- and woman-owned business owners to be qualified to do business with the City through an across-the-board small business training initiative which caters to all businesses irrespective of race, gender or ethnicity. For those businesses that are qualified to do business with the City, the Council member recommends that the City should encourage these businesses to bid by making efforts to dispel the perception of the existence of a "good old boy network" in the City's contracting system. In addition, the City should provide these businesses with incentives to hire the hardcore unemployed in the City's blighted areas. These incentives should include: (a) providing credit or tax breaks to businesses in the City's relevant market area of the unemployed. The need for more clearly defined procurement classification of M/WBE availability; (b) expand the M/WBE program to other commodity areas, not only construction; and (c) establish trust and horizontal linkages between the City, minority community, M/WBEs and non-M/WBEs in the local community. A Council member suggested that there should be provisions in the M/WBE ordinance to provide ongoing assistance to M/WBEs in accounting, business planning, bid/RFP responses, and cost estimating.

Government Contracting Education

A City Council member suggested that the City should shift its focus from quick handout of City funds to M/WBEs whose qualification and credit history are questionable, to a loan guarantee program which emphasizes a careful review of each applicant's business plan. With regards to the bidding on City contracts, the Council person suggested that the City should establish a mechanism to educate M/WBEs on how to apply and complete a bid application, and upon contract award, how to manage a government contract. In effect, the Council person recommended that the City should focus on educating M/WBEs on government contracting from which a pool of qualified M/WBEs can be derived to do business with the City. Without such an education initiative, the Council person asserted, the City may be vulnerable to waste and legal problems. By way of example, the Council member cited an incident involving a prime MBE contractor who hired local subcontractors to perform work on a City contract. When the project was completed, the prime MBE refused to pay the local subcontractors, resulting in a lawsuit which was still in progress.

Expansion of Race Preference Program

Most of the city official and community leaders interviewed wanted to see the city's race preference program expanded to other commodity and service areas. For example, a Council member recommended that the M/WBE program should be expanded to other commodity areas. Meanwhile, a City purchasing agent suggested that the city's race preference program be expanded to the entire City's major commodity areas, and assistance to all local small businesses irrespective of racial ethnic or gender of the owner. The purchasing agent felt that such an expanded program will better serve the M/WBEs in the City's relevant market area if it is a separate entity (Department), not as office within a City department. A number of city directors suggested that the city's race preference initiative should shift its focus to capacity-building and expansion of the program to other procurement areas. To accomplish this goal, the directors recommended that the City should invest in M/WBE education, staffing of the M/WBE office, and increasing the budget for business assistance. A city administrator recommended that, if legally feasible, the program should be expanded into other commodity areas.

Monitoring of Prime Contractors

A City Administrator recommended that the City should, if legally possible, formalize the monitoring of prime contractors to make sure they are utilizing M/WBEs as specified in contract award documents. He also recommended that the City should fine-tune its efforts in: (a) verifying the M/WBE status of contractors and vendors; and (b) payment of M/WBEs by prime contractors; (c) outreach and networking efforts.

Race Neutral Small Business Program

A City Administrator suggested that the City should modify the race preference program to include all small businesses irrespective of race, gender or ethnicity of the owner. A City Administrator said that a problem that seems to arise occasionally is when a subcontractor (minority or otherwise) gets in a dispute with a prime contractor, and the City gets caught in the middle. Such an incident is often not in the direct control of the City, but the City project may be negatively impacted. The Administrator suggested that procedures to address this beforehand could be helpful. He also was in favor of expanding the City's M/WBE initiative into other commodity areas, and if legally feasible to all small businesses, irrespective of the racial, gender or ethnicity of the owner.

Race Preference Policy and Law Update

A Purchasing Agent suggested that there should be a periodic in-house briefing to update City Officials about the City's race preference policy and other laws affecting M/WBEs.

Consistency of Procurement Procedures across City Departments

A purchasing agent recommended that the Engineering Department's procurement procedures be amended to be more compatible with that of Purchasing Department.

Summary

The findings and suggestions of these interviews seem to corroborate the results of verified anecdotes presented earlier in this chapter.

Contractors Survey Results

This section presents the results of a survey administered to contractors or vendors (M/WBEs and non-M/WBEs) in the City of St. Petersburg's relevant market area. The purpose of the survey was to identify administrative barriers and requirements that inhibited effective implementation of the city's procurement policy. A total of 364 surveyed were mailed to a randomly selected firms on the city's contract awards list. Of this total number of surveys, 89 contractors (or vendors) responded, representing a response rate of approximately 25 percent. Approximately

55 percent of the respondents were M/WBEs, while and 45 percent were non-M/WBEs. The survey focused on four major dimensions of the City's contracting process such as: (a) the quality of the M/WBE Office assistance; (b) bonding and financial position of the contractors; (c) effectiveness of prompt payment by the City; and (d) effectiveness of the M/WBE certification process. The result of the survey is presented below.

Quality of M/WBE Office Assistance

Table 12-1 displays the M/WBE owners' opinion regarding the quality of assistance received from the City of St. Petersburg M/WBE office. The data indicates that a large majority (90.6 percent) of respondents rate the quality of assistance received from the M/WBE office as fair to excellent. When the data was disaggregated by racial, gender or ethnicity of the owners, the result was consistent with the overall finding. Hence, it can be concluded that M/WBEs in the City of St. Petersburg's relevant market area are generally satisfied with the quality of assistance received from the M/WBE office.

Contractors Bonding Requirement and Financial Position

Table 13-1 shows the contractors' response to bonding requirements needed to contract with the City of St. Petersburg. The result indicates that a large proportion (70.2 percent) of the respondents do not require bonding, compared to only 29.8 percent that do require bonding. When the data was disaggregated by racial, gender or ethnic group, each group exhibited the same outcome as the overall finding in that a large proportion (over 61 percent) of each group does not require bonding. Of the few contractors that required bonding, a majority (58.4 percent) of them have bonding level ranging from $0.00 to $1,000,000, while 38.7 percent of them have a bonding level of over $1,500,000. (*see* Table 13-2)

Table 12-1
Rating of quality of assistance received from the City's M/WBE office
by race, gender or ethnic group
City of St. Petersburg

Rating	M/WBE													
	Non-minority		Woman		Black		Hispanic		Other		Total M/WBE		All Races	
	#	%	#	%	#	%	#	%	#	%	#	%	#	%
Very Poor	1	50.00	1	7.69	1	20.00	0	0.00	0	0.00	2	6.67	3	9.38
Poor	0	0.00	0	0.00	0	0.00	0	0.00	0	0.00	0	0.00	0	0.00
Fair	0	0.00	3	23.08	1	20.00	4	36.36	0	0.00	8	26.67	8	25.00
Good	1	50.00	6	46.15	3	60.00	3	27.27	0	0.00	12	40.00	13	40.63
Excellent	0	0.00	3	23.08	0	0.00	4	36.36	1	100.00	8	26.67	8	25.00
Total	2	100	13	100	5	100	11	100	1	100	30	100	32	100

Table 13-1
Frequency of business requiring bonding by race, gender or ethnic group
City of St. Petersburg

Rating	M/WBE													
	Non-minority		Woman		Black		Hispanic		Other		Total M/WBE		All Races	
	#	%	#	%	#	%	#	%	#	%	#	%	#	%
NO	27	71.95	14	63.64	7	87.50	7	63.64	4	80.00	32	69.57	59	70.24
YES	11	28.95	8	36.36	1	12.50	4	36.36	1	20.00	14	30.43	25	29.76
Total	38	100.00	22	100.00	8	100.00	11	100.00	5	100.00	46	100.00	84	100.00

Table 13-2
City of St. Petersburg
Bonding level by race, gender or ethnic group

Rating	M/WBE													
	Non-minority		Woman		Black		Hispanic		Other		Total M/WBE		All Races	
	#	%	#	%	#	%	#	%	#	%	#	%	#	%
$0 - $100,00	5	38.46	0	0.00	1	50.00	1	20.00	1	50.00	3	16.67	8	25.81
$100,001 - $500,000	1	7.69	4	44.44	1	50.00	0	0.00	0	0.00	5	27.78	6	19.35
$500,001 – $1,000,000	1	7.69	0	0.00	0	0.00	0	0.00	0	0.00	0	0.00	1	3.23
$1,000,001 - $1,500,000	1	7.69	1	11.11	0	0.00	2	40.00	0	0.00	3	16.67	4	12.90
OVER $1,500,000	5	38.46	4	44.44	0	0.00	2	40.00	1	50.00	7	38.89	12	38.71
Total	13	100	9	100	2	100	5	100	2	100	18	100	31	100

Tables 14-1 to 14-4 displays the results of the analysis of the respondents' opinion regarding their financial position. The data indicates that a majority of the respondents viewed their financial position as fair to excellent in terms of net worth, revenue, credit history, access to credit, and cash flow. However, a majority of the respondents have not (and do not currently) financed their business through government grants and loans, and private loans. Instead they rely on personal savings for financial capital to run their businesses. (*see* Tables 15-1 to 16-7). These overall findings are the same for each the racial, gender or ethnic groups analyzed. Hence, it can be inferred that the bonding and financial position of contractors in the City of St. Petersburg's relevant market area is good. However, a majority of the respondent contractors in the City's relevant market area rely on personal savings, and not public and private institutions, to finance their businesses.

Prompt Payment Effectiveness

Tables 17-1 and 17-2 displays the result of the analysis of the contractors' opinion regarding prompt payment by the City of St. Petersburg and prime contractors for services or product provided. When asked how frequently the City has paid them beyond 30 days from submission of an invoice, a majority (58 percent) of the respondents said seldom to never. (*see* Table 17-1). When the data was disaggregated by racial, gender or ethnic group, with the exception of Hispanic-owned firms, the opinion of each of the groups was consistent with that of all the groups combined. In regards to payment of subcontractors by prime contractors, however, the result was opposite. For example, a majority (57.2 percent) of the respondents said prime contractors often to always delay paying them beyond 30 days from submission of invoice, and 16.6 percent said seldom to never. (*see* Table 17-2). Hence, it can be concluded that the City of St. Petersburg generally is prompt in paying contractors for services and supplies provided, while prime contractors doing business with the City delay paying subcontractors services and supplies provided.

Table 14-1
City of St. Petersburg
Firm's current cashflow by race, gender or ethnic group

Rating	M/WBE													
	Non-minority		Woman		Black		Hispanic		Other		Total M/WBE		All Races	
	#	%	#	%	#	%	#	%	#	%	#	%	#	%
Very Poor	0	0.00	1	4.55	2	25.00	0	0.00	1	16.67	4	8.33	4	4.60
Poor	3	7.69	1	4.55	0	0.00	2	16.67	0	0.00	3	6.25	6	6.90
Fair	4	10.26	7	31.82	2	25.00	1	8.33	0	0.00	10	20.83	14	16.09
Good	14	35.90	11	50.00	3	37.50	4	33.33	3	50.00	21	43.75	35	40.23
Excellent	18	46.15	2	9.09	1	12.50	5	41.67	2	33.33	10	20.83	28	32.18
Total	39	100	22	100	8	100	12	100	6	100	48	100	87	100

Table 14-2
City of St. Petersburg
Firm's gross annual revenue by race, gender or ethnic group

Rating	M/WBE													
	Non-minority		Woman		Black		Hispanic		Other		Total M/WBE		All Races	
	#	%	#	%	#	%	#	%	#	%	#	%	#	%
$0 - $100,00	3	8.11	1	4.76	2	25.00	0	0.00	0	0.00	3	6.53	6	7.23
$100,001 - $500,000	12	32.43	7	33.33	1	12.50	0	0.00	0	0.00	8	17.39	20	24.10
$500,001 – $1,000,000	7	18.92	6	28.57	2	25.00	3	25.00	1	20.00	12	26.09	19	22.89
$1,000,001 - $ 1,500,000	1	2.70	2	9.52	1	12.50	2	16.67	0	0.00	5	10.87	6	7.23
OVER $1,500,000	14	37.84	5	23.81	2	25.00	7	58.33	4	80.00	18	39.13	32	38.55
Total	37	100	21	100	8	100	12	100	5	100	46	100	83	100

Table 14-3
City of St. Petersburg
Firm's net worth by race, gender or ethnic group

Rating	M/WBE													
	Non-minority		Woman		Black		Hispanic		Other		Total M/WBE		All Races	
	#	%	#	%	#	%	#	%	#	%	#	%	#	%
Very Poor	1	2.63	0	0.00	2	25.00	0	0.00	1	16.67	3	6.25	4	4.65
Poor	1	2.63	2	9.09	0	0.00	0	0.00	0	0.00	2	4.17	3	3.49
Fair	4	10.53	5	22.73	3	37.50	4	33.33	0	0.00	12	25.00	16	18.60
Good	17	44.74	12	54.55	2	25.00	4	33.33	2	33.33	20	41.67	37	43.02
Excellent	15	39.47	3	13.64	1	12.50	4	33.33	3	50.00	11	22.92	26	30.23
Total	38	100	22	100	8	100	12	100	6	100	48	100	86	100

Table 14-4
City of St. Petersburg
Frequency of credit denial by race, gender or ethnic group

Rating	M/WBE													
	Non-minority		Woman		Black		Hispanic		Other		Total M/WBE		All Races	
	#	%	#	%	#	%	#	%	#	%	#	%	#	%
Never	18	50.00	8	36.36	2	25.00	6	50.00	2	33.33	18	37.50	36	42.86
Seldom	8	22.22	6	27.27	2	25.00	1	8.33	2	33.33	11	22.92	19	22.62
Sometimes	3	8.33	3	13.64	2	25.00	5	41.67	0	0.00	10	20.83	13	15.48
Often	2	5.56	2	9.09	0	0.00	0	0.00	0	0.00	2	4.17	4	4.76
Always	5	13.89	3	13.64	2	25.00	0	0.00	2	33.33	7	14.58	12	14.29
Total	36	100	22	100	8	100	12	100	6	100	48	100	84	100

Table 15-1
City of St. Petersburg
Frequency of initial financing from other sources
by race, gender or ethnic group

Rating	M/WBE													
	Non-minority		Woman		Black		Hispanic		Other		Total M/WBE		All Races	
	#	%	#	%	#	%	#	%	#	%	#	%	#	%
No	23	67.65	16	80.00	6	85.71	11	100	3	60.00	36	83.72	59	76.62
Yes	11	32.35	4	20.00	1	14.29	0	0.00	2	40.00	7	16.28	18	23.38
Total	34	100.00	20	100.00	7	100.00	11	100.00	5	100.00	43	100.00	77	100.00

Table 15-2
City of St. Petersburg
Frequency of initial financing from government grants
by race, gender or ethnic group

Rating			M/WBE											
	Non-minority		Woman		Black		Hispanic		Other		Total M/WBE		All Races	
	#	%	#	%	#	%	#	%	#	%	#	%	#	%
No	30	100.00	20	100.00	7	100.00	11	100.00	4	100.00	42	100.00	72	100.00
Yes	0	0.00	0	0.00	0	0.00	0	0.00	0	0.00	0	0.00	0	0.00
Total	30	100.00	20	100.00	7	100.00	11	100.00	4	100.00	42	100.00	72	100.00

Table 15-3
City of St. Petersburg
Frequency of initial financing from government loan
by race, gender or ethnic group

Rating	M/WBE													
	Non-minority		Woman		Black		Hispanic		Other		Total M/WBE		All Races	
	#	%	#	%	#	%	#	%	#	%	#	%	#	%
No	30	100.00	20	100.00	7	100.00	11	100.00	3	75.00	41	97.62	71	98.61
Yes	0	0.00	0	0.00	0	0.00	0	0.00	1	25.00	1	2.38	1	1.39
Total	30	100.00	20	100.00	7	100.00	11	100	4	100.00	42	100.00	72	100.00

Table 15-4
City of St. Petersburg
Frequency of initial financing from friends loan
by race, gender or ethnic group

Rating	M/WBE													
	Non-minority		Woman		Black		Hispanic		Other		Total M/WBE		All Races	
	#	%	#	%	#	%	#	%	#	%	#	%	#	%
No	25	83.33	18	90.00	6	85.71	10	90.91	3	75.00	37	88.10	62	86.11
Yes	5	16.67	2	10.00	1	14.29	1	9.09	1	25.00	5	11.90	10	13.89
Total	30	100.00	20	100.00	7	100.00	11	100.00	4	100.00	42	100.00	72	100.00

Table 15-5
City of St. Petersburg
Frequency of initial financing from personal loan
by race, gender or ethnic group

Rating	M/WBE													
	Non-minority		Woman		Black		Hispanic		Other		Total M/WBE		All Races	
	#	%	#	%	#	%	#	%	#	%	#	%	#	%
No	18	60.00	11	55.00	1	12.50	3	25.00	3	75.00	18	40.91	36	48.65
Yes	12	40.00	9	45.00	7	87.50	9	75.00	1	25.00	26	59.09	38	51.35
Total	30	100.00	20	100.00	8	100.00	12	100.00	4	100.00	44	100.00	74	100.00

Table 15-6
City of St. Petersburg
Frequency of initial financing from saving
by race, gender or ethnic group

Rating	M/WBE													
	Non-minority		Woman		Black		Hispanic		Other		Total M/WBE		All Races	
	#	%	#	%	#	%	#	%	#	%	#	%	#	%
No	12	37.50	6	28.57	2	28.57	4	36.36	3	75.00	15	34.88	27	36.00
Yes	20	62.50	15	71.43	5	71.43	7	63.64	1	25.00	28	65.12	48	64.00
Total	32	100.00	21	100.00	7	100.00	11	100.00	4	100.00	43	100.00	75	100.00

Table 16-1
City of St. Petersburg
Frequency of current funding from friend loans
by race, gender or ethnic group

Rating	M/WBE													
	Non-minority		Woman		Black		Hispanic		Other		Total M/WBE		All Races	
	#	%	#	%	#	%	#	%	#	%	#	%	#	%
No	26	96.30	19	90.48	6	85.71	9	100.00	4	100.00	38	92.68	64	94.12
Yes	1	3.70	2	9.53	1	14.29	0	0.00	0	0.00	3	7.32	4	5.88
Total	27	100.00	21	100.00	7	100.00	9	100.00	4	100.00	41	100.00	68	100.00

Table 16-2
City of St. Petersburg
Frequency of current funding from government grant
by race, gender or ethnic group

Rating	M/WBE													
	Non-minority		Woman		Black		Hispanic		Other		Total M/WBE		All Races	
	#	%	#	%	#	%	#	%	#	%	#	%	#	%
No	27	100.00	20	100.00	7	100.00	9	100.00	4	100.00	40	100.00	67	100.00
Yes	0	0.00	0	0.00	0	0.00	0	0.00	0	0.00	0	0.00	0	0.00
Total	27	100.00	20	100.00	7	100.00	9	100.00	4	100.00	40	100.00	67	100.00

Table 16-3
City of St. Petersburg
Frequency of current funding from government loan
by race, gender or ethnic group

Rating	M/WBE													
	Non-minority		Woman		Black		Hispanic		Other		Total M/WBE		All Races	
	#	%	#	%	#	%	#	%	#	%	#	%	#	%
No	27	100.00	20	100.00	7	100.00	9	100.00	4	100.00	40	100.00	67	100.00
Yes	0	0.00	0	0.00	0	0.00	0	0.00	0	0.00	0	0.00	0	0.00
Total	27	100.00	20	100.00	7	100.00	9	100.00	4	100.00	40	100.00	67	100.00

Table 16-4
City of St. Petersburg
Frequency of current funding from other sources

Rating	M/WBE													
	Non-minority		Woman		Black		Hispanic		Other		Total M/WBE		All Races	
	#	%	#	%	#	%	#	%	#	%	#	%	#	%
No	16	48.48	10	50.00	5	71.43	7	77.78	2	40.00	24	58.54	40	54.05
Yes	17	51.52	10	50.00	2	28.57	2	22.22	3	60.00	17	41.46	34	45.95
Total	33	100.00	20	100.00	7	100.00	9	100.00	5	100.00	41	100.00	74	100.00

Table 16-5
City of St. Petersburg
Frequency of current funding from personal loan
by race, gender or ethnic group

Rating	M/WBE													
	Non-minority		Woman		Black		Hispanic		Other		Total M/WBE		All Races	
	#	%	#	%	#	%	#	%	#	%	#	%	#	%
No	20	74.07	17	80.95	5	71.43	6	60.00	4	100.00	32	76.19	52	75.36
Yes	7	25.93	4	19.05	2	28.57	4	40.00	0	0.00	10	23.81	17	24.64
Total	27	100.00	21	100.00	7	100.00	10	100.00	4	100.00	42	100.00	69	100.00

Table 16-6
City of St. Petersburg
Frequency of current funding from relatives loan
by race, gender or ethnic group

Rating	M/WBE													
	Non-minority		Woman		Black		Hispanic		Other		Total M/WBE		All Races	
	#	%	#	%	#	%	#	%	#	%	#	%	#	%
No	27	100.00	20	100.00	7	87.50	9	90.00	4	100.00	40	95.24	67	97.10
Yes	0	0.00	0	0.00	1	12.50	1	10.00	0	0.00	2	4.76	2	2.90
Total	27	100.00	20	100.00	8	100.00	10	100.00	4	100.00	42	100.00	69	100.00

Table 16-7
City of St. Petersburg
Frequency of current funding from savings
by race, gender or ethnic group

Rating	M/WBE													
	Non-minority		Woman		Black		Hispanic		Other		Total M/WBE		All Races	
	#	%	#	%	#	%	#	%	#	%	#	%	#	%
No	13	44.83	13	61.90	2	28.57	4	44.44	2	50.00	21	51.22	34	48.57
Yes	16	55.17	8	38.10	5	71.43	5	55.56	2	50.00	20	48.78	36	51.43
Total	29	100.00	21	100.00	7	100.00	9	100.00	4	100.00	41	100.00	70	100.00

Table 17-1
City of St. Petersburg
Rating of how frequently has the City paid beyond 30 days from invoice submission by race, gender or ethnic group

Rating	M/WBE													
	Non-minority		Woman		Black		Hispanic		Other		Total M/WBE		All Races	
	#	%	#	%	#	%	#	%	#	%	#	%	#	%
Never	11	47.83	3	25.00	3	50.00	2	40.00	2	50.00	10	37.04	21	42.00
Seldom	4	17.39	3	25.00	0	0.00	0	0.00	1	25.00	4	14.81	8	16.00
Sometimes	4	17.39	5	41.67	1	16.67	3	60.00	0	0.00	9	33.33	13	26.00
Often	1	4.35	1	8.33	1	16.67	0	0.00	0	0.00	2	7.41	3	6.00
Always	3	13.04	0	0.00	1	16.67	0	0.00	1	25.00	2	7.41	5	10.00
Total	23	100.00	12	100.00	6	100.00	5	100.00	4	100.00	27	100.00	50	100.00

Table 17-2
City of St. Petersburg
Rating of how frequently prime contractors paid subcontractor beyond 30 days by race, gender or ethnic group

Rating	M/WBE													
	Non-minority		Woman		Black		Hispanic		Other		Total M/WBE		All Races	
	#	%	#	%	#	%	#	%	#	%	#	%	#	%
Never	7	41.18	2	22.22	1	33.33	2	22.22	2	50.00	7	28.00	14	33.33
Seldom	3	17.65	1	11.11	0	0.00	0	0.00	0	0.00	1	4.00	4	9.52
Sometimes	3	17.65	3	33.33	0	0.00	5	55.56	1	25.00	9	36.00	12	28.57
Often	2	11.76	2	22.22	2	66.67	1	11.11	0	0.00	5	20.00	7	16.67
Always	2	11.76	1	11.11	0	0.00	1	11.11	1	25.00	3	12.00	5	11.90
Total	17	100.00	9	100.00	3	100.00	9	100.00	4	100.00	25	100.00	42	100.00

M/WBE Certification Process Effectiveness

The result of the frequency distribution of the M/WBEs' opinion effectiveness of the City of St. Petersburg's certification process is exhibited in Tables 18-1 to 18-6. Table 18-1 indicates that majority (60.5 percent) of the respondents are certified with the City, while 39.5 percent are not certified. Table 18-2 shows the M/WBEs response regarding the City of St. Petersburg's certification appeals process. The Table indicates that only 15.63 percent of the total respondents have been involved in the appeals process. Of this total, a majority was uncertain whether the process was unfair.

The M/WBE owners' rating of the City of St. Petersburg's practice of reciprocal certification is presented in Table 18-3. The data indicates that a majority (64.71 percent) of the respondents as a good gauge for determining M/WBE eligibility. The data also indicate that a majority of the M/WBE owners viewed the certification form and process as neither cumbersome nor complicated (see Tables 18-4 and 18-5).

Table 18-6 presents the frequency distribution of the respondents' opinion regarding the time it takes the city to process an applicant's request for certification. The result indicates that a majority (60.6 percent) of the respondents view the time it takes for the City to respond to an applicant's request for certification as not too long.

When asked how helpful certification has been in improving the M/WBEs chances of getting prime contracts and subcontracts, a majority of the respondents (58.8 percent for prime contracts and 62.9 percent for subcontracts) viewed the City's certification as somewhat helpful to extremely helpful in improving their chances of getting both prime contracts and subcontracts (see Tables 18-7 and 18-8).

In summary, it can be concluded that the M/WBEs surveyed in the City of St. Petersburg's relevant market area are generally satisfied with the quality of the City's M/WBE certification and appeals process. In addition, the M/WBEs view certification as improving their prospect in getting City contracts.

Table 18-1
City of St. Petersburg
Frequency of Firms Certified as MWBE by race, gender or ethnic group

Rating	M/WBE													
	Non-minority		Woman		Black		Hispanic		Other		Total M/WBE		All Races	
	#	%	#	%	#	%	#	%	#	%	#	%	#	%
No	16	88.89	3	15.00	1	14.29	10	83.33	3	75.00	17	39.53	33	54.10
Yes	2	11.11	17	85.00	6	85.71	2	16.67	1	25.00	26	60.47	28	45.90
Total	18	100.00	20	100.00	7	100.00	12	100.00	4	100.00	43	100.00	61	100.00

Table 18-2
City of St. Petersburg
Frequency of MWBE Certification Appeal
by race, gender or ethnic group

Rating	M/WBE													
	Non-minority		Woman		Black		Hispanic		Other		Total M/WBE		All Races	
	#	%	#	%	#	%	#	%	#	%	#	%	#	%
No	2	100.00	11	73.33	6	85.71	9	100.00	1	100.00	27	84.38	29	85.29
Yes	0	0.00	4	26.67	1	14.29	0	0.00	0	0.00	5	15.63	5	14.71
Total	2	100.00	15	100.00	7	100.00	9	100.00	1	100.00	32	100.00	34	100.00

Table 18-3
City of St. Petersburg
Rating of how the practice of reciprocal certification is a good gauge for determining M/WBE eligibility by race, gender or ethnic group

Rating	M/WBE													
	Non-minority		Woman		Black		Hispanic		Other		Total M/WBE		All Races	
	#	%	#	%	#	%	#	%	#	%	#	%	#	%
Strongly Disagree	0	0.00	1	5.88	2	28.57	1	9.09	0	0.00	4	11.11	4	10.00
Disagree	0	0.00	1	5.88	0	0.00	0	0.00	0	0.00	1	2.78	1	2.50
No Opinion	1	25.00	3	17.65	3	42.86	2	18.18	0	0.00	8	22.22	9	22.50
Agree	2	50.00	5	29.41	1	14.29	2	18.18	1	100.00	9	25.00	11	27.50
Strongly Agree	1	25.00	7	41.18	1	14.29	6	54.55	0	0.00	14	38.89	15	37.50
Total	4	100.00	17	100.00	7	100.00	11	100.00	1	100.00	36	100.00	40	100.00

Table 18-4
City of St. Petersburg
Rating of how cumbersome the City's Certification Process is by race, gender or ethnic group

Rating	M/WBE													
	Non-minority		Woman		Black		Hispanic		Other		Total M/WBE		All Races	
	#	%	#	%	#	%	#	%	#	%	#	%	#	%
Not cumbersome	2	100.00	7	46.67	3	50.00	4	40.00	0	0.00	14	43.75	16	47.06
Somewhat cumbersome	0	0.00	4	26.67	1	16.67	5	50.00	0	0.00	10	31.25	10	29.41
Cumbersome	0	0.00	2	13.33	2	33.33	0	0.00	0	0.00	4	12.50	4	11.76
Very cumbersome	0	0.00	2	13.33	0	0.00	0	0.00	0	0.00	2	6.25	2	5.88
Extremely cumbersome	0	0.00	0	0.00	0	0.00	1	10.00	1	100.00	2	6.25	2	8.88
Total	2	100.00	15	100.00	6	100.00	10	100.00	1	100.00	32	100.00	34	100.00

Table 18-5
City of St. Petersburg
Rating of how complicated the certification form is
by race, gender or ethnic group

Rating	M/WBE													
	Non-minority		Woman		Black		Hispanic		Other		Total M/WBE		All Races	
	#	%	#	%	#	%	#	%	#	%	#	%	#	%
Not complicated	2	100.00	11	68.75	5	83.33	5	45.45	1	100.00	22	64.71	24	66.67
Somewhat complicated	0	0.00	1	6.25	0	0.00	5	45.45	0	0.00	6	17.65	6	16.67
Complicated	0	0.00	3	18.75	0	0.00	0	0.00	0	0.00	3	8.82	3	8.33
Very complicated	0	0.00	1	6.25	1	16.67	0	0.00	0	0.00	2	5.88	2	5.56
Extremely complicated	0	0.00	0	0.00	0	0.00	1	9.09	0	0.00	1	2.94	1	2.78
Total	2	100.00	16	100.00	6	100.00	11	100.00	1	100.00	34	100.00	36	100.00

Table 18-6
City of St. Petersburg
Rating of how long it takes the city to process an applicant's request for certification by race, gender or ethnic group

Rating	M/WBE													
	Non-minority		Woman		Black		Hispanic		Other		Total M/WBE		All Races	
	#	%	#	%	#	%	#	%	#	%	#	%	#	%
Not long at all	0	0.00	5	29.41	1	16.67	1	11.11	0	0.00	7	21.21	7	20.00
Not long	0	0.00	4	23.53	0	0.00	8	88.89	1	100.00	13	39.39	13	37.14
No Opinion	2	100.00	7	41.18	2	33.33	0	0.00	0	0.00	9	27.27	11	31.43
Long	0	0.00	1	5.88	1	16.67	0	0.00	0	0.00	2	6.06	2	5.71
Too long	0	0.00	0	0.00	2	33.33	0	0.00	0	0.00	2	6.06	2	5.71
Total	2	100.00	17	100.00	6	100.00	9	100.00	1	100.00	33	100.00	35	100.00

Table 18-7
City of St. Petersburg
Rating of how helpful certification has been in improving chance of getting prime contracts by race, gender or ethnic group

Rating	M/WBE													
	Non-minority		Woman		Black		Hispanic		Other		Total M/WBE		All Races	
	#	%	#	%	#	%	#	%	#	%	#	%	#	%
Not helpful	1	50.00	7	43.75	2	33.33	5	45.45	0	0.00	14	41.18	15	41.67
Somewhat helpful	0	0.00	2	12.50	2	33.33	0	0.00	0	0.00	4	11.76	4	11.11
Helpful	0	0.00	5	31.25	1	16.67	3	27.27	0	0.00	9	26.47	9	25.00
Very helpful	0	0.00	0	0.00	0	0.00	2	18.18	0	0.00	2	5.88	2	5.56
Extremely helpful	1	50.00	2	12.50	1	16.67	1	9.09	1	100.00	5	14.71	6	16.67
Total	2	100.00	16	100.00	6	100.00	11	100.00	1	100.00	34	100.00	36	100.00

Table 18-8
City of St. Petersburg
Rating of how helpful certification been in improving your chance of getting subcontracts with the city by race, gender or ethnic group

Rating	M/WBE													
	Non-minority		Woman		Black		Hispanic		Other		Total M/WBE		All Races	
	#	%	#	%	#	%	#	%	#	%	#	%	#	%
Not helpful	1	50.00	6	37.50	3	42.86	4	36.36	0	0.00	13	37.14	14	37.84
Somewhat helpful	0	0.00	2	12.50	0	0.00	1	9.09	0	0.00	3	8.57	3	8.11
Helpful	0	0.00	0	0.00	2	28.57	1	9.09	0	0.00	3	8.57	3	8.11
Very helpful	1	50.00	2	12.50	1	14.29	3	27.27	0	0.00	6	17.14	7	18.92
Extremely helpful	0	0.00	6	37.50	1	14.29	2	18.18	1	100.00	10	28.57	10	27.03
Total	2	100.00	16	100.00	7	100.00	11	100.00	1	100.00	35	100.00	37	100.00

Contractors' Experience in contracting with the City of St. Petersburg

A number of the contractors surveyed provided the following comments regarding their experience in contracting with the City of St. Petersburg.

- ***Good Contracting Opportunities but Sluggish Bureaucracy***
  Several respondents felt that the city had good contracting opportunities. However, the city bureaucracy was slow in responding to the contractors requests and processing paper work. For example, a non-minority maintenance contractor commented that the City is great with the exception of the Purchasing Department. They are overloaded with work that does not get completed. The City does not follow up on important issues. The payment system and the contracting opportunities are good. A non-minority equipment rental and sales contractor said that he was still waiting to hear on a purchase of personnel lift for the Coliseum and Bayfront Center. It seems like the City is taking too long to make a decision and he could not figure out why because both of these facilities need this equipment. A non-minority painting contractor commented that the City of St. Petersburg does not give out bid results easily. Other agencies fax or relay bid results as soon a possible. A WBE general construction contractor commented that Permitting Department needs serious changes – takes much too long to get a commercial permit.

- ***Good Monitoring System***
  A WBE said that the City of St. Petersburg monitors their projects much better than any other municipality.

- ***No problem Doing Business with the City***
  A non-minority contractor commented that he had had no problems with the City. In particular, he felt that the City's Traffic Engineering Department has been polite, helpful and prompt in arranging all matters.

- ***No Bid Notification***
  A number of respondents expressed concerns about not being notified of contracting opportunities. For example, a non-minority electrical equipment manufacturer would like to be notified of bids. A non-minority computer-related software and hardware consulting

contractor said that he had never received a bid package from the City of St. Petersburg. A non-minority Engineering and Architecture contractor wished the City of St. Petersburg would send notices for upcoming engineering opportunities.

- ***Reverse Discrimination***
  A non-minority lawn sprinkler systems supplier said that the City of St. Petersburg left him with a bad feeling of being treated unfairly. He was told that he was to hire blacks and was even told which people to hire. Such as poor blacks, poor or black women, and poor black handicapped persons. Even though he does hire minorities, he did not want to be given orders to do it in order to receive a contract. He felt that the remainder of the questions on the survey is examples of how the City discriminates against Caucasian/white privately owned companies.

- ***Poor Management***
  A non-minority building construction contractor said that the entire Baseball Stadium project was poorly run, under staffed, had a poor pay history and not professional. Having Hubert, Hunt and Nichols as a supervisor team was a joke. The City was ripped off and so were the Devil Rays. The Devil Rays also should not be in the construction business. But rather it should stick with baseball.

- ***Prompt Payment***
  A non-minority supplier of canine training equipment for police dogs commented that the City of St. Petersburg has always paid beyond 30 days from the date that you submitted an invoice for work or services that you performed. Meanwhile, non-minority professional contractor said that getting paid on time by the City of St. Petersburg is a problem.

- ***Guarantee Subcontractor's Payment by Prime Contractors***
  A black MBE construction contractor suggested that the City of St. Petersburg needs to be stricter on general contractors in the way they treat subcontractors in getting paid on contract negotiations. There must be a program that would guarantee subcontractors their money beyond completion. They must stop holding all trader money until the project is completed because there are subs that finish their trades before others.

- ***Economic Status Discrimination***
  A Hispanic MBE professional service contractor said that the City has a "good old boy network" discrimination contracting system based on "perceived status." By way of example, he said that he bid on a local HUD project involving lead base paint assessment for a local public park located in a black neighborhood. He said they were committed to hiring people from the black neighborhood where the park was located, and had a ready pool of local individuals qualified to do the work. But the City awarded the contract to a firm from out of town. Upon probing, the contractor said other Cities are much easier to work with than the City of St. Petersburg, and he remarked that the City of St. Petersburg should note that Hispanics are minorities as well, and their population is increasing daily. In addition, he said the City's procurement system is too cumbersome, and the bulk of the contract is for construction only. However, in an interview with City officials, it was revealed that that this particular contract was awarded by the St. Petersburg Housing Authority, and not the City of St. Petersburg. Hence, the allegation of disparate treatment by the city was not corroborated.

Summary of City Official Interview and Contractors Survey Results

The findings of the assessment above indicate that, with a few exceptions, the City of St. Petersburg has generally been effective in enforcing its race preference program. However, comments and observations from contractors and leaders of local community organizations seem to suggest that the race preference program has achieved modest gain in enhancing minority participation in the city's contracting process. It stand to reason, therefore, that other non-racial factors may be prohibiting M/WBE firms in the City's relevant market area from actively participating in the city's contracting process. This finding seems to be consistent with the findings and conclusions derived from verified anecdotes.

Overall Summary of Study Results

The results of the disparity analyses of the City of St. Petersburg's contracting data indicate that during FY 1989 to FY 1999 no "gross" or statistically significant disparity in awarding prime contracts to M/WBEs was exhibited amongst M/WBEs in twelve (12) major procurement categories analyzed[311]. With regards to subcontracts, no conclusion was made because the City has kept no data on the number and amount of subcontracts going to non-M/WBEs or on which firms are available for subcontracting. Thus, no disparity analyses for subcontracting could be performed. Altogether, during the period studied (FY 1989 to FY 1999), M/WBEs supplied 8.8 percent of the total number of prime bids and received 9.1 percent of the total number of prime contracts awarded by the City of St. Petersburg. Meanwhile, M/WBEs submitted 6.5 percent of the total dollar value of bids and received 6.6 percent of the total dollars awarded by the City. Therefore, when M/WBE bid on the City of St. Petersburg's contracts, the outcomes are proportionate. The problem is that M/WBEs in the City of St. Petersburg's relevant market area do not bid very often.

The results of verification of specific incidents or instances of alleged discrimination against M/WBEs in the award of contracts or subcontracts in the City of St. Petersburg's contracting process indicate that the city has not been an active participant in a discriminatory contract award process against minority-owned firms. This finding is corroborated by the survey results which indicate that a majority of the respondents did not view the city as discriminatory against minorities in the award of contracts. However, some of the verified anecdotes do suggest that the City has been a passive participant in a discriminatory subcontracting system. With the exception of two M/WBE contractors, the anecdotal data indicate that the M/WBEs

[311] See Chapter Nine for a detailed summary of the disparity findings for each of the twelve procurement categories analyzed.

in the City's relevant market area generally attribute their lack of full participation in the city's contracting process to unfair "aggressive market behavior" of their more affluent and privileged competitors, manufacturers and suppliers. This attitude may have discouraged some M/WBEs from actively participating in the City's contracting process.

An interesting finding is that a majority of the M/WBE contractors and representatives of community organizations interviewed were of the opinion the City's existing race preference program has actually limited the opportunity of M/WBEs to actively participate in the City's contracting process, and that the establishment of a small business program may remedy some of the contracting problems that M/WBEs are experiencing under the City's existing race preference program. The results of the anecdotal evidence of disrimination and survey analyses corroborate the disparity and bid analyses findings which indicate that no significant disparity exist between the proportion of M/WBEs available in the City of St. Petersburg's relevant market area and their utilization by the City, and that the M/WBEs are not actively pursuing the City of St. Petersburg contracting opportunities as expected. Discrimination was not found to be a reason for the depressed level of participation of minority-owned firms in the city's contracting process. Rather, the major reason seems to be that minority-owned firms are less endowed with market competitive attributes than non-minority firms in the City of St. Petersburg's relevant market area. These attributes include the lack of social capital, financial capital and human capital that has been found to enhance a business chances of competing effectively in the market place, the City of St. Peterburg being one such markets.

Chapter Nine

Predicate Study Conclusions and Policy Recommendations

This study was designed to address four major questions within the context set forth in the *Croson* decision and subsequent court rulings. The questions are:

(1) Is there a disparity between the proportion of available minority- and woman-owned firms in the City of St. Petersburg's relevant market area and the proportion of these firms that have participated in the City's contracts?

(2) If disparities exist, are they the product of discrimination or market competitive attributes of contractors in the City of St. Petersburg's relevant market area?

(3) If disparity exists which is evidence of discrimination, in what procurement category should race conscious policies be established within the constitutional parameters of the *Croson* decision and subsequent Federal courts interpretation of that ruling?

(4) If disparity does not exist, what race neutral policies should the City of St. Petersburg establish?

These four questions were central to the methodological design and conclusions of this study. The subsections that follow summarize major conclusions and recommendations as they relate to the above questions, as well as questions which have evolved while completing the study. Hence, in order to appreciate the scope of the conclusions and recommendations, a thorough review of the preceding chapters is highly recommended.

Study Conclusions

Based on the quantitative and qualitative analyses and the conceptual framework outline in the Introduction and Chapters One through Five of this book, the following summary of findings and conclusions are made regarding the City of St. Petersburg procurement practice:

Disparity Analyses

The results of the disparity analyses of the City of St. Petersburg's contracting data indicate that during FY 1989 to FY 1999 no "gross" disparity in awarding prime contracts to M/WBEs was exhibited amongst M/WBEs in twelve (12) major procurement categories analyzed[313]. With regards to subcontracts, there are no conclusions made because the City has kept no data on the number and amount of subcontracts going to non-M/WBEs or on which firms are available for subcontracting. Thus, no disparity analyses for subcontracting could be performed.

Bid Analysis

Prime Contract Bidding Pattern

1. Non-minority-owned firms significantly over-bid relative to their potential availability in the City's relevant market area.
2. All the M/WBE groups combined significantly under-bid.
3. Each of the M/WBE groups under-bid relative to their potential availability, with the under-bidding significant among woman-, black- and Hispanic-owned firms.
4. Non-minority firms consistently bid high in each of the dollar value levels analyzed.
5. All the M/WBE groups combined bid low on extremely low and extremely high dollar value contracts.
6. Hispanic-owned firms generally bid more on large dollar value contracts, while black-owned and the other M/WBE firms bid low in each the dollar value level of contracts.

---

[313] See *Appendix A* for a detailed outline of the disparity findings for each of the twelve procurement categories analyzed.

7. The bidding pattern for woman-owned firms is mixed, but generally steady at each of the dollar value levels analyzed.

Altogether, during the period studied (FY 1989 to FY 1999), M/WBEs supplied 8.83 percent of the total number of prime bids, they received 9.12 percent of the total number of prime contracts awarded by the City of St. Petersburg. As for the dollar value of bids and awards, M/WBEs submitted 6.50 percent of the total dollar value of bids and received 6.58 percent of the total dollars awarded by the City. Therefore, when M/WBE bid on the City of St. Petersburg's contracts, the outcomes are proportional. The problem is that M/WBEs in the City of St. Petersburg's relevant market area do not bid very often.

Reasons for Not Bidding on Prime Contracts

The major reasons provided by the contractors for not bidding on the City's prime contracts are:

1. specialized field;
2. lack of information; and
3. other reasons.

Reasons for Not Bidding on Subcontracts

The major reasons cited by the City's potentially available contractors for not bidding on subcontracts were:

1. lack of information;
2. specialized field;
3. discrimination by prime contractors;
4. other reasons.

Number of Prime Contract Bids Submitted by Racial, Ethnic or Gender Group

1. The contractors in the City of St. Petersburg's relevant market area submitted a total of 269 prime contract bids during the nine fiscal years studied.

2. Non-minority firms submitted a large majority (91.86 percent) of the total prime contract bids, followed by Hispanic-owned firms with 3.89 percent of the total bids, third place was woman-owned firms with 2.61 of the total number of bids, fourth were black-owned firms with 1.60 percent of the total bids, and the least were the other M/WBE group with 0.04 percent of the total bids submitted during FY 1989 to FY 1997.

Dollar Level of Prime Contract Bids Submitted by Racial, Ethnic or gender Group

1. Non-minority firms consistently submitted over 88 percent of the total number of bids at each of the dollar levels of bids analyzed.
2. All the M/WBE groups combined tended to bid low on extremely low and extremely high ticket contracts, and highest on contracts with dollars values ranging from $50,000 to $500,000.
3. Woman-owned firms bid low on contracts with dollar value ranges from $0 to $25,000 and contracts with dollar value within the range of $500,000 to $1,000,000 dollar value, and higher in all the other dollar value levels analyzed.
4. Black-owned firms consistently bid less than 3.00 percent in each of the dollar levels analyzed, with the lowest proportion of number of bids submitted occurring at the extremely low ($0 to $25,000) and extremely high range (over $1000,000).
5. Hispanic-owned firms, with the exception of the over $1000,000 range, bid more on large dollar value contracts and less on small dollar value contracts.
6. The other M/WBE group bid only once (that is, at the $50,000 to $100,000 level) during the nine fiscal years analyzed.

Anecdotal Evidence of Discrimination in Contracting by the City of St. Petersburg

1. M/WBEs in the City of St. Petersburg's relevant market area generally attribute the cause of the unfair or disparate treatment they have received in either attempting to or

actually contracting with the City of St. Petersburg to unfair "aggressive market behavior" of their more affluent and privileged competitors, manufacturers and suppliers.

2. The contractors interviewed view the City of St. Petersburg as a "passive participant" in a system that subjects M/WBEs to unfair or disparate treatment in contracting with the City. This attitude may have discouraged some M/WBEs from actively participating in the City's contracting process.
3. A majority of the M/WBEs surveyed view the City of St. Petersburg's contracting and subcontracting system as not discriminatory on the basis of race, gender or ethnicity.
4. A majority of the M/WBE contractors and community organizations interviewed or surveyed are of the opinion the City's existing race conscious program have limited the opportunity of M/WBEs to actively participate in the City's contracting process, and that the establishment of a Small Business Program may remedy some of the contracting problems that M/WBEs are experiencing under the City's existing race-conscious program.
5. The results of the qualitative analysis of discrimination allegations substantiates the disparity and bid analyses findings which indicate that no "gross" disparity exist between the proportion of M/WBEs available in the City of St. Petersburg's relevant market area and their utilization by the City, and that the M/WBEs are not bidding relative to their potential availability in the City of St. Petersburg's relevant market because of other market competitive factors, and not discrimination. However, the analysis also suggests that the city of St. Petersburg is a "passive" participant in a relevant market area that discriminates against minorities.

Contracting Discrimination Survey

1. A majority of the contractors and vendors surveyed in the City of St. Petersburg's relevant market area contend that they have seldom to never been denied contracting opportunities because of their race, gender or ethnicity.
2. A majority of contractors and vendors surveyed in the City of St. Petersburg's relevant market area surveyed view race or

gender as not a determining factor in the award of prime contracts by the City, and the award of subcontracts by prime contractors. However, most black contractors surveyed view race, ethnicity or gender as a determining factor in the award of prime contracts by the City. Meanwhile, a majority of M/WBEs surveyed view race, ethnicity and gender as a determining factor in the award of subcontracts by prime contractors.

3. A majority of contractors and vendors surveyed in the City of St. Petersburg's relevant market area view race, gender or ethnicity as not an important factor in the award of subcontracts by the City. However, this majority opinion is not shared by a majority of black-, Hispanic- and woman-owned business contractors and vendors who view race, gender, or ethnicity as a somewhat to extremely important factor in the award of subcontracts by prime contractors in the City's relevant market area.[313]

4. A majority of contractors and vendors in the City of St. Petersburg's relevant market area do not view race, gender or ethnicity as a determining factor in the selection of subcontractors by prime contractors. However, a majority of M/WBE respondents, especially woman- and other minority-owned contractors, view race, gender or ethnicity as a determining factor in the selection of subcontractors by prime contractors.[314]

5. A majority of contractors and vendors in the City of St. Petersburg's relevant market area view race, gender or ethnicity as not a determining factor in the selection of contractors and subcontractors, the provision of technical assistance to effectively compete for the City's contracts, fair treatment by the City, and being informed of contracting opportunities.

---

[313] It is, however, uncertain if this majority opinion is influenced by the City's existing race conscious policy.
[314] *Id.*

M/WBE Policy Awareness

1. The officials and political leaders of the City of St. Petersburg are generally aware of the City's M/WBE policy, its goal and coordination structure.
2. The City of St. Petersburg's M/WBE awareness and tracking system is generally well organized and consistent with the provisions of the City's M/WBE ordinance.

Coordination and Implementation Structure Effectiveness

1. The City officials and community organizations interviewed are, for the most part, satisfied with the existing coordination (and implementation) structure of the City M/WBE program.
2. Most of the interviewees view the recently established Business Development Center under the Economic Development and Property Management Department as a positive step in facilitating and enhancing an effective implementation (and coordination) of the City's M/WBE policy.

Awareness, Coordination and Tracking Effectiveness

1. The City of St. Petersburg departments' awareness, coordination and tracking of W/MBE are generally organized and consistent with the provisions specified in the City's M/WBE ordinance and Administrative Code.
2. Most of the City officials do seem to understand their role regarding tracking, coordinating and promoting M/WBE awareness as specified in the City's M/WBE Ordinance.

Targeted Technical Assistance Effectiveness

1. The City of St. Petersburg departments, have effectively implemented the targeted technical assistance provisions as specified in the City's M/WBE ordinance and the City's Administrative Code.

2. The City has established a sound working relationship with community organizations to assist M/WBEs in the City's relevant market area to participate in the City's contracting process.

Networking and Outreach Effectiveness

1. The effectiveness of the City of St. Petersburg's efforts in providing networking and outreach assistance to M/WBEs is inclusive.

Tracking and Monitoring of M/WBE Participation

1. The City of St. Petersburg departments' tracking and monitoring of M/WBE participation in the City's contracting and subcontracting activities are coordinated, organized and consistent with the provisions of the City's M/WBE ordinance.
2. The two departments and the M/WBE office responsible for implementing the City's M/WBE policy seem to understand their role in tracking and monitoring M/WBE participation as specified in the City's M/WBE ordinance.

Bonding and Financial Position of Contractors

1. The bonding and financial positions of contractors in the City of St. Petersburg's relevant market area are generally good.
2. A majority of the respondent contractors in the City's relevant market area rely on personal savings, and not public and private institutions, to finance their businesses.

Prompt Payment and Bonding of M/WBEs

1. Although the City departments have different time frames for paying contractors doing business with the City, the departments have generally been effective in enforcing the

City's prompt payment provision as specified in the City's M/WBE ordinance.

2. The City of St. Petersburg generally is prompt in paying contractors for services and supplies provided, while prime contractors doing business with the City delay paying subcontractors services and supplies provided.
3. Most of the City departments do have a bond waiver provision for M/WBEs.

M/WBE Office Assistance Effectiveness

The M/WBEs in the City of St. Petersburg's relevant market area are generally satisfied with the quality of assistance received from the M/WBE office.

Certification and Appeals Process Effectiveness

1. A majority of M/WBEs surveyed in the City of St. Petersburg's relevant market area are generally satisfied with the quality of the City's M/WBE certification and appeals process.
2. A majority of M/WBEs surveyed view certification as improving their prospect in getting City contracts.

Policy Implications and Recommendations

As discussed in Chapter One of this book, the goal of this predicate study was to provide the City of St. Petersburg with empirically grounded data that will assist the City's decision makers to determine the need for a race preference policy and program under the strict scrutiny standard of review specified by the United States Supreme Court's ruling in the case of the *City of Richmond, Virginia v. J.A. Croson Company* and subsequent court decisions; as well as federal, state of Florida, and the City of St. Petersburg anti-discrimination laws. The standard and laws, as outlined in Chapters Four and Five of this book respectively include the identification of discrimination directly or indirectly related to the City of St. Petersburg's contracting, evaluation of non-racial, ethnic or gender remedies, and development of a solution that is consistent with the public policy problem, within the strict scrutiny limits and guidelines set forth in the *Croson* decision.

The findings of this study clearly suggest that the problems facing minority businesses in the City of St. Petersburg contracting process has very little to do with their race. Rather, the problem facing these firms revolves around their ability to effectively compete for government contracts due to the small size of businesses, and lack of human capital, financial capital, and social capital. Hence, under the strict scrutiny standard of review, a compelling need for race preference in the City's contracting process has not been established. Rather, the findings seem to suggest the need for race neutral remedies and active enforcement of Title VI of the Civil Rights Act of 1964. Hence, the following recommendations can be made:

The City of St. Petersburg should consider discontinuing its Race Preference Policy.

The *Croson* decision stipulates that race conscious remedies should be in place only for as long as documented evidence indicates the existence of the present effects of past discrimination. Recently, the federal judiciary has made it clear that the role of race conscious programs is extremely limited in scope and duration. Since the Supreme Court ruled in *Croson* that strict scrutiny was the necessary judicial test in reviewing race conscious programs, the last local race conscious procurement program to be upheld was in Denver in 1993. The Denver decision was subsequently reversed and remanded by the tenth Circuit. Since then, Philadelphia, Columbus, Jackson (Mississippi), The District of Columbia, Metropolitan Dade County (Florida), Fulton County (Georgia), Atlanta Public Schools, Memphis City Schools, Cuyahoga Community College (Ohio), and the States of Florida, California and Ohio have all lost in court when their Race Preference Programs were challenged. Other jurisdictions, such as Cincinnati, New York, the Washington Suburban Sanitation district and the South Florida Water Management district have signed expensive settlements to avoid adverse judicial decisions. Cities such as San Diego and Elyria (Ohio) that did not have disparity studies lost their Race Preference Programs quickly when lawsuits were brought. Even with a methodologically sound (or legally defensible) disparity study, race preference remedies should be "narrowly tailored" to statistically identified factors that inhibit minorities from competing for government contracts. The analysis of the City of St. Petersburg contracting data indicate that no disparity in M/WBE contracting was exhibited in all twelve (12) of the City's major procurement categories. Moreover, a bidding pattern analysis indicates that when M/WBEs in the City's relevant market area do bid, they receive a proportional number and dollar value of the City's contracts. These major statistical findings are substantiated by the results of surveys and verified anecdotal comments from M/WBEs, Community organizations, non-M/WBEs, and City officials which indicate that the City has not discriminated on the basis of race, gender or ethnicity in the award of contracts to M/WBEs. Hence, we recommend that the City of St. Petersburg should consider discontinuing its race preference program.

The City of St. Petersburg should consider establishing a Targeted Race Neutral Small Business Policy.

Croson and recent federal courts decisions have endorsed the active use of race neutral policy such as the targeted small business concept which we recommend. By way of example, in *Croson*, the Supreme Court said: "Even in the absence of evidence of discrimination, the City has at its disposal a whole array of race-neutral devices to increase the accessibility of City contracting opportunities to small entrepreneurs of all races."[315] This philosophy has been recently summarized and endorsed by the Fifth Circuit in *Walker v. Mesquite*, decided March 19, 1999. In that case, the Court found that both the federal Department of Housing and Urban

---

[315] *Croson*, 488 U.S. 469, 509-10 (1089)

Development and the City of Dallas had discriminated in the City's public housing program. But the Court rejected the City's race conscious remedy by declaring: "In application, arriving at an exact fit between harm and remedy requires consideration of whether a race neutral or less restrictive remedy could be used...This is because a race conscious remedy should be explicitly a matter of last resort...A race conscious remedy will not be deemed narrowly-tailored until a less sweeping alternative – particularly race neutral ones – have been considered and tried."[316] The results of bidding analysis indicate that M/WBEs accounted for less than 10 percent of the total number and dollar value of bids submitted during the nine fiscal years studied. Furthermore, the analysis indicates that when M/WBEs do bid, they receive a proportional number and dollar value of the City's contracts. The anecdotal evidence collected from interviews with M/WBEs indicated that most M/WBEs are discouraged from participating in the City's contracting process because they cannot compete with larger and more experienced firms in the City's relevant market area. In particular, these M/WBEs asserted that most major wholesalers and suppliers in the area will more likely give discounted prices and line of credit to their more affluent and larger companies that make larger purchases than to smaller less experienced firms. Hence, we recommend that the City of St. Petersburg should consider establishing a targeted race neutral small business program.

The City of St. Petersburg procurement code should consider separating prime contracting from subcontracting activities.

The City of St. Petersburg ordinance does not clearly separate prime contracting from subcontracting activities. Neither does the City's M/WBE ordinance require soliciting department to track, monitoring and keep record of subcontracting activities, especially bid and quote data. The *Columbus* case, the

---

316 *Walker v. Mesquite*, 169 F. 3rd 973, 982-983 (5th Cir. 1999).

Court, in assessing the validity of the disparity study upon which the City of Columbus M/WBE program was established, indicated that subcontracting data should be separated from prime contracting data in establishing disparity and therefore, set-aside goals. This separation is essential in meeting the factual predicate specification of *Croson*. Since no disparity in the award of contracts to M/WBE firms was observed in this study, the City may have to sunset its M/WBE ordinance. However, the City of St. Petersburg can amend it's procurement code to require the reporting of all subcontracting and at least on larger prime contracts, where subcontracting is probable, require that primes make subcontracting opportunities publicly known and kept records on who submitted subcontracting quotes. Hence, we recommend that the City of St. Petersburg M/WBE ordinance should be modified to separate contracting from subcontracting activities, and require soliciting departments to strictly monitor, track and document subcontracting and prime contracting data separately.

The City of St. Petersburg should consider monitoring and tracking prime contracting activities in the twelve (12) particular service areas identified in this study.

The *Croson* decision calls for measurement of disparities by particular services, so as to avoid results that are over-inclusive and might mask underlying patterns. To measure particular services, the study used the National Institute of Government Purchasing (NIGP) classifications which are the standard in procurement systems across the country. During the time period covered by the study, St. Petersburg purchased in 103 different NIGP classes, but in many of these codes the number of contracts or the amount of dollars purchased was too small to perform a meaningful statistical analysis. To make this data more manageable, related four digit NIGP classes were combined into 2-digit NIGP codes.

In order to focus on those NIGP classes where the greatest amount of purchases took place, disparity analysis was confined to those classes which represented more than 5 percent of the contracts or dollars in a particular year. Tables 1-1 to 1-9 and 2-1 to 2-9 display this data. If an NIGP class met the 5 percent threshold in a particular fiscal year, it was analyzed in all the fiscal years. Data from NIGP classes that did not meet the 5 percent threshold in a particular year were placed in a residual category which, because that category represents many particular services, was not analyzed. Overall, approximately only 20 percent of the total number of contracts and 3 percent of dollar value of contracts awarded by the City of St. Petersburg were in this category. Therefore, the statistical analysis presented in this report captures an overwhelming proportion of the data from the number and dollar value of competitively bid contracts awarded by the City of St. Petersburg during the period studied.

The City of St. Petersburg should consider monitoring and tracking prime contracting activities by racial, ethnic or gender group per particular service area.

Although this study has found no disparity in the award of contracts to M/WBEs, and hence a recommendation to discontinue the City's race conscious policy, it does not, however, eliminate the possibility of a need to establish *Croson's* "compelling State interest" in the future for re-institution of a race conscious remedy. The City's monitoring and tracking of prime contracting activities is well organized and consistent with the City's procurement code and administrative procedures. However, during the course of this study, we realized that the City's procurement data had several missing values for racial, ethnic or gender type of the contractor or vendors. *Croson* requires that should the need arise for a "compelling State interest", the City must establish a factual predicate by comparing the proportion of available firms to the proportion of their utilization for each racial, gender or ethnic group in a particular service area. Hence, we recommend that the City should consider monitoring and tracking prime contracting activities by ethnic, racial or gender group per particular service area.

The City of St. Petersburg should consider monitoring and tracking subcontracting activities by racial, ethnic or gender group per particular service area.

The City does not monitor or track its subcontracting activities. This missing data makes it impossible to establish *Croson's* factual predicate in City's contracting, should in case the need arises in the future for the City to establish a "compelling State interest" in remedying the present effects of past discrimination. Hence, we recommend that the City of St. Petersburg should consider monitoring and tracking subcontracting activities by racial, ethnic or gender group per particular service area.

The City should consider continuing to implement its targeted technical assistance provisions as specified in the procurement ordinance and administrative procedures.

Research has shown that most new and small businesses need technical assistance in business planning and management to more effectively compete for, and manage, government contracts. This study has also revealed that most contractors and community organizations interviewed and surveyed in the City's relevant market area favor the continuation of the City's technical assistance provisions to small businesses as specified in the City's Procurement code and Administrative procedures. Hence, we recommend that the City of St. Petersburg should consider continuing to provide technical assistance to small businesses in the City's relevant market area.

The City should consider continuing to maintain a sound working relationship with Community organizations to assist small businesses in the City's relevant market area to participate in the City's contracting process.

Interviews from community organizations indicate that the City's relationship with these organizations has been good, and has contributed to effectively identifying, encouraging and soliciting qualified small businesses in the City's relevant market area to participate in the City's contracting process. Hence, we recommend that the City of St. Petersburg should consider maintaining a sound working relationship with community organizations in the City's relevant market area.

The City should consider intensifying its efforts to provide networking and outreach assistance to M/WBEs in the City's relevant market area.

Our analysis indicates that a major reason why M/WBE's are not bidding on the City's contracts is lack of information. Similar to establishing a sound working relationship with community organizations, a networking and outreach initiative may be an effective mechanism for identifying, encouraging and soliciting qualified small businesses in the city's relevant market area to participate in the City's contracting process. Hence, we recommend the City of St. Petersburg should consider intensifying its efforts to provide networking and outreach assistance to M/WBEs in the City's relevant market area.

The City should consider continuing to provide funding for micro-loans to small businesses in the area.

Research on small business financing indicates that most small businesses lack start-up and working capital.[317] This renders them ineffective in competing for government contracts. In addition, most of these businesses do not have an established credit to obtain financing from private sources. Our analysis indicate that most of the firms surveyed indicated that their initial and current funding source is personal savings, not public or private funding. Hence, we recommend that the City

---

[317]See Faith H. Ando, "Capital Issues and Minority-owned Businesses," *The Review of Black Political Economy*, 16 (1988); pp. 33-49; Jawanza Kunjufu, *Black Economics, African American Images*, (Chicago, IL: 1991); Nancy McCrae, Minority Enterprise Development, National Council for Urban Economic Development, 1989.

should consider continuing to provide funding for micro-loans to small businesses in the City's relevant market area.

The City should consider continuing to enforce its prompt payment policy for small businesses.

The City's procurement staff generally understands its role in implementing the M/WBE Policy. Hence, to effectively continue this trend we recommend that the City should consider continuing to enforce its prompt payment policy for small businesses.

The City should consider maintaining its existing procurement awareness coordination and tracking system.

The City officials and community organizations were, for the most part, satisfied with the existing procurement awareness, coordination and implementation system. Moreover, our assessment indicate that the City departments' awareness, coordination and tracking system is generally well organized and consistent with the City's procurement and administrative codes. Hence, we recommend that the City should consider maintaining its existing procurement awareness, coordination and tracking system.

The City should consider establishing a certification and appeal process for participation in the newly established Targeted Small Business Program.

Since a targeted small business program requires defining participants on the basis of business size, the establishment of a small business certification and appeal process may effectively target the program towards intended beneficiaries. Hence, we recommend that the City should consider establishing a certification and appeals process for participation in the newly established targeted small business program.

The City should consider intensifying its efforts in encouraging small minority businesses to bid on City contracts.

Our analysis indicated that non-minority firms significantly over bid in the City's relevant market area. Meanwhile, minority-owned firms significantly under bid. The results of the statistical analysis of the City's contracting data indicates that M/WBE's submitted only 8.83 percent of the total number of bids and received 9.12 percent of the total number of contracts awarded by the City of St. Petersburg. Meanwhile, M/WBE's submitted 6.58 percent of the total dollar amount of contracts awarded by the City. Therefore when the M/WBEs bid on the City contracts the outcome are proportional. The problem is that M/WBE's in the City's relevant market area do not bid very often. Hence, we recommend that the City of St. Petersburg should consider intensifying its efforts in encouraging minority businesses to bid on City contracts.

The City should consider working with manufacturers and wholesale suppliers to maintain a standard uniform pricing system for all buyers.

A number of M/WBEs interviewed (or surveyed) indicated that they were discouraged from bidding on the City of St. Petersburg contracts because manufacturers and wholesalers in the City's relevant market area tend to quote them higher prices than their non-M/WBE competitors for products being solicited by the City. These M/WBEs asserted that this practice has also placed them in a competitively disadvantaged position when competing for the City's contracts. Hence, we recommend that the City should consider making a concerted effort to work with manufacturers and wholesalers to maintain a uniform standard of pricing for all businesses in the city's relevant market area.

The City should consider conducting a study every two years to assess the the efficacy of its race neutral initiative in improving M/WBE participation in the City's contracting process.

The recommendations outlined above are based on the quantitative and qualitative analyses findings, which show: (a) no statistically significant under-representation of minority-owned firms in the award of contracts by the City of St. Petersburg; (b) a general lack of market competitive attributes among MBEs; and (c) "passive" discrimination by the City of St. Petersburg. However, the adoption of any or all of these recommendations by the City of St. Petersburg may be contingent upon how feasible they fit within the constitution mandate and administrative procedure framework of the City. To assist in this process, suggestions derived from our interviews of the City's political leaders and officials, contractors in the City's relevant market area and community organizations are presented below.

City Officials and Political Leaders' Suggestions for Improving M/WBE Contracting Participation

- A City Council member suggested that the emphasis in M/WBE development should be in assisting minority- and woman-owned business owners to be qualified to do business with the City through an across-the-board small business training initiative which caters to all businesses irrespective of race, gender or ethnicity. For those businesses that are qualified to do business with the City, the Councilman recommends that the City should encourage these businesses to bid by making efforts to dispel the perception of the existence of a "good old boy network" in the City's contracting system. In addition, the City should provide these businesses with incentives to hire the hardcore unemployed in the City's blighted areas. These incentives should include: (a) providing credit or tax breaks to businesses in the City's relevant market area of the unemployed. The need for more clearly defined procurement classification of M/WBE availability; (b) expand the M/WBE program to other commodity areas, not only construction; and (c) establish trust and horizontal linkages between the City, minority community, M/WBEs and non-M/WBEs in the local community.

- A City Council member suggested that the City should shift its focus from quick handout of City funds to M/WBEs whose qualification and credit history are questionable, to a loan guarantee program which emphasizes a careful review of each applicant's business plan. With regards to the bidding on City contracts, the Council member suggested that the City should establish a mechanism to educate M/WBEs on how to apply and complete a bid application, and upon contract award, how to manage a government contract. In effect, the Council person recommended that the City should focus on educating M/WBEs on government contracting from which a pool of qualified M/WBEs can be derived to do business with the City. Without such an education initiative, the Council person asserted, the City may be vulnerable to waste and legal problems. By way of example, the Council person cited an incident involving a prime MBE contractor who hired local subcontractors to perform work on a City contract. When to project was completed, the prime MBE refused to pay the local subcontractors, resulting in a lawsuit which was still in progress.

- A Council member recommended that the M/WBE program should be expanded to other commodity areas.

- A City Administrator recommended that the City should, if legally possible, formalize the monitoring of prime contractors to make sure they are utilizing M/WBEs as specified in contract award documents. He also recommended that the City should fine-tune its efforts in: (a) verifying the M/WBE status of contractors and vendors; and (b) payment of M/WBEs by prime contractors; (c) outreach and networking efforts.

- A City Purchasing Agent suggested that the M/WBE program should be expanded to all the City's major commodity areas, and assistance to all local small businesses irrespective of racial ethnic or gender of the owner. The Purchasing Agent feels that such an expanded program will better serve the M/WBEs in the City's relevant market area if it is a separate entity (i.e. Department), not as office within a City department.

- A City Director suggested that the City's M/WBE initiative should shift its focus to capacity-building and expansion of the program to other procurement areas. To accomplish this goal, the Director recommended that the City should invest in M/WBE education, staffing of the M/WBE office, and increasing the budget for business assistance.

- A City Administrator suggested that the City should expand the M/WBE program to include all small businesses irrespective of race, gender or ethnicity of the owner. In addition, he recommends that, if legally feasible, the program should be expanded into other commodity areas.

- A City Administrator said that a problem that seems to arise occasionally is when a subcontractor (minority or otherwise) gets in a dispute with a prime contractor, and the City gets caught in the middle. Such an incident is often not in the direct control of the City, but the City project may be negatively impacted. The Administrator suggested that procedures to address this beforehand could be helpful. He also was in favor of expansion the City's M/WBE initiative into other commodity areas, and if legally feasible to all small businesses, irrespective of the racial, gender or ethnicity of the owner.

- A City Director recommended that the City's M/WBE program should be expanded to other procurement area such as goods and professional services.
- A Purchasing Agent suggested that there should be a periodic in-house briefing to update City Officials about the City's M/WBE policy and other laws affecting M/WBEs.

- A Purchasing Agent recommended that the Engineering Department's procurement procedures be amended to be more compatible with that of Purchasing Department.

- A Council member suggested that there should be provisions in the M/WBE ordinance to provide ongoing assistance to M/WBEs in accounting, business planning, bid/RFP responses, and cost estimating.

Comments on City's Contracting Process by M/WBE

- A non-minority maintenance contractor commented that the City is great with the exception of the Purchasing Department. They are overloaded with work that doesn't get completed. The City doesn't follow up on important issues. The payment system and the contracting opportunities are good.

- A WBE said that the City of St. Petersburg monitors their projects much better than any other municipality.

- A non-minority equipment rental and sales contractor said that he was still waiting to hear on a purchase of personnel lift for the Coliseum and Bayfront Center. It seems like the City is taking too long to make a decision and he cannot figure out why because both of these facilities need this equipment.

- A non-minority contractor commented that he has had no problems with the City. In particular, he felt that the City's Traffic Engineering Department has been polite, helpful and prompt in arranging all matters.

- A non-minority electrical equipment manufacturer would like to be notified of bids.

- A non-minority lawn sprinkler systems supplier said that the City of St. Petersburg left him with a bad feeling of being treated unfairly. He was told that he was to hire blacks and was even told which people to hire. Such as poor blacks, poor or black women or poor black handicapped persons. Even though he does hire minorities, he did not want to be given orders to do it in order to receive a contract. He felt that the remainder of the questions on the survey is examples of how the City discriminates against Caucasian/white privately owned companies.

- A non-minority painting contractor commented that the City of St. Petersburg does not give out bid results easily. Other agencies fax or relay bid results as soon a possible. This needs to be changed.

- A non-minority building construction contractor said that the entire Baseball Stadium project was poorly run, under staffed, had a poor pay history and not professional. Having Hubert, Hunt and Nichols as a supervisor team was a joke. The City was ripped off and so were the Devil Rays. The Devil Rays also should not be in the construction business.

- A non-minority supplier of canine training equipment for police dogs commented that the City of St. Petersburg has always paid beyond 30 days from the date that you submitted an invoice for work or services that you performed.

- A non-minority professional contractor said that getting paid on time by the City of St. Petersburg is a problem.

- A non-minority computer related software and hardware consulting contractor said that he had never received a bid package from the City of St. Petersburg.

- A non-minority Engineering and Architecture contractor wished the City of St. Petersburg would send notices for upcoming engineering opportunities.

- A black MBE construction contractor suggested that the City of St. Petersburg needs to be stricter on general contracts in the way they treat subcontractors in getting paid on contract negotiations. There must be a program that would guarantee subcontractors their money beyond completion. They must stop holding all trader money until the project is completed because there are subs that finish their trades before others.

- A WBE general construction contractor commented that the City's Permitting Department needs serious changes – takes much too long to get a commercial permit.

- A Hispanic MBE professional service contractor said that the City has "good old boy network" discrimination contracting system based on "perceived status" By way of example, he said that he bid on a local HUD project, and the City awarded the contract to an out of town firm. He said they were committed to hiring people from south side, had the talents local, but a company from Tampa got the job! The project was lead base paint assessment for Jordan Park. Upon probing for more explanation by We, the contractor said other Cities are much easier to work with than the City of St. Petersburg, and he remarked that the City of St. Petersburg should note that Hispanics are minorities as well, and their population is increasing daily. In addition, he said the City's procurement system is too cumbersome, and the bulk of the contract is for construction only. However, an interview with city officials, revealed that that this particular contract was awarded by the St. Petersburg Housing Authority, and not the City of St. Petersburg.

Bibliography

Adarand Constructors, Inc. v. Pena, 115 S. Ct. 2097, 132 L. Ed. 2d 158 (1995).

AGC v. Columbus, 936 F. Supp. at 1414, 1426 (S.D. Ohio 1996).

Ando, Faith H. "Capital Issues and Minority-owned Businesses," *The Review of Black Political Economy*, 16 (1988).

Bates, Timothy. "The Changing Nature of Minority Business: A Comparative Analysis of Asian, Non-minority, and Black-owned Businesses." *The Review of Black Political Economy* 17 (November 1989), pp. 25-42.

Black, T.G. "Small Business Contracting with the Federal government." *Journal of Small Business Management* (October 1982), pp. 64-70.

Cantor, J.A. "The Small Business" In The Federal Marketplace-A Study of Barriers." *Journal of Small Business Management* (January 1989), pp. 74-77.

City of Richmond v. Croson, 109 S. Ct. 706, (1989).

City of St. Petersburg Administrative Policy and Procedure, Sections 6.03.02, 6.05.01, 9.01.01, 8.04.01 and 8.09.

City of St. Petersburg Code, Art. II, § 70-36, *et seq.*

City of St. Petersburg MBE Annual Report, 1985.

City of St. Petersburg M/WBE Annual Reports, FY1989, FY1990, FY1991, FY1992, FY1993, FY1994, FY1995, FY1996, FY1997, and FY1998.

City of St. Petersburg Ordinance 102-G, 1, July 1, 1993.

City of St. Petersburg Ordinance 127-G, Section (f), 1994.

City of St. Petersburg Ordinance No. 362-F, 1, June 21, 1979.

City of St. Petersburg Ordinance No. 714-F, 1, January 19, 1984.

City of St. Petersburg Ordinance No. 744-F, 1, May 17, 1984.

City of St. Petersburg Ordinance No. 2023-F, 1990.

City of St. Petersburg Procurement Code, Sections 2-177, 2-226, 2-228, 2-229, 2-230, 2-231

City of St. Petersburg Purchasing and Material Management Policy and Procedure Manual, February 1, 1989.

City of St. Petersburg M/WBE Policy and Procedure, 1990.

Civil Rights Restoration Act amendment to Rehabilitation Act , 29 U.S.C. § 794(b), 1988.

Code of Federal Regulations, 14 C.F.R., 40 C.F.R., 41 C.F.R. and 49 C.F.R.

Consent Order dated May 21, 1997.

Consultant Competitive Negotiation Agreement (Section 287.055, Florida Statute), 2004.

Contractors Association of Eastern Philadelphia v. Secretary of Labor, 442 F.2d 159 (3d Cir. 1971).

Contractors Assoc. of Eastern Pennsylvania v. Philadelphia, 735 F. Supp. 1274 (E.D. Pa. 1990).

Contractors Assoc. of Eastern Pennsylvania v. Philadelphia, Civ. No. 89-2737, 1992 WL 245851 (Sept. 22, 1992).

Contractors Assoc. of Eastern Pennsylvania v. Philadelphia, 6 F.3d 990 (3d Cir. 1993).

Contractors Assoc. of Eastern Pennsylvania v. Philadelphia, 893 F. Supp. 419, 423 (E.D. Pa. 1995).

Contractors Assoc. of Eastern Pennsylvania v. Philadelphia, 91 F.3d 586, 609-10 (3d Cir. 1996).

Cooper, A.C. and C.M. Daily, "Entrepreneurial Team." In Don Sexton and Ray Smilor (eds.), *Entrepreneurship 2000*. (Chicago, IL: Upstart Publishing Company, 1997), pp. 127-150.

Cooper, R.B. and R.W. Zmud, "Information Technology Implementation Research: A Technology Diffusion Approach." *Management Science*, 36(2), 1990, 31-42.

Coral Construction Co. v. King County, 941 F.2d 910, 941 (9th Cir. 1991).

Croson v. City of Richmond, 779 F.2d 181, 191 (4th Cir. 1985).

Davis, J.W. *Perceived Effects of Federal Procurement Legislation on Small Disadvantaged Businesses*. (Dissertation, School of Business Management, United States International University.

Defendants' Suggestion of Mootness dated May 21, 1997.

Defendants' Status Report at ¶6.

Denzin, Norman K. and Yvonne S. Lincoln, Editors, *Handbook of Qualitative Research* (Newbury Park: Sage Publications, 1998).

Doukidis, G.I., S. Smithson and T. Lyberes, "Trends in Information Technology in Small Businesses." *Journal of End User Computing*, 6(4), 1994, 15-25.

Engineering Contractors Association of South Florida, Inc. v. Metropolitan Dade County, 122 F. 3rd 895 (11th Cir. 1997).

Engineering Contractors Association of South Florida, Inc. v. Metropolitan Dade County, 943 F. Supp. 1546 (S.D. Fla. 1996).

Ensley Branch, N.A.A.C.P., et al. v. Seibels, 31 F.3d 1548, 1569 (11th Cir. 1994).

Federal Railroad Administration (U. S. Department of Transportation), *The Railroad Revitalization and Regulatory Reform Act of 1976* (aka the Rail Passenger Service Act).

Flora, J.L. "Social Capital and Communities of Place." *Rural* Sociology, 63(4), (1998), pp. 481-506.

Flora, J.L., J. Sharpe, B.L. Newlon and C. Flora, "Entrepreneurial Social Infrastructure and Locally Initiated Economic Development in the Non-metropolitan United States." *The Sociological Quarterly*, 38(4) (1997), pp. 623-645.

Florida Administrative Code, F.A.C. § 14-98.007(24)

Florida Statutes, Art. II, § 15-21, et seq.

Florida Statutes, Chapter 760, § 112.042.

Florida Statute 166.045.

Fratoe, Frank A. "Social Capital of Black Business Owners.' *The Review of Black Political Economy*, 16 (1988), pp. 25-32.

Fullilove v. Klutznick, 448 U.S. 448, 454, 65 L. Ed. 2d (1980) (quoting 91 Stat. 116, 42, U.S.C. § 6705(f)(2)).

Giorgi, Amedeo. *Phenomenology and Psychological Research* (Pittsburgh: Duquesne University Press, 1985).

Giventer, Lawrence L. *Statistical Analysis for Public Administration* (Belmont, CA: Wadsworth Publishing Company, 1996).

Gosepath, Stefan. "Equality" In Edward N. Zelta (ed.), *The Encyclopedia of Philosophy* (Winter 2001 Edition).

Grishman, V.L. Jr. *Tupelo: The Evolution of Community* (Dayton, OH: Kettering Foundation Press, 1999).

Hartman, A.E., C.B. Tower and T.C. Sebora, "Information Sources and their Relationship to Organizational Innovation in Small Businesses." *Journal of Small Business Management*, (January 1994).

Hazelwood School District v. United States, 433 U.S. 299, 307-08, 53 L. Ed.2d 768 [1977]).

Holzinger, A. "The Virtual Future." *Nation's Business*, (May 1995), 45-47.

House Government Operations Committee, U.S. Congress, *Problems Facing Minority and Women-owned Small Business Including SBA Section 8(a) Firms in Procuring U.S. Government Contracts: An Interim Report HRPT. No. 103-870* (November, 1994).

Julien, P. "New Technologies and Technological Information in Small Business." *Journal of Business Venturing*, Vol. 10 (1995), 459-475.

Kunjufu, Jawanza. *Black Economics, African American Images*, (Chicago, IL: 1991).

Laws of Florida (1931), Chapter 15505, 17(a)

Laws of Florida, Chapter 69-1557, 1.

Laws of Florida (1951) Chapter 27873

Lin, N., "Building a Network Theory of Social Capital." *Connections*. 22(1), 28-51.

Master, J., G.B. Hartmann; and A. Safari, "Small Business Strategic Planning and Technology Transfer: The Use of Publicly Supported Technology Assistance Agencies." *Journal of Small Business Management*, (July 1995), 26-37.

McCrea, Nancy *Minority Enterprise Development* (Washington D.C.: National Council for Urban Economic Development, 1989).

McManus, Susan .*Doing Business With Government* (New York: Paragon House, 1992).

Monterey Mechanical Co. v. Wilson, F.3d, 1997 WL 535626 (11th Cir. 1997).

Monterey Mechanical Co. v. Wilson, F.3d, 1997 WL 538757 (9th Cir. 1997)

Nachmias, David and Chava Nachmias, *Research Methods in Social Sciences*, New York: St. Martins Press (1987).

National Institute of Government Purchasers (NIGP), NIGP Code, 1984.

O' Donnell Construction Co. v. District of Columbia, 963 F.2d 420, 427 (D.C. Cir. 1992).

Order on Motions for Summary Judgment in Prior Tire Enterprises v. Atlanta Public School District, Case No. Civ. 1:95-CV-825-JEC (N.D. Ga. 1997).

Patton, Michael Quinn. *Qualitative Evaluation and Research Methods*, (Newbury Park: Sage Publications, 1990).

Peightal v. Metropolitan Dade County, 26 F.3d 1545, 1558 (11th Cir. 1994).

Phillips and Jordan v. Watts, 13 F. Supp. 2d 1308, 1314 (N.D. Fla. 1998).

Pinellas County Code, 1995.

Prior Tire Enterprises v. Atlanta Public School District, Case No. Civ. 1:95-CV-825-JEC (N.D. Ga. 1997).

Rehabilitation Act of 1973, 29 U.S.C. § 794(a).

Schafer, S. "How Technology is Leveling the Playing Field." *Inc. Technology*, Vol. 4 (1995), 57-62.

Server, A.E. "Path to Wealth in the New Economy." *Fortune*, 20 February, 57-62.

Servon, L.J. "Credit and Social Capital: The Community Development Potential of US Microenterprise Programs." *Housing Policy Debate*, 9(1) (1998), pp. 115-149.

Shaw v. Reno, *509 U.S. 630, 642, 125 L. Ed. 2d 511* (1993).

Small Business Administration, "Planning for EDI Implementation." *On-line Business Adviser* (June 1995), pp. 1-13.

Small Business Administration, *Electronic Commerce/Electronic Exchange Data Interchange* (March 1996), pp. 1-9.

Smith, Owen J., Mitchell F. Rice, and Woodrow Jones, Jr., *Blacks and American Government*. (Kendall Publishers, Dubuque, Iowa, 1991), Chapter 10.

Strong Rodney, *Disparity study – Construction*, (Atlanta Public School District, Atlanta, Georgia, 1998).

Suggs, R.E. "Racial Discrimination in Business Transactions." *The Hastings Law Journal,* 42 (1991).

Title VI of the Civil Rights Act of 1964.

Tolbert, C.M., C.M. Lyson and M.D. Irwin, "Local Capitalism, Civil Engagement, and Socioeconomic Well-being." *Social Forces,* 77(2), (1998), pp. 401-427.

U.S. v. Paradise, *480 U.S. 149, 171* (1987))

U.S. Commission on Minority Business Development, *Interim Report, 1990 Executive Summary*, (Washington D.C.: U.S. Commission on Minority Business Development, 1990).

Van Manen, Max. *Researching Lived Experience: Human Science for an Action Sensitive Pedagogy* (NewYork: New York University Press, 1990).

Vietnam Era Veterans Readjustment Assistance Act of 1974, 38 U.S.C. § 4212

Walker v. Mesquite, 169 F. 3rd 973, 982-983 (5th Cir. 1999).

Wozniak, Gregory D. "Human Capital, Information, and Early Adoption of New Technology." *The Journal of Human Resources* (Winter 1987), pp.101-112.

Zelta, Edward N. (ed.). *The Standard Encyclopedia of Philosophy* (Winter 2001 Edition).

Index